MULTISPECIES STORYTELLING IN INTERMEDIAL PRACTICES

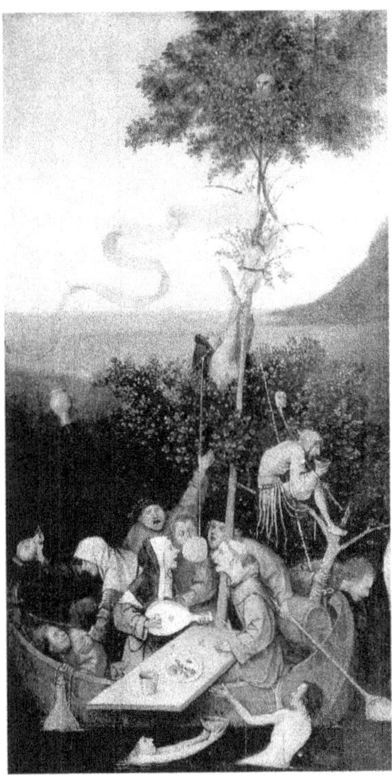

Fig. 1. Hieronymus Bosch, *Ship of Fools* (1490–1500)

First published in 2022 by punctum books, Earth, Milky Way.
https://punctumbooks.com

ISBN-13: 978-1-68571-022-4 (print)
ISBN-13: 978-1-68571-023-1 (ePDF)

DOI: 10.53288/0338.1.00

LCCN: 2022932942
Library of Congress Cataloging Data is available from the Library of Congress

Book design: Vincent W.J. van Gerven Oei
Cover photograph: Adam Dickinson

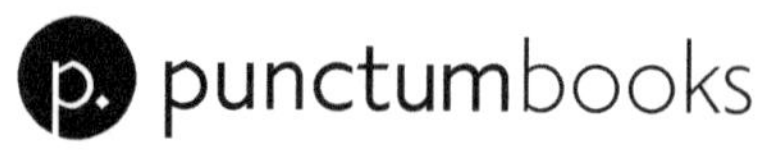

spontaneous acts of scholarly combustion

MULTISPECIES STORYTELLING in INTERMEDIAL PRACTICES

Edited by Ida Bencke
and Jørgen Bruhn

Contents

Introduction

Ida Bencke and Jørgen Bruhn

*My multispecies storytelling is about recuperation in complex
histories that are as full of dying as living, as full of endings,
even genocides, as beginnings. In the face of unrelenting historically specific surplus suffering in companion species knottings, I
am not interested in reconciliation or restoration, but I am deeply
committed to the more modest possibilities of partial recuperation and getting on together. Call that staying with the trouble.*
— Donna Haraway, *Staying with the Trouble*

*There are many kinds of life, said Spike [a robot], mild-
ly. Humans always assumed that theirs was the only kind
that mattered. That's how you destroyed your planet.*
— Jeanette Winterson, *The Stone Gods*

I

Within Western institutional thinking, the human is constituted through an ability to speak, defined as the sole creature who holds language and consequently is
capable of articulating, representing, and reflecting upon the world. Along with
language comes the power of naming, of choreographing the semantic categories
put in place, continually reproduced and negotiated to make sense of the world.
Language is a kind of gathering technology that enables collectivity and continuity
between bodies and ideas. It is also a tool of separation and control, which holds
a promise of mastery.

Language is commonly thought of as that which sets "us" apart from the rest of
species, as that which lifts and divides us from an otherwise mute or unintelligible
materiality.

And yet, the world is made and remade by ongoing and many-tongued conversations between various organisms reverberating with sound, movement, gestures,
hormones, electrical signals. Everywhere, life is making itself known, heard, and
understood in a wide variety of media and modalities; some of these registers are
available to our human senses, while some are not.

And still, we often think of ourselves as the sole creature in this universe capable of actively producing meaning. This is a story of separation through semantics:
that we, as humans, are separated from the rest of nature by that crucial dividing
line called language that runs between those who speak and those who are spoken
of. In this story, Man is master of nature, and nature is consequently reduced to a

beautiful "out there," an exotic other, pacified, and devoid of voice, lacking both political agency and legal rights.

However, entering the vast and humming fields of multispecies storytelling comes with a set of urgent problems. Merging linguistics with the more-than-human world opens questions of anthropomorphism (i.e., adorning nonhumans with human faculties of speech) and problems of centering certain kinds of semiotic faculties on the expense of others. All too often, the human becomes a sort of spokesperson, a well-meaning ventriloquist assuming the right to speak on behalf of the nonhuman other and hereby confirming, rather than challenging, the normative taxonomical hierarchy of Western science.

At the same time, as the multispecies philosopher and animal trainer Vicky Hearne reminds us, while the obstacles to transversal conversations between species are many, our lived, everyday experiences of multispecies cohabitation tell us that in practice, "we" often manage to understand each other. Beyond the boundaries of species, of different kinds of bodies, different dialects and their different apparatuses of communication, meaning is reproduced and confirmed within more-than-human encounters. Haraway, Despret, and likeminded thinkers have accounted for a kind of generative, open-ended, and ongoing multispecies morphology in which bodies, materials and ontologies are always negotiated, in which the contours of "we" are always morphing and emerging anew through a kind of deep contact founded within play, intercession, digestion.

The question remains: how do we narrate and (re)present these encounters in ways that do not negate, annul, or overwrite the distinctive qualities and logics of a nonhuman semiotics?

A (self-)critical multispecies philosophy must interrogate and qualify the broad and seemingly neutral concept of humanity utilized in and around conversations grounded within Western science and academia. The notion of the human, as we know, comes with its own fraught history of exclusion. Who gets to be included in the "we" employed by scientific, social and political discourses, and who is pushed to the margins and beyond of this seemingly neutral category is a violent story of making invisible, of disenfranchisement, of marginalized bodies and their epistemologies.

And still, facing a not-so-distant future catastrophe, which in many ways and for many of us is already here, it is becoming painstakingly clear that our common imaginaries are in dire need of replacements. As Indigenous scholar and botanist Robin Wall Kimmerer asks, how are we supposed to avoid environmental collapse when we are unable to even imagine non-harmful ways of existence? How do we cultivate, nourish, and share those other kinds of stories that may hold promises of modest yet radical hope? As long as we keep reproducing the same kind of languages, the same kinds of scientific gatekeeping, the same kinds of stories about "our" place in nature, we remain numb in the face of collapse.

What is needed, it seems, is to change the story by radically reimagining who we are, what we may become and in alliances with whom. We may ask, what kinds of political, cultural, aesthetic, and scientific prejudices police our speculative abilities to think and act differently, and how do we break with the stories that enable and justify this policing?

This is not merely a question of thematics but one of form as well. In order to accommodate those different kinds of stories, we need to come up with new ways of telling them — with and for whom. Here, we return to the question of narrative strategies, and media: what would our stories look like, were we to take the signals, traces and voices of other beings serious? What if we, instead of telling story upon story about nature, were to engage in collaborative storytelling activities with that humming, throbbing murmur of countless critters that all, collectively, make up "our" world?

Multispecies Storytelling in Intermedial Practices is a speculative endeavor asking how we may represent, relay, and read worlds differently by taking other species serious as protagonists in their own rights. What other stories are to be invented and told from within those murky and many-tongued chatters of multispecies camaraderie, allies, and collectivity? Could such stories teach us how to become human otherwise?

II

Like it so often happens, it was a coincidence that marked the beginnings of what was initially a loose idea, which then became a conference, exhibition, and performance event, and now this finalizing book project that — due to the medial affordances of the book as media type — showcases a small but illustrative part of the diversity and richness of the conference.

We, that is Ida Bencke and Jørgen Bruhn, had met at the university of Copenhagen years before and bumped into each other at a poetry reading with the Swedish poet Johannes Heldén, an intermedial, multispecies storytelling writer in his own right. Ida was an art curator and editor, interested in ecology and multispecies aesthetics and co-founder of the curatorial collective Laboratory of Aesthetics and Ecology; Jørgen was immersed in intermedial theory and ecocritical questions in the Linnæus University Centre for Intermedial and Multimodal Studies. We were both trained in literary studies and had interests in narrative forms in different media, and therefore it seemed obvious to open an investigation into the possible correspondences between media studies and multispecies thinking by way of a common denominator of both fields, namely storytelling. We formulated a broad title early on that circled in on what we wished to focus — Multispecies Storytelling in Intermedial Practices.

Multispecies philosophies and intermediality are both rich and emerging fields of research and practice in themselves, but, at our conference, we wished to instigate messy meetings, transversalities, and rich crosspollinations rather than traditional academic deep-diving that specify and clarify terminological intricacies.

In this project, therefore, we operated with generous working definitions of the key terms, meaning that *multispecies,* for us, signaled the lively, and in some cases quite revolutionizing, ongoing conversations pointing towards less hierarchical, less anthropocentric positions of more-than-human lifeworlds currently under construction.

The *intermedial* perspective signaled, in its basic sense, our wish to welcome all sorts of stories and contributions in all sorts of media, but it also indicated the a priori, intermedial notion that all media and all meaning making are basically intermedial. A conversation between two persons employs verbal language as well as gestures, and our clothes, our spatial position, and other aspects factor in, too. An eco-documentary produces its meaning by way of sound, images, editing, and often a narrating voice-over in a complex combination. A poem employs language, but it also organizes the page in a spatial pattern, and the words not only represent an outer world or inner feelings but also has rhythmic and musical aspects. All media are mixed media. *Storytelling* was equally and openly understood as the immense field of different narratives and narrative voices or positions, human or not, across the fiction or non-fiction divide — all the different narratives in different media forms that engage in mostly contemporary artistic and philosophical dialogues but also in historical or political contexts. Stories that represent aspects of the world and stories that acts in and acts upon the world.

As always, the funding question came in as an early priority, and when applying for external funding we envisioned a relatively modest thirty- to forty-person exploratory workshop-slash-symposium with a strong setup of keynote speakers. Linköping University's Seedbox funding supported the idea. However, when disseminating the call for papers for the January 2019 conference in Växjö, it turned out that more than 130 people wanted to present work or discuss multispecies storytelling in intermedial practices with us. We were happy to see that our hopes for a truly transdisciplinary and global group of diverse guests came true. In the end, the generous engagement of so many wonderful minds, bodies and institutions manifested in three days and nights of talks, debates, art exhibitions, video screenings, performances, experimental workshops, experimental dinner sessions, and a lot of fun. The participants included an intergenerational mix of academics of many disciplines whose work met and merged with artists, designers, and activists who discussed burning issues while taking pleasure in each other's company.

III

It does not really make sense to try to paraphrase the three days' lively engagements, but the rich and diverse contributions to this volume are a sample of the diversity of the generous contributions. After a thought-provoking opening address from Dean of Faculty Gunlög Fur, briefly discussed in one of the contributions to the volume, Vinciane Despret gave the first keynote presentation at the conference, which also opens this volume. Her text opens on a modest, everyday experience — being awakened by a blackbird at 4 o'clock in the morning. Despret integrates this initial experience into speculations concerning animal behavior and continental philosophy, spiraling into visions of being together, and sharing life and the goods of the world, which ultimately ended up in questions of what it means to live. The blackbird's beautiful fabulations initiated ideas about how all animals inhabit the world. Octopuses, for instance: "As we see with octopuses, the habitat not only designs the shapes of relationships, but, what's more, it has the function of actively establishing social beings." Animals — and we humans, of course, are animals too — are defined by our habitats, and a bird's singing becomes a social vision. Despret borrows a reflection from Latour, when she notes that "the two meanings of the French term *partition* as a 'partaking agreement,' or more precisely as a 'sharing granted' and as a 'musical script,' can be brought together. A new vision of territory, and co-habitation, perhaps?" Seeing the traditional, territorial marking of animals as rather the event of sharing space, Despret surprisingly finds that "the territory reorganizes the aggressive functions [of animals] into expressive functions." The blackbird's song, then, demonstrates that in the animal kingdom, "we are far from the idea of the territory as private property, as a place of exclusive possession to which our modern legal and philosophical tradition has accustomed us." As with so many contributions at the conference, Despret's talk was, deep down, about learning from animal practices without anthropomorphizing or romanticizing these animal life forms.

Also, Karin Bolender's contribution has a lot to say about learning from animals. Bolender, self-characterizing as "artist-researcher, and more recently as a maternal linguistic transmitter," opens her text with her memories from giving birth and dreams of a radical, multispecies beginning to a new life that, for medical reasons, turned into a wholly hospitalized birth. This probably saved her and her child's life, but it also hindered the dreamed-of, multispecies birth experience. Only a while after the actual birth is the child, then, "messily inoculated into a family full of barn-dust bodies and muzzles and mud, local grass hay, forest edges, and the millioning motes and swarms of untold, often sub-visible others that proliferate as both allies and enemies in every crack and fold." Being an artist and linguistic transmitter, she is not only offering her newborn some of the microbial tongues, but she acknowledges that "we each also pass on the seeds of linguistic 'mother tongues' to fetuses and neonates—all the heritable names, stories, cultures, and categorical cuts carried forth in particular languages and ontologies." From this personal birth story to larger learning and storying projects, she welcomes the readers of her essay and everybody else to the project of the Secretome, which "explores one creative proposal for how we might make space for mysterious, sub-visible agencies of microbial meshes in collective storying, at different nexuses of ecologies and imaginative encounters—with the recognition that they are always already involved in the stories of our collective lives in ways we barely grasp." Imagining new ways of living with other species, creating new homes and deterritorialized *territories,* a phrase she lifts from Despret, Bolender ends her text on an inviting note: "Home is where the unknown is. *Welcome to the Secretome.*"

Staying in the subject of learning from animals, Hörner/Antlfinger's "Tales of a Modern Parrot: Living Entangled Lives in an Interspecies Art Collective" describes decades of the artists' lives, living with and thinking about and creating art about and with animals. Describing such a long-time cooperation, the text also describes changes in the collective's work that reflects changes in philosophy and politics concerning general shifts in multispecies co-habitations. It offers valuable insights into "a more reflective kind of anthropomorphism. One that does neither overestimate, nor does it underestimate the similarities between human and non-human animals." Also, the parrots taught their human cohabitants and co-workers about new balances between work and play, a well-known relation for many artists – and perhaps academics, too — and the artwork with animals therefore poses fascinating questions relating to what "work" is. Does it make sense to say that pets work? And is it only human beings that create art?

In "The Laudable Cow: Poetics of Human/Cattle Relationships," Emily McGiffin begins by quickly going through the immense — and immensely inhuman — human-cattle relationship as we know it today in Europe and North America. McGiffin investigates aspects of the "growing human, environmental, and animal injustices of industrialized meat production" that "require us not only to shift our eating habits but also our sympathies, by rekindling relationships of kinship and care with the animals we are reliant upon." Her entry to these issues is sung and written poetry, from South Africa and North America respectively; observing that "when cattle are given a degree of independence to direct their own lives and movements, they enjoy many of the same things people do. They like hanging out in parks. They like sunbathing on the beach or by a river. They like watching the surf." This aspect of cattle-human relationships is more evident, though, in the praise-poetry of South African poets than it is in the cowboy songs from the second half of the nineteenth century. For her, cowboy literature is less an expression of human-animal entanglements and more an aspect of the settler and capitalist mechanism of today.

For a conference hosted at a faculty of Arts and Humanities, there was unusually much talk about natural sciences, in particular biology and the so-called life sciences. Péter Kristóf Makai's article, "The Representation of the 'Tree of Life' Metaphor across Media," goes directly to one of the founding scientific set of ideas ruminating behind almost all the presentations at the conference, namely the idea of evolution. The article responds quite explicitly to the key words of the conference, namely "multispecies," "storytelling," and "intermedial practices." Establishing early on the central message of Darwin's revolutionary thinking — "that all life on earth is fundamentally connected: every species is kin to every other species that has ever lived on earth" — Makai directly goes on to posit this as a design or representational problem, noting that "[n]o visual metaphor has captured this fact so succinctly as the Tree of Life." In an archetypical intermedial methodology, Makai gathers a sample of different media responses to this "design problem" that ranges from documentary film to digital online-design and more narrative versions in popular science book and, finally, to a board game. All of these demonstrate "how evolution as an abstract scientific concept tests the limits of medial expression, broadening the affordances and constraints of the media in question." Representing evolution is a grand challenge because of both the complexity and in the numbers of species and the immense time frames. Another problem is that there are no protagonists in evolution, a basic fact that makes it difficult for creators in different media and different scientific or aesthetic domains to find suitable narrative forms. Many, therefore, succumb to what Makai with a neologism terms "protagonification."

Evolution, seen in the efficient light of comparative intermedial studies, tests the limits of visual metaphors (i.e., the tree itself), narrative form, and the idea of a central hero. One of the takeaways of Makai's investigation is Dawkins's insight that the comprehensive story he told in *The Ancestor's Tale: A Pilgrimage to the Dawn of Life* could be multiplied in endless, different versions. Written as it is from a human point of view, "another book could have been written in parallel for any of 10 million starting pilgrims," which means all the different results of the overwhelmingly rich evolutionary process. That is yet another sign of how Uexküll's idea of the affordances created by each specific species' *Umwelt* are present, implicitly or explicitly, in so many of the contributions in this volume.

One of the explicit references to Uexküll is in the visual artist Fröydi Laszlo's text "The Plant-story? Listening and Multispecies Storytelling." Here, she invites the reader to come behind the scenes for a video art project, "The Pest." This piece mimics several genres, including the love story and the nature documentary. The description of the making of this project takes up less space, however, than a series of wide-reaching reflections relating to the philosophical backgrounds to Laszlo's artistic practices. Ernst Cassirer's Neo-Kantian philosophy of symbolic forms is proposed as an essential dialogue partner for contemporary multispecies considerations and media theory. Laszlo demonstrates that the supporting, central aspects of Cassirer's philosophy is Uexküll's *Umwelt* theory. Laszlo argues for better ways to understand and to appreciate meandering in a world of human and nonhuman relations: the world, it is argued here, is much richer than conventional, anthropocentric worldviews can see, and Laszlo leads the way in meeting the world halfway between all the living features of human animals, animals, and plants.

Apart from Uexküll's realization of the different affordances that characterizes different species, another leitmotif in this book (often in critical discussions) is the idea of the Anthropocene. In her contribution, Melanie Boehi reminds the reader about the critical discussions surrounding the concept of the Anthropocene. She wishes to change the geographical and social imbalances and blind spots in the concept by thinking about an "African Anthropocene." Her starting point for doing this is the "impact of the climate crisis on the Adderley Street flower market" in Cape Town, South Africa. This setting enables her to open a discussion of "the complex entanglements of human and plant lives [that] make the Adderley Street flower market a suitable site for examining life in an African Anthropocene." The art project investigates how the flower vendors tell stories by way of their local produce, and, at the art show described by Boehi, the public was invited to do so too. Boehi describes the tradition of arranging flowers — selecting, collecting, organizing — as a form of storytelling that "allows humans to make arrangements together with plants, and be themselves arranged by plants." Adding layer after layer to her argument — flower arrangements, flower wrapping papers, sound — Boehi shows how these media types "inhabit a space between conventional forms of media, and how they are constantly evolving from one form to another: Flower arrangements turn into stories; flower wrapping papers are recycled into newspapers; and a music composition becomes a flower arrangement." Storytelling and intermedial practices from the living, and dying, languages of plants.

To politicize the too easy globalist heritage of much talk about the Anthropocene is also an issue in "'You have to learn the language of how to communicate with the plants' and other selva stories" by Kristina Van Dexter. Van Dexter leaves the Global North to discuss aspects of the ongoing war in Colombia after the peace settlement with the Revolutionary Armed Forces of Colombia (FARC) in 2016. Blending field notes of interviews with historical overviews, photographs, and Colombian original texts, Van Dexter explores new ways of thinking about war, peace, and the forests, selva. Selva, though, is much more than concentrated amounts of trees as a conventional anthropocentric view would have it: "the selva refers to the living forests of Amazonia, a lively entanglement of soils, seeds, trees, pollinators, forest spirits, and farmers." The Selva are communicative, social, life-producing environments under threat of both the increasing number of cattle, and the coca industries. Van Dexter wants to create a response to ecocidal destruction, which requires the act of writing; writing witness and the telling of stories that entangle us within the selva's temporalities and communicative relationalities." And therefore, the essay "looks to the selva's relational poetics and generative rhythms death nourishing life for guidance on how to inherit ecocidal destruction toward the possibilities of peace." Farming in the spirit of selva means defying several threats and temptations and applying traditional practices — for instance, singing to and with coca and tobacco plants — to try and reestablish the lifegiving relations to selva. Under dire conditions and very high risks, the writer manages to create hope by contributing with yet another nice neologism appropriate to this particular setting, when she is talking about "restorying peace."

The politics of the Anthropocene and other definitions is also central for Cassandra Troyan and Helen V. Pritchard. In "The Anti Menagerie: Fictions for Interrogating the Supremacy of World-shaping Violence," they take the cue from the inaugural conference speech from Dean of the faculty of arts and humanities Gunlög Fur, who is a postcolonial historian by training. Troyan and Pritchard acknowledges the need for historical facts concerning the ideological backgrounds for contemporary and historical Anthropocene effects, but they want to add to the academic perspective of history: "Fur's analysis as a historian is greatly appreciated and crucial in contextualizing this moment, yet we believe the work of fiction provides a critical intervention by calling into question the relations between fact, fiction, narration, and who is given the voice and authority to be able to make claims to the category of history, in or of itself." Therefore, the strategy of this text is to "propose multispecies solidarity stories" that "address the role of colonial rule in actively constructing a narrative of dominance and subjugation to all living organisms under its purview." Following this critical frame, the authors offer what may perhaps be characterized as speculative, multispecies storytelling, that deconstructs and narrates versions of possible weird and queered multispecies constellations; recognizable and uncanny fables for life in the contested world of the Anthropocene.

Troyan and Pritchard's menagerie is hardly paraphrasable, nor is Gillian Wylde's work printed here. Titled "*#FEELSWeoutheregettinthisbread*," Wylde sets in motion funny, burlesque, but also strangely alienated settings and situations that might have been picked up at more or less random internet travels. She collects and represents "multispecies inter-relationships and stories that circulate rapidly and widely on the internet" and, by cutting up, rewriting, adding and subtracting, shows "how they replicate, mutate and evolve." Intertextually dumbfounding, where the colorful illustrations add to the complexity, the text finds, or, rather produces a voice and vision that seems disembodied and floating and immersed in many bodily matters at the same time. The result is text and images that you have probably not seen before, and that, without explain crutches or pedagogical hints, creates and critically comments on the commercialized and click-baiting, multispecies, internet life.

From Wylde's digital visions and down to something analog: a lake, and what to learn from it. In "Learning from the Lake," Katie Lawson asks if "curatorial work — as a kind of storytelling — [can] be reshaped by aqueous thinking, by multispecies and more-than-human relationalities, by watery territories." Lawson critically questions her own and others' curatorial efforts in the exhibition with the same name as her article and she is well aware of the limitations of an art show or an ecofeminist philosophical treatise when facing the grand challenges of what she, like many others, only hesitatingly names the Anthropocene. However, after considerations she chooses to believe that exhibitions, storytelling, thinking "does hold the potential to present possibilities for being otherwise, to prefigure certain kinds of ethical relations with water or watery others." Lawson discuss ecofeminist attempts to find new fluid logics, insists on thinking metaphorically and concretely at the same time, and offers glimpses into the art exhibition that included the work of Maggie Groat and Kelly Jazvac. These artists, along with the lake and the tradition of (eco)feminist theory, all contributed to Lawson's curated show, and their artistic work helped Lawson create her curatorial, ecofeminist metaphors.

In "Lagomorph Lessons: Feminist Methods for Environmental Sensing and Sensemaking," Maya Livio asks, "[w]hat is at stake when already marginalized nonhuman beings are leveraged as sensemaking apparatus, and how can these practices be made more ethical and just?" She modestly offers her work "as a few preliminary provocations, tactics that might serve as methodological breadcrumbs for more ethical sensemaking with nonhuman beings." It is all about the pikas: the "(*Ochotona princeps*) is a small lagomorph, a relative of rabbits and hares," but they are not only that. Rather, the pikas that are often considered as an "indicator species" should not be seen only as an indicator for human life; rather Livio discuss them as a sign of the broader nonhuman turn in thinking and the arts. Coworking with pikas opens up new ways of multispecies sensemaking and cooperations, where nonhuman species are not only instruments or indicators for human utilitarian interests. Thermoregulation, a truly central notion in times of global warming, is at center in the pikas' sophisticated adaptation strategies to changing surroundings. Livio's reflections touches upon questions of nesting, burrowing, and other technologies of making homes, and her article's thorough description of the preparations for the intermedial film project *Thermopower* offers insights to both the possibilities of rethinking human-nonhuman relations in arts and science and to which degree this definition includes questions of storytelling and intermediality. "Through sensors placed inside their bodies, biologists have learned about thermoregulation. More ambiently, pikas have helped me to make sense of multispecies, thermoregulatory processes and to notice how technological thermoregulation maps thermopower across species lines." Pikas, for Livio, are like the canaries in the coalmines, and she seems to ask implicitly whether we humans too are canaries in the fossil-fuel-driven, capitalist coalmine.

Moving from the larger mammals to Kafkaesque bugs, Adam Dickinson opens his piece, "The Blattarians," dramatically, stating that "[w]e write our environment as our environment writes us." The phrase mirrors major insights of his books, *The Polymers* and *Anatomic,* which are part of Dickinson's attempt to create a "metabolic poetics." He describes his poetics as "a research-creation practice concerned with the potential of expanded modes of reading and writing to shift the frames and scales of conventional forms of signification in order to bring into focus the often inscrutable biological and cultural writing intrinsic to the Anthropocene and its interconnected global and local metabolic processes." Partly by experimenting with his own body, he moves to the question of heat and thermoregulatory processes, nicely echoing Livio's contribution to this book. Dickinson implicitly constructs yet another kind of poetic "canary in a coal mine" experiment when he tested his physical and cognitive performances when put under the pressure of 1.5 degrees raised temperature — referring to the 1.5 limit of the Paris Agreement. Moving his heat experiments from his own body to cockroaches in a de-hierarchizing gesture, Dickinson investigates how they react to two things: the first, a two-degree change in temperature and, second, a habitat change to see how they react upon literally living upon a paper copy of Kafka's famous text on the transformation of a human being into a cockroach. The poems testify to a multispecies practice by being created in a mixture of human intention and agency, nonhuman animal agency (including excrements that, when reproduced look quite beautiful), and his personal dreams. The poems are "illustrated," or, rather, accompanied by photographs and thermal camera copies documenting the cockroach work-in-progress. Adam Dickinson generously let us use one of this great photos for the front cover of this book.

Carol Padberg's text, "WERT: Interspecies Weaving and Becoming," posits the ancient craft of weaving textiles within an experimental, multimodal, and multispecies art and research practice. Weaving wearable sculptures with wool and mycelium, Padberg's practice assembles at least two different weaving practices, one of the human and the other of the mycelia that spread its "hyphal threads into multiple directions" in order to break down organic matter and grow. Padberg's practice is one of radical collaboration: "For four years we have been making these ecological weavings. As we weave, we are part of a multispecies expanded art practice that includes local sheep; dye plants from our garden; and the chickens, insects, worms, and protozoa that maintain our soil's vitality. Our creative group includes representatives from each major family of Eukaryota organisms: animals, fungi, plants and protists." The sculptures are later put to use in somatic workshops, where the human participants are invited to wear the weaving, assisting a kind of multispecies sensorial experience and allowing the mycelia to enter the human body, making tangible the multispecies morphology that always already exists at the very core of any living entity or body: "By helping humans to sense fungal beings through their skin, we are cultivating the human ability to sense fungal communities that already live right on their skin, as well as microorganisms that live in their gut and in their lungs. Rehabilitating these senses helps to increase human awareness of the interconnectivity of the myriad forms of life on planet earth."

From the ancient technology of weaving to a contemporary technology of remote-camera viewing in capturing wildlife: Elizabeth Vander Meer's contribution explores the ethics and power dynamics of capturing the lives of animals via camera traps and discusses what kinds of stories this particular technology is able to unfold. Between dominance and care, distance and proximity, Vander Meer investigates the unique gaze facilitated in and by remote camera viewing, as well as the ethics and politics of this gaze. Her text blends media and discourse analysis with autoethnography, discusses questions of affective logics, micropolitics, and biopower, and considers practices of both care and harm expressed in different ways of viewing and narrating the lives of indigenous wildlife.

When Loup Rivière presented a draft at the conference for what is here printed as "Dancing is an Ecosystem Service, and So Is Being Trans," the atmosphere was intense, highly expectant, and curious. After Loup Rivière's performance the night before with her Dance for Plants group at the opening of the exhibition at Växjö Konsthall, the audience possibly hoped to get the dance practice explained and framed. It was, but many other aspects are opened in the rich text, too. First, perhaps, it offers a manifesto for radically different and liberating ways of seeing and being in the world. Initially, the text gives an explanation of *dancing for plants,* an activity that turns out to have political as well as philosophical outcomes. The philosophical system service of dancing for plants is "to become capable of dancing in their presence, not seeking to transform into them or to imitate them but rather to present yourself to them, to dance for them and *because* of them, to let them become, for a while, a reason for you to be in the world." Going further, however, means that any idea of Ecosystem Services needs to be criticized, rethought, and rearranged. Actually, Ecosystem Services must be transformed into the diametrically opposite to what was originally meant to specify — as quoted by Loup Rivière, "production of oxygen in the air, the natural purification of water, the biomass that feeds domesticated animals, the pollination of crops, etc. Also included are the 'amenities offered by nature like the beauty of landscapes.'" A first, remarkable rhetorical turn of the text is to make the dance for plants practice, defined as a relay-function or putting things into relation, a blueprint for another life practice, namely being trans. The second rhetorical turn is to make the practice of being trans a kind of blueprint for all beings in this world. This turn occupies the last third of the text where the reflective mode changes into a mode very directly related to the reader: to me, and to you.

IV

Multispecies Storytelling in Intermedial Practices was a many-armed event whose tentacles touched a large number of people and institutions. As an extension and parallel dimension to the conference, Växjö Konsthall opened a group exhibition co-curated with Ida Bencke with the same title, hosting art works and performances. Växjö Konsthall proved to be the perfect host environment for generous and playful conversations around experimental artistic practices and multispecies thinking. In addition, the local art and farming collective Kultivator Öland provided a much-needed satellite: in collaboration with the Rural Alchemy Workshop (R.A.W.), Kultivator Öland organized a roundtable discussion that was situated in a large barn with humans, horses, dogs, and their microbial companions, along with those of cows and sheep, who joined the conversation while engaging in a shared meal. The roundtable became a dining table, reminding us of the root of the word "companion," *cum panis,* "with bread." As Haraway reminds us, multispecies encounters are all about digestion, about eating and being eaten in the best possible, most nourishing, and least harmful ways. As it were, this multispecies roundtable was centered around questions of bacteria and regimes of hygiene — how some of our tiniest but nonetheless crucial companions often go unnoticed in our stories about what constitute health, selves, communities, and worlds.

This more-than-human panel was invested in efforts of getting to know some of the microbial critters that inhabit our bodies and our homes. Bacteria cultured by Karin Bolender and companions at R.A.W. in Oregon were traced onto a large tablecloth, which was first used on the roundtable for the communal meal at Kultivator and then installed in the hallway of the conference at the university. Upon arrival, each conference participant was given thread and a needle and was encouraged to spend some time embroidering the traces of the microbial companions who shared the roundtable. This was our way of inviting the more-than-human into the academic conference setting in a playful yet contemplative way.

Of course, the question of hygiene, of sharing tables with many companions, has now entirely changed in the face of the global pandemic that has ravaged our world. The conference took place in January 2019, one year before the global health and economic Corona crisis. The crisis was a result, as far as we know, of an unhealthy multispecies relation, and it was unfortunately a sign that many of the dire and slightly pessimistic ideas weathered at the conference came true shockingly quickly. COVID-19 offers, among many other things, a lecture on the vulnerability that we share. It is a testament to the porosity of our bodies and communities. It has also been a lesson of the consequences of our particular way of administrating and producing multispecies relations.

The crisis also made some of the editing and collecting processes somewhat slower than planned, but after a while we found the perfect seedbox for the book at punctum books, with the aid of publisher Vincent W.J. van Gerven Oei.

Nothing of this would have happened had it not been for the generous economic funding from, primarily, the Seedbox funding agency based at the time at Linköping University. Secondly, the faculty of arts and humanities of Linnæus University added necessary funding, in particular when the size of the conference grew unexpectedly. The Linnæus University Centre for Intermedial and Multimodal Studies supported some of the hours spent in the project, and the department of Design at Linnæus was particularly important in providing spaces, ideas, and essential collaborators; among them Zeenath Hasan, Eric Snodgrass and not least Leah Ireland, who worked tirelessly to facilitate a smooth and caring infrastructure of such a large and complex event. A huge thanks to the amazing students from the Design+Change program who provided extraordinarily delicious, playful., and conceptual food experiences throughout the conference.

Gratitude goes to the team at Växjö Konsthall, Filippa de Vos and Ragnhild Lekberg, for an excellent collaboration on the *Multispecies Storytelling* exhibition, and to Kultivator Öland for arranging a truly multispecies roundtable in their barn. Finally, we would like to acknowledge and thank the administrative assistance of Martina Wilmén and Martina Slättman Hansson from the university conference assistance office.

CHAPTER 1

Politics of Terristories

Vinciane Despret

For the past two or three years, I have been questioning what it means to *inhabit*. Ethology is a precious science in this matter. Not that animals can provide models; we know too well that when they are summoned to do so, they only illustrate social and economic theories that seek to legitimize their claims in nature. The study of multiple ways of living and inhabiting could instead open our imaginary to other ways of conceiving what it means to find a place in the world and to make this place a home with others who have themselves found a home.

Maybe I should first recall how a few years ago, before I began this research on the way animals inhabit their (and our) world, I was awakened by the song of a blackbird. If I mention it, it is not only because this experience touched me deeply at the time, but because it accompanied all the research that followed. The black bird sang. It was around 4 o'clock in the morning. My window was open. He was nearby, probably perched on a neighboring chimney. I could not go back to sleep. He sang with all his heart, with all his strength, with all his talent as a blackbird. Another answered him in the distance, probably from another nearby chimney. I could not go back to sleep. This blackbird sang with the enthusiasm of his body, as philosopher Étienne Souriau says of animals totally taken by the game and simulations of the pretense. But it was not this enthusiasm that kept me awake, nor what a grumpy biologist might call a noisy evolutionary success. It was the constant attention of this blackbird to his variation of each series of notes. I was captured, from the second or third call of this blackbird, by what appeared to me as an audiophonic novel, and I found myself eagerly calling for the next melodic episode with an "and again?" Each sequence differed from the previous and was invented, each time, in the form of a new counterpoint.

My window has remained open every night since. With every insomnia that followed this first episode, I returned to the same joy, the same surprise, the same waiting that prevented me from finding (or even wishing to find) sleep. The blackbird was singing. But never had singing, at the same time, seemed so close to speech. These are sentences, we can recognize them, and they also hold my ear exactly where the words of language will stick; yet never would singing at the same time be further from talk, in this effort held by a demand of non-repetition. It was sentences, but in tension of beauty and of which every word matters. The silence held its breath. I felt it trembling to attune itself to the song. I had the strongest, most obvious feeling that the fate of the whole earth, or perhaps the existence of beauty itself, at this moment rested on the shoulders of this blackbird. Souriau, talking about young animals playing, spoke of enthusiasm of the body[1]; some or-

---

1   Étienne Souriau, *Le sens artistique des animaux* (Paris: Hachette, 1965), 92.

nithologists evoke, with regard to the skylark, the exaltation. For this blackbird, it is the term "importance" that should prevail. Something matters, more than anything else, and nothing else matters except singing. The importance was invented in a song of a blackbird, and the song carried it, sent it to the furthest reaches of the song, to others, to the other blackbird over there, to my body tensed to hear, to the edges of where the power carried it. And probably the feeling that I had of a total silence, undoubtedly impossible in the urbanized environment in which I live, testified that this importance had captured me so fully that it had erased all that was not that singing. The song had given me silence. The importance had touched me.

But perhaps I was so touched by this song because I had previously read Donna Haraway's *Companion Species Manifesto*.[2] Haraway describes how the relationship with her dog, Cayenne, has profoundly affected her way of relating to other beings, or more specifically to "significant others"; how this rendered her better able to learn how to make herself more present in the world — more listening, more curious — and how she hopes that the stories she lives with Cayenne can stir the appetite for new commitments with significant others who come to count. What the writings of Haraway do — I discovered their effectiveness in this experience — is to arouse, induce, make exist, and make desirable other modes of attention. And to invite others to attend to these modes of attention. Not to become more sensitive (a catch-all that is a little too convenient and that might just lead to allergies), but to learn to and become able to grant attention. Granting attention here takes on the dual meaning of "paying attention to" and recognizing how other beings themselves cultivate the "art of noticing," as Anna Tsing calls it.[3] This is another way of declaring importance.

The ethnologist Daniel Fabre used to say about his work that it leads him to look out for what prevents people from sleeping. The anthropologist Eduardo Viveiros de Castro proposes a definition very similar: anthropology is, he says, the study of variations of importance. He also writes that anthropology does not have the task of "explaining the world of others, but that of multiplying our world."[4] I believe that the ethologists and naturalists who observe and study animals propose a similar project: to multiply ways of being, or as philosopher Didier Debaise puts it, "the ways of experiencing, feeling, making sense and giving importance to things."[5]

"Each animal is a way of knowing [the world]," writes the cognitive ethologist Mark Bekoff.[6] This proposition invites us to think of living beings in terms of "ways of being." As a result, it echoes the finest definition I've found of ethology—that of Gilles Deleuze, who sustains that ethology (which he traces back to

2   Donna Haraway, *The Companion Species Manifesto: Dogs, People and Significant Otherness* (Chicago: Prickly Paradigm Press, 2003).

3   Anna Lowenhaupt Tsing, *The Mushroom at the End of the World: On the Possibility of Life in Capitalist Ruins* (Princeton: Princeton University Press, 2017).

4   Eduardo Viveiros de Castro, *Métaphysiques cannibales: Lignes d'anthropologie post-structurale* (Paris: P.U.F., 2009), 169.

5   Didier Debaise, *L'appât des possibles* (Dijon: Presses de Réel, 2015).

6   Marc Bekoff, "Animal Passions and Beastly Virtues: Cognitive Ethology as the Unifying Science for Understanding the Subjective, Emotional, Empathic and Moral Lives of Animals." *Zygon* 41, no. 1 (2006): 71–104.

Spinoza's Ethics) is the practical science (stress the "practice") that explores what beings are capable of, that explores their powers, their ways of being affected.[7]

But what does "knowing" mean? If knowing is the expression of a desire, or rather the expression of a desire to engage with the world, Mark Bekoff's statement opens itself to many other verbs. Amid all the verbs that are and remain possible, I have chosen to give one particular meaning to his proposal: each animal is a way of *inhabiting* the world. I don't forget that the blackbird's song was about this. As I have discovered when I began my research, it was clearly a territorial song.

Let us first note that when I began this research on the question of habiting and cohabiting, I observed that these questions have undergone, in recent years, really interesting changes; I will not analyze them in detail but just mention a few. I'll start with a comparison: in the early 1970s, Karl von Frisch, the great bee specialist, published a very large book on animal architecture.[8] It includes the construction of nests, termite mounds, burrows, wasp's nests, bees, and so on. Some examples of interspecific cohabitation are mentioned. For the most part, von Frisch suggested, these were cases of parasitism.

Nearly forty years later, zoologist Mike Hansell publishes another important book on animal architecture.[9] There are birds and their nests, termites, bees and wasps, very similar to von Frisch's book. Of course, some theories have changed as to construction techniques, but overall this book continues and extends the work of von Frisch, except on one point: this time an entire chapter is devoted to innumerable interspecific cohabitations.

And parasitism is no longer mentioned. To put it simply, many animals enjoy living together, or at least they find some benefit from it. Narratives change, and no doubt they reflect changes in our concerns and questions. But I do not want to insist too much on this because to do so would be to forget that animals also change: that they face new challenges, and that they try to attune themselves as best as possible to the changes that this world imposes, or, sometimes, offers them. Didn't spiders of various species gathered by the artist Tomas Saraceno for his *Hybrid Webs* exhibition—whether they were social, solitary, or semi-social—end up making innovative webs based on different styles of composition and weaving?

Another brief example concerns research on social wasps. In the late 1990s, it was discovered that, contrary to what was previously thought, wasps weren't always busy protecting their nests from intruders from other nests. A group of London researchers discovered that the nests they observed in Panama had an average 56 percent of wasps that had migrated from other nests and been accepted into the new community.[10]

7   Gilles Deleuze, *Spinoza: Practical Philosophy,* trans. Robert Hurley (San Francisco: City Lights Books, 1988), 125.

8   Karl von Frisch, *Architecture animale,* trans. Paul Kessler (Paris: Albin Michel, 1975).

9   Mike Hansell, *Built by Animals. The Natural History of Animal Architecture* (Oxford: Oxford University Press, 2008).

10   Seirian Summer, Eric Lucas, Jessie Barker, and Nick Isaac, "Radio-tagging Technology Reveals Extreme Nest-drifting Behavior in a Eusocial Insect," *Current Biology* 17, no. 2 (2007): 140–45.

Architect Luca Merlini has asserted that architecture shapes human relations.[11] We should, I think, relieve this assertion of its anthropomorphism. In the book *Le monde du silence* [*The Silent World*], Jacques-Yves Cousteau and Frédéric Dumas recount how in the waters close to Porquerolles Island, in the south of France, they came upon a village of octopuses.[12] They saw true villas there: one had a flat roof made of a large slab supported by two lintels of stone and brick, with a rampart in front of its entrance made of pebbles, shards of bottles and pottery, and oyster and other shells. Since then, other villages have been discovered, notably in 2009 in Jervis Bay on the eastern coast of Australia: a "city" to be called Octopolis, and, more recently, not far from there, another that has been dubbed Octlantis.

Octopuses were thought to be solitary and not very social. Clearly, they are capable of changing their habits or, more precisely, dealing in unprecedented ways with an environment that gives them options. This is what Mike Hansell calls an "ecological route," to account for the fact that the transformation of the environment being carried out by the creatures will itself provoke changes in habits, ways of doing things, and ways of living and organizing in these creatures.

As we see with octopuses, the habitat not only designs the shapes of relationships, but it has the function of actively establishing social beings. And it is in this sense that I would propose understanding habitats and territories. They are the establishers of new relationships, of other ways of "relating" to others. When a couple of weaverbirds make their nest, attaching it to the thorny branches of a tree, other weavers come soon afterward to build next door, in the same tree. And others arrive and do the same. And then each couple arranges bridges between the nests with twigs.[13] In a short time, a collective of weaver birds is created in a nest that continues to grow, each couple with their own room to sleep in, another for the brood, and, at the bottom of each nest, an independent entry. Sociable weavers, on the other hand, begin collectively with the fabrication of a large roof on a sturdy branch, and from that they build separate chambers.

And from here, we may be interested in the jet black ants (*Lasius fuliginosus*) whose chamber walls in underground galleries are made of paper amalgamated with the excrement of aphids, which they care for; they also cultivate and nourish a mushroom that, by growing, consolidates the galleries. We also find strange cohabitations in a variety of fish (including gobies), either with shrimp or within much larger interspecies colonies. "Messmates," as Donna Haraway would call them.

We might then consider that these constructions are what transform individuals or couples into collectives, at times interspecies, and that "home" is what institutes this collective and gives it its existence. In other words, the collective does not preexist the creation of the territory or the habitat; it is the habitat that establishes the collective. This, it seems to me, might open our minds to other stories — less marked by exclusivity — of what "home," or even "our home," might mean.

11   Luca Merlini, "Indices d'architectures," *Revue Malaquais* 1 (2014): 9.
12   Jacques-Yves Cousteau and Frédéric Dumas, *Le monde du silence* (Paris: Editions de Paris, 1953).
13   John Hurrell Crook, "The Adaptative Significance of Avian Social Organizations," *Symposia of the Zoolological Society of London* 14 (1965): 182–218.

While thinking about the relationships between animals and home, nests or territories has changed in recent years, ideas about the ways of inhabiting aural space have undergone a similar metamorphosis. I am thinking, for instance, of the recent work of musician and bio-acoustician Bernie Krause.

Bernie Krause broke with the research methodologies concerning sound that scientists had been carrying out in animals. In effect, a large part of the traditional research relied on a way of collecting sound that was similar to how one collects specimens in a museum — without taking into account the kinds of relations that can be maintained between different species, let alone different kingdoms. As a composer and a musician, Bernie Krause instead looked for how animals compose together and how they compose with what surrounds them, such as wind, water, other organisms, and the movements of vegetation; how these animals create silences that build harmony; how they share frequencies; and how they harmonize anew. True, they still rely a regime of differentiation, but one that is very different from the *passive* regime of differentiation of visual forms, such as the voices, in this context, are the effect of a differentiation that actively attunes itself with the particularities of other sound productions. Krause explains: "First one bird, insect, or frog might sing, then others when that one quits." What Krause calls "[vying] for acoustic bandwidth" becomes visible for us in a spectrogram showing a group of singers, wherein one can clearly distinguish the succession of channels. Each of the participants — bird, frog, insect, mammal — occupies their own temporal frequency and spatial niches. This creative *agencement,* or as Deleuze's translator Brian Massumi proposes, "assemblage," tells a story.

> Where disparate groups of animals have evolved together over a long period, their voices tend to split into a series of unoccupied channels. So each sonic frequency and temporal niche is acoustically defined by a type of vocal organism: insects tend to occupy very specific bands of the spectrum, while different birds, mammals, amphibians, and reptiles occupy various other bands, where there are fewer chances of frequency or temporal overlap and masking.[14]

This led Bernie Krause to theorize that the members of this "acoustic collective [...] vocalize in distinctive kinship to one another."[15] Due to this segmentation of sound niches and division of acoustic bandwidth that mitigates conflicts over sonic territory, songs rarely overlap. One bird falls silent while others take over and then fall quiet in their own turn, leaving some others to launch into their own melody, as if to say "it's your turn now." The sounds and songs of the world are shaped in a composition. In other words, the song of the world translates into what in French we call a *partition*. In French, a *partition* refers both to the score, the musical script or composition, and (as in English) to the division of a space into differentiated territories — with this precision that the French term has lost today its sense of "division" in favor of that of "partaking."

This happy semantic duality of the French language — the fact that the same term, *partition,* designates both a musical composition and a way of distributing

---

14   Bernie Krause, *The Great Animal Orchestra: Finding the Origins of Music in the World's Wild Places* (Boston: Little, Brown and Company, 2012), 98.
15   Ibid., 88.

places — opens then to a double, inseparable dimension of inhabiting: an *expressive* dimension and a *geopolitical* one.

In a very inspiring paper, "'Prova d'orchestra' or Society as Possession," Bruno Latour revisits the commonly accepted, traditional idea that sees a political organization as a social contract based on possession. According to the social contract theory, it is by cutting up the space of goods into exclusive zones of property that society is established, and by the contract tied to this division it protects its members from a war of all-against-all and assures relatively stable peace. "That is yours, this is mine" would be, under this perspective (that, notably, of Hobbes' social contract), the political act par excellence of leaving the state of nature, a state considered in this sense to represent total disorganization of possessions.

As Latour proposes, however, is this not moving a little too fast in understanding the "that is yours, this is mine" as the claim and demand for protection of properties? "That is yours, this is mine" could take on a completely different resonance which could even define the reason for political composition in a manner very similar to how Bernie Krause describes biophonic orchestras. Here is what Latour writes, spinning the metaphor of the orchestra:

> Sentences like "It's my turn," "Careful! Now it's yours," can also serve to give *rhythm* to a joint action in which the successive phases require the actors to coordinate their participation in a rehearsed global sequence of actions. The conductor's baton signals to the viola players that "it's their turn" to play. [… While] the violists are not playing — as it's not "their turn" — they must nevertheless, in a luminal, subdued but attentive and alert way, still possess *the entire* score under the conductor's watchful eye. [...] We thus see that the same terms of property or appropriation can refer to two entirely different regimes: the spatial regime of the exclusive zone of interest delimited by clear-cut boundaries; and the temporal regime of a point in a script shared by all but in which each protagonist plays only one part.[16]

Following the way some territorial birds establish their territories — another way of operating the distribution of space — I propose, we may imagine a property regime that is not an "exclusive zone of interest" but rather one that appears more like the "the temporal regime of a point in a script shared by all but in which each protagonist plays only one part," as Latour writes. Thus, the two meanings of the French term *partition* as a "partaking agreement," or more precisely as a "sharing granted" and as a "musical script," can be brought together. If this is the case, and it seems to me that this is with territorial birds, the expressive functions and the geopolitical functions would become practically indistinguishable. At the same time, the question of the limits of individuality would be replayed.

When I visited Tomas Saraceno's *Hybrid Webs* exhibition in the Palais de Tokyo in Paris I found a very fruitful image of what could be a territory from the point of view of the territorial animal's body. Before meeting these spiders, I could hardly say anything about arachnids, as most of my research has been devoted to birds. The only thing I probably could have said is that many northern birds use

---

16   Bruno Latour, "'Prova d'orchestra' or Society as Possession," in Matea Candea, ed., *The Social After Gabriel Tarde: Debates and Assessments* (London: Routledge Press, 2016), 299–310.

spider webs to make their nests. This is just a detail, without doubt, but for me it testifies to this great game of exchanges, mischievous embezzlements, and acts of recycling that so creatively engage the living. But by looking further at spider webs, I realized that these webs were in fact giving me privileged access to certain crucial characteristics of the territorial behavior of birds. To state it briefly: the spider web is a technology that gives spiders the power to make a self with a non-self. The web that a spider weaves extends the limits of the body of her owner in space; moreover, the web is the body of the spider, and all this space thus taken in the web, which becomes space-of-web, space-of-body, this space which hitherto was a milieu or an environment, becomes not a property of the spider but something that is the very being herself. This is an act of appropriation, in the sense that French philosopher David Lapoujade commenting on Souriau recalls: to appropriate is to make oneself appropriate to, to make something properly exist.[17] Under this perspective, we can understand why Deleuze chose to translate *Umwelt* not as "the surrounding world" or "phenomenal world" but as the "associated world." Because the web, and therefore the space that the web fills, is a world associated with the body of the spider, an extended body—as my arm is associated with my body while being both a component of it and its extension. As Jean Luc Nancy wonders, if my arm is a constituent of what I call myself or me, why don't I say is "me" instead of "mine"?[18]

In other words, the spider constantly re-enacts the boundaries of her identity by giving what constitutes her self an extension replayed each time. It is in the light of these webs transforming non-self into self that I would suggest we might understand the territorial song of birds, *le chant de l'oiseau fait corps avec l'espace,* that is, "the song of the bird is/becomes one with space," or "the song of the birds transforms the space into their own body." Which means that singing transforms what is "around," what was "space" into an extension of the bird's body. What ornithologists call "a song territory." We find a lovely example of this idea that "home" is an extension of the self in Uexküll, when he investigates this enigma.[19] Why do so many small birds make their nests in proximity to those of their predators? Are they unaware? And yet it would seem this choice is judicious, if considered from the predator's point of view. For the latter, everything surrounding his nest and bearing his mark and scent is an extension of himself, like a great self that spreads itself out. That's why those close to the nest have nothing to fear.

Observing a bird who is becoming territorial, one cannot miss the theatricalization, or even more, the incessant repetitions. In the beginning of the territorial season the bird sets himself on a site and chooses a promontory, a raised place, a particular shrub. Then he moves from this center within a space that will constitute itself gradually as a space of appropriation.[20] By repeated trips and returns,

---

17   See David Lapoujade, *Les existences moindres* (Paris: Minuit, 2017), 60–61.

18   Jean-Luc Nancy, *L'intrus* (Paris: Gallilée, 2000).

19   Jakob von Uexküll, *A Foray into the Worlds of Animals and Humans: With a Theory of Meaning,* trans. Joseph D. O'Neil (Minneapolis: University of Minnesota Press, 2010).

20   See for example early depictions made by ornithologist amateur, Eliot Howard, *Territory in Bird Life* (London: Collins, 1948, and later by Margaret Morse Nice, "The Role of Territory in Bird Life," *The American Midland Naturalist* 26, no. 3 (1941): 441–87, and David Lack, "Early References to Territory in Bird Life," *The*

rhythmic surveys, the bird is pacing the entire space, as if drawing a dense web in invisible ink over the space progressively filled with his presence. The singing accompanies it, creating, as one can read in *A Thousand Plateaus*," A wall of the sound, or at least a wall with some sort of sonic bricks in it."[21] I would compare this invisible web to the equally invisible web of the spider in its expressive dimension. Such is the dimension of any form of territoriality: it is expressive.

Deleuze and Guattari add: "There is territory precisely when milieu components [...] cease to be functional to become expressive. [...] What defines the territory is the emergence of matters of expressions [qualities]."[22] In this regard, the term "self-expression" could take on a literal meaning: if it is a matter of making a site into a place, it is as much about appropriating oneself to this place, to make it a self-expression, as it is to say, to make it a "self."

Singing, as an extension of the body in space, fulfills the same role as these rhythmic surveys. It also creates an invisible web of sound stretched over a space that becomes a place; it organizes an interior and an exterior, and it is not impossible that the power of song, its rhythm, determines in part the possible extension of the territory, just as must the possibilities of surveying a certain surface. The song becomes *partition,* in the double sense of the term, musical and geopolitical.

The territorial song is a very specific song. During the long history of evolution, the song of the birds could have developed for many biological reasons, most of them being mainly expressive, that is, to seduce the females, to communicate with the others, to alert, to signify certain things. The territorial song is singular in the sense that it is both an expression of the territory ("I am here and I am the resident of this place"), and it forges the territory, making it exist and become as such. The song is both addressed to others as an expression of a "home" and at the same time oriented towards the environment, which it metamorphoses into "territory". It means partaking, sharing the space, but at the same time it actively produces (and transforms a space into) territory. And we can as well affirm that the bird sings to affirm its territory and that the territory is what gives the bird the opportunity to sing, that the territory is put at the service of the song. The song functions both as *partition* and as song, that is to say, as both signifier and signified. As a result, singing can assume both a geopolitical dimension (i.e., partaking and claiming) and an expressive function (i.e., the territory "makes the bird sing").

The territory is an event. And the song of the bird both creates and expresses this event. Deleuze and Guattari insist that the territory is first and foremost an act. And it is first and foremost an expressive act. For example, if we go back to the spider, the web that captures insects, as functionally adapted to this capture, is not yet a territory. It will become so as soon as there is a reorganization of the functional characteristics that take on an expressive value. In the same way, in birds, singing may serve to attract a female. It becomes expressive, with this behavior of territorialization. This does not prevent the song from being de-territorialized, to become functional within the territory and to call the female to subsequently

Condor 46 (1944): 108–11.

21   Gilles Deleuze and Félix Guattari, *A Thousand Plateaus: Capitalism and Schizophrenia,* trans. Brian Massumi (Minneapolis: University of Minnesota Press, 1987), 311.

22   Ibid., 315.

be re-territorialized as a territorial behavior—many birds continue to sing after mating. Similarly, and I would like to insist on this last point, aggressive functions don't make the territory. The territory is not an effect of interspecific aggression, as Konrad Lorenz suggested; instead the territory reorganizes the aggressive functions into expressive functions, and the aggressive function, as Deleuze and Guattari said, "change[s] the pace."[23]

The territory reorganizes the aggressive functions into expressive functions: this accounts for the theatricalization that so impressed the first researchers, who, in the beginning of the twentieth century, decided to study territorial behavior. The disputes that arise in regards to border definition or that result from intrusion of an invader are spectacular. And that is exactly what they mean to be. This could explain why the scientists who studied them, in the early research on territories in the first part of the twentieth century, were so impressed: these birds are so pugnacious, so aggressive in their addresses to each other. Only a very fierce competition could explain that. But as time passed, scientists noted that these conflicts hardly ever end up in real fights. And not only that. Not only did the conflicts mostly consist of threatening postures, but the outcomes were also largely foreseeable. The inhabitant of the place is almost always the winner.

Several theories have been proposed to account for these observations. It was first found that the defensive vigor of the occupant or resident, is always greater than the aggressiveness of the intruder. As well, the closer the inhabitant of the place was to the center of his territory, the more he displayed aggression, and the more the intruder became hesitant and timid. The dimensions of the territory are not extensive but intensive and traversed by gradients of affects, forces, strengths. There is a partition of the powers.

But another feature was overshadowed. It progressively appears that birds prefer to settle where others have settled. Certainly, we can think of the effect of mimicry, related to the quality of the chosen places, and scientists first interpreted this phenomenon in relation to the quality of the privileged places. But more cautious observations had shown that if quality is at stake, it is not the sole reason. Often there are places of equivalent quality nearby, which will only be occupied when the privileged space is saturated. If quality of the site was not their sole reason for choosing these places, then birds might have social or even political motives for choosing to live near each other.

Here appears the more specifically geopolitical dimension of territorialization, which is inspired by the work of Baptiste Morizot and by the writings of the ornithologist James Fisher,[24] himself inspired by Franck Fraser Darling. There is a characteristic of the territories that should be taken into account: they are always adjacent. In Fraser Darling's words, one of the most important functions of "territory in breeding birds is the provision of periphery."[25] What is outside the borders is as important as what is inside. In Deleuze and Guattari's words, all territorialization engages, at the same time, a de-territorialization that is in reality a re-territorialization.

---

23   Ibid., 388.
24   James Fisher, "Evolution and Bird Sociality," in *Evolution As a Process,* eds. J. Huxley, A.C. Hardy and E.B. Ford (London: Allen & Unwin, 1954), 71–83.
25   Frank Fraser Darling, "Social Behavior and Survival," *The Auk* 69 (1952): 183–91.

In other words, what territories do is to create *neighbors,* and therefore neighborhood relations: this re-territorialization is a social device. It is a social organization that makes neighbors. Or, if we refer to the geopolitical dimension, it constitutes what Morizot calls a "conventional device of pacification."[26] In other words, and quite counter-intuitively, the territory socializes the birds. It forms a constant reinvention of social relations. For example, in many cases intruders of the same species are tolerated as long as they only feed themselves, but they are chased away if they start parading or singing. Baptiste Morizot, in this regard, thinks that wolves also support this hypothesis of pacifying convention. When they cross a border, they stop marking. According to this conception, the territory would be a spatial configuration that requires good manners, that is, some things shouldn't be done from here, from this border onwards. This is what I would call respect of the forms, a respect for forms created in space (i.e., the territories) and a lifestyle respectful of conventions; a composition, both a partition of space to make living together as good as possible, and a musical script, a series of musical chords ("now it is your turn"). It is a device-place that, in a way, both protects community life from disorder and allows the social life of a group. It is a musical device, as being mostly made of songs in birds, a political musical invention. That is cosmopolitics. And this may lead us to think that for birds, the birth of art was a political invention.

To sing for a bird is both to transform oneself into a being that becomes territorial — because as we have seen, the song, far from only expressing the territory participates in the metamorphosis of the bird — and it is to transform a place that becomes a territory. Thus, in each song, a story is created and told. And we can even imagine that the song tells something of the stories of the place itself, that it echoes the stream that flows through it, that it adjusts to the density of vegetation, that it attests to the presence of other birds, other animals (or predators), that it perhaps even tells past conflicts in which the bird has been involved. And may be it anticipates those that will occur in the future. Many stories meet in these songs and ours are added to them. That is in that sense that one might say that the birds, in singing (or even celebrating) their territories, take an active part in the world's cosmopolitics — cosmophonic stories.

But what matters most for me is that with these stories, we are far from the idea of the territory as private property, as a place of exclusive possession to which our modern legal and philosophical tradition has accustomed us. Territorial issues are often heavily burdened. I do not expect that birds will help us find solutions to learn how to live, and I really do not want to burden them with that, or to take them as hostages to our problems. Perhaps they may just help us to detox from all the obvious ideas about territories that have so far been imposed. Or they may inspire the poetic purpose of ethology: multiplying our world and the ways we can inhabit it, and finding alongside them the courage that the French singer Dominique A. celebrates: the courage of birds singing in the icy wind.

---

26 Baptiste Morizot, *Les diplomates: Cohabiter avec les loups sur une autre carte du vivant* (Marseille: Wild Project, 2016).

References

Bekoff, Mark. "Animal Passions and Beastly Virtues: Cognitive Ethology as the Unifying Science for Understanding the Subjective, Emotional, Empathic and Moral Lives of Animals." *Zygon* 41, no. 1 (2006): 71–104. DOI: 10.1111/j.1467-9744.2006.00727.x

Cousteau, Jacques-Yves, and Frédéric Dumas. *Le monde du silence.* Paris: Editions de Paris, 1953.

Debaise, Didier. *L'appât des possibles.* Dijon: Les presses du réel, 2015.

Deleuze, Gilles. *Spinoza: Practical Philosophy.* Translated by Robert Hurley. San Francisco: City Lights Books, 1988.

Deleuze, Gilles, and Félix Guattari. *A Thousand Plateaus: Capitalism and Schizophrenia.* Translated by Brian Massumi. Minneapolis: University of Minnesota Press, 1987.

Fisher, Jane. "Evolution and Bird Sociality." In *Evolution as a Process,* edited by J. Huxley, A.C. Hardy, and E.B. Ford. London: Allen & Unwin, 1954: 71-83.

Fraser Darling, Frank. "Social Behavior and Survival." *The Auk* 69 (1952): 183–91. DOI: 10.2307/4081268.

Hansell, Mike. *Built by Animals: The Natural History of Animal Architecture.* Oxford: Oxford University Press, 2008.

Haraway, Donna. *The Companion Species Manifesto: Dogs, People, and Significant Otherness.* Chicago: Prickly Paradigm Press, 2003.

Howard, Eliot. *Territory in Bird Life.* London: Collins, 1948 [1920].

Hurrell Crook, John. "The Adaptative Significance of Avian Social Organizations." *Symposia of the Zoolological Society of London* 14 (1965): 182–218. DOI: 10.1016/0003-3472(64)90041-7.

Krause, Bernie. *The Great Animal Orchestra: Finding the Origins of Music in the World's Wild Places.* Boston: Little, Brown and Company, 2012.

Lack, David. "Early References to Territory in Bird Life." *The Condor* 46, no. 3 (1944): 108–11. DOI: 10.2307/1364276.

Lapoujade, David. *Les existences moindres.* Paris: Minuit, 2017.

Latour, Bruno. "'Prova d'orchestra' or Society as Possession." In *The Social after Gabriel Tarde: Debates and Assessments,* edited by Matea Candea, 299–310. London: Routledge, 2016.

Lowenhaupt Tsing, Anna. *The Mushroom at the End of the World: On the Possibility of Life in Capitalist Ruins.* Princeton: Princeton University Press, 2017.

Merlini, Luca. "Indices d'architectures." *Revue Malaquais* 1 (2014): 9.

Morizot, Baptiste. *Les diplomates: Cohabiter avec les loups sur une autre carte du vivant.* Marseille: Wild Project, 2016.

Morse Nice, Margaret. "The Role of Territory in Bird Life." *The American Midland Naturalist* 26, no. 3 (1941): 441–87. DOI: 10.2307/2420732.

Nancy, Jean-Luc. *L'intrus.* Paris: Galilée, 2000.

Seirian, Summer, Eric Lucas, Jessie Barker, and Nick Isaac. "Radio-tagging Technology Reveals Extreme Nest-drifting Behavior in a Eusocial Insect." *Current Biology* 17, no. 2 (2007): 140–45. DOI: 10.1016/j.cub.2006.11.064.

Souriau, Étienne. *Le sens artistique des animaux.* Paris: Hachette, 1965.

Viveiros de Castro, Eduardo. *Métaphysiques cannibales: Lignes d'anthropologie post-structurale.* Paris: P.U.F., 2009.

von Frisch, Karl. *Architecture animale*. Translated by Paul Kessler. Paris: Albin Michel, 1975.
von Uexküll, Jacob. *A Foray into the Worlds of Animals and Humans: With a Theory of Meaning*. Translated by Joseph D. O'Neil. Minneapolis: University of Minnesota Press, 2010.

CHAPTER 2

Secretome Perpetua

Karin Bolender

Homebirth (Borne in the Barn Dust)

In the weeks before the birth of Possible, we parents-to-be were encouraged by midwives, friends, and recommended books to devise what they call a birth plan, which at the very least sketches a hopeful vision of how things might go once labor begins. The vision we landed on was simple: a homebirth, with trusted midwives present and a warm bathtub at the ready and a fire crackling in the hearth. Yet my own real and visceral maternal gut desire was otherwise, and, for a number of reasons, wildly implausible. I wanted Possible to be born in the barn.

Secretly and deeply, I wanted newborn Possible to be licked clean by Aliass, my dear, long-eared equine companion of many years and miles. Odd, perhaps, and of course forbidden, but this wish held a fierce desire to sidestep sterile exclusions of western birth practices (i.e., allopathic, colonial, human-exceptionalist) and instead nurture a new human from the get-go within deeper ecological meshes, to immerse them in radically different possibilities for more diverse, earthly m<other tongues. We recognize that "human" birth is regulated by numerous laws and cultural taboos. No one would have let us do this, not even our heroically empowering midwives. So when labor began, we hunkered down inside the relatively less dusty house, which at least was only a short distance from the barn where the herd chewed hay and dozed. As it happens, complications arose during sixteen hours of labor at home. Later at the hospital, an emergency Caesarean section revealed that Possible had made what they call a "true knot" in the umbilical cord — a tricky little loop, truly knotted, that must have been crossed over and swam through at roughly twenty weeks of fetushood. Surgery saved our lives, no doubt. Yet the hospital was about as far from the familial barnyard as we could get. Meanwhile Possible also missed out on the significant early microbial "seeding" –passage of maternal microbiome to a newborn mammal — that comes with natural passage through the birth canal.[1]

---

1   Though the science is not decisive, a number of studies have shown positive health effects of "vaginal seeding" for infants born by preplanned C-section. Mothers swab their vaginal microbiomes ahead of the birth and then rub the swab over the newborn's skin. See Maria Dominguez-Bello et al., "Partial Restoration of the Microbiota of Cesarean-born Infants via Vaginal Microbial Transfer," *Nature Medicine* 22, no. 3 (2016): 250–53. Other studies have contradicted this finding.

Possible's unexpected knot precluded earliest inheritance of a maternal microbiome at birth, but we soon came home to a matrix of far-from-sterile relations, visible and unseen: constant knotty encounters of all kinds. And we have been immersed ever since in the kinds of dense webs that Natalie Loveless describes as "ecologies of care," which in our case involve the macro and micro biomes of a familial herd of asses, dogs, cats, an old rodeo horse, swallows, kestrels, grasses, mice, and many others — to name only some of the lives that entwine amidst daily comings and goings.[2] So Possible was messily inoculated into a family full of barn-dust bodies and muzzles and mud, local grass hay, forest edges, and the millioning motes and swarms of untold, often sub-visible others that proliferate as both allies and enemies in every crack and fold.

As a kid who was privileged to grow up amidst thick beams and drafts of barn aisles and haylofts myself, as a mother I was inclined to be pleased by a 2017 scientific study that suggested surprising immunological benefits of childhood exposure to microbial inhabitants of barn dust. Through a long-term tracking of children growing up in two distinct, us religious communities that maintain distance from modern urban life and technologies, the Amish and the Hutterites, researchers found significant differences. Among the Amish children, who grow up immersed in family barns and work and play in close daily contact with cows, horses, hay, and many sub-visible associates, incidences of allergies were notably lower than among the Hutterite kids, who have less direct contact with communal livestock, mostly dairy cows quartered in centralized facilities.[3] Pitch the implications of these findings against rampant Antibacterial Wars that have raged in medical facilities, classrooms, and nuclear-family bathrooms for decades, where the weapons of choice are ubiquitous hand-sanitizers and widespread beliefs that all bacteria are evil germs to fear and fight. Meanwhile, researchers into microbial biodiversity find increasing evidence that successful antibacterial campaigns may well be killing off some of our most ancient and beneficent biological "old friends," whose roles in our enmeshed well-beings are wildly unknown.[4]

Questions of old friends and new possibilities, of dangers and solaces tangled up in dreams of intra-species maternal hygiene, bring us back by a brand-new path to the dream of the birth of Possible, almost in our own muddy ass family barnyard. While the benefits of Amish dust might seem to vindicate immersion in swarms of invisible allies among barn-beam motes and dusty hay, these findings still would not convince anyone it was safe for me to give birth in the barn — and rightly so, I suppose. Even a post-Pasteurian profligate knows that some risks are not worth taking. Who knows what sorts of slavering, sub-visible villains lie in

---

2   Natalie Loveless, "Maternal Ecologies: A Story in Three Parts," in *Performing Motherhood: Artistic, Activist, and Everyday Enactments,* eds. Amber E. Kinser, Terri Hawkes, and Kryn Freehling-Burton (Bradford: Demeter Press, 2014), 149.

3   This particular study on childhood asthma shows marked benefits to children exposed to barnyard dust, called by researchers "the farm effect." See Gina Kolata, "Barnyard Dust Offers a Clue to Stopping Asthma in Children," *The New York Times,* August 3, 2016, http://www.nytimes.com/2016/08/04/health/dust-asthma-children.html/. Note that other studies have shown different findings.

4   On the "Old Friends Hypothesis" that proposes significant beneficial co-evolutions in multispecies assemblages of early domesticates, especially bovines and humans, see G.A. Rook and L.R. Brunet, "Microbes, Immunoregulation, and the Gut," *Gut* 54, no. 3 (2005): 317–20.

wait in such wild and messy places, waiting to take advantage of vulnerable openings?

Any mammalian mother might tell you, and not only in words, that giving birth is most vulnerable and ragged opening there is, and also one that never ever closes. Often thereafter, desire to protect loved ones can make us want to close ranks against all unfamiliar others, by whatever unequally distributed means are afforded to us. But a certain mode of closing ranks around dangerously exclusive, antibacterial so-called "Human" fortresses is one trend I wished to buck in the dream of Possible being born in the barn and licked clean by Aliass. Why couldn't they be, just as Aliass's own Passenger was on that night in 2002 in the dusty midnight bare-bulb glow of a Virginia barn? Just as every foal and whelp and kit and cub is, welcomed and warmed into the world by the licks of a mammalian mother tongue.

But true enough, too, that not every element in a given mother tongue is warm and worldly-welcoming. Like the maternal microbiome passed to newborns, whether through natural birth or newfangled seeding practices, we each also pass on the seeds of linguistic "mother tongues" to fetuses and neonates — all the heritable names, stories, cultures, and categorical cuts carried forth in different languages and ontologies. While "mother tongue" is a loaded metaphor for the language that human children grow up into in various ways, we are becoming more and more aware these days that both languages and microbial worlds invisibly and inextricably shape the parameters of embodied lives and ecologies in unequal ways. In 2020, viral microbes significantly changed life around the world. The global COVID-19 pandemic has also drawn stark attention in new ways to how the category of the "human" has been policed by prevailing systemic racism, as environmental and reproductive justice activists have known for ages.[5] In this consideration of microbial and linguistic inheritances, then, I must recognize the racial and economic privileges that allow some of us to make choices at all regarding the kinds of birth and hygiene practices we want to engage, while many, or most, mothers are deprived of choices regarding how to give birth and protect loved ones: from lacks of reproductive health care and accumulation of toxic legacies in racially marked zones to the seemingly infinite and often obfuscated other ways in which choices and protections are unequally distributed.

As an artist–researcher and more recently as a maternal linguistic transmitter, I have long sought ways to intervene in elements of mother tongues that bear toxic and false tales about who, what, where, and how we coexist within barely reckoned, living meshes and within systems and institutions that define Human and Other-than in woeful ways. For many years, Aliass and our family herd have been steadfast companions in this effort to probe spaces between arbitrary and damaging material-semiotic categories, thanks in large part to the implosive charge of the word "ass" from within my own mother tongue, mixed with deep maternal regard for wordless, embodied human-equine-other ways of living.[6] Various projects

---

5   See Adele Clarke and Donna Haraway, eds., *Making Kin Not Population* (Chicago: Prickly Paradigm Press, 2018).

6   See Karin Bolender, *The Unnaming of Aliass* (Earth: punctum books, 2020). In particular, a project called "R.A.W. Assmilk Soap" draws on the parapoetic and immunological properties of mammalian colostrum (neonatal milk) to imagine ways that bodies intra-act with environments in unseen ways.

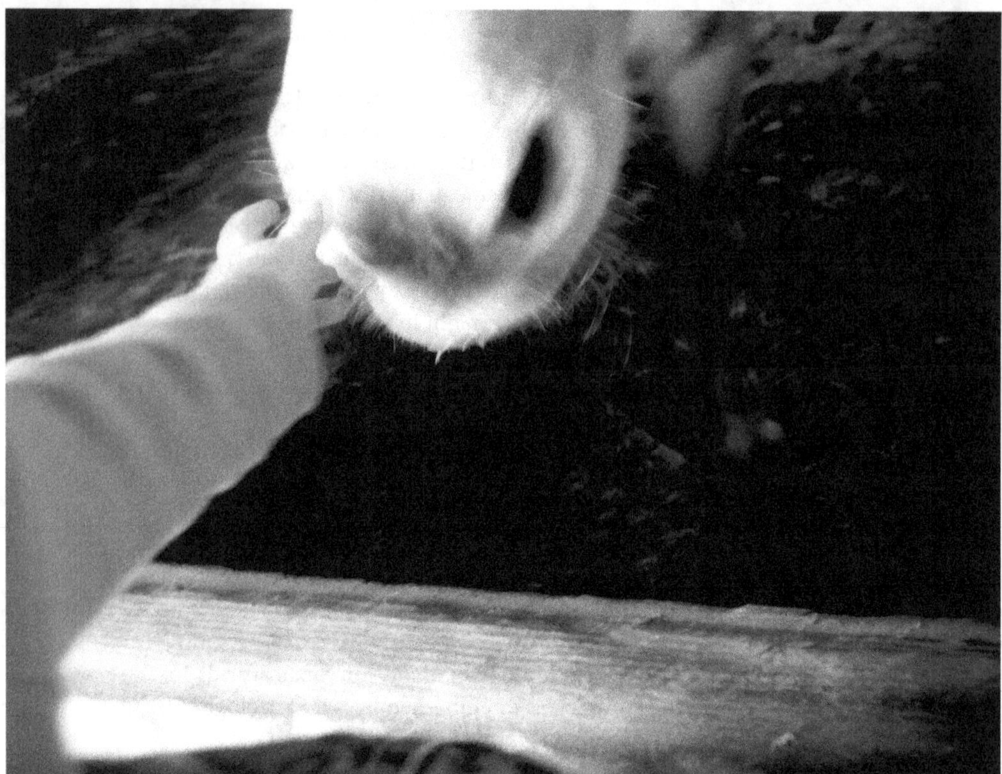

Fig. 2.1. Possible meets the mysterious muzzle of Aliass in the barn. Photograph by the author.

over the years have imaginatively engaged with invisible-ass embodied processes and myriad parapoetic possibilities therein. But it was not until I began to ponder the influences of microbial and other sub-visible becomings within tangled lives and practices that I found another vital opening into the thick of all this mother-tongue questioning. Beginning with the prohibition against barn birth and inter-species licking, I discovered a kind of portal into new hopeful possibilities for "seeding" Possible's m<other tongue, in a process of culturing Aliass's warm, wet, and sweetly hay-smelling one.

In the summer of 2016, a local art-science collaboration offered artists the chance to sample different aspects of local environments and examine our cultures in the Oregon State University Microbiology lab. Through this invitation, I came back around to my old born-in-the-barn dream, and so I knew exactly where to go for my act of culturing. After all, if the presence of unknown bacteria in the barn, or any hygienically untamed place for that matter, is what makes the stable an unsafe place to bring forth a newborn human, I would like to get a sense of just who these nefarious agents might be. The first culturing act was to sample the dust of the barn, not that I expected to recognize any particular species of bacterium or protist, per se. Then it occurred to me to go to the source, the motherlode of m<other tongue possibility. I swabbed Aliass's lovely pale-pink tongue as she chewed contemplatively on a muzzleful of local grass hay in the paddock sun one summer day. And that is how I came to meet — and so slowly begin to admire and

absorb into the mesh of familial relations — a sweet-ass microbe called (maybe) *Bacillus subtilis.*[7]

Bacillus, I have been told, is a common family of bacteria with some special charisma, including exceptional motility — they move around a lot. I knew little about these new friends, except that they live within the muzzle of the wisest and loveliest beast I know, that they also associate with grasses and hay, and that they make beautiful, webbed traces of their wanderings around the agar in a petri dish as they seek whatever it is they are seeking. I know they can be dangerous, too, in certain concentrations. *Bacillus* is in the family of anthrax. Little knowledge that this is, this unforeseen meeting, mediated by Aliass's lovely muzzle and the observations of a poetic microbiologist, was enough to peak a passionate interest and incline me to welcome *Bacillus* as an agent and collaborator into our imaginative worldings. And, so, with this dramatic entry of *Bacillus* on the scene, we began slowly to consider all kinds of known and unknown microbial presences in daily worldings and especially into the long task of seeding m<other tongues: to cultivate new openings and alliances, in hopes of becoming more inclusive of the truly knotted and constant immersions in and through other lives, both those we recognize and love and those we barely fathom.

Welcome to the Secretome

It happened at home one Saturday, in the rare mysterious glow of an October morning when the sun hovers just on the other side of a ghostly glowing mist. In this singular autumn weather phenomenon, influenced by the forested mountains and the westward Pacific Ocean, the trees loom and spider webs everywhere leap quivering into the visible light: delicate webs you would never see otherwise, except in this special luminous weather. That morning we happened to be out wandering around in the pond pasture — humans, pups, asses, and so on — and something happened. Oddly I can't recall how it was that I came to be holding that image of Aliass's tongue culture; but when I held it up just so in that special light, it became a sort of portal, an opening into invisible layers of the place in a never-before-noticed way. And then, as another moment passed, it became something else: a kind of (im)possible "treasure map."

Layered onto the landscape with this vague suggestion of scrutability, the paths inscribed in agar by movement of hungry, desiring lives suggested hidden meshes, like the suddenly visible spider webs and other less visible threads of care, connection, and desire that bind lives together in timeplaces in various ways. All this came into focus, if sub-visibly, like tales scrawled through the earth in translucent ink. At the time this was more of a gut recognition. The evocation of sub-visible living webs layered into the visible landscape was just the sort of imaginative ecological opening I had been searching for, if unwittingly. Here was a new kind of on-

---

7 The visual identification of *Bacillus* was an educated guess by one of the microbiologists at the OSU lab that day, Kyle Asfahl, who was helping artists interpret what we saw under the microscopes. Asfahl could not claim to be sure which, if any, *Bacillus* it was without DNA analysis, but its wild traces of wandering movement around the petri dish indicated a great deal of flagellar motility. So, I take a degree of poetic license here in identifying *Bacillus subtilis,* also known as "hay bacillus" or "grass bacillus."

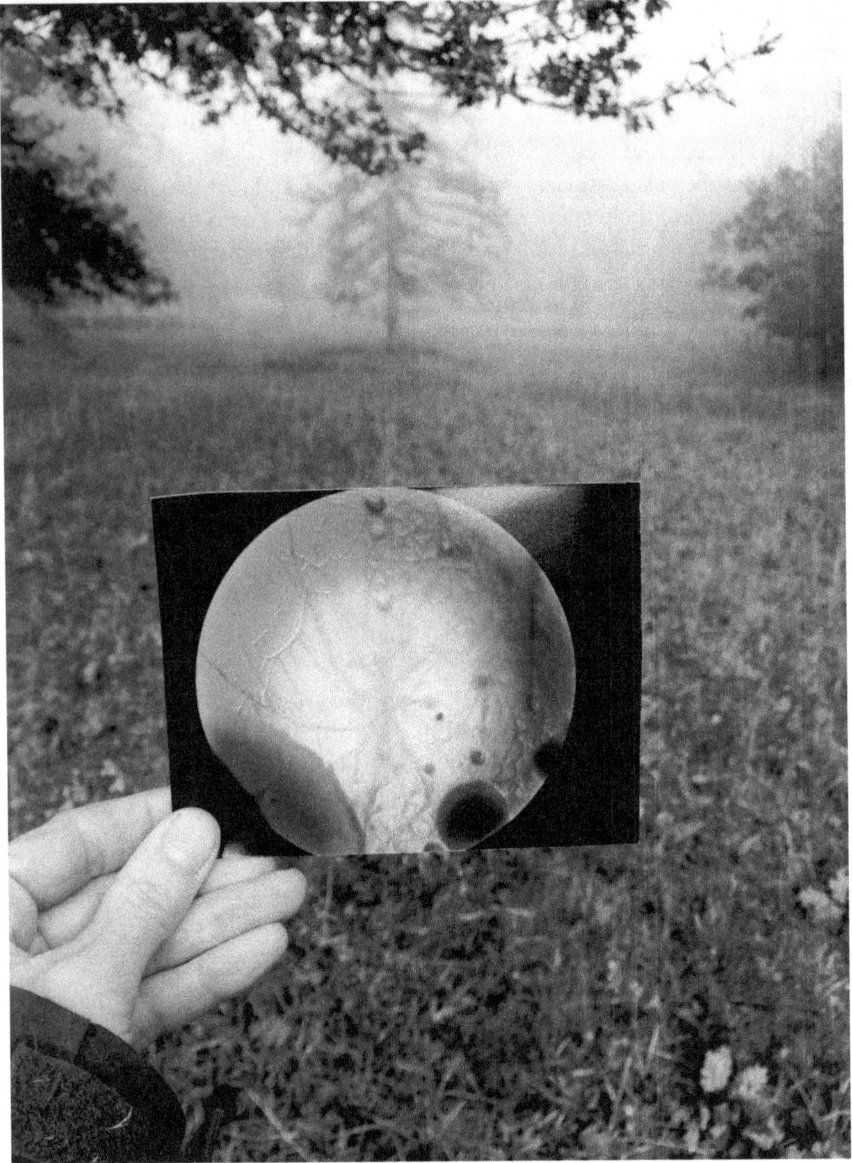

Fig. 2.2. The muzzle-tongue culture from Aliass emerging as locally-grown Secretome treasure (not)map in the R.A.W. pasture. Photograph by the author.

tological opening into specific ecologies — a kind of opaque portal into active un/knowing of places, habitats, territories, a kind of hole through which to dive into layered living meshes we inhabit, as inscribed in tales flowing secretively through a specific habitats.[8] So the so-called Secretome emerged as an alluring, elusive des-

8   Marisol de la Cadena, "Matters of Method: Or, Why Method Matters toward a Not Only Colonial Anthropology," HAU: *Journal of Ethnographic Theory* 7, no. 2 (2017): 2.

ignation for an experimental mode of exploring habitats, hunting idiosyncratic "treasures" and seeking paths into active un/knowing in timeplaces.[9]

From this first voluptuous slide into what I have come to call "the Secretome," I began dreaming up new and different ways to invite others to come along, to explore hidden relations with seemingly familiar places through this inscrutable quasi-bio-semiotic portal. In the spring of 2017, as part of the *Microbiomes: To See the Unseen* exhibition in Corvallis, Oregon, this impulse took the form of an invitation to local humans to come participate in an experimental workshop called "R.A.W. Welcome to the Secretome." That first workshop was performed with interdisciplinary artist Emily Stone and fifteen participants in and around the Rural Alchemy Workshop (R.A.W.) home barnyard in Philomath. After Emily led us in a series of movement exercises around the barn, we presented the treasure maps made from Aliass's muzzle-tongue culture. We then invited all to explore the deep mud of the barnyard and the wet, grassy pasture and steamy hot manure pile, while actively and imaginatively seeking whatever treasures or openings they might each discover, and with the caveat (via Gregory Bateson, via Alfred Korzybski) that "the map is not the territory."[10]

"Welcome to the Secretome" events have since unfolded in a number of different places, inviting different gatherings of participants to explore sub-visible layerings and treasure-seeking through portals into various places: from culturing maps from a semi-wild deer's muzzle on the Pacific shores of Washington to exploring revelatory soils of a farm in Norway to reveling in the wonderfully biodiverse, dirty, and vibrant assemblages, including the conjuring by Beth Stephens of a little spotted ass named Benito and his lovely human caretaker, Eva, that came together for E.A.R.T.H. Lab's SEEDBED: Soil Symposium in Santa Cruz, California.[11] In various ways, "Welcome to the Secretome" explores one creative proposal for how we might make space for mysterious, sub-visible agencies of microbial meshes in collective storying, at different nexuses of ecologies and imaginative encounters with the recognition that they are always already involved in the stories of our collective lives in ways we barely grasp.[12]

First and foremost, the Secretome project invites an experimental, creative mode of experiencing embodied presence and time-in-places, while acknowledging the myriad other unknown lives also present in that timeplace, at peripheries of perception where the seemingly familiar becomes wildly unknown. The Secretome is about honoring that wild complexity, playing and poking at the frayed edges of what we know about the places we call home. This practice finds resonance in Vinciane Despret's proposition for how all kinds of inhabitants co-com-

---

9   The term "secretome" was something I came across in earliest research into "hay bacillus." As it happens, *Bacillus* has played a significant role in the emerging scientific field of secretomics.

10   Gregory Bateson, *Mind and Nature: A Necessary Unity* (Cresskill: Hampton Press, 2002), 27.

11   In April 2018, E.A.R.T.H. Lab's SEEDBED: A Soil Symposium, hosted by Annie Sprinkle and Beth Stephens and UCSC Center for Agroecology and Sustainable Agriculture, cultivated two days of fertile creative and critical dialogues with and about the wonders and significances of dirt and all the living matters it supports. See the site: https://earthlab.ucsc.edu/soil-symposium/.

12   Check out the emerging field of psychobiotics to dig into fascinating ways that microbiomes shape mammalian psychological experiences.

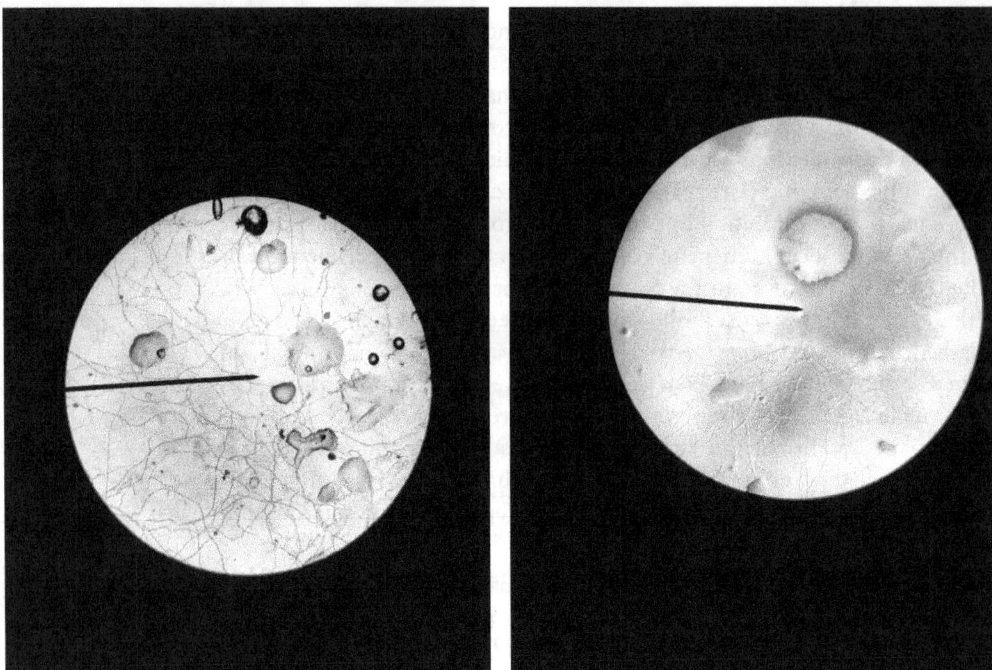

Figs. 2.3, 2.4, 2.5. The muzzle-tongue culture emerging as locally-grown treasure (not) map. Photographs by the author.

pose overlapping stories together in places, as each expresses their world's dimensions in their own ways. In "Politics of Territstories," Despret describes how a bird's movements and songs together both express and enact a territory "as if drawing a dense web in invisible ink over the space progressively filled with his presence. […] I would compare this invisible web to the equally invisible web of the spider in its expressive dimension. Such is the dimension of any form of territoriality: it is expressive."[13] The Secretome project echoes this sense of "territory" as "terri(s) tories" always in-the-making as both a special mode of creative expression and an inherently collaborative endeavor, where all the collaborators can never be named or known or translated.

Muddy Creek Secretomes

In spring 2019, a R.A.W. collaboration with a local elementary school in Corvallis, Oregon invited third- and fourth-grade kids (ages 9 and 10) to explore their own Secretomes through culturings around the ecological restoration area of their school grounds. Guided by teachers (the mysterious "Mr. O" and assistant Ms. Ellen), we invited the kids to wander around the familiar grounds, seeking special "portals" that called to them as a possible openings into other worlds. We handed out swab-sticks and agar "lenses" to each kid, with which to culture their own unique portals, and then we asked them each to go out and find a spot that might

13   Despret, "Politics of Territstories," this volume.

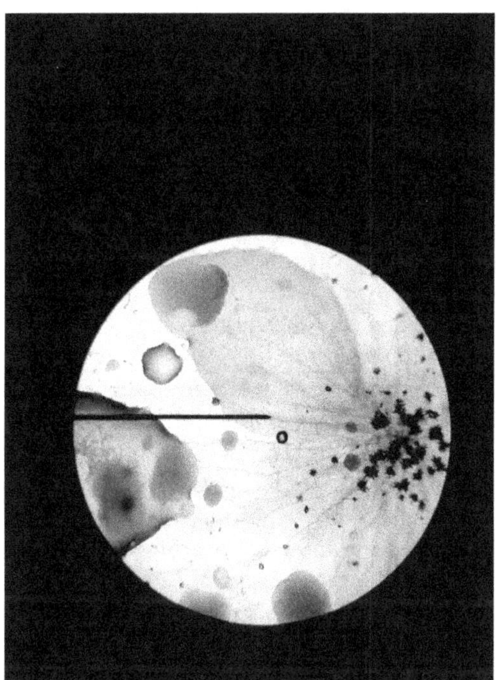

imaginatively transport them into sub-visible realms of multilayered worlds. Once they had done this, with a separate swab, they layered in cultures from their own tongues and so mixed in the different storytelling capacities of human linguistic imaginations. I took the individual cultures home and let them grow for a few days, then created unique images from each kid's culture and gave them back as "treasure maps." The kids then engaged their unique Secretome maps as visual material with which to create stories of imaginary adventures, passing through their microbial portals into hidden geographies of the actual landscape, simultaneously familiar and unknown.

The kids' stories that emerged from this process are wild and strange assemblages of genre, grammar, and scale, mixes of geographic names and plot lines, influenced by their favorite stories and characters and each as different and distinct as the maps they draw from. One of my favorite adventures, written by Noe, follows the narrator on a winding path into the heart of a strange forest of flower stalks and thorny brambles, through jolting encounters with a benevolent, giant spider and an ambiguous, three-legged fox. Others feature hybrid meldings of mythical beasts and local ecologies, where narrators enter realms of poetically named dragons and tiny magic narwhals accessed through native oaks or ubiquitous puddles. They penetrate surfaces of bark and soil and scramble up and down the roots and stems of familiar plant species to converse with beautiful maples, giant grasses, or rhizomatic spore-bearing plants known as horsetail, a gnarly local relic of the Paleozoic understory.

This interesting juxtaposition of local biomes and creative imagination is where we shift back for a moment to thorny questions of raising (generations of) Possible(s), in a time of jarring ecological uncertainty. As it happens, the grounds of this Secretome workshop with Muddy Creek kids is also where my own child attends elementary school, a place where they are learning to name and read and categorize the world, by means of an innovative, integrated art-science curriculum focused on the local bioregion. This learning is wondrous and essential to their future worldings, so we hope.[14] But certain fraught questions loom at the peripheries of all formal colonial education, especially as children are raised in tattered legacies that have, in many cases, precipitated many of the toxic consequences they and their planet inherit. It's worth asking, though if not for immediate answers: What do we lose in learning the names of all the things and species, and all the categories and assumptions that go with them, when those names so often erase other present, past, and possible ways of knowing places? What other grammars and connective ways of un/knowing, listening, and inhabiting in-betweens go by the wayside as western colonial classifications calcify?[15]

These are wonderings that the Secretome projects aim to activate, in embodied gestures toward active (un)knowing, and with respect for multitudes of untold authors weaving and warping stories together all the time, in every timeplace. The vagueness is not accidental but strategic, as we seek to cultivate a mode of "unthinking mastery" and move toward different, more respectful and inquisitive approaches to encountering places in all their un/knowable layerings.[16] Secretome projects proceed with the sense that composing less-exploitative earthly stories requires us to seek creative modes of finding ourselves within assemblages of unfolding tales, co-composed with unthinkable lives and temporalities at the edges of forests, seas, and other familiar places we do not know.[17]

14   Many schoolchildren around the world have experienced extended hiatus from collective school attendance in response to the global COVID-19 pandemic. With their educations suddenly laid in the laps of families and home territories (and through the agency of a microbial actor, I might add), these questions seem ever more urgently in need of careful attention and exploration.

15   We are indebted in countless ways to the Champinefu band of the Kalapuya tribe on whose traditional lands we are uninvited guests, and we have much to learn from them and other tribes of this region. In a different register and mostly within European and colonial contexts, Adriana Benzaquen's *Encounters with Wild Children* describes a fraught push and pull of desires and resistance embedded in historical accounts of feral children and explores how these gnarly old tales of wild children (with)hold vital questions and hidden desires about possible other ways of knowing worlds we inhabit. See Adriana Benzaquen, *Encounters with Wild Children: Temptation and Disappointment in the Study of Human Nature* (Montreal: McGill-Queen's University Press, 2006).

16   Julietta Singh, *Unthinking Mastery: Dehumanism and Decolonial Entanglements* (Durham: Duke University Press, 2018).

17   I come back again and again to a quotation by Deborah Bird Rose that evokes the humility we so desperately need: "Frank Egler is reported to have said, 'ecosystems may not only be more complex than we think, they may be more complex than we can think.' One cannot remove one's self from the system under examination, and because one is a part of the system, the whole remains outside the possibility of one's comprehension." Deborah Bird Rose, *Reports from a Wild Country: Ethics for Decolonization* (Sydney: University of New South Wales Press, 2014), 188.

Secretome Perpetua

> *One Saturday in October 2018, a crew of Secretome explor-*
> *ers — five humans and two canines — set out to hunt un-*
> *told stories and hidden treasures in a storied forest at the edge*
> *of the sea, a place known to some as Cape Perpetua…*

"Secretome Perpetua" is a participatory performance that hopes to expand sto-rying modes and temporalities by seeking sub-visible "treasures" and modes of exploration within layered meshes of specific places.[18] Navigating again by sug-gestion of microbial (un)mappings and other experimental modes of encounter, "Secretome Perpetua" performs a foray into a specific landscape that happens to be in the region we call home, in hopes of playing within other sub-visible layers of possible significance and connection. We have a ways to go toward grasping m<other tongues capable of narrating what happens in wildly different scales and temporalities, what has been and will happen across these layers-of-places. But if there was ever a time to try to honor and attune to the complexity of lives that have been systematically exploited, ignored, or erased in the colonial landscapes we call home, the time is now and always.[19]

Engaging the basic Secretome score, "Secretome Perpetua" first took place one Saturday in October 2018, when we assembled a crew to hunt untold treasures in the landscape and trails of Cape Perpetua, a mountainous state forest perched at the edge of the Pacific Ocean near Yachats, Oregon. Our gang as we knew it that day included two adult humans (photographer Chris Cearnal and myself), three human children (then aged 5, 7, and 10), two family dogs (one a recent rescue by transport from Tyler, Texas), and billions of trees, plants, and nameless others. From the parking lot at Cape Perpetua, we entered the forest at the main trailhead behind the whale-watching visitor center, perched on a windblown cliff overlook-ing the Pacific horizon. Equipped with the original Secretome maps from Aliass's muzzle-tongue (which the kids refused), various mediating devices, agar for cul-turing, and a special rope, we set out on the path to trace both knotty tensions and bright camaraderies that push and pull our familial tales and evolving m<other tongues through the places where we find ourselves. As we chased the kids clum-sily up the mountain on steep and winding trails, tripping on roots and tangling

---

18   As situated within the larger *True Knots of Possible* project, this performance and the video work that documents it were made in conversation with Multispecies Storytelling in Intermedial Practices at Växjö Konsthall in Växjö, Sweden in 2019. The installation at Växjö Konsthall featured three interrelated videos on separate monitors. The "Secretome Perpetua" video looped on a monitor that was set on a table with a significant stick brought home by the kids and dog from Perpetua and the Rope. Two other video works, mounted on the wall to either side of the table, document related *True Knots of Possible* projects: "Gut Sounds Lullaby" (2012) and "True Knots of Possible (culturing m<other tongues)," 2018.

19   For Indigenous perspectives on vastly different scales of time in relation to caretaking of land, see Noriko Ishiyama and Kim TallBear's work on native per-ceptions of nuclear waste legacies. Noriko Ishiyama and Kim TallBear, "Nuclear Waste and Relational Accountability in Indian Country," in *The Promise of Mul-tispecies Justice*, eds. Sophie Chao, Karin Bolender, and Eben Kirksey (Durham: Duke University Press, forthcoming 2022).

in plastic cords and the dogs' leashes, Chris and I shot the day's unfoldings in various digital and analog visual media. We immersed in ferny forest understories, following indeterminate whims, on and off the trail and moving with a different speeds and awarenesses through mostly invisible meshes. So we ventured out into this local forest in hopes that our wanderings might lead us to better understand who, how, and what we see and don't see, who and how we ignore or might better attend to hidden layers that animate worlds and ways of knowing in the places we call home.

"Secretome Perpetua" incorporates another kind of sub-visible storying layer to the Secretome score. We were lured along the mountain trails by specific, long-gone cinematic ghosts that have passed through this specific coastal forest, and so spectral traces of particular stories that have shaped us. This adventure in Cape Perpetua was haunted in certain ways by affective knots and narrative involutions of the 1987 family film, *Benji the Hunted.* Shot on location in this Siuslaw National Forest and other local forests and mountain slopes and meadows, this movie uniquely features very little human action. The plot unfolds almost entirely through scenes with animal actors, featuring the phenomenal canine movie star Benji/ne, mother cougars and cubs, a dark wolf, and many others.[20] The plot, while preposterous from perspectives of traditional ethology, is milky-rich with significant knots of interspecies connection, which lace traces of longed-for wild intimacies through the forest landscape. Hence the dense conifer forests of Cape Perpetua offered a richly significant location for this Secretome foray into meshes of multilayered, multi-temporal, intra-generational stories-in-places.

This layer of cinematic storying brings in another element specific to questions of multispecies storytelling. In a sense, we set out to explore how the more traditional "animal stories" we each carry in the folds of our lives and tongues, from childhood onward, might shape our experiences in different ways. As we do or do not pass such stories on, they shape how and with whom we make our worlds and our homes. Yet this inquiry is far from sociological, or anything I would aim to quantify with data. These are traces we seek otherwise in the forests of Perpetua and elsewhere, and with an awareness of Indigenous peoples whose stories have been erased in certain ways (but not all) from the land.

Meanwhile, this quest for ghostly traces of *Benji the Hunted* in the invisibly storied forests of Perpetua is deeply personal. The twists and turns and winding paths of the *Benji* plot, as it is played out by real and, incredibly charismatic actors of canine, feline, and other persuasions in this Perpetua forest, also happen to be a kind of subterranean (subcutaneous?) cinemecological layering in the homemade landscape of Possible's m<other tongue. As it happens, this film became a staple

---

20   Joe Camp, dir., *Benji the Hunted* (Walt Disney Pictures, 1987). In a volume called *Animal Stars: Behind the Scenes with Your Favorite Animal Actors,* I came across important details about the history of animal welfare in filmmaking, among tips from cinema's top animal trainers. The book also briefly narrates the rise to stardom of a death-row shelter mutt named Huggins (who played the original Benji in the seventies), and the later inheritance of both Huggins's incredible acting skills and global stardom by his daughter, Benjine, who portrays Benji as the lead in *Benji the Hunted.* Robin Ganzert, Allen Anderson, and Linda Anderson, *Animal Stars: Behind the Scenes with Your Favorite Animal Actors* (Novato: New World Library, 2014).

of storying entertainment and learning in the early days of Possible's language acquisition, in what was a very limited, screen-based catalog. Given that the film has little human action or dialogue, the story is told through mise-en-scenes that Possible learned to parse by asking many, many questions as we watched together. The exchanges that emerged from this habitual watching of *Benji the Hunted* became layered into the landscape we inhabit, through the presence of familiar ferns and trees, colors and textures both on the screen and right outside, while they were also layered into fleshly neural networks of a language-hungry brain. Given a mother tongue's unique power to shape worldings across and among different lifeforms, I am compelled to pay attention to the unique role of this film's storytelling, and my own maternal acts of translation, in the making-of possible m<other tongues and what it means to claim, to know, to make a home among myriad unknown others.

In her keynote for *Multispecies Storytelling,* Vinciane Despret describes attention to others' forms of storying and place-making as a powerful way to expand and enrich how we imagine the making of "home." Considering various ethological examples of multispecies cohabitation and collective nesting, denning, and other forms of habitat-architecture, Despret suggests that "the collective does not preexist the creation of the territory or the habitat; it is the habitat that establishes the collective. This, it seems to me, might open our minds to other stories — less marked by exclusivity — of what 'home,' or even 'our home,' might mean."[21]

What happens when we practice new ways to collectively and respectfully (un) map contested places we share with so many sub-visible lives and marked and unmarked erasures? What new kinds of collective storying might find expression in such acts? These are open(ing) questions, more like speculations. Recognizing the limits of its human lenses (even or especially the microscopic ones), "Secretome Perpetua" plays with(in) a new kind of map-less territory that is also in some ways our "home territory," as it brims with inscrutable stories writ in sub-visible traces. Here ghostly marks of faded cinematic mise-en-scènes meet with our own fleeting mammalian intimacies, never-finished stories flowing through bodies-in-time across layered ecological and temporal unfoldings.[22] To actively crack open the

---

21 Despret, "Politics of 'Terristories.'"

22 Though I didn't fully catch it at the time, a secret of the Secretome was revealed by Vinciane Despret in a casual conversation at the vernissage of the *Multispecies Storytelling* exhibition in Växjö. We happened to be standing near the looping video installation of "Secretome Perpetua," and I was trying to describe my fascination with the idea of Perpetua containing vanished traces of certain cinematographic choreographies in the making-of scenes for films with animal actors, where the actors must hit their "marks" on the forest floor in order to make the scene sensible for visual narrative. The dogs, mountain lions, wolves, and others involved in these scenes in *Benji the Hunted* experienced this narrative matrix in different modes of smell, sound, and other ways of making sense of the landscape. It struck me that these marks, long vanished, might still represent a constellation of traces in the land, like an invisible layer of interwoven nodes of human, canine, feline, and other presences and perceptions. As I fumbled with this articulation, Vinciane Despret offered the idea that the figure of the rope — which features in the "Secretome Perpetua" video installation and all through *True Knots of Possible* — might suggest a desire to stitch together different layers of time unfolding in places, visibly and invisibly. In this sense, the rope's presence suggests an effort to interweave temporalities — to stitch

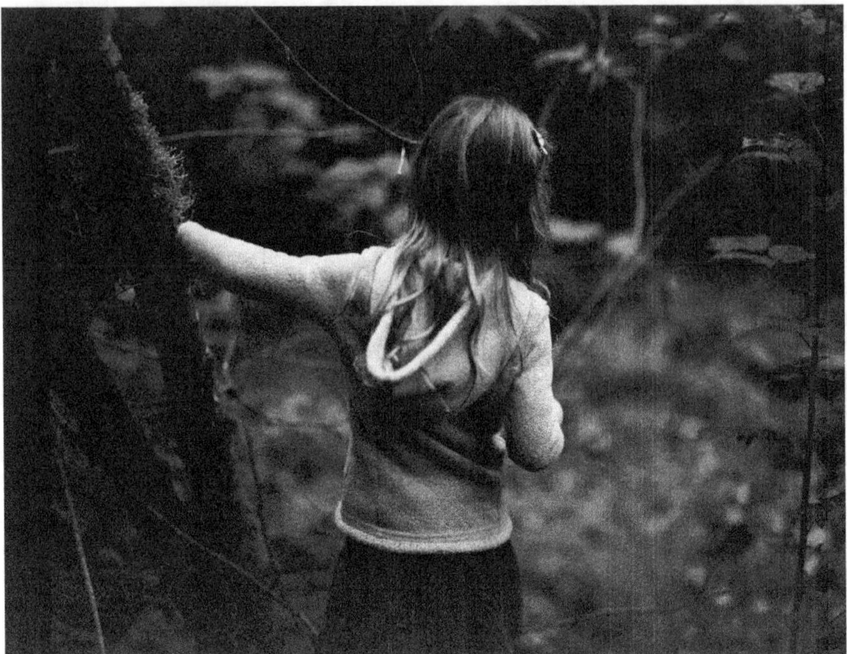

Fig. 2.6. Still from "Welcome to the Secretome (Perpetua): An Invitation" (2018), performance and Super8/digital video (8:20), rope, stick, microbial "treasure maps." Photograph by Chris Cearnal.

barbed-and-rusty, anthropocentric, colonial narratives we absorb and perpetuate, we seek new secretory paths for nameless tales through bodies-in-places. We dig into bigger questions of how we might dissolve stubborn forms of generic Western storying and make space for the layered and interwoven agencies of all kinds of others, who have been making worlds with(in) our anthropocentric hero's journeys all along.

Of course, the stories we make are not ours to claim, either, nor do they conform to the frames of lenses, languages, maps, or mediating devices. The "Secretome Perpetua" video is scrapped together from digital and Super 8 footage we shot that day in the forest. Edited roughly, it is a sketchy document, not a record of what happened but more of a montage of partial assemblages, ropy tangles of care and culturing and intraspecies connection, and knots of ghostly aspiration. In other words, an invitation.

And so here I wish to extend it again. "Welcome to the Secretome (Perpetua)" invites everyone to go Secretoming, in any vital and significant place, to seek hidden openings through active, experimental explorations of these places, through and beyond the edges of familiar ways of making homes with others. The Secretome project cultivates the kind of attentions Despret calls forth to "open our

together past, present, and future happening through looping layers of invisible lives. Secretome Perpetua, then, might also suggest a mode where we can disrupt the supposed linearity of time, across different bodies and generations, looping instead of linear, weaving untold stories into possible futures..

imaginary to other ways of conceiving what it means to find a place in the world and make this place a home with others who have themselves found a home."[23] In this mode we proceed with slow and careful steps, watching and listening and looping, not-knowing what living tales we may be perpetually passing through. With opaquely biosemiotic "treasure maps" as visual provocations, we might explore untold stories in unforeseen ways, finding tales inscribed across desires-materialized and ghostly sub-visible encounters. So we might humbly imagine our ways into the seams and cracks of places and the ways of life and richly elusive stories that comprise them, which bodies of all kinds are bound to carry into uncertain earthly futures.[24]

Home is where the unknown is. *Welcome to the Secretome.*

23　Despret, "Politics of Terristories."
24　As Loup Rivière proposes, acts of moving through in-betweens are not only a creative human mode of exploration but can also perform the role of transforming ecologies in unforeseen material ways. Rivière, "Dancing Is an Ecosystem Service, and So Is Being Trans," this volume.

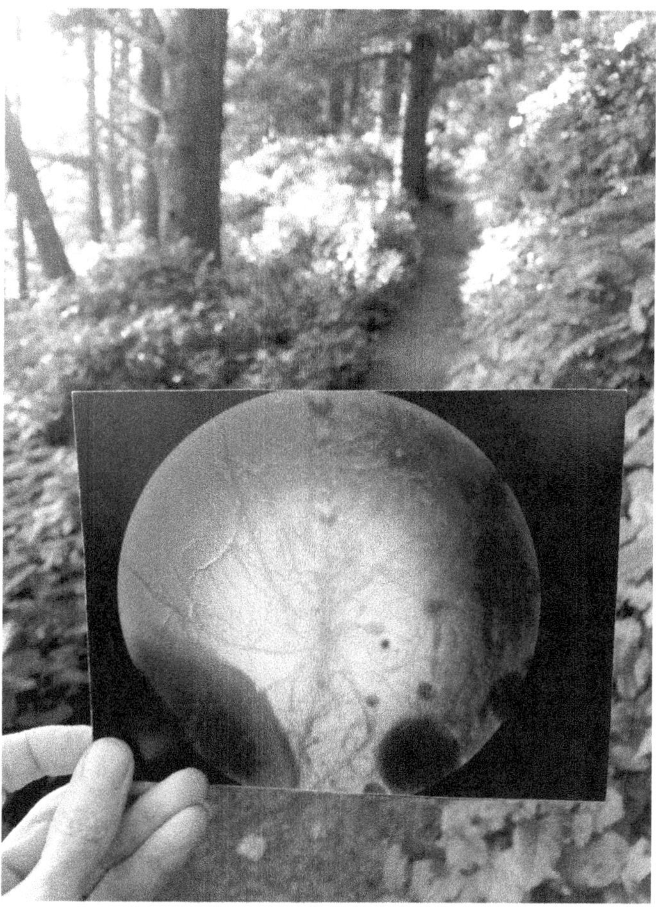

Figs. 2.7. Entering the Perpetua forest with a Secretome map. Photograph by the author.

References

Bateson, Gregory. *Mind and Nature: A Necessary Unity.* Cresskill: Hampton Press, 2002.

Benzaquen, Adriana. *Encounters with Wild Children: Temptation and Disappointment in the Study of Human Nature.* Montreal: McGill-Queen's University Press, 2006.

Bolender, Karin. *The Unnaming of Aliass.* Earth: punctum books, 2020.

Camp, Joe, dir. *Benji the Hunted.* Walt Disney Pictures, 1987.

Clarke, Adele, and Donna Haraway, eds., *Making Kin Not Population.* Chicago: Prickly Paradigm Press, 2018.

de la Cadena, Marisol. "Matters of Method: Or, Why Method Matters toward a Not Only Colonial Anthropology." *HAU: Journal of Ethnographic Theory* 7, no. 2 (2017). DOI: 10.14318/hau7.2.002. https://www.haujournal.org/index.php/hau/article/view/hau7.2.002.

Dominguez-Bello, Maria, Kassandra Jesus-Laboy, Nan Shen, Laura Cox, Amnon Amir, Antonio González, Nicolas Bokulish, Se Jin Song, Marina Hoashi, Juana I. Rivera-Vinas, Keimari Mendez, Rob Knight, and Jose Clemente. "Partial Restoration of the Microbiota of Cesarean-born Infants via Vaginal Microbial Transfer." *Nature Medicine* 22, no. 3 (2016): 250–53. DOI: 10.1038/nm.4039/.

Ganzert, Robin, Allen Anderson, and Linda Anderson. *Animal Stars: Behind the Scenes with Your Favorite Animal Actors.* Novato: New World Library, 2014.

Ishiyama, Noriko, and Kim TallBear. "Nuclear Waste and Relational Accountability in Indian Country." In *The Promise of Multispecies Justice,* edited by Sophie Chao, Karin Bolender, and Eben Kirksey. Durham: Duke University Press, forthcoming 2022.

Kolata, Gina. "Barnyard Dust Offers a Clue to Stopping Asthma in Children." *The New York Times,* August 3, 2016. http://www.nytimes.com/2016/08/04/health/dust-asthma-children.html/.

Loveless, Natalie. "Maternal Ecologies: A Story in Three Parts." In *Performing Motherhood: Artistic, Activist, and Everyday Enactments,* edited by Amber E. Kinser, Terri Hawkes, and Kryn Freehling-Burton, 149–69. Bradford: Demeter Press, 2014.

Rook, G.A., and L.R. Brunet. "Microbes, Immunoregulation, and the Gut." *Gut* 54, no. 3 (2005): 317–20. DOI: 10.1136/gut.2004.053785/.

Rose, Deborah Bird. *Reports from a Wild Country: Ethics for Decolonization.* Sydney: University of New South Wales Press, 2014.

Singh, Julietta. *Unthinking Mastery: Dehumanism and Decolonial Entanglements.* Durham: Duke University Press, 2018.

CHAPTER 3

Tales of a Modern Parrot: Living Entangled Lives in an Interspecies Art Collective

Hörner/Antlfinger

As media artists we always had a strong interest in the development of new media technologies. Those have undergone a rapid development since the euphoria of the eighties and early nineties, when the internet was a new and unknown territory, an endless playground without physical restraints — or so we thought. Things are a bit more complicated nowadays, as we all witness the impact of the technosphere on our social life and the planet. The interdependence between the virtual and the physical played a major role in many of our narrative works and culminated in a project titled *Factory≠Farm* in 2012 about the computerization of animal farming — a high-tech industry in which animals, humans, and machines are connected in the most extreme way. The research on this project was traumatizing, and we urgently needed a theory to understand what we had witnessed.[1] At that time we came across the still fairly new human-animal studies. Since then, human-animal studies have become a major influence on our personal artistic work as well as an important aspect of our teaching at the Academy of Media Arts Cologne.

Our animal companions are part of our teaching team. Especially Clara, a 21-year-old grey parrot lady, seems to enjoy being with the students as much as they enjoy being with her. She's a great teacher, who listens and observes very carefully in class, spreading her attention by wandering from student to student and laughing along enthusiastically whenever the human flock starts to do so.

Eventually, the change of perspective demanded by human-animal studies made us rethink our own relationship with the animals we lived with. A new thread developed in our work — everyday observations of the life we share with our parrot companions. With our increasing awareness of their extraordinary capacities, they became more and more important, not only as protagonists in some

---

1   For this highly loaded topic we decided to start with our own entanglement with animal production in everyday life (as in KRAMFORS). Other elements are a real-time simulation of a barn with 120,000 chickens situated in *Farmer Kyber's Oops-Room,* which we developed on the basis of information that was provided by manufacturers of animal factories. We spent many hours every day watching video material filmed by animal rights activists. The images they recorded were hard to bear, painful, and disturbing. At that time hardly anyone talked about the traumatizing effect the mediated images can have on the recipients, nor about the post-traumatic stress disorders from which animal activists suffer.

of our early videos but also as partners in a collaborative art practice — which is of course a fragile claim, notably in an environment shaped by humans. The desire to create conditions for the most equitable coexistence possible led to the founding of the CMUK *interspecies collective* in 2014.[2]

We will now tell the story of our interagency, including both the power to influence each other — as Humberto Maturana puts it, potentially down to our nervous systems[3] — and the possibilities each of us has to act individually. Even though it is us, the humans, who put this story into words and establish the historical references, our animal companions are involved in this narration as co-authors of our shared experience. As acting subjects, whose artistic destructions, interventions, and remnants shape our everyday life, they are present in our collaborative works. In parallel with these works, we will try to describe our development, from reflecting our relationship from a more distanced position, to the idea of "becoming-with" or of growing together as companions and investigating how an interspecies partnership could work.

This process is in no way completed, there are moments of affection, joy, and trust but also misunderstandings, failures, and ideas that need to get revised. Anthropomorphic attributions are something we cannot completely avoid when telling this story. In order to empathize with another being, to ask what it wants and why it does something, we can't help but draw conclusions from ourselves first, before we abstract from our own perspective in the next step. And sometimes it seems necessary to bring a strategic anthropomorphism into play, in order to make things more sharp, indicating that anthropodenial is the problem we need to be more aware of.[4]

2   The word CMUK is an acronym composed of the forenames of the founding members — Clara, Mathias, Ute, and Karl. In Slovakian it means something like "a little kiss."

3   One of the key stories in Humberto Maturana's book *Was ist Erkennen? (What Is Recognition?)* — at least for us — is about a chicken named Bigote (Mustache), with whom he had lived as a child. The daytime it spent with its human flock — "it came to the table, picked something from the plates, shit on the table and jumped on one's shoulder or on the head" (Humberto Maturana, *Was ist erkennen? Die Welt entsteht im Auge des Betrachters* [Munich: Goldmann Verlag, 2001], 87). The night it spent together with the other chickens in the stable. One night, Bigote came to his mother's door, knocking its beak several times vehemently against it. When the mother finally looked what was going on, she noticed that a predator had entered the barn. Bigote had come for help. This behavior was more than unusual for a chicken. Maturana assumes that Bigote's nervous system had changed considerably as a result of living together with humans and subsequently considers it possible that these changes could work vice versa. Perhaps the chicken Bigote opened the young Humberto Maturana's eyes to what would later occupy him as a neurobiologist and philosopher.

4   As the primatologist and ethologist Frans de Waal points out, "[a]t the same time that anthropomorphism is rejected on the grounds that it tends to overestimate animal mental complexity, should not we be equally worried about the possible underestimation of similarities between humans and animals, and the possible underestimation of animal mental complexity? Alternatively, could it be that we routinely overestimate human mental complexity? [... T]o cover this kind of error, I have coined the term anthropodenial for the a priori rejection of shared characteristics between humans and animals when in fact they may exist.

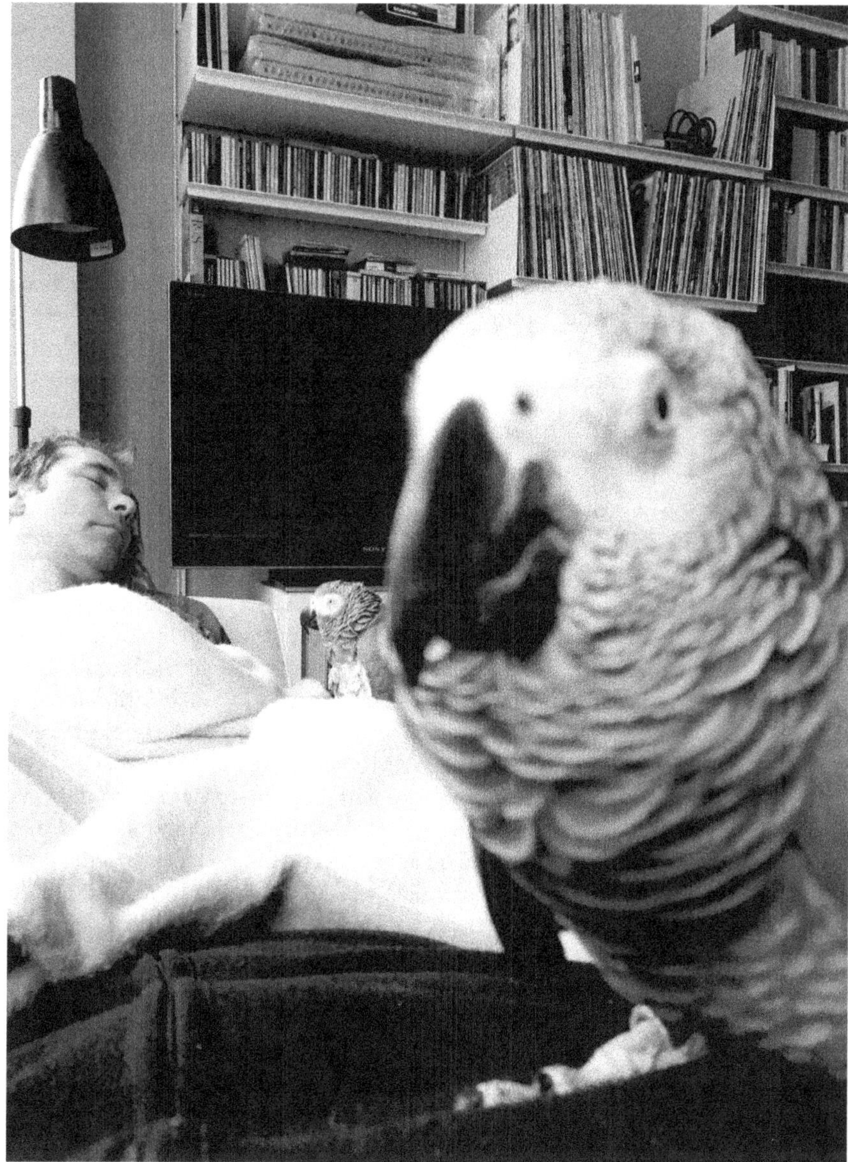

Fig. 3.1. Afternoon nap with Theo and Clara from *Tales of a Modern Parrot* (2019). Photograph by the authors.

Learning How to Live Together

Clara came to us as a young bird in 2000 along with her brother Francesco. When it became clear that they would not become a pair (parrots reach puberty at around

Anthropodenial is a blindness to the human-like characteristics of animals, or the animal-like characteristics of ourselves." Frans B.M. de Waal, "Anthropomorphism and Anthropodenial: Consistency in Our Thinking about Humans and Other Animals," *Zoological Philosophy* 27, no. 1 (1999): 255–80.

six years of age and from that time on they couldn't stand each other anymore), we decided to give them the chance to find new partners. To this end they lived at a pairing facility in an animal shelter in Berlin for almost a year. Here, Clara found Karl and Francesco joined another family with his new partner. No one could tell us back then exactly how old Karl was, but his ring was made before official records began, so he must have been at least fifty years old.

Our cohabitation has gone through various phases. At first, now almost twenty years ago, there was the curiosity and the interest in the communication capabilities of these extraordinary animals. We worked with language as artists and to "talk" with nonhuman animals was something we were very excited about at that time. We had read about Irene Pepperberg's research on the cognitive and communicative skills of Grey Parrots in the lab,[5] but, to be honest, we had no idea what it would mean to live with parrots, that is, with individual animals that are so intelligent and not adjusted to living with humans by domestication.[6]

I (Ute) remember when they had just become fledged and screeched out at the top of their lungs from the highest branch of a tree that we had installed in the flat. They swooped over our heads and attacked us. One could say they were exercising resistant practices on us. When we were at a complete loss of what to do, we got hold of some handbooks. They contained a variety of rules for cohabitation. For example, companion parrots are not allowed to climb out or into their cage autonomously; they must be placed. They are not allowed to run around on the floor; that is our territory. They are not allowed to sit on our shoulders and certainly not on our heads; that expresses dominance. Most of the books were full of things that parrots were not allowed to do, much more than what they were allowed to do. By now, the idea that parrots are dominant has proved itself to be a genuine human construct. Even though most of this advice proved unusable, it became clear to us that the journey would be about socializing each other to the point that cohabitation became possible. And as we had little interest in giving orders, we only did what was absolutely necessary, that is, just enough to avoiding being bitten.

At the same time, it dawned on us just how vulnerable and dependent on us they were. We had entered a "complicated arrangement" that offers no consistent way out. In the words of philosopher Lori Gruen, "[e]ven the most thoughtful, compassionate domesticated relationships can't erase the fact that companion animals are forced to live by our cultural standards. Companion animals are, in a very real sense, our captives."[7] Suddenly the old question of whether there can be a right life in the wrong, which had occupied us as artists for a long time, reappeared. But we could not turn back time, we had taken responsibility for these birds and even if we had wanted to, we could not have released them into the wild. They had lived

---

<ol start="5">
<li>Irene Pepperberg, The Alex Studies: Cognitive and Communicative Abilities of Grey Parrots (Cambridge: Harvard University Press, 1999).</li>
<li>Domesticated animals are animals that have been bred for centuries to live together with humans and whose genetic characteristics have been altered to make them so. This is not the case with parrots. They are no different from their wild counterparts.</li>
<li>Lori Gruen, "Facing Death and Practicing Grief," in Ecofeminism: Feminist Intersections with Other Animals and the Earth, eds. Carol J. Adams and Lori Gruen (New York City: Bloomsbury Academic, 2014), 130.</li>
</ol>

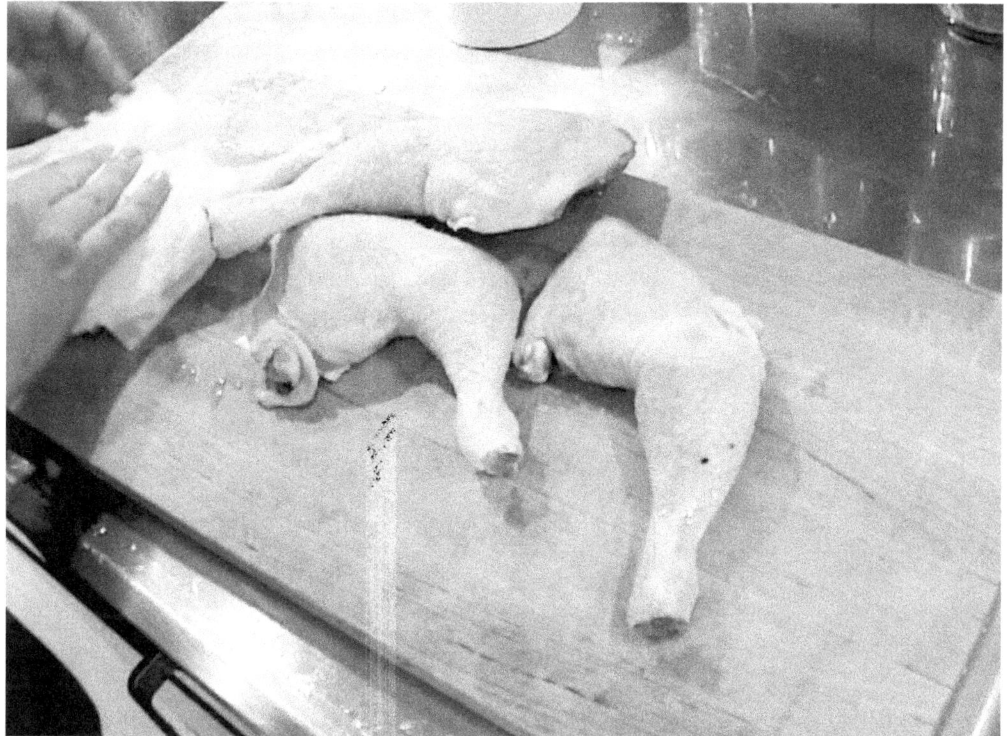

Fig. 3.2. Still from *Lunch in a Cross-species Household* (2002). Digital video, 1:30 min.

with humans from childhood and would have been as helpless in the wilderness as we would be.

Lunch in a Cross-species Household

Clara and Francesco were still so-called "pets" at this point and we as "pet owners" tried to care for them the best we could. Parrots don't like to eat alone, and the single channel video *Lunch in a Cross-species Household* (2002) gave a first insight into our interspecies household at that time. Together we share something that many people might call a "balanced meal." To make the picture more complete, we slipped into animal costumes from an IKEA family toy set, donning one suit of a monkey and the other of a dog, two species very close to humans in different ways. *Lunch in a Cross-species Household* was presented at many festivals, but the more often it was shown and the more often we saw it, the more we asked ourselves: how was it possible to love these birds and to eat other birds? Wasn't this interspecies cannibalism, as one of our students calls it today? And did we perhaps dress up in these costumes to distract from the fact that we belong to our own species and the moral claims associated with it? The family table is the first place where we practice anthropological difference. As the philosopher Cora Diamond puts it: "[w]hat a human being is, we learn, among other things, by sitting at a table where they

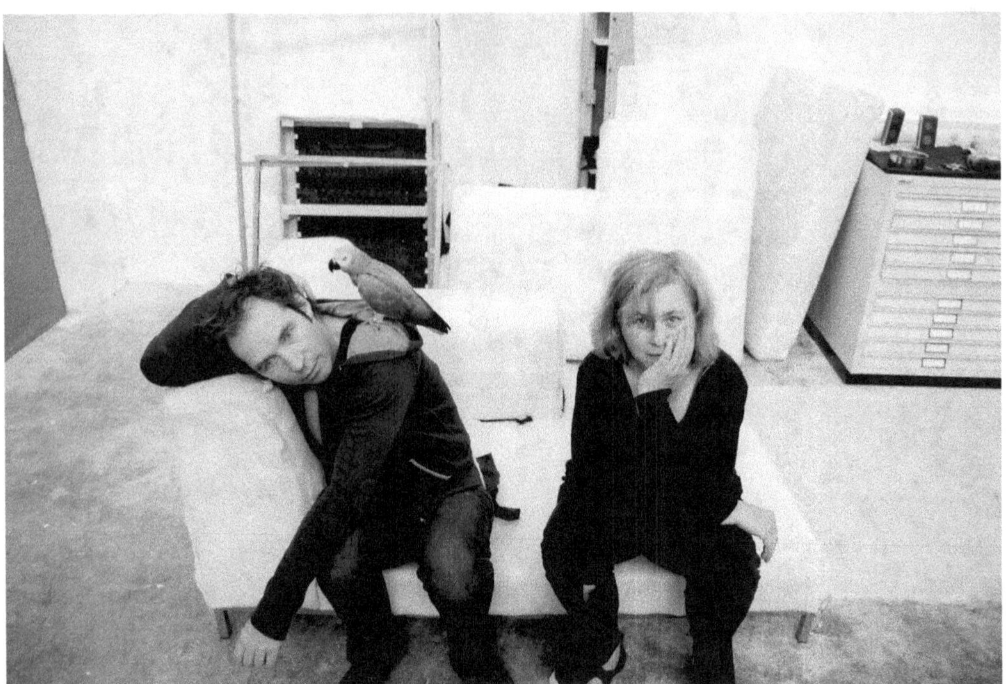

Fig. 3.3a. Still from KRAMFORS (2012). Digital video, 4:30 min.

[the animals] are eaten by us."[8] In our video we and the birds sit together at the table and eat other birds. The transgression that manifests in sharing table and meat with them points to their status that parrots are, compared to chickens, privileged animals. That is what makes this short, at first glance funny, video subsequently awkward.

Lunch in a Cross-species Household was the first work in which we addressed the cognitive dissonances that the cohabitation in our multispecies household triggered in us. KRAMFORS (2012) was created ten years later as part of the project *Factory≠Farm*, which we mentioned earlier. The installation is based on the deconstruction of the eponymous leather sofa from the Swedish furniture chain IKEA. It had been in our possession for many years, and copies of it presumably still exist in thousands of households all over the world. In the DIY video on the production of KRAMFORS, Clara and Karl appear like founding figures in medieval paintings — often at the edge of the picture, not involved in the depicted scene but still very present. In our perception today they were the initiators for this piece. They were the ones who had made us aware of animal rights and the contradictions in which we lived.

The video documents the sculptural process, in which an individual creature reemerges from the anonymous skin of a mass-produced product: a handmade calf, resting on the now-naked sofa as if on a pedestal and presented to the viewer at eye level. Accompanied by Clara and Karl (who observed the whole process from the farewell to the sofa in our living room, via the transport to the studio,

8   Cora Diamond, "Fleisch essen, Menschen essen," in *Menschen, Tiere und Begriffe: Aufsätze zur Moralphilosophie* (Berlin: Suhrkamp, 2012), 91.

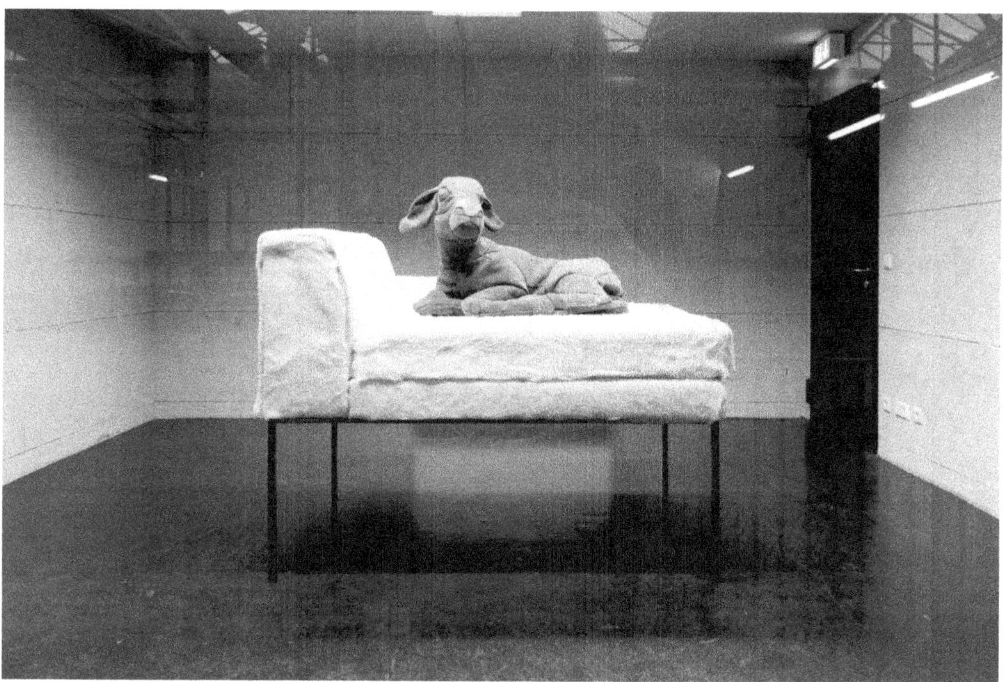

Fig. 3.3b. KRAMFORS (2012). Installation view Weltkunstzimmer, Düsseldorf. Photograph by the authors

to the removal of the skin, the cutting of the leather, all the way to the final sculpture), the viewers are invited to follow up, "to move from the abstraction of social compacts towards the concrete, in order to grasp the real significance of such compacts."[9] In order to make this possible not only on a theoretical level but also practically, we made our sewing pattern available to the audience. The first image shows us in our studio resting on the now naked sofa, Clara sitting on Mathias's shoulder. It was created when the process of disassembling and skinning was just finished. The second image shows the sculpture *KRAMFORS* in an exhibition situation, the sensitive object protected by a pane of glass.

Contact Call (2006) was the first work in which the parrots themselves "had their say." The work examines their way of communicating with us, which was quite different to how we had imagined it would be. Although they used human vocalizations such as "hello" or "come here," they clearly preferred the "utterances" of nonhuman protagonists, electronic devices such as the telephone, fax and desktop sounds, the voices of their rivals with whom they would compete for our attention. We used this behavior for an interactive installation in which the viewer, attracted by these sounds, approached two white boxes with proximity sensors and peepholes that were installed above head-height on the wall.

To be able to see where the sounds came from, the viewers had to step up onto the small podiums, similar to those used for circus tricks with nonhuman animals. From there they could identify the origin of the sounds through the peepholes. It

---

9   Barbara Engelbach, "Of Images and Thoughts," in Hörner/Antlfinger, *Discrete Farms* (Berlin: Revolver Verlag, 2012), 20.

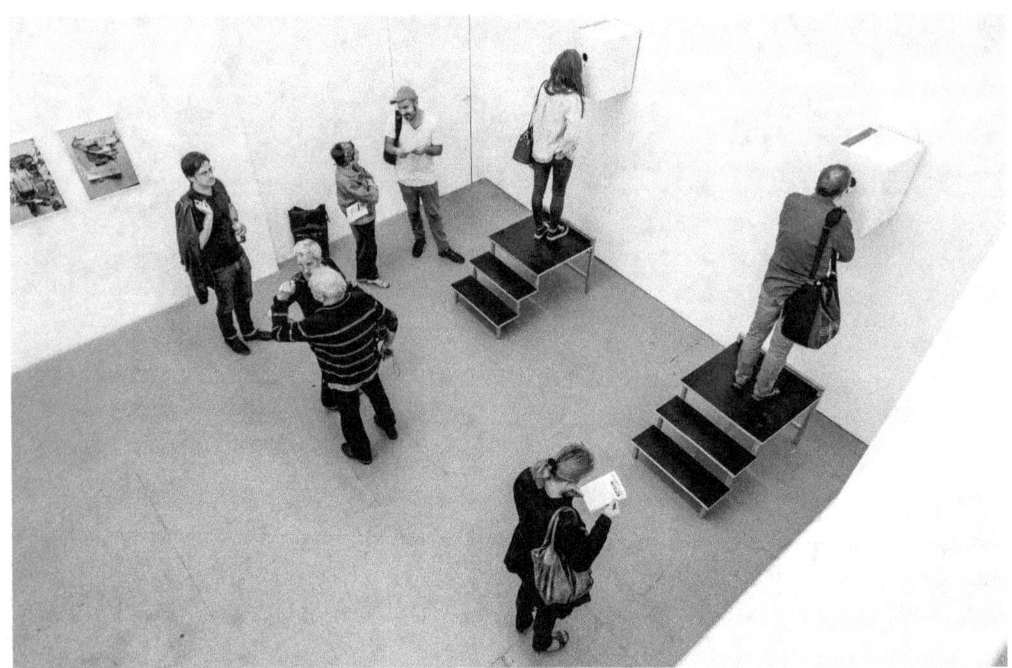

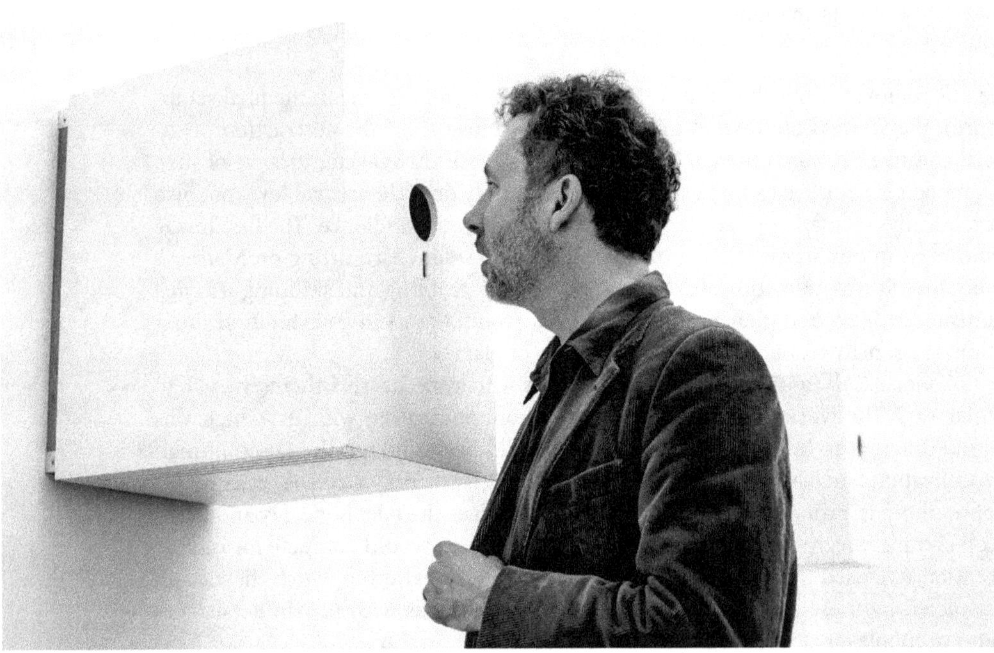

Figs. 3.4a, 3.4b. Contact Call (2006). Installation views Meinblau Project Space, Berlin.
Photographs by Andreas-Michael Velten.

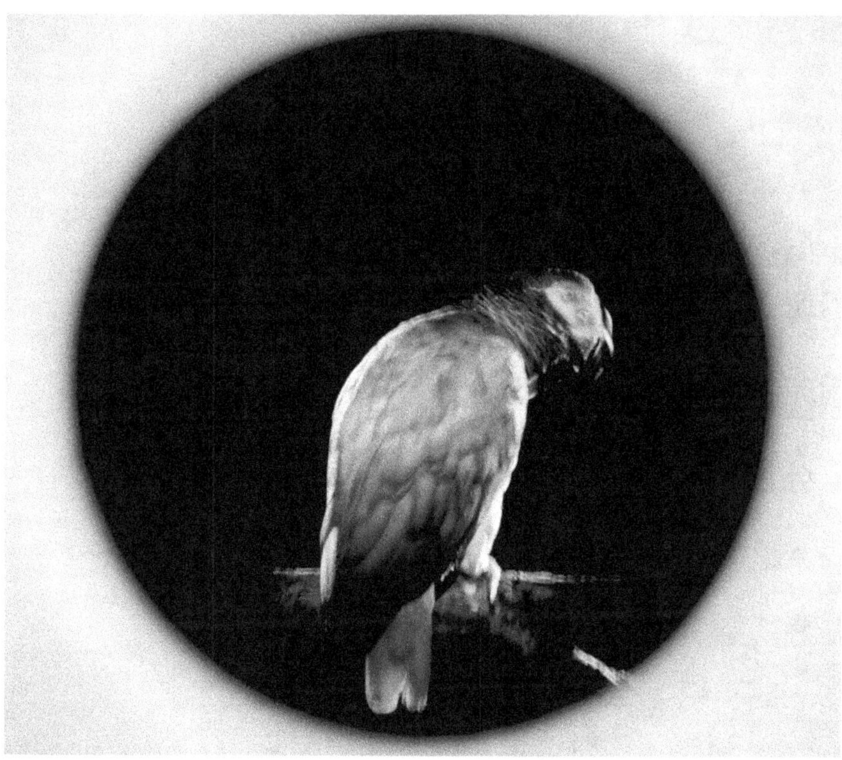

Fig. 3.4c. Video projection of Clara sitting inside the box. Photograph by the authors.

was parrots who looked out at them from inside the boxes and remained silent just as long as their gaze was reciprocated, that is, as long as they were given attention. The video recordings seemed eerily real: we used a visual effect called the "Pepper's Ghost Effect"[10] that gave the birds the appearance of floating in space, like in a hologram. The inside of the box was exactly matched to the size of the birds to enhance the illusion. As soon as the visitors stopped looking, or, more precisely, moved away from the sensors, the ring tone calls would resume. Those viewers who observed the birds for a long time were rewarded with small surprises, such as the appearance of a stick suddenly handed in from above that helped the bird to climb up to the ceiling and disappear through an invisible hole.

In the video installation *Tales of a Parrot, Rereading the Tooti Nameh* (2015), we tried to get the attention of a parrot ourselves. The "Tooti Nameh" or "Tales of a Parrot" is a collection of stories of Indian origin form the twelfth century, written down in Persia in the fourteenth century.[11] In the late sixteenth century, the Mughal emperor, Akbar, commissioned an illustrated version of the work with 250 miniature illustrations, now located in the Cleveland Museum of Art in Ohio. It is

10   The Pepper's Ghost effect was invented and popularized by the scientist John Henry Pepper in the nineteeth century. It was used in magic shows as well as in natural history museums.

11   Ziyā' al-Dīn Nakhshabī, *The Tooti Nameh, or, Tales of a Parrot: In the Persian Language with an English Translation* (Calcutta: J. Debrett, 1801).

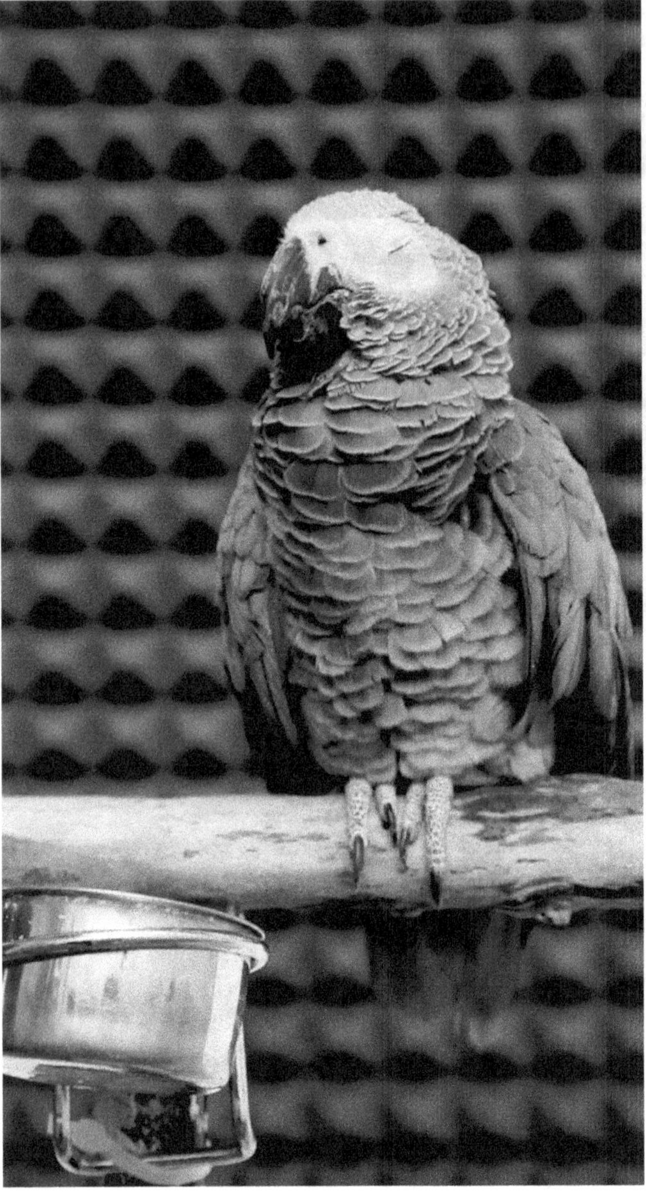

Fig. 3.5a. Still from *Tales of a Parrot, Rereading the Tooti Nameh* (2015). Digital video, 20:00 min.

believed that Akbar was strongly influenced by these narratives in his youth. The moral of the stories, primarily aimed at controlling women, were of great interest to him, as he was the owner of a large harem. The main narrator is a parrot that has been given the task of looking after the wife of his owner, a travelling salesman. His skill and cunning in telling her compelling stories evening after evening prevents her from visiting a lover and saves the parrot's life.

On the one hand, the "Tooti Nameh" is a classic fable in which nonhuman animals discuss moral issues that concern people. On the other hand, parrots can

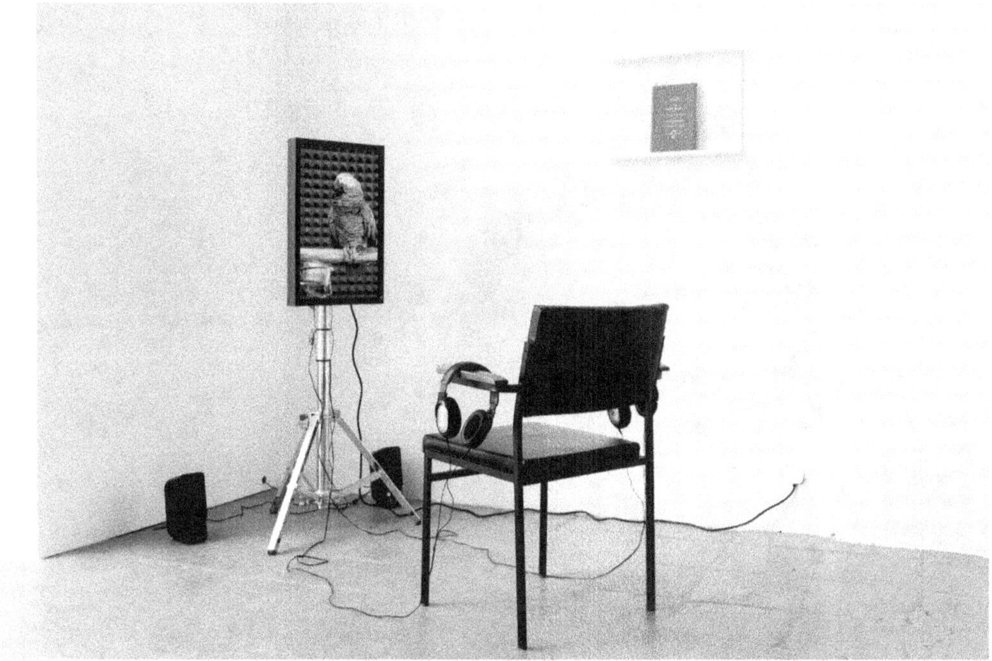

Fig. 3.5b. Tales of a Parrot, Rereading the Tooti Nameh (2015). Installation view Meinblau Project Space, Berlin. Photograph by the authors.

indeed communicate by using human vocalizations, and the "Tales of a Parrot" were created at a time when nonhuman animals were, maybe more likely than today, regarded as persons with moral agency. For example, we may think of medieval animal trials where nonhuman animals could be convicted for their "misconduct." In our piece *Tales of a Parrot, Rereading the Tooti Nameh,* we deal with what human animals think nonhuman animals might be capable of over the course of time, which cannot be disentangled from what they think about themselves. Furthermore, we invite the viewers to look at fables from an animal point of view in order to achieve a more reflective kind of anthropomorphism; one that neither overestimates nor underestimates the similarities between human and nonhuman animals.

The video in the installation shows a modern parrot, Karl sitting in a speaker's booth. Being a gray parrot, he belongs to a species that, due to its intelligence and unique faculty of speech, has been kept in the human environment since medieval times. They were regarded as mystical, prestigious, and, not least of all, entertaining animals.

Karl was presumably born in the late 1960s or early '70s in the Congo, caught as a young bird, and sold in Europe where he lived with one or more owners. Finally, at the age of about fifty, he was given to an animal shelter, and it was from there that he came to us. On a summer afternoon, we read to him from the "Tooti Nameh," curious about how he would react to the tales of a fellow parrot from the fourteenth century. In the video, after several minutes of listening attentively,

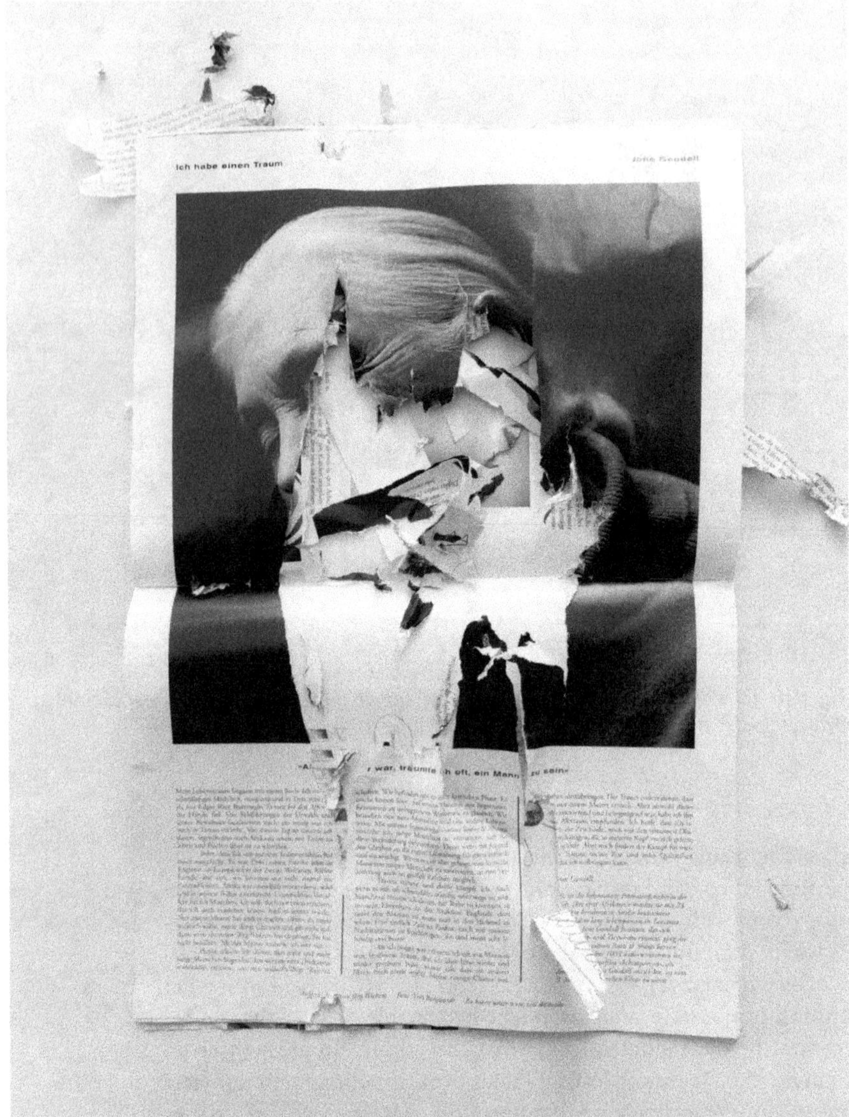

Fig. 3.6a. weekly No. 4 (2014). Décollage/Photography, 40 × 60 cm.

he falls asleep. Occasionally he opens one eye as if something in the story or the melody of the voice has aroused his interest.

In the installation we use a tripod as a monitor mount, which gives the impression that Karl is sitting on a so-called Freisitz ("free seat"), a piece of furniture intended for the interaction between parrots and people outside the cage. An armchair invites the viewers to take a seat and listen to the story together with a real parrot and imagine what the reading might mean to him. The historical edition of "Tooti Nameh," which we used for our work, is displayed as a reference in a showcase on the wall.

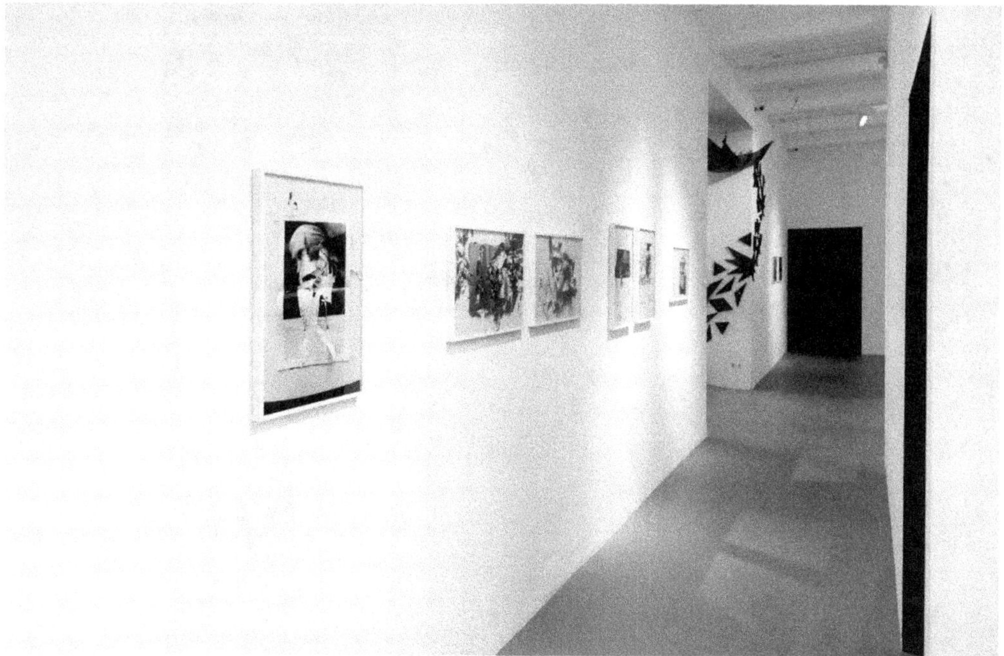

Fig. 3.6b. weekly, ongoing series (since 2014). Installation view NGBK, Berlin. Photograph by the Anne Hölck.

We Play All Day

Clara and Karl had begun to work with us long before we became aware of it. First there was the work of being a so-called pet, to adjust to our way of living and to ensure emotional balance in the family, which is a difficult task for a parrot. Then there were activities that they carried out with great enthusiasm. In summer 2014, we began to focus on the parrots' own creative agency which became apparent, above all, in the destruction of objects in our communal environment. Some of these destructions quite obviously had an aesthetic quality and we began to capture them in photographs.

In this way among others, the series weekly, based on reworked magazines from the German weekly newspaper *Die Zeit,* came into being. While we read the black-and-white part of the newspaper, Clara and Karl grabbed for themselves the color magazine and reworked it by climbing between the pages, gnawing them with their beaks and scratching them with their claws. This activity was carried out with great passion. Occasionally they took a step back to have a drink or something to eat before getting back to work, just as we do in our studio. They developed their own individual signatures. Karl was very precise. He bit the magazine pages into the smallest of scraps, whereas Clara picked and plucked bigger pieces with the help of her claws. This was by no means automatic behavior. Before they started working, they needed a certain context or atmosphere to be initiated, for example, by a long breakfast, with time and leisure that we participated in. It soon became a ritual between us in which each of us explored the newspaper in her or his own way. But was this work or was it play?

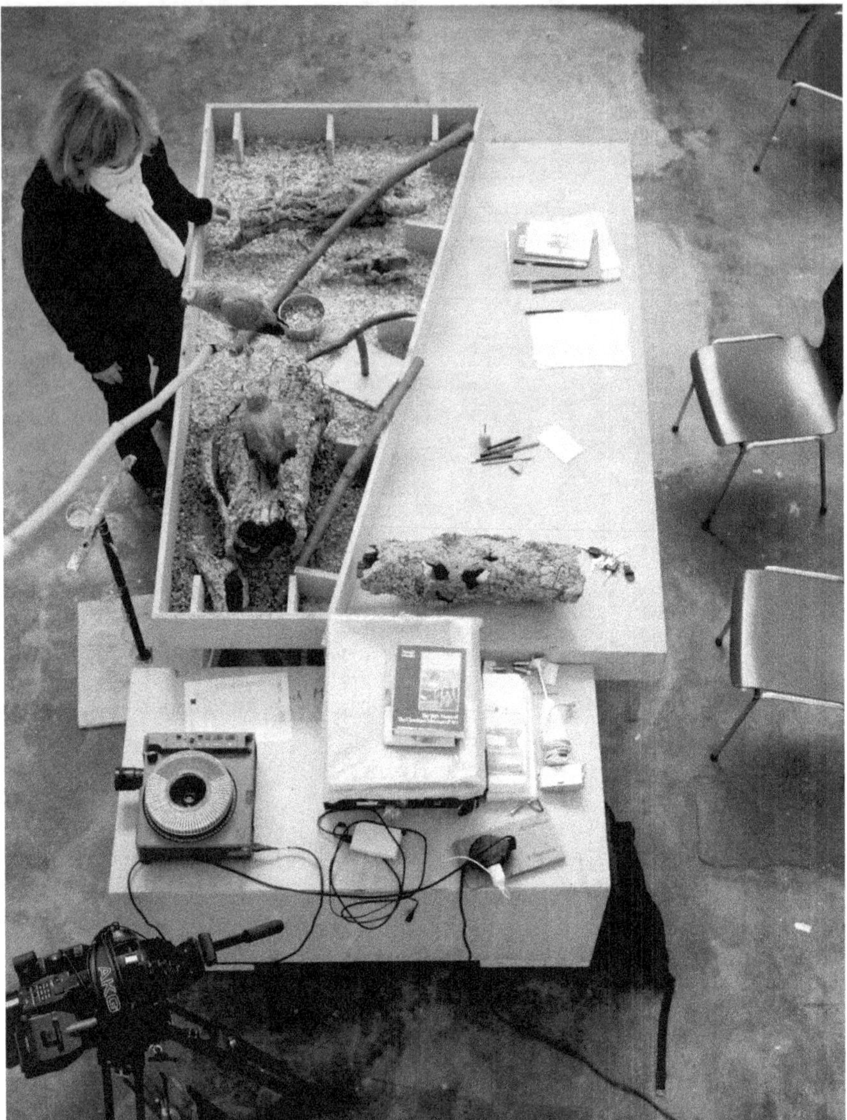

Fig. 3.7. Clara, Karl, and Ute at their shared workbench in the studio (2016). Photograph by the authors.

"Work or play?" is a question that is quite common when it comes to art. Some artists will state that all art is playing; as Lynn Hershman-Leeson puts it self-ironically: "we play all day."[12] The notion that artistic creation is work isn't a very old one at all. Human and perhaps also nonhuman animals of antiquity clearly preferred idleness — work was a banal activity that had to be avoided. It wasn't until the eighteenth century when the change in the concept of work put work at the center of Western construction of the self, and this certainly didn't exclude artists.

12   Lynn Hershman-Leeson, in an interview about her relationship to computers, see Hörner/Antlfinger, *Two Lives? A Debate,* 1999, http://h—a.org/en/project/ zwei-leben-eine-debatte/.

Work had become something valuable, something that defines and refines us. Can nonhuman animals also define themselves by the work they do? Are they doing that perhaps in cohabitation with us?

"Do animals work?" Vinciane Despret asks in her book *What Would Animals Say If We Asked the Right Questions?* She writes, "The sociologist Jocelyne Porcher, who is a specialist in animal farming, made this question the subject of her research. She began by asking farmers whether it makes any sense for them to think that their animals collaborate and work with them. The proposition is not an easy one — neither for us, nor for many of the farmers."[13] As Despret further explains, Porcher reports that the farmers initially answered no; only people would work, the animals would not work. What is recognized for "work animals," such as workhorses or assistance dogs, remains invisible in the case of livestock, such as cows or pigs and, interestingly as we would like to add, also in the case of pets. But Porcher doesn't stop at a one-time inquiry. As a sociologist she's interested in what the question can change. She asks the farmers to think about it and to explore with her what the proposal to think of their animals as employees would change in their relationship. And what "working" in this context could mean.

But even when animals no longer live in economic contexts, such as the animal residents of farm sanctuaries, where, as a rule, great care is taken to not give the impression that the animals are working, the question arises as to whether the idea that all work means exploitation disregards the fact that "work, activity, cooperation, and contribution can be critical dimensions of flourishing," as Sue Donaldsen and Will Kymlicka point out. They ask, "[w]hat do animals like to do? All farmed animals belong to social species. Like us, they tend to be intensely interested in what others are up to, and have a strong inclination to be part of things, to participate, to belong."[14] As ambivalent as our own relationship to work is, especially as work and performance are so internalised today, and doing nothing can be regarded as a necessary act of resistance — understanding Clara's and Karl's activities as work enabled us to perceive them not only as kin (which we already did), but also as colleagues, which again changed our relationship.

The Expertise of the Other

As we thought about the conditions of our cooperation, we agreed that the most important thing was that all involved would enjoy what they do. And we made a list of possible activities. Many of them may not be covered by the conventional concept of work, but as we know, the concept is a broad one in art. The list serves as a starting point and can always be referred to and revised. We also thought about our different competences and about what we could do so that we didn't tinker in each other's work. As the art historian Gesa Ziemer points out, "[t]he

---

13   Vinciane Despret, "W for Work, Why Do We Say Cows Don't Do Anything," in *What Would Animals Say If We Asked the Right Questions?* (Minneapolis: University of Minnesota Press, 2016), 177.

14   Sue Donaldsen and Will Kymlicka, "Farmed Animal Sanctuaries: The Heart of the Movement? A Socio-political Perspective," *Politics and Animals* 1 (2015), https://journals.lub.lu.se/index.php/pa/article/view/15045.

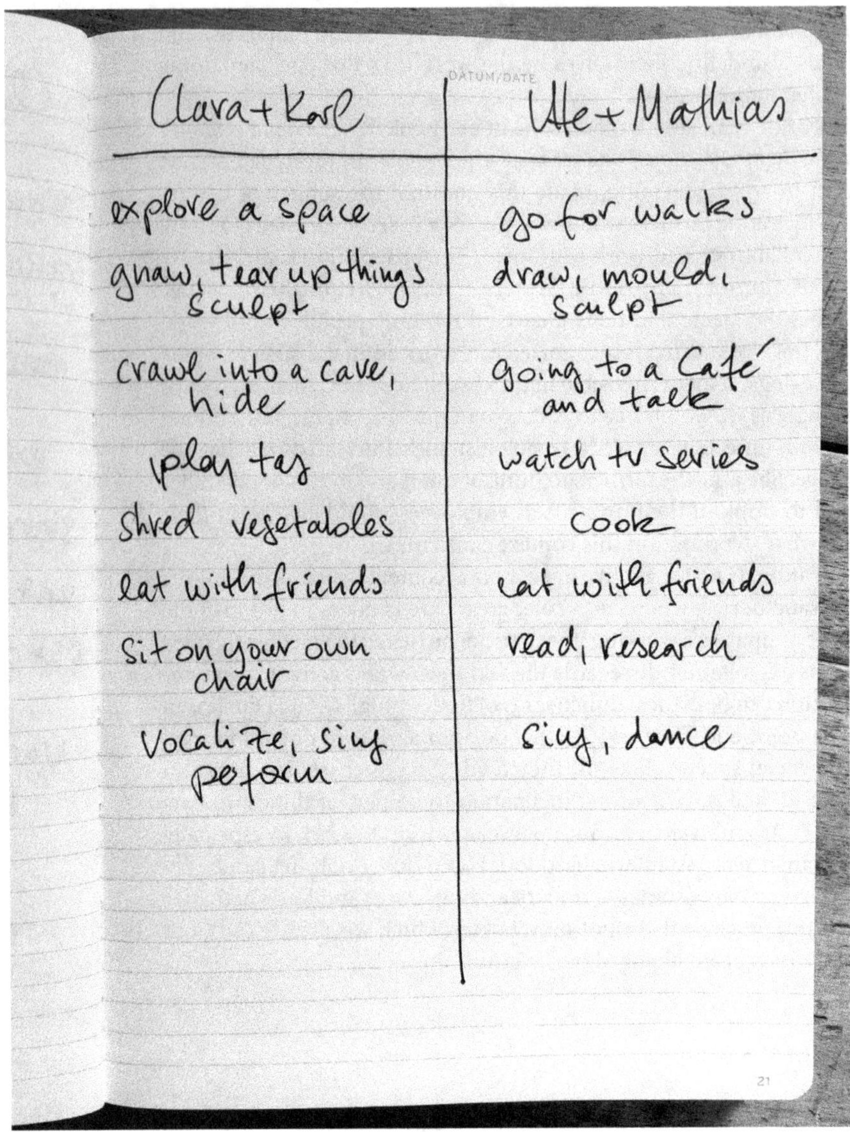

Fig. 3.8. List of things we like to do (2016). Photograph by the authors.

basic prerequisite for collective work is the recognition of various subject cultures and the trust in the expertise of the other."[15]

The collaboration with Clara and Karl also brought us back to our artistic roots and thus to an expertise that we had acquired a long time ago, without which we might not have been able to recognize their work as such. Before we became media artists, we considered ourselves sculptors. In art school we had learned to work with different materials such as concrete, ceramics, polyester, and bronze; we knew how to make casting molds and how to create complex sewing patterns.

15   Gesa Ziemer, "Kollektives Arbeiten," in *Künstlerische Forschung: Ein Handbuch* (Zurich: Diaphanes Verlag, 2015), 171.

And through my (Ute's) training in wood carving, I probably have a keen eye for tools and their traces.

Clara and Karl's amorphous and fragile creations reminded us of the pleasures of this kind of work, and we, "computer workers," wanted to have it back, without becoming nostalgic. It had been our interest in narration that had brought us to work with electronic media, which led in the early 2000s to 3D real-time animations, interactive storytelling, and computer installations. As an interspecies collective, we are transmedial narrators. Drifting in the transitions and transformations between the media, a book can evolve into an installation, and a sculpture can generate a narrative. The borders between different media, like those between different species, are there to be played with. While the video works (e.g., *KRAMFORS* or *Lunch in a Cross-species Household*) remain rough documents of our everyday life and recorded with a handheld camera and edited with hard cuts, in other works, we use rather sophisticated visual effects, like Pepper's Ghost or Virtual Reality (VR). We appreciate these effects because of their "unsafe" origins, more attached to variété and entertainment than to "serious" art. In the installations we use them to involve the audience in a play, changing roles like climbing a small podium in *Contact Call,* being called or controlled by the birds. Or as in *Jurassic!,* where the camera perspective gives the viewers the illusion to see through the eyes of someone else. Finally, the objects that are created by Clara and Karl are presented very elaborately, emphasizing their aesthetic appeal, framing them as delicate works of art. Taking their expertise seriously is our way to counter the idea of human superiority, and to call into question one of the last largely unchallenged features of anthropological difference: the exclusively human ability to create art.[16]

An Unusual Object That Causes People to Start Talking

When we showed the installation *Subtraction One* for the first time in 2016, we realized that it functions as a "conversation piece."[17] On a black, squared table there is a collection of cork objects that Clara and Karl worked on over a period of roughly a year. Many parrot keepers offer their birds pieces of cork for activity. It's a natural material that offers a pleasant resistance. At the same time, cork has a long history as an artistic material, such as for architecture models. (At the courts of Europe cork models with their highly sensorial surface were considered precious collectors' items.) Parrots in turn are born sculptors; their beaks are extremely sensitive "tools" with which they elaborately shape their material, each in their own way.

As the ones who arranged their objects, we have tried to keep the interpretation as open as possible, consciously not positioning them so that faces, figures, and so on were to be recognized. Rather, we looked for a balanced arrangement, paying attention to how the volumes and shapes corresponded with each other.

Human visitors to the exhibition in Cologne moved around the table and looked at the objects very attentively. The fine surfaces that the parrots had carved out with their beaks, which represented its shape just as the shape of the tool is

16   Other features thought to be exclusively human have been, amongst others, tool usage, language, consciousness, and culture.

17   An unusual object that causes people to start talking. *Cambridge Dictionary,* s.v. "conversation piece."

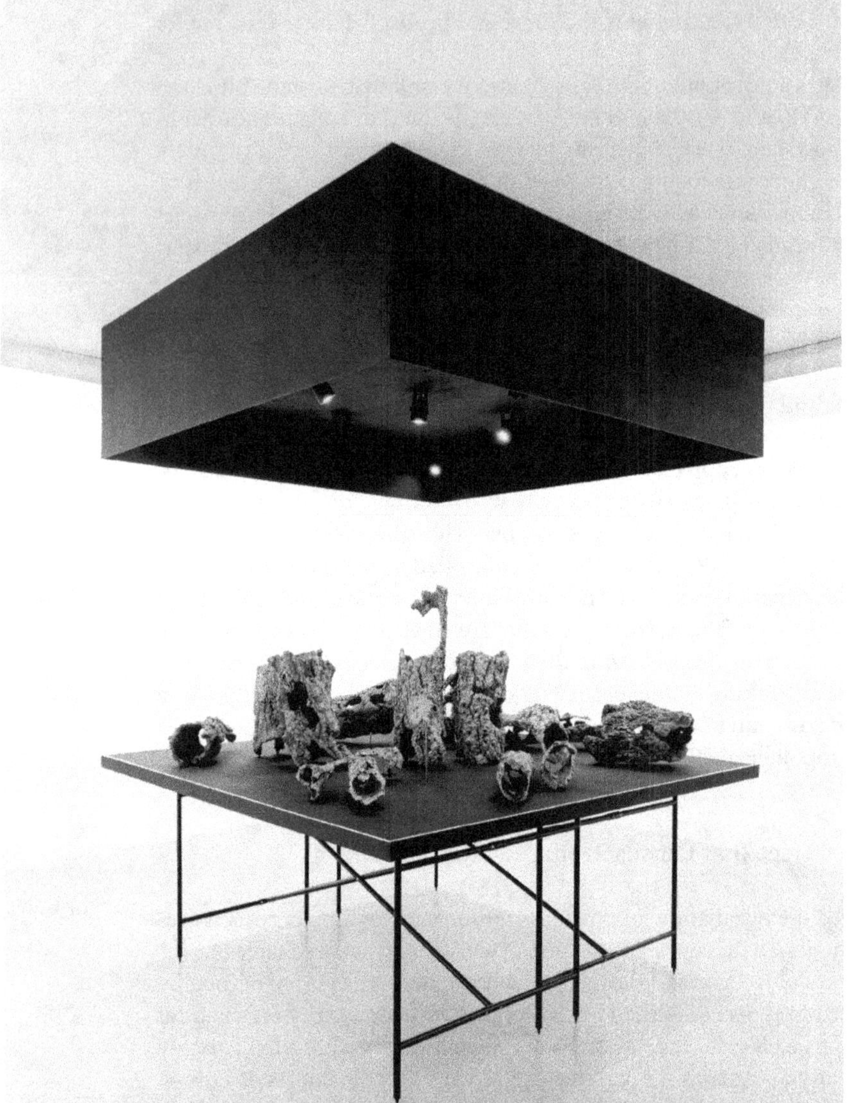

Fig. 3.9. Subtraction One (2016). Installation view Kjubh Kunstverein, Cologne. Photograph by the authors.

present in woodcarving, together with the delicate illumination coming from the black square ceiling element, gave the objects the impression of being bronze casts. Visitors who didn't know that they were made by the parrots were especially interested in their aesthetic appeal and that of their unique materiality.

With the knowledge of interspecies collaboration, questions of process and the conditions of creation came into play: how do the birds do it and is it something they do instinctively? Is it fun for them or are they forced to do it? Are they rewarded for it? Are Clara and Karl attached to their objects? What are they thinking about them being shown? And who decides when the piece is finished? [18] Fundamental questions that they probably would never have asked us as a human artist couple but that nevertheless provoked intense conversations about issues like the balance of power or the effects of rewards which are not only related to interspecies art.

For the same exhibition Clara and Karl reworked one of the most famous books of the last century. *The World We Live In,* originally conceived by Lincoln Barnett for *Time Life Magazine* and published in Germany by Knaur, tells the natural history of the world, from the genesis of the planets to the present.[19] Its lush illustrations are inscribed into the visual memory of a whole generation. As a child I (Ute) was torn between fascination and disgust. There were pages I could only look at for a short while, but which I kept going back to, with pictures called "Tyrannosaurus Rex mauls a herbivore" or "desert rat escapes from a snake." *The World We Live In* not only aspired to make the cutting-edge scientific knowledge of the time comprehensible to everyone. It also incidentally told the thoroughly American story of "eat or be eaten" and conveyed what was still a completely intact anthropocentric world view. It is absolutely clear who was meant by the "we" in the title. We are humans, and it was time to submit this to a fundamental revision.

It was the first cloth-bound book for Clara and Karl, and by the way they treated it we got the impression that it was a particular pleasure. While our relationship to particular books was paramount for us, for Clara and Karl it was probably their materiality, the strength of the bindings, the varying resistance of the paper. Perhaps it was also the sound of the materials when gnawed; the rule is, especially with cardboard, the crispier the better. After all, it is possible as Jessica Ullrich notes that Clara and Karl experience their artistic creation in dimensions that human observers, including us, cannot even guess at.[20]

18   In the studio but also at home in the kitchen all members of the collective have their working places, which they can enter and leave independently. We have a variety of materials there, such as cork, paper, and fabrics, and Clara and Karl are free to use them or not. Gnawing and scraping have a "natural" function in nesting as parrots are cave breeders. But we are pretty sure that they know that they are not building nests on the workbench. For us it rather looks like they really enjoy what they do. They spend a lot of time with these activities, sometimes many hours a day, and don't like to be disturbed. They also show signs of contentment like fluffing their feathers, and beak grinding after a work session, chilling on top of their pieces. We never force them to perform in any way, and we don't need rewards such as treats, which are commonly used in trick training or to create "desired" behavior, because they only do what they want to do. But recognition and praise certainly play a role between us. As long as Clara or Karl work on a piece, they can be highly attached to the objects, and it can be difficult to ask them to give them away. We cannot really know what they think about them being shown in an exhibition. But what we can perceive is that they like the attention when we look at their objects and comment on them, and, to a certain extent, the attention they get at an opening when they accompany us.

19   Lincoln Barnett, ed., *The World We Live In* (New York: Time Incorporated, 1955).

20   Parrots' sensorium differs from ours. They have an almost 360-degree field of view, richer color vision, and they can see up to 150 images per second, to name only a few examples. They might have senses we don't even know about. "To assume that this is completely impossible would be pure anthropocentrism." Jessica Ullrich, "Schwarmästhetik, Distributive Agency in der Interspezies Kol-

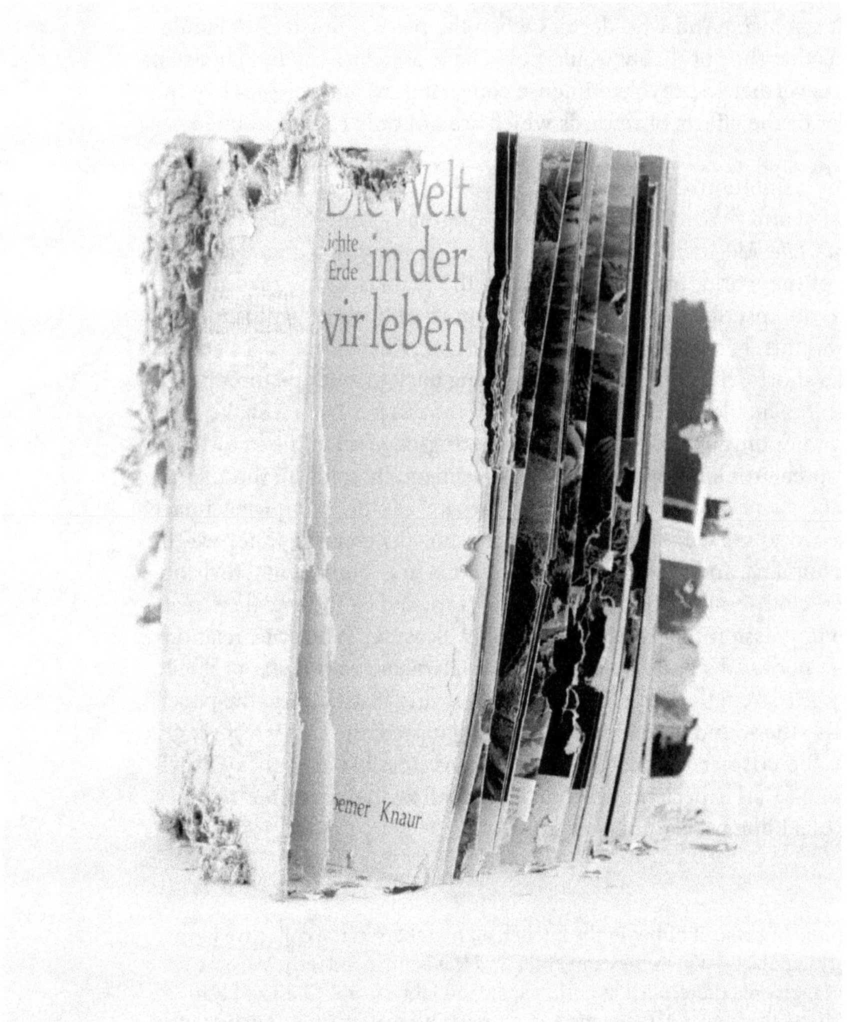

Fig. 3.10a. The World We Live In (2016). Book object in a glass case. Photograph by the authors.

Reading has become an everyday practice for many people, and so it comes as no surprise that parrots are interested in the associated media, especially books. Another one we've been exploring together is Michael Crichton's novel *Jurassic Park* from 1990.[21] Birds are dinosaurs — not just relatives or descendants of them, as paleontologists Darren Naish and Paul Barrett emphasize. They have emerged from a group of relatively small predatory dinosaurs (e.g., the velociraptor or the raptor for short), whose ability to cooperate we could admire in the film. The intelligence and speed with which their three-dimensional representations know how

laboration CMUK," in Hörner/Antlfinger und das Interspezies Kollektiv CMUK, *Die Welt in der wir leben* (Cologne: Verlag der KHM, 2016), 33–41.

21   Michael Crichton, *Jurassic Park* (New York: Ballantine, 1990).

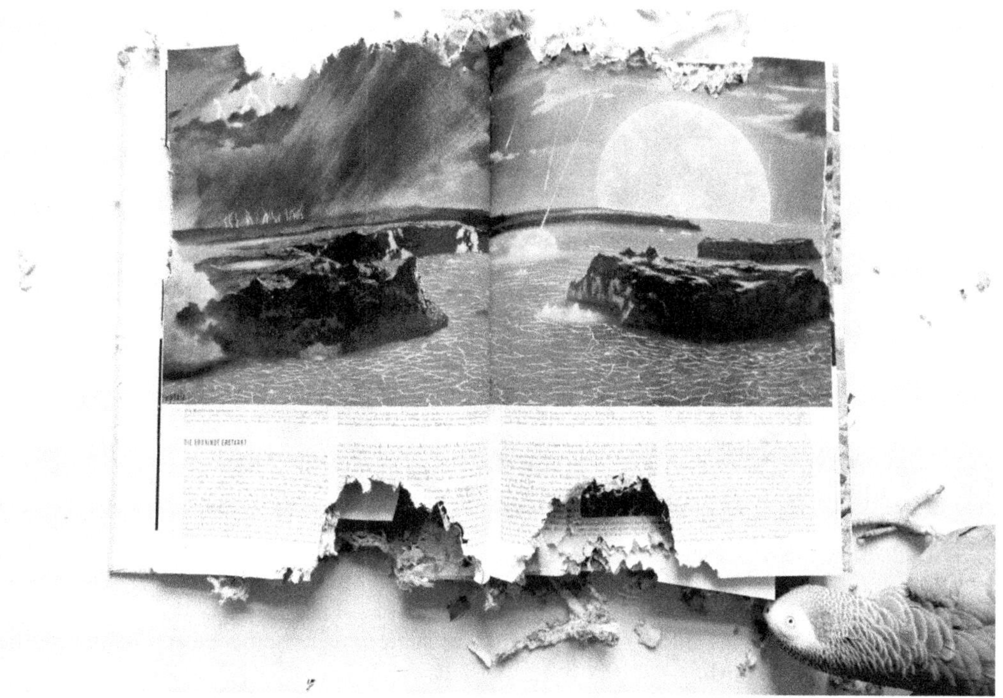

Fig. 3.10b. Clara working on the *The Word We Live In* (2016). Photograph by the authors.

to immediately use any human inattentiveness to their advantage made us think of experiences with our parrots: short moments of inattentiveness that are used to attack their worst rivals: laptops and mobile phones, wooden window frames and doors, soft sneaker soles, musical instruments, and other things that are valuable to us humans.

For *Jurassic!* we worked with what was left after the avian exploration of the book; like archaeologists we searched amongst the remains of a past culture for the pieces that fit. In laborious work we put the scraps, into which the parrots had disassembled the book, together again on one large sheet of paper. In this way the first multispecies version of "Michael Crichton's Text" emerged.

In addition, a VR headset — something no natural history presentation can do without — opened up a view of the everyday life of dinosaurs in their natural habitat. Birds can see almost 360 degrees around, and we have adapted our recording technology accordingly. When we installed the camera on our breakfast table, we realized to our surprise and joy that the VR camera's perspective made us feel like in the body of a bird, as if we were miniaturized. The plates looked like pools. Mathias and I were giants! Another shot shows us together in the aviary, you can see how I (Ute) am trying to understand how the new VR camera works, and the birds, too, approach the strange, little, three-legged box with curiosity.

The remains of the book and the reconstruction of the text were presented in a glass case together with other publications on dinosaurs, for example, *Ausgestorben um zu bleiben* (*Extinct in Order to Remain*) by Bernhard Kegel, in which the before mentioned paleontologists have their say. A table and chair beside the glass case invited the audience to take a seat, put on the VR Glasses, and watch the videos. As in *Contact Call,* we used a visual effect to create an illusion, this time

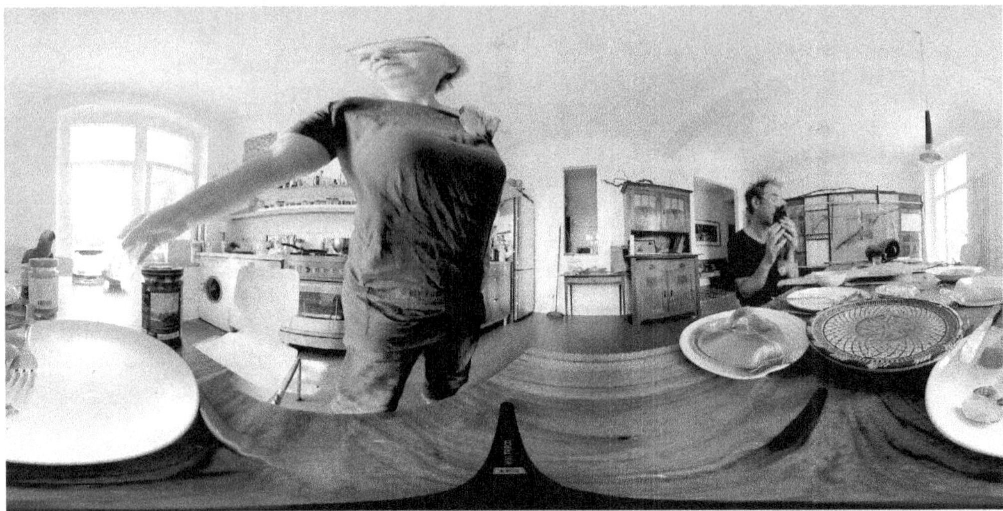

Fig. 3.11. Still from *Jurassic!* (2018). 360° Video, 2:30 min.

to be in the middle of the situation, as something or someone approximately the size of a bird.

When we took these VR pictures, they were supposed to be test records. We didn't know that these recordings were to be the last with Karl in it. He died in June 2018 after having been with us for almost ten years. He reached a very old age, even for a parrot, though nevertheless, we miss him greatly. All of a sudden, we understood and had to face the fact that the idea of "becoming-with" — to live and work together — also means dying together. This photography shows Karl at the beach in Brittany where we often spent our holidays together. He looks at us from the center of the image, behind him being the sea he must once have crossed.

> *"[L]ife is a product of putrefaction, and it de-*
> *pends on both death and the dung heap."*[22]

Karl's Islands (2019), a piece that we had just started to work on, finally became a homage to him. A couple of years ago, we made a series of photos of his morning manifestations, which he used to present to us with great emphasis. The constellations that are reflected in them and the various substances that they are made up of had long fascinated us. Some of his droppings looked like complicated signs or symbols — perhaps someone could read the future in them? Others looked like far-off landscapes covered in mist, seen from a bird's-eye perspective. We had the impression that Karl also took these apparitions seriously, deemed them important, and wanted us to look at them. A good digestion is important, especially for an old creature, since it is a question of the ecology of one's own body. We laid them on a green background — the color assigned to love and nature in medieval thinking — an era of thought when the separation between human beings and other living creatures was not yet as pronounced as it is today. Then we had them

22   Georges Bataille, "Death," in *The Bataille Reader,* eds. Fred Botting and Scott Wilson (Oxford: Blackwell, 1997), 242.

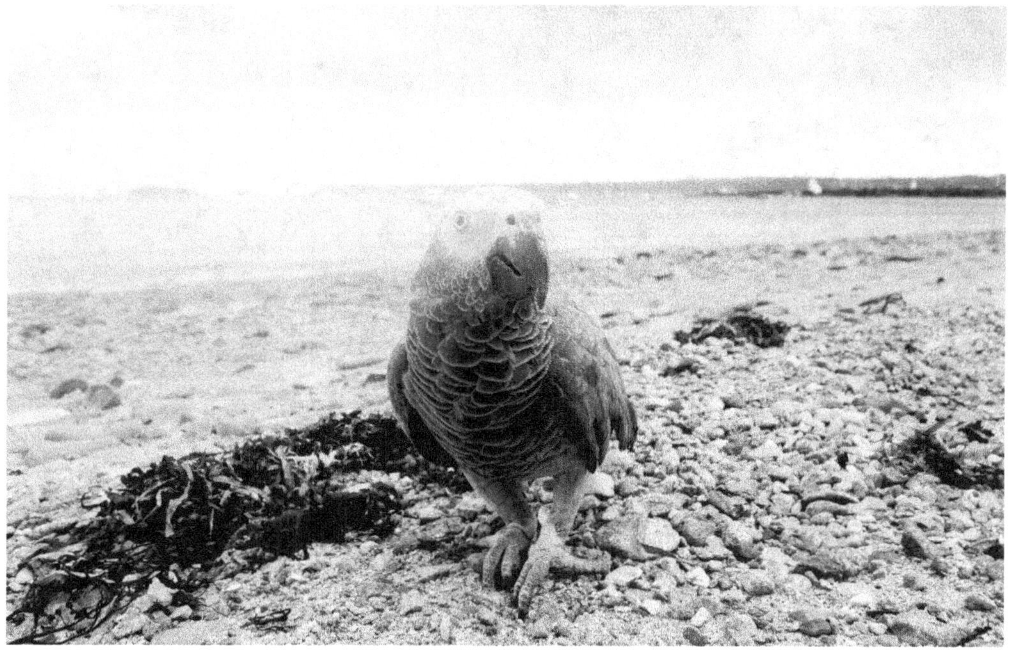

Fig. 3.12. Karl at the beach in Brittany where we often spent our holidays together (2016). Photograph by the authors.

printed on velvet, one of the most precious fabrics of that period, and assembled them to form a magnificent quilt.

In the installation, the quilt is spread out on the floor like a splendid coat. Below, the contours of a sleeping or dreaming human figure can be seen. On one side, the quilt is lifted — as if someone or something were let in or out. Many parrots love to crawl under blankets. Karl had always been too careful to get involved in this game — he didn't want to be touched except at the beak, most likely he has had bad experiences with people. But as he grew older, he often slept in his little box right next to our bed so that we could be there for him when he wasn't feeling well. Before falling asleep he sometimes made a little rustling noise with his beak. The noise emerges when the two halves of the beak, which are equipped on the inside with a riffled structure, are rubbed against each other. It is a comfort sound, similar to the purring of a cat. In the installation, a recording of this sound and a weathered old branch coming out from under the blanket form a bridge to the surrounding space.

Since Karl passed away, we reflected a lot on his story. No one could tell us where he came from, where he had spent the first four or five decades of his life. We think it was part of our mourning for him. Since we could not find out anything about him as an individual, we developed an interest in the history of the African Grey Parrots in Europe, which is closely related to the history of slavery. The first paintings in which they appear are Francesco Melzi's *Portrait of Man with a Parrot* (1525) and Lucas Cranach the Elder's *Cardinal Albrecht* (1526). Both date from the period in which the transatlantic slave trade began.

African Grey Parrots came to Europe on the same trade routes and on the same ships — in other words with the same companies — that traded in sugar and slaves.

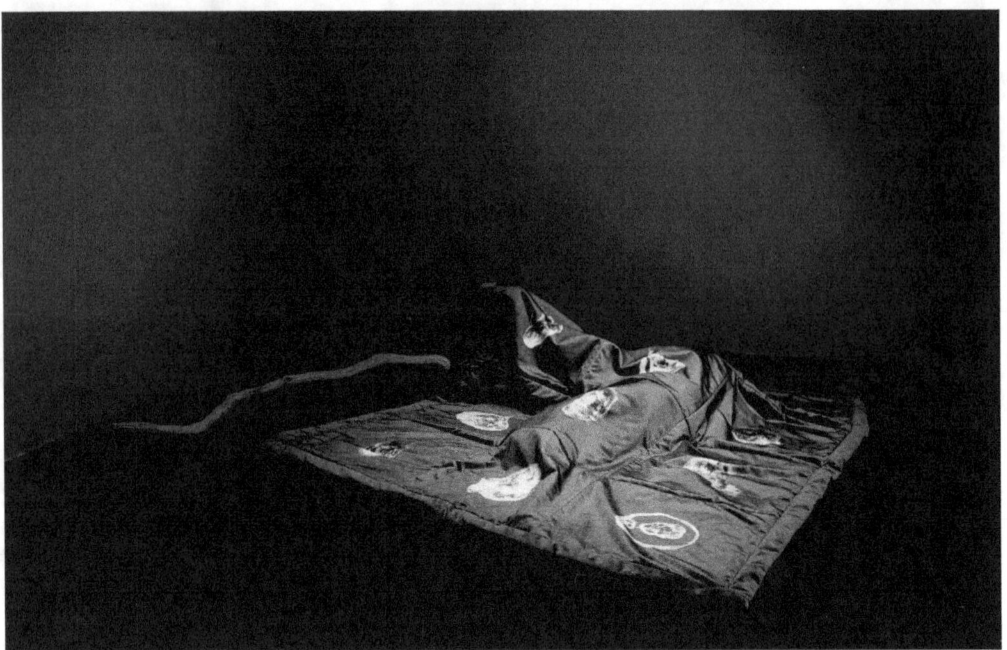

Fig. 3.13a. Karl's Islands (2019). Installation view Temporary Gallery, Cologne. Photograph by Pascal Dreier.

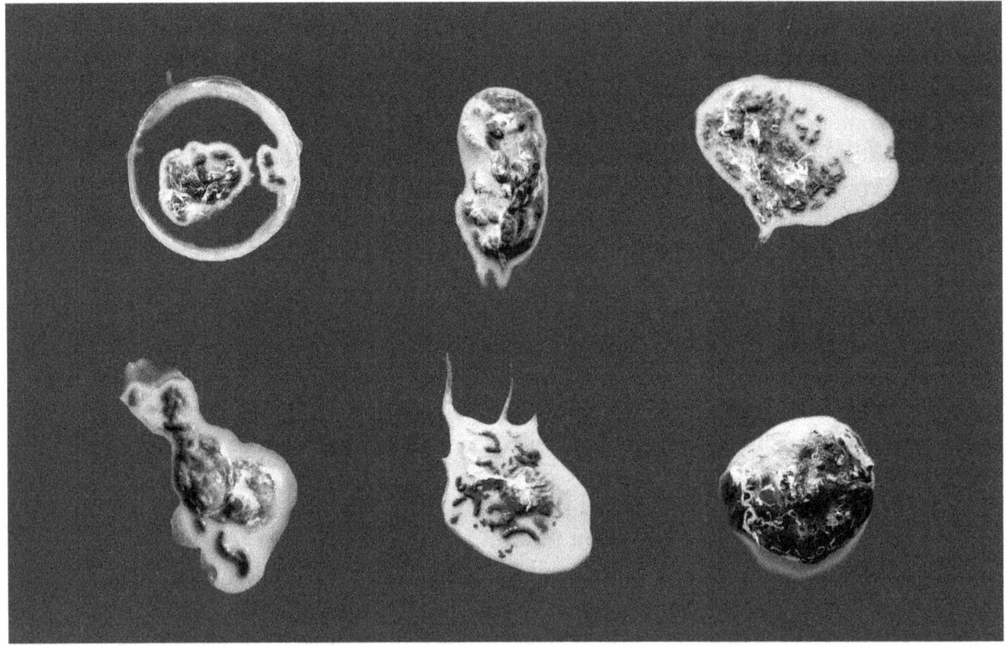

Fig. 3.13b. Various droppings, printing patterns. Photograph by the authors.

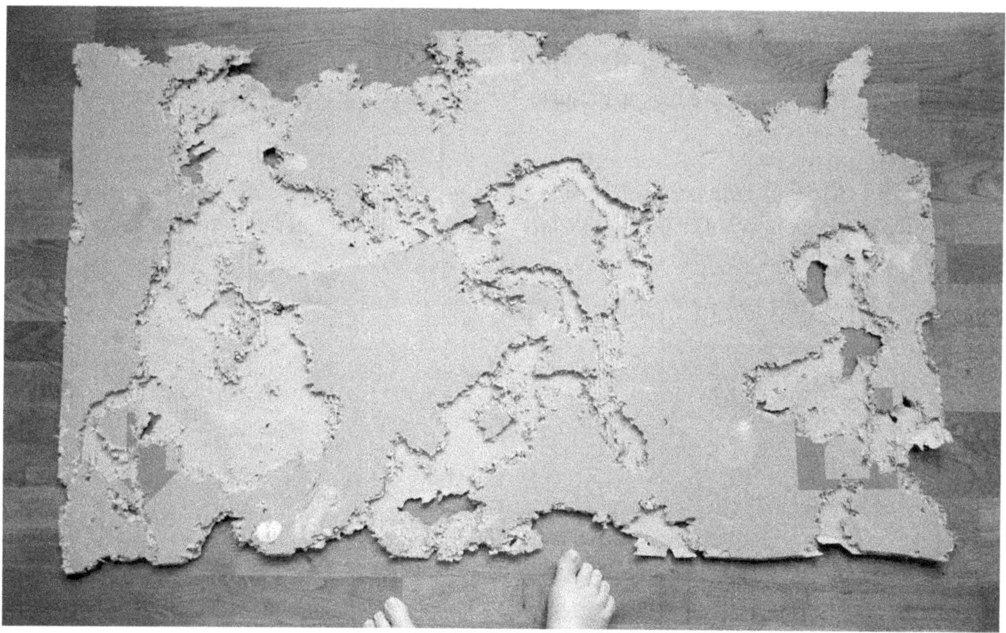

Fig. 3.14 "World map" gnawed into packaging carton (2018). Photograph by the authors.

Many did not survive the passage, and many more died in this new environment. The trade with Karl's wild conspecifics and the destruction of their environment made the African Grey Parrot an endangered species in many regions of Africa. It can be assumed that more now live in America, Europe, and Asia than in their countries of origin. In our current research we are working on a map that depicts this factual entanglement of the lives of humans and parrots. The map is to show the migration movements of the birds and their original and their new habitats, and we will show this map together with "maps" made by birds. Maps that may seem puzzling to us, like Karl's islands or the two "world maps" that Clara and Karl gnawed into the sides of a large shipping box.

Living and working together with Clara and Karl has shaped us significantly in recent years. We learned to regard nonhuman animals as individuals with own desires and interests that we must respect. This had of course consequences for how we relate to nonhuman animals in general. To us, they are no longer material, neither in art nor in everyday life or when it comes to food or clothing. Is it possible to have an equal, interspecies partnership? Maybe not quite as there are power gaps that remain especially in a human environment, but we can try to get as close as possible. What helps is politeness — paying attention to the interests of animals, as Vinciane Despret puts it. To think about the implications of what we want from each other and whether it is meaningful for everyone involved.

The avian part of our collective is probably not interested in the art context or in exhibition, but that does not mean that they have no sense of or interest in aesthetics. Long before humans appeared, birds were singing, dancing, and building architectures and staging spaces (just think of the elaborately designed arcades of the Bowerbird). And there are many indications that they enjoy it. The human part of the flock hopes that our joint work succeeds in creating an awareness for the desires, interests, and rights of nonhuman animals; for their obstinacy, their knowledge, and their sense of humor. And that the proposition of a collaboration between human and nonhuman animals in the field of art has the power to open the view to the bigger picture — to recognize the world as an ongoing *communal* project.

Note: In January 2019 Theo, a thirty-year-old African Grey Parrot, became part of the flock after he met with Clara on neutral territory at a friend's place. We are very glad that he stays with us.

References

Barnett, Lincoln, ed. *The World We Live In.* New York: Time Incorporated, 1955.

Bataille, Georges. "Death." In *The Bataille Reader,* edited by Fred Botting and Scott Wilson, 242–45. Oxford: Blackwell, 1997.

Crichton, Michael. *Jurassic Park.* New York: Ballantine, 1990.

Despret, Vinciane. "W for Work: Why Do We Say Cows Don't Do Anything." In *What Would Animals Say If We Asked the Right Questions?,* 177–83. Minneapolis: University of Minnesota Press, 2016.

de Waal, Frans B.M. "Anthropomorphism and Anthropodenial: Consistency in Our Thinking about Humans and Other Animals." *Zoological Philosophy* 27, no. 1 (1999): 255–80. https://www.jstor.org/stable/43154308.

Diamond, Cora. "Fleisch essen, Menschen essen." In *Menschen, Tiere und Begriffe: Aufsätze zur Moralphilosophie,* 83–107. Berlin: Suhrkamp, 2012.

Donaldsen, Sue, and Will Kymlicka. "Farmed Animal Sanctuaries: The Heart of the Movement? A Socio-Political Perspective." *Politics and Animals* 1 (2015). https://journals.lub.lu.se/index.php/pa/article/view/15045.

Engelbach, Barbara. "Of Images and Thoughts." In Hörner/Antlfinger, *Discrete Farms,* 20–23. Berlin: Revolver Verlag, 2012.

Gruen, Lori. "Facing Death and Practicing Grief." In *Ecofeminism: Feminist Intersections with Other Animals and the Earth,* 127–41. New York: Bloomsbury Academic, 2014.

Hörner/Antlfinger. *Two Lives? A Debate.* 1999. http://h—a.org/en/project/zwei-leben-eine-debatte/.

Maturana, Humberto. *Was ist erkennen? Die Welt entsteht im Auge des Betrachters.* Munich: Goldmann Verlag, 2001.

Nakhshabī, Ziyā' al-Dīn. *The Tooti Nameh, or, Tales of a Parrot: In the Persian Language with an English Translation.* Calcutta: J. Debrett, 1801.

Pepperberg, Irene. *The Alex Studies: Cognitive and Communicative Abilities of Grey Parrots.* Cambridge: Harvard University Press, 1999.

Ullrich, Jessica. "Schwarmästhetik: Distributive Agency in der Interspezies Kollaboration CMUK." In Hörner/Antlfinger und das Interspezies Kollektiv CMUK, *Die Welt in der wir leben,* 33–41. Cologne: Verlag der KHM, 2016.

Ziemer, Gesa. "Kollektives Arbeiten." In *Künstlerische Forschung: Ein Handbuch,* 169–72. Zurich: Diaphanes Verlag, 2015.

CHAPTER 4

The Laudable Cow: Poetics of Human/ Cattle Relationships

Emily McGiffin

It is an unhappy reality that most people in the postindustrial societies of North America and Europe rarely come into contact with living cattle. One of our closest companion species throughout much of human history, cattle in industrialized societies are now mainly impounded in distant confined animal feedlot operations (CAFOS) and raised as commodities far from human communities and out of the public eye. Yet despite this geographical separation, most of us who live in these societies remain intimately connected with cattle. Cattle nourish us with their flesh and milk while their skins provide the raw material for cherished everyday goods. Our estrangement from cattle is yet another of the paradoxes of contemporary life: despite being more absent from everyday human lives than perhaps at any point in the last several thousand years, cattle have never been more abundant. Over 33 million head of cattle were slaughtered in the United States in 2019, a new record that marked a 2 percent increase over 2018.[1] In 2020, total beef production in the US will exceed 10 million metric tons, up 1.2 percent from 2019 despite the impacts of the COVID-19 pandemic.[2] The vast majority of these animals spent their lives confined in overpopulated enclosures where they were fattened on unhealthy diets of industrially produced and genetically modified corn and soy, to which their digestive tracks are not suited, before being shipped to killing factories that slaughter and dismember thousands of animals an hour.

Rising numbers of cattle under industrial production regimes have resulted not only in "an environmental catastrophe"[3] in the form of rampant deforestation, water pollution, and climate change. They have also resulted in a human catastrophe: foreign workers and marginalized rural communities are left to bear the brunt of increased pollution, crime, and mental health issues that accompany the proliferation of CAFOS and abattoirs, while healthcare systems shoulder the burdens of obesity, cancer, and heart disease linked to the overconsumption of beef.[4]

1   United States Department of Agriculture, "Livestock Slaughter: 2019 Summary," *USDA, National Agriculture Statistics Service*, 2020.
2   Chris Torres, "Look for Large Growth in Meat Production, Exports in 2020," *Corn and Soybean Digest*, 2020.
3   Karyn Pilgrim, "'Happy Cows,' 'Happy Beef': A Critique of the Rationales for Ethical Meat," *Environmental Humanities* 3, no. 1 (2013): 125.
4   Jody Emel and Harvey Neo, *Political Ecologies of Meat* (London: Routledge, 2015), and Amy J. Fitzgerald, Linda Kalof, and Thomas Dietz, "Slaughterhouses and Increased Crime Rates," *Organization & Environment* 22, no. 2 (2009):

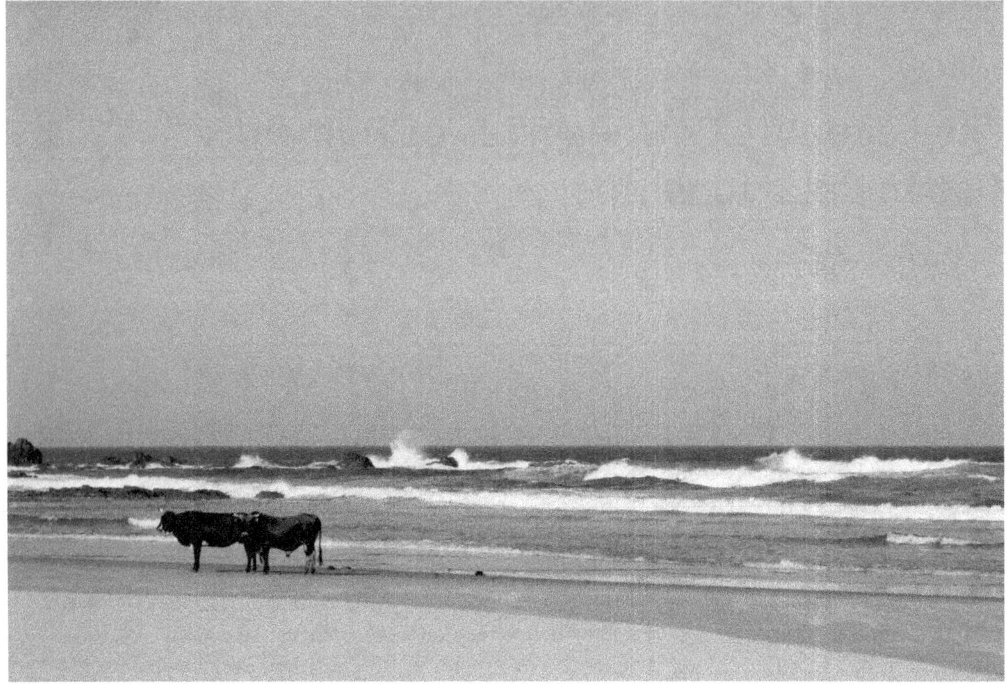

Fig. 4.1. Cattle enjoy a day at the beach in sunny Port St. Johns, South Africa. Photograph by the author.

Industrialized food production has made nourishment much more abundant than at any time in human history, in part by alleviating the threat of insufficiency that had plagued much of our species in pre-industrial times, but more significantly by ushering in the opposite problem of overabundance and overconsumption. Many of us are now over-nourished and, despite an unprecedented cornucopia of other foodstuffs to choose from, the majority of us opt to indulge in an ever-growing amount of dairy products and meat. This situation of harm is made possible by a deficit of human sympathy for other creatures, which enables us to "overlook the enormity of animal suffering."[5] Addressing the growing human, environmental, and animal injustices of industrialized meat production requires us to shift both our eating habits and our sympathies by rekindling relationships of kinship and care with the animals we are reliant upon.

Factory meat production is the relationship that connects most people in industrialized societies to the animals that have been our close companions for vast stretches of human history. However, this separation of humans and living cattle is far from the only human relationship with these animals in practice today. Cattle remain prominent in the culture and daily lifeways of small farmers, ranchers, and pastoralists around the world. Working at the margins or outside of industrial, food-production systems, these animal husbandry practitioners open space for alternative relations of kinship and care that are only possible through prox-

158–84.

5   Greta Gaard, "Vegetarian Ecofeminism: A Review Essay," *Frontiers: A Journal of Women Studies* 23, no. 3 (2002): 119.

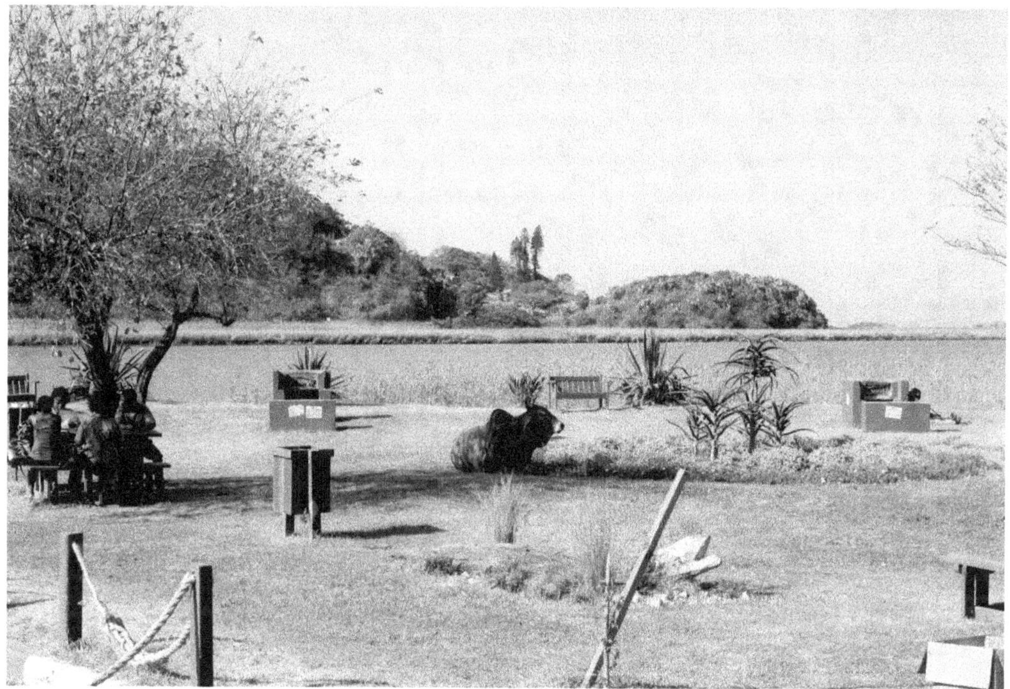

Fig. 4.2. A head of cattle appreciating a recent town beautification and landscaping project in Port St. Johns, South Africa. Photograph by the author.

imity. Over the past six years, my research on South African and West African poetic genres has brought me into close contact with people for whom cattle are very much present in day-to-day life. For amaXhosa people living in rural parts of South Africa's Eastern Cape province, cattle are everyday companions, much as they have been for hundreds, if not thousands, of years. During my time in rural and peri-urban settings throughout the province, I found that cattle often enjoy a large degree of autonomy and freedom of movement. In Port St. Johns, a seaside community at the mouth of the Mzimvubu River, I watched a group of cows enjoy an afternoon at the beach before filing home along the roadside at the end of the day (see Fig. 4.1). A lone bull passed the afternoon ruminating calmly under a tree in a nearby municipal park in the company of small groups of picnickers (see Fig. 4.2). At other points along the coast, I saw large crowds of cattle gathered on the beach, enjoying the fresh salt air rolling in off the breakers (see Fig. 4.3). In the small Eastern Cape city of Makhanda (formerly Grahamstown), cattle are commonplace in neighborhoods surrounding the downtown core, where they graze the boulevards and occasional flower gardens and are herded home at the end of the day.

As such observations accumulated, it became clear to me that when cattle are given a degree of independence to direct their own lives and movements, they enjoy many of the same things people do. They like hanging out in parks. They like sunbathing on the beach or by a river. They like watching the surf. They saunter home before it gets dark. They enjoy one another's company and the company of their companion species. With respect to humans, their relationships have practical elements, to be sure, but in these contexts their place within the social fabric

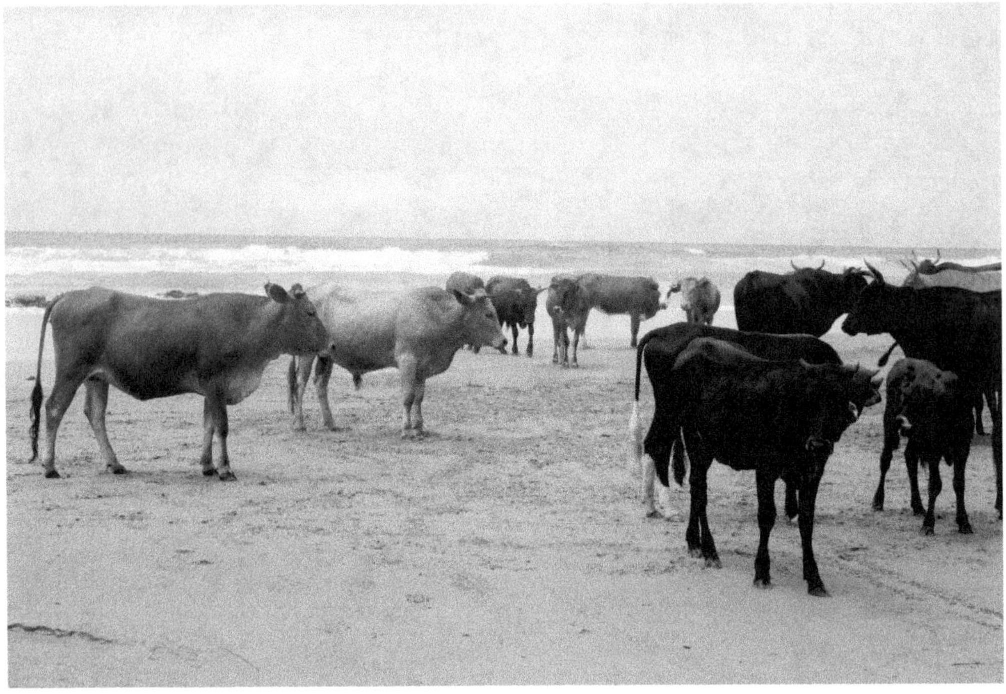

Fig. 4.3. Freely roaming cattle congregate at the beach along South Africa's Eastern Cape. Photograph by the author.

is complex, and not merely utilitarian. Whether grazing in the pasture beside a home, or snuffling at the grass outside the front gate, or standing affably in the middle of the dirt road between villages, their calm and welcome presence is reassuring. Gentle observers of the bustle of human life, they are easy-going reminders that the human way of understanding and being in the world is only one of thousands of alternatives.

This kind of easy-going relationship is part of Britain's not-so-distant past. As John Clare wrote in a lament about the enclosure movements and subsequent loss of the remaining agricultural commons in the late-eighteenth and early-nineteenth centuries,

> Unbounded freedom ruled the wandering scene
> Nor fence of ownership crept in between
> To hide the prospect of the following eye —
> Its only bondage was the circling sky.
> …
> The sheep and cows were free to range as then
> Where change might prompt nor felt the bonds of men:
> Cows went and came, with evening, morn and night,
> To the wild pasture as their common right.[6]

---

6   John Clare, "The Moors," in *Selected Poems,* ed. Jonathan Bate (New York: Faber and Faber, 2003), 89–91.

The freedom of movement enjoyed by both humans and animals prior to the imposition of private property regimes was perhaps not fully appreciated by agrarian commoners such as John Clare until it was lost. The friendly awareness of and regard for the sensibilities and distinctive personalities of individual cattle that I witnessed in the Eastern Cape is part of our history in Europe and North America despite being far from the norm in contemporary life.

No doubt there are a raft of factors that account for the vastly different lives of cattle within different cultures and at different points in space and time. The array of differences between societies, urban and rural, agro-pastoralist and industrialized, includes different property regimes, differing political economies, different life expectations, different histories, different cosmologies. But my research in South Africa centred on oral poetry, and it almost immediately became clear to me that the cultural politics of cattle in amaXhosa society was enmeshed with the centrality of cattle to poets and their art. Specifically, my research examined *iimbongi* (sg. *imbongi*), respected oral poets traditionally associated with chiefs and dignitaries, who practice an extemporaneous panegyric genre known as *izibongo*. This poetic form is largely structured by names: family names, given names, and praise names of lineages of chiefs, kings, and their bulls. Izibongo, particularly that of rural communities, is very clearly a multispecies poetics of place that names not only human inhabitants of a landscape but also their ever-present forbears, the wild plants and animals that they share the landscape with, and the animal companions that share their homesteads. Poets I spoke with, like those of earlier times, describe honing their crafts by praising cattle during hours spent tending them in their youth. Izibongo express the beauty and dignity of cattle and highlight the importance of the animals both as valued companions and as social metaphors.

In response to my encounters with iimbongi and their multispecies entanglements, I found myself curious about parallels in western North America. On landscapes transformed by industrial agriculture that are now dedicated in large part to industrial beef production, were there ever relationships with cattle similar to those of amaXhosa pastoralists? What equivalent poetry might be present in the literary tradition of Western North American? How have North American poets written about cattle and how might their literature have shaped our relationships with these animals? To answer these questions, I turned to the cultural figure most closely associated with cattle in North America: the cowboy. In the nineteenth century, during long cattle drives between grazing lands and shipping points, cowboys lived with the herd for months on end, caring for the animals and fending off both predators and thieves. While many other poets before and since cowboys have no doubt had things to say about cattle, I felt that cowboy poetry in particular might reveal a lifestyle and sensibility akin to that of pastoralist peoples in other places.

I begin this chapter with a closer look at isiXhosa poetry and examples of what it might reveal about human-cattle relationships in the South Africa's Eastern Cape. Drawing on my research on izibongo, I discuss the importance of cattle in amaXhosa and amaZulu tradition and the representation of cattle in two selections of transcribed oral poetry. I then shift to an examination of cowboy oral poetry — songs and ballads collected in *Cowboy Songs and Frontier Ballads* and *Songs of the Cattle Camp and Cow Trail* — to consider how human-cattle relationships are represented in this poetic tradition. From these samples of poetry, I speculate as to what these two poetic traditions reveal about two very different societies and their relationships with cattle. I also ask what these poetics might reveal when it comes to regenerating what has been, and in many cases remains, a sacred connection to an animal we shouldn't live without.

Lauding the Cow

Over the course of a multi-year research project on the cultural politics of izibongo, commonly translated as "praise poetry," I learned that cattle play a key role in this literature. At the time of the arrival of European colonizers, amaXhosa people, like various other nations in the region, lived largely as an agro-pastoralist society in what is now South Africa's Eastern Cape province. Despite enormous social changes in the intervening years, many people in rural areas throughout the province continue to rely heavily on land-based livelihoods and to live in close association with cattle. Young poets often hone their talents by praising cattle during long days spent tending and working with them and cattle appear in poems both as a subject of praises and metaphor for praiseworthy human qualities.

As an overseas visitor to the region, my research into this ephemeral art form is necessarily limited. Beyond the relatively few performances I was able to attend and poets I was able to speak with, my discussion here includes one of the relatively few transcribed poems available in translation. While I can't claim that these examples are wholly representative of the genre or culture, they are certainly illustrative of alternative relations with cattle.

During 2015 and 2016, the Mthatha-based imbongi Thukela Poswayo performed several poems for chiefs and dignitaries at various public events in the Transkei that I attended.[7] The excerpts below are call-and-response openings to poems delivered to King Zwelonke, the monarch of the amaXhosa nation at the time. In this poem, chief and bull are synonymous. The poem illustrates linkages between king and cattle that go beyond metaphor alone: the poet names the king's father — and by extension the king himself — as a strong and powerful leader and warrior by referring to him as a bull. In doing so, Poswayo creates an association between cattle and nobility that flows in both directions, directly bestowing the animal qualities of strength and fecundity onto the human dignitary while simultaneously lauding the patrician nature of cattle.

> *Imbongi: A Zwelonke!*
> *Abantu: A Zwelonke!*
> *Imbongi: A! Zweloooonke!*
> *Abantu: A! Zweloooonke*
> *Iyakhumbulana mntane nkosi.*
> *Iyakhumbulana thole leduna.*
> *Ndelula amehlo ndayibona imilambo,*
> *Ndanga ndinga qhayisa ndixele uthekwane*
> *Ndithi ndimbi ngapha ndimhle ngapha.*
> *Ewe kaloku thole leduna*
> *Siyinqamle imilambo.*
> *[…]*

7   The Transkei is a former land reserve designated an amaXhosa "homeland" during apartheid times.

Ke kambe okwethu kukungqina
Sithi nal'ithole lika Xolilizwe.
Nants' inkonyane yohlanga
Eyabizwa ingekaveli.

Imbongi: Hail Zwelonke!
Audience: Hail Zwelonke!
Imbongi: Hail! Zweloooonke!
Audience: Hail! Zweloooonke!
We miss each other, child of a chief.
We miss each other, son of a bull.
I stretched my eyes and saw the rivers,
I wish I can boast like the thekwane,
Saying I'm ugly on this side, beautiful on that.
Yes then, son of a bull,
We crossed rivers.
[…]
Now we need only witness,
Saying that this is Xolilizwe's calf.[8]
This is the calf of the nation,
Named before he was born.

This second poem also opens with the same characteristic call and response before shifting to praises of landscape and cattle.

Mntan'omhle
Amehl'am ath'akukhangela ndabon'imilambo
Ndathi ndakujonga ngaphesheya
Ndazibon'iinkomo zako kwenu
Ndazibon'iinkomo zako kwethu
Ndiyazaz'ezako kwenu
Ndiyazaz'ezako kwethu
Ndiyazehlula ngemibala
Kuba zingaphesheya kwemilambo zicacile.
Zicacile zizakuhle
Zibonakala ngok'tyhobo

Honorable one,
Opening my eyes, I saw rivers.
When I looked across
I saw your family's cattle,
I saw my family's cattle.
I know those of your family
I know those of my family.
I know them by their colors
For even across the river they are distinct.
They are beautifully distinct

8   Xolilizwe: King Zwelonke's father.

They appear now, charging.

Both poems illustrate the importance of cattle to this society by placing the animals within the opening lines of extremely important poems. An invitation to praise the king is perhaps the highest honor that a poet in this tradition can receive. In speaking here, Poswayo not only performs not only for king, dignitaries, and a gathered audience of several hundred people; he also performs for and surrounded by an ancestral lineage that extends into past and future. In the passage above, Poswayo praises the singularity of the cattle while highlighting the association between herds and particular families. He lauds the wealth of families associated with such beautiful and plentiful beasts and references the splendid and varied coloration of Nguni cattle that can even be recognized from afar thanks to their markings — at least by the poet, who knows them personally.

Like many other iimbongi, Poswayo developed his talents praising cattle in his boyhood: "[s]ince a young age I was [an imbongi]. But the platform then was different from the platform I'm using now. I was following cattle and all those things. I would sing praises for the cattle."[9] Poswayo's praises of cattle continue a long-established tradition that is also evident in earlier examples of transcribed izibongo by the late David Livingstone Phakamile Yali-Manisi. Manisi describes similar poetic roots. His earliest poems were praises for cattle that over time developed into praises for his nation's chiefs and political pieces decrying the poverty and dispossession of his people under the apartheid state.[10] Indeed, reports of the importance of cattle in isiXhosa poetry date back as far as the mid-nineteenth century. In his southern Africa travel account, made between 1864 and 1866, Gustav Fritsch noted, "[t]he ideal of the [umXhosa], the object of his daydreams and the favorite subject of his songs (*Liedern*), is his oxen, which are his most valuable possession. With the praise songs (*Lobgesängen*) of the cattle those of the chief mix themselves, and in these in turn the chief's cattle figure prominently."[11]

Marguerite Poland and David Hammond-Tooke pay tribute to the similarly intimate relationships between the neighboring amaZulu and cattle in their book *The Abundant Herd,* which documents the richly poetic terms for the diverse markings and coloration of the animals. Of poems spoken in honor of cattle, the authors write, "[c]attle are praised to encourage them to plough harder, to thank them for producing milk, to admire them for their virility, to coax them into the byre, and generally to affirm them in the eyes of their owners."[12] The complex and imaginative names given to the multicolored cattle illustrate not only the close relationships with and high regard for these animals in amaZulu culture; the names also illustrate the associations and interconnections drawn between the cattle col-

9   Thukela Poswayo, personal communication, Eastern Cape, 2016.

10   Jeff Opland, *The Dassie and the Hunter: A South African Meeting* (Scottsville: University of KwaZulu-Natal Press, 2005), and D.L.P. Yali-Manisi, *Imbongi entsha: Iimbali Zamanyange: Historical Poems,* trans. Jeff Opland and Pamela Maseko (Pietermaritzburg: University of KwaZulu-Natal Press, 2015).

11   Jeff Opland, *Xhosa Oral Poetry: Aspects of a Black South African Tradition* (Cambridge: Cambridge University Press, 1983), 22.

12   Marguerite Poland, W.D. Hammond-Tooke, and Leigh Voigt, *The Abundant Herds: A Celebration of the Cattle of the Zulu People* (Vlaeberg: Fernwood, 2003), 85.

oration and the many other creatures — birds, reptiles, plants, and antelope, for instance — with which people and cattle share the landscape. Cattle markings are also named for entities as diverse as stones, shadows, clouds, household implements and crops such as sorghum or sugar beans. Not only are markings named, bulls themselves may receive intricate praise names.[13] These names and poems are expressions of respect and admiration in contexts where cattle are much-loved companions and important actors in rural economies and lifeways. They provide labor, fertilizer, milk, meat, and hides, as well as building and cleaning materials, and serve as important symbols of cultural and spiritual continuity.

Prodding the Cow

In the settler-colonial nations of Canada and the United States, cattle became prolific with the expansion of the western frontier following the US civil war, the opening of new grazing lands, and the establishment of new meat packing plants in the US Midwest. By the 1870s, cowboys had become iconic figures within a growing industry that through the mid-1800s spread across the continent's central grasslands from Texas to Canada and westward to the Rocky Mountains. With their long, seasonal migrations that moved vast herds of cattle hundreds of kilometers between breeding grounds, feeding grounds and markets, the movements of cowboys and their herds had much in common with the annual transhumance movements of Eastern Cape pastoralists in precolonial times.

Curious about the lifeways of cowboys and their possible parallels with pastoralist societies I had encountered, I located two collections of historical songs and poems from the western United States collected and compiled by Harvard scholar John A. Lomax in 1919 and 1929. Both *Songs of the Cattle Trail and Cow Camp* and its companion collection, *Cowboy Songs and Other Frontier Ballads,* are freely available as downloadable ebooks on Project Gutenberg.[14] Project Gutenberg houses a large selection of Western texts (i.e., "cowboy" genre), yet these two collections are the only ones I found that specifically contained cowboy *poetry* composed and sung by the cowboys themselves rather than being fictionalized accounts of life on the range. The fact that these ballads are the lyrics of popular cowboy songs means that they are well-worn and often-repeated interpretations and expressions of western frontier life. Lomax describes his collection technique as "haphazard," jotting down the oral texts on scraps of paper and backs of envelopes as he crisscrossed the American West. As he explained, "I put together what seemed to me to be the best of the songs created and sung by the cowboys as they went about their work."[15]

Describing the communal lives of cowboys, horse-wranglers, and cooks working together on the range, Lomax overserved that "songs sprang up naturally" as a means of entertainment, "the joint product of a number of them, telling perhaps the story of some stampede they had all fought to turn, some crime in which they

---

13   Opland, *Xhosa Oral Poetry.*

14   John A. Lomax, ed., *Songs of the Cattle Trail and Cow Camp* (New York: MacMillan, 1919), and John A. Lomax, ed., *Cowboy Songs and Other Frontier Ballads* (New York: MacMillan, 1929).

15   Lomax, *Songs of the Cattle Trail.*

had all shared equally, some comrade's death which they had all witnessed."[16] On the trail, cattle songs, not unlike praise poems, served practical purposes, stirring cattle that lagged behind, and, during long night-watches, calming restless animals to sleep. Of these lullabies, Lomax remarked, "some of the best of the so called 'dogie songs' seem to have been created for the purpose of preventing cattle stampedes" that were so dangerous to the life and limb of cowboys and of their horses and herds. These songs, spoken "familiarly to his herd in the stillness of the night," came "straight from the heart of the cowboy."[17] To examine how often cattle figure in the poems and how the relationship between cows and cowboys are depicted in them, I began by conducting a series of searches of both books (including both poems and scholarly introductions) for instances of key terms. In *Cowboy Songs and Other Frontier Ballads,* a search for the word "cow" produced 396 hits, but when I removed cowboy, cow-ranch, cow-punch, and other instances where the was used to describe cattle handlers, I found only seven references to the animals themselves. The words "bull" and "calf" each appear twice. "Heifer" appears four times. "Dogie," an abandoned calf, and "steer," a castrated bull, are more common referents with twenty-seven and twenty-eight mentions respectively. The plural "cattle" appears fifty-six times and "herd," twenty-nine. In *Songs of the Cattle Trail and Cow Camp,* "cow" as a stand-alone word produced twenty matches, "steer" produced eighteen, "bull" five, "calf" two, "heifer" four, and "cattle" forty-seven. Across both books, cattle in their various forms were mentioned 188 times. Importantly, across both books, the primary subject of the songs is not cattle but rather the men who tended them. "Cowboy" and "cowpuncher" appear a total of 300 times across the two collections, "man" an additional ninety times, "cowman" thirteen. The word "woman" also appears thirteen time. Like the isiXhosa poems, these cowboy poems are highly gendered, reflecting women's exclusion from these particular relationships with cattle.

From these searches, I moved on to closer readings to investigate how the poems respond to this situation of intimacy with cattle, cows, and steers and how the animals are depicted. This first example, taken from a "dogie song" entitled "The Cowboy's Dream" draws direct comparison between men and beast, likening cowboys to their wards with the lines

> They say there will be a great round-up,
> And cowboys, like dogies, will stand,
> To be marked by the Riders of Judgment
> Who are posted and know every brand.
>
> ....
>
> For they, like the cows that are locoed,
> Stampede at the sight of a hand,
> Are dragged with a rope to the round-up,
> Or get marked with some crooked man's brand.[18]

Even the chorus, "Roll on, roll on; / roll on little dogies, roll on, roll on," while ostensibly addressed to the calves, in the context of the poem seems a form of gentle

---

16   Lomax, *Cowboy Songs.*
17   Ibid.
18   Ibid.

encouragement and empathy from one cowboy to another. Similarly, "A Cowboy's Worrying Love," attributed to James Barton Adams, uses the language of cattle handling to describe romantic love:

> I'm a-goin' to brace her by an' by to see if there's any hope,
> To see if she's liable to shy when I'm ready to pitch the rope;
> To see if she's goin' to make a stand, or fly like a skeered up dove
> When I make a pass with the brandin' iron that's hot in the fire o' love.
> I'll open the little home corral an' give her the level hunch
> To make a run for the open gate when I cut her out o' the bunch.[19]

In other examples, the rowdy, unruly animals are referred to in the tone of loving, long-suffering exasperation that parents might use when describing their children. For instance, the cowboys in "John Garner's Trail Herd" suffered the "merry hell" of being wakened every night by the "circus" of stampeding cattle.

> All things went on well till we reached the open ground,
> And then them cattle turned and they gave us merry hell.
> They stampeded every night that came and did it without fail,—
> Oh, you know we had a circus as we all went up the trail.[20]

Other examples are more concerned with cattle as a form of wealth. This selection below from "The Cowman's Prayer" is an innocently comical supplication for prosperity, gentle weather, and reproductive health. The poem, whose title plays on *The Book of Common Prayer*, opens tongue-in-cheek in the language of a pious supplicant:

> Now, O Lord, please lend me thine ear,
> The prayer of a cattleman to hear,
> No doubt the prayers may seem strange,
> But I want you to bless our cattle range.
> Bless the round-ups year by year,
> and don't forget the growing steer;
> Water the lands with brooks and rills
> For my cattle that roam on a thousand hills.

Yet by the third stanza, the comedic undertone has shifted from subtle to overtly wry:

> Prairie fires, won't you please stop?
> Let thunder roll and water drop.
> It frightens me to see the smoke;
> Unless it's stopped, I'll go dead broke.

Of course, with these lines we also learn the true motive for the prayer, which is the cowman's prosperity. This theme continues in the final two stanzas:

19 Lomax, *Songs of the Cattle Trail.*
20 Lomax, *Cowboy Songs.*

> As you, O Lord, my herd behold,
> It represents a sack of gold;
> I think at least five cents a pound
> Will be the price of beef the year around.
> One thing more and then I'm through,—
> Instead of one calf, give my cows two.
> I may pray different from other men
> But I've had my say, and now, Amen.[21]

Like pastoralists elsewhere, this cattleman's wealth lies in his herd. Unlike many pastoralists, however, the extent of his wealth is tightly bound to fluctuating commodity values. His lifestyle as a cattleman is one that he prizes but its continuance is largely a matter of economic viability — determined by both God and the market's continued provision of favorable circumstances.

However, in other instances in the book, cattle do not appear as prized possessions at all. Instead, they are subject to abuse and domination in which they are pulled by their sensitive tails and roped by their horns, an action that typically precedes the animal being immobilized or wrestled to the ground. Singular animals are occasionally mentioned but by and large cattle remain generic rather than being recognized as distinctive individuals. The ballad "Whose Old Cow?" is one notable instance of a poem that speaks at length about a cow as a particular individual, rather than a plural mass. Much of this poem is written in the dialect of Ol' Add, the Black man tasked with branding the cattle. The patois is difficult to make sense of for unfamiliar audiences, but essentially the poem tells of a cow so thoroughly scarred by a multitude of different branding irons, her ears so tattered by identifying cuts that it is impossible to know whose property she is. She is an old and ugly cow, deformed by human assertions of ownership over many years. In the closing lines, Add decides to claim the cow for his employer, adding a further brand and stating that such an addition won't do the animal any harm.

> Well, after each outfit had worked on the band
> There was only three head of them left;
> When [Ol']* Add from LFD outfit rode in,—
> A dictionary on earmarks and brands.
>
> He cut the two head out, told where they belonged;
> But when the last cow stood there alone
> Add's eyes bulged so he didn't know just what to say,
> 'Ceptin', "Boss, dere's something here monstrous wrong!
>
> "White folks smarter'n Add, and maybe I'se wrong;
> But here's six months' wages dat I'll give
> If anyone'll tell me when I reads dis mark
> To who dis longhorned cow belong!
>
> "Overslope in right ear an' de underbill,
> Lef' ear swaller fork an' de undercrop,

---

21 Ibid.

Hole punched in center, an' de jinglebob
Under half crop, an' de slash an' split.

"She's got O Block an' Lightnin' Rod,
Nine Forty-Six an' A Bar Eleven,
T Terrapin an' Ninety-Seven,
Rafter Cross an' de Double Prod.

"Half circle A an' Diamond D,
Four Cross L and Three P Z,
B W I bar, X V V,
Bar N cross an' A L C.

"So, if none o' you punchers claims dis cow,
Mr. Stock 'Sociation needn't git 'larmed;
For one more brand more or less won't do no harm,
So old [*] Add'l just brand her now."[22]

Overall, the crude and racist portrayal of the cattle hand combined with the violent treatment of the cow produce a poem that is revealing of a vicious side of cowboy life that the comedic ballad makes light of.

In the history of the industrialized west, the semi-nomadic, animal-oriented lifestyle of cowboys is anomalous to almost any other. I had hoped that it might hold wisdom that could help shift our present dysfunctional relationship with cattle, or at least suggest where we might have gone wrong. Given the long stretches of time that cowboys spent outside, away from human communities and in close contact with cattle and landscape, I was optimistic about what they might have to say about these relationships. The results are mixed. Although environmental and animal entities are certainly important in these ballads, the collections suggest that the human-cattle relationships among cowboys of the North American West are significantly unlike those experienced in pastoralist cultures. This should come as no surprise, of course, particularly considering the cowboy's economic role: poorly-paid servants tasked with transporting someone else's goods to market, they moved "on the skirmish line of civilization," fighting back Indigenous peoples as they carried out "a work that was necessary in winning the West."[23] In their poems, cattle are rarely referred to as particular, singular animals with sensibilities and personalities and are instead much more likely to be described as an undifferentiated mass whose chief tendency is to stampede.

The cowboy's economic relationship with cattle aligns with his political place in North American history: ruggedly independent men at the frontier of an expanding imperial power, they were a colonizing force implicated in the dispossession of Indigenous peoples and the privatization and industrialization of the landscape. As John Lomax affirms, "to the cowboy, more than to the goldseekers, more than to Uncle Sam's soldiers, is due the conquest of the west [...]. The cowboy has fought back the Indians ever since ranching became a business and as long

---

22 Lomax, *Cowboy Songs*. The asterisk indicates a deleted racial slur.
23 Ibid.

as Indians remained to be fought."[24] In the words of one poet, the cowboy was "the plowman's pioneer."[25] The arrival of cowboys and cattle culture to the North American West brought a wave of extermination as millions of bison were slaughtered through the nineteenth century. The preexisting relationships between humans and wild buffalo that had defined the landscape of the North American plains were deliberately destroyed and replaced by new human-cattle relationships in which the animals were a subservient mass owned, controlled, and herded by humans. The genre of the western, including novels, poems, and songs, contributed to this transformation, lending strength to a particular vision of history and justifying brutalities against Indigenous peoples and their exclusion from contemporary society. In this final example, the cowboy's role as an agent of colonialism is clear:

> While taking refreshment we heard a low yell,
> The whoop of Sioux Indians coming up from the dell;
> We sprang to our rifles with a flash in each eye,
> "Boys," says our brave leader, "we'll fight till we die."
>
> They made a bold dash and came near to our train
> And the arrows fell around us like hail and like rain,
> But with our long rifles we fed them cold lead
> Till many a brave warrior around us lay dead.[26]

In this poem, Indigenous peoples resisting the incursion of masses of cattle and their violent, armed herders onto their territory are described as being as dangerous and senseless as a mass of stampeding cattle — and are dispatched with as little sentiment.

Through the nineteenth century, the onslaught of colonialism almost entirely dispossessed the continent's First Peoples. Ironically, cowboys too were soon to find themselves swept off the landscape. By the turn of the twentieth century, the open ranges throughout much of the North American West had been converted to private ranches fenced with barbed wire. New private property regimes closed the commons that had briefly supported a culture that has become a defining North American mythology, and the expanding railway system created new ways of moving beasts to market that were more economical than cattle droving.[27] The new society of private farms and ranches would transform with increasing speed into today's vertically integrated system of commercial agriculture dominated by a handful of multinational corporations. Arguably, this transition was eased by ways of thinking and speaking about cattle as masses of mindless animals to be dominated by physical prowess rather than as intelligent companions with much to offer and teach.

24 Ibid.

25 Lomax, *Songs of the Cattle Trail.*

26 Lomax, *Cowboy Songs.*

27 Anne Kerr and Edmund Wright, eds., *A Dictionary of World History,* 3rd edn. (Oxford: Oxford University Press, 2015), s.v. "Cowboy," https://www.oxfordreference.com/view/10.1093/acref/9780199685691.001.0001/acref-9780199685691-e-952.

Re-placing the Cow

While I was living in the village of Ngxoyana, my friend and host told me that in amaXhosa culture, to draw comparisons between a woman and a cow is to say that she is beautiful, that she moves gorgeously with leisurely dignity and grace. In Western culture, any such comparison is the height of insult. Cattle, for westerners, are symbols of docility, of stupidity, of a vacuous herd instinct. The Oxford English Dictionary offers two definitions of bovine: the first, "belonging to, or characteristic of, the ox tribe," the second, "inert, sluggish; dull, stupid." Such drastically different cultural ideas of this animal are indicative of its treatment in very different societies. The differences also illustrate how the debasement or ridicule of a creature can assist in its transformation from loved and respected companion to unseen commodity. Debasement predisposes us towards mistreatment and eventually wholesale exploitation.

This is not to romanticize or essentialize the complex realities of other traditions. In amaXhosa tradition, bulls are also metaphors of male virility and, traditionally, were very literally the route to reproduction via lobola or bride price.[28] Gendered codes of conduct governing who can touch, approach, or handle cattle extend the differential freedoms and unfreedoms experienced by men and women in traditional society. Furthermore, it can be argued that in the South African context, cattle played a role in the displacement of Indigenous peoples as successive waves of pastoralists from northern parts of the continent arrived to inhabit the terrain of earlier groups of hunter-gatherer peoples. Finally, even in these pastoralist cultures with their high regard for these animals, cattle are not free entities but are items of property that confer personal status and wealth and that may find their lives cut short at any time by human need or whim.[29]

Rather than revealing enthrallment with cattle as beautiful and particular companions imbued with symbolic significance, the cowboy ballads in Lomax's collections are a very different kind of poem. They are not the spontaneous utterances of a single imbongi moved by the particularities of place and circumstance; rather they are collective works, communally shaped and embellished, that have passed from hand to hand over decades on the dusty trail. They describe a lifestyle of physical proximity to cattle, but one in which cattle are economic entities in a burgeoning capitalist society unfettered by lack of space or resources. The cattle — moving together in herds that may have been thousands strong — are too numerous to be particular and are most often referred to in the collective: cattle, herd, longhorns, little dogies. The only ballad that treated a cow as an individual entity was racist and derisory. There is a clear sense of comradery in these poems, of cattle and lonely cowboys weathering the dangers of the trail together as they make their way jointly toward a distant destination, and the lexicon of the collec-

---

28 J.B. Peires, *The House of Phalo: A History of the Xhosa People in the Days of Their Independence* (Berkeley: University of California Press, 1982).

29 The Eastern Cape's disastrous nineteenth-century cattle-killing movement illustrates that even in relationships of care cattle are subject to the whims of humans and that under duress, pastoralists might massacre their animals by the hundreds of thousands, with disastrous results for both cattle and their people. See J.B. Peires, *The Dead Will Arise: Nongqawuse and the Great Xhosa Cattle-Killing Movement of 1856–7* (Johannesburg: Ravan Press, 1989).

tions doesn't include the words inert, sluggish, dull, or stupid. However, neither are the animals portrayed as beautiful, intelligent, or noble. Rather, in their penchant for stampeding they might more aptly be described as dangerous slaves to a herd mentality.

The poems in Lomax's collections are cultural works from an era of cultural and economic transformation, whose lasting violences are evident in the landscape of the North American West. Cattle droving in North America is a consubstantial aspect of colonial genocide and the replacement of vibrant, diverse prairie ecosystems with monoculture plantations and densely packed animal-rearing and slaughtering facilities. In the settler colonial nations of Canada and the United States, cattle droving was a colonial import that became intimately bound up in a frontier mythos of freedom, of strength and virility, of rugged independence and self-sufficient masculinity on the open range. Songs that glorified this lifestyle played their own part in the conquest, colonization, and, ultimately, industrial transformation, of western North American landscapes and animals. The mythology of the cowboy, wild and free, was a chapter in the story of the creation of a commodity fetish and the conquest, colonization, and, ultimately, industrial transformation of western North America.

At the same time, while North American cowboys were surely part of the commoditization of cattle that has led to their current inhumane treatment in western society, it would be wrong to suggest that this process began with colonization. The various peoples of the British Isles and Ireland, the origins of many North American settlers, were pastoralist from early Neolithic times, and droving emerged gradually from seasonal needs to move their herds and flocks.[30] As an economic activity, the occupation of cattle droving grew in economic importance with the rise of industrialization from the seventeenth century onward, yet it is far older than capitalism. Large cattle markets had developed in England by the early medieval era and before that, evidence suggests that drovers brought cattle on the hoof to feed the several thousand Roman soldiers garrisoned in northern Britain.[31] And before Roman times? The Greeks lived with cattle, as did Egyptians. Strong relationships with cattle have persisted throughout the Indian subcontinent for millennia, and they remain highly respected members of human societies. In east and west, in Africa, Europe, and Asia human relationships with cattle are older than history itself. The relationship itself is unstable; with cattle so often a representation of wealth, with more of them too easily equating to a higher human social status, the relationship shimmers at the boundary between companion and currency, mutual dependence and enslavement. Human freedom and survival have often relied upon cattle, but as both species — and the constrained world order of late capitalism — have proliferated, it's been all too easy to cast that memory aside. What remains to be recovered and relearned from the North American cowboy may be the simple fact that while not everyone thrives in proximity with cattle, many people do.

---

30   William Thompson, "Cattle Droving between Scotland and England," *Journal of the British Archaeological Association* 37, no. 2 (2017): 172–83.

31   Sue Stallibrass, "The Way to a Roman Soldier's Heart: A Post-Medieval Model for Cattle Droving to the Hadrian's Wall Area," *Theoretical Roman Archaeology Journal* (2008), https://traj.openlibhums.org/article/id/3888/.

Indeed, human thriving in proximity with cattle is emerging as a new wellness trend. *Koe knuffelen,* literally "cow hugging," is a therapeutic practice with Dutch origins. Now well over a decade old in the Netherlands, the practice has since spread to Switzerland and the United States, where eager cow huggers may drive hours to visit a farm. As the BBC reports,

> The cow's warmer body temperature, slower heartbeat and mammoth size can make hugging them an incredibly soothing experience, and giving the animal a backrub, reclining against them or even getting licked is all part of the therapeutic encounter. Cow cuddling is believed to promote positivity and reduce stress by boosting oxytocin in humans, the hormone released in social bonding. The calming effects of curling up with a pet or emotional support animal, it seems, are accentuated when cuddling with larger mammals.[32]

As the Dutch farmer interviewed in the accompanying BBC news reel explains, not every cow is suited to cow-hugging. Those that are well-suited to the endeavor exhibit traits of relaxed sociability from a young age, while others might be demonstrably less sociable. For instance, as the farmer explains, "[w]e have one jealous cow. When she's not being hugged she's just jealous."[33] Although cowboys, with thousands of transient cattle in their care, may have sung less about the particular characters among them, the individual personality of each animal remains clear to their more sedentary farming counterparts. As it turns out, the benefits of happy, cow-hugging sessions flow both ways. Folk wisdom points to the value of gentle tactile contact in successful dairy farming, and so does veterinary science. Recent studies confirm that animal handling practices that mimic social licking lower a cow's heart rate and lead to better human interactions.[34]

As animal therapy is increasingly valued as a means of relieving social anxieties, it's heartening to see cattle join the ranks of more familiar dogs, cats, and horses. It suggests possibilities when it comes to recreating relationships with species that have fallen from grace, that exist on the far margins of social consciousness even as we interact with them daily. In reforming such relationships, we transform ourselves from a mass of stampeding consumers into humans defined by webs of kinship and care. Cattle, like dogs and horses, are animals with whom we've developed many contemporary societies and cultures, however problematic the results. Our task, in my view, is not to further remove cattle from landscapes and societies in the name of environmental protection but rather to resolve the underlying problem in our present scenario, which is the severing of a sacred relationship with a companion species that has historically been, and remains, a major source of human wellbeing. Rather than expelling the animals we rely upon further and further to the margins of industrial societies through blanket calls for abstinence

---

32 BBC Reel, "Is Cow Hugging the World's New Wellness Trend?" *BBC,* October 9, 2020, http://www.bbc.com/travel/story/20201008-is-cow-hugging-the-worlds-new-wellness-trend/.

33 Ibid.

34 Claudia Schmied et al., "Stroking of Different Body Regions by a Human: Effects on Behaviour and Heart Rate of Dairy Cows," *Applied Animal Behaviour Science* 109, no. 1 (2008): 25–38.

in the form of vegetarianism and veganism (as important as such actions are), perhaps social behaviors might change more readily were we to embrace the logic of the cow-huggers and look for ways to draw these animals further in. Were we to invite sheep and cattle to graze our lawns, boulevards and city parks, perhaps they would become more to us than merely the absent referents of their body parts. If the sights and smells of urban farms and their multispecies collectives were on our urban doorsteps, perhaps we would develop a deeper sense of what it means to be cattle and what it means to live in right relationship with the creatures we depend upon. While proximity in and of itself is no guarantee of more ethical or respectful relationships between humans and animals, it guarantees a mutual *regard,* both literal and figurative, that cannot exist in absentia. The forming of kinship bonds through relations of awareness and care becomes more possible, if not always actual, through proximate dwelling. Such dwelling might be fodder for our poets. As we learn, unlearn, and relearn who we are in the world, the work of the imagination remains as central to the process as ever.

References

BBC Reel. "Is Cow Hugging the World's New Wellness Trend?" *BBC*, October 9, 2020. http://www.bbc.com/travel/story/20201008-is-cow-hugging-the-worlds-new-wellness-trend

Clare, John. "The Moors." In *Selected Poems*, edited by Jonathan Bate, 89–91. New York: Faber and Faber, 2003.

Emel, Jody, and Harvey Neo. *Political Ecologies of Meat*. London: Routledge, 2015.

Fitzgerald, Amy J., Linda Kalof, and Thomas Dietz. "Slaughterhouses and Increased Crime Rates." *Organization & Environment* 22, no. 2 (2009): 158–84. DOI: 10.1177/1086026609338164.

Gaard, Greta. "Vegetarian Ecofeminism: A Review Essay." *Frontiers: A Journal of Women Studies* 23, no. 3 (2002): 117–46. https://www.jstor.org/stable/3347337.

Kerr, Anne, and Edmund Wright, eds. *A Dictionary of World History*, 3rd edn. Oxford: Oxford University Press, 2015.

Lomax, John A., ed. *Cowboy Songs and Other Frontier Ballads*. New York: MacMillan, 1929.

———, ed. *Songs of the Cattle Trail and Cow Camp*. New York: MacMillan, 1919.

Opland, Jeff. *The Dassie and the Hunter: A South African Meeting*. Scottsville: University of KwaZulu-Natal Press, 2005.

Peires, J.B. *The Dead Will Arise: Nongqawuse and the Great Xhosa Cattle-Killing Movement of 1856–7*. Johannesburg: Ravan Press, 1989.

———. *The House of Phalo: A History of the Xhosa People in the Days of Their Independence*. Berkeley: University of California Press, 1982.

Pilgrim, Karyn. "'Happy Cows,' 'Happy Beef': A Critique of the Rationales for Ethical Meat." *Environmental Humanities* 3, no. 1 (2013): 111–27. DOI: 10.1215/22011919-3611257.

Poland, Marguerite, W.D. Hammond-Tooke, and Leigh Voigt. *The Abundant Herds: A Celebration of the Cattle of the Zulu People*. Vlaeberg: Fernwood, 2003.

Schmied, Claudia, Susanne Waiblinger, Theresa Scharl, Friedrich Leisch, and Xavier Boivin. "Stroking of Different Body Regions by a Human: Effects on Behaviour and Heart Rate of Dairy Cows." *Applied Animal Behaviour Science* 109, no. 1 (2008): 25–38. DOI: 10.1016/j.applanim.2007.01.013/.

Stallibrass, Sue. "The Way to a Roman Soldier's Heart: A Post-Medieval Model for Cattle Droving to the Hadrian's Wall Area." *Theoretical Roman Archaeology Journal* (2008). https://traj.openlibhums.org/article/id/3888/. DOI: 10.16995/TRAC2008_101_112.

Thompson, William. "Cattle Droving between Scotland and England." *Journal of the British Archaeological Association* 37, no. 2 (2017): 172–83. DOI: 10.1080/00681288.1932.11894305.

Torres, Chris. "Look for Large Growth in Meat Production, Exports in 2020." *Corn and Soybean Digest*, 2020.

United States Department of Agriculture, "Livestock Slaughter: 2019 Summary." *USDA, National Agriculture Statistics Service*, 2020.

Yali-Manisi, D.L.P. *Imbongi entsha: Iimbali Zamanyange: Historical Poems*. Translated by Jeff Opland and Pamela Maseko. Pietermaritzburg: University of KwaZulu-Natal Press, 2015.

CHAPTER 5

The Forest of Life: The Representation of the "Tree of Life" Metaphor across Media

Péter Kristóf Makai

If there is one central message to Charles Darwin's theory of evolution, it is that all life on earth is fundamentally connected: every species is kin to every other species that has ever lived on earth. No visual metaphor has captured this fact so succinctly as the "tree of life." Although the tree of life is a metaphor that has been part and parcel of religious symbolism in both pagan and Abrahamic religions,[1] it has also had a long and illustrious career in the field of biology since at least the late-eighteenth century.[2] Many an august figure, including Carl von Linné, Georges-Louis Leclerc, Comte de Buffon, and Augustin Augier, have already drawn "botanical trees," but it wasn't until Jean-Baptiste de Lamarck, followed by Edward Hitchcock, Robert Chambers, and later Teilhard de Chardin, among others, to draw evolutionary trees. Whether evolutionary or not, naturalists have used the metaphor to point toward the relationship between species by way of analogy with human genealogy.[3] Appearing in Chapter 4 of On the *Origin of Species* is a neat branching diagram, an expanded version of his famous "I think…" illustration from the transmutation notebooks drawn in July 1837, which is Darwin's version of the tree of life that shows how from a single species many can arise due to a small number of variations.[4] Since then, virtually all media have found ways of communicating the interconnectedness of all life using the tree of life as a visual and conceptual shorthand.

---

1   I thank one anonymous reviewer for reminding me of the history of the tree of life as a mythological and religious symbol. However, since this paper deals with the metaphor as it is used in natural philosophical and biological theories, I encourage the reader to pick up Douglas Estes's (2020) edited collection that explores the rich symbolism of this metaphor. Indeed, an obvious extension of the article would be to tie together both mythological, religious, and biological representations, since the newest media I work with, computer games, call the genre of games in which player-controlled evolution appears "god games." Unpacking that metaphor alone is worthy of a separate study.

2   Theodore W. Pietsch, *Trees of Life: A Visual History of Evolution* (Baltimore: Johns Hopkins University Press, 2012).

3   For a representative sample list, see Appendix 1 in Marie Fisler et al., "The Treeness of the Tree of Historical Trees of Life," *PLoS One* 15, no. 1 (2021): e0226567.

4   Charles Darwin, *On the Origin of Species by Means of Natural Selection: Or, The Preservation of Favoured Races in the Struggle for Life* (London: J. Murray, 1859).

The purpose of this study is to examine some contemporary attempts to bring the tree of life metaphor alive in diverse media. By investigating how they translate this biological insight into verbal, visual, or interactive reality for people to perceive, we gain a better understanding of how evolution as an abstract scientific concept tests the limits of medial expression, which broadens the affordances and constraints of the media in question. After a brief summary of the central tenets of evolution, I demonstrate with examples from fiction and nonfiction, the TV documentary and the computer game medium how the tree of life metaphor has been utilized to provide a narrative drive for an all-encompassing multispecies storytelling.

By definition, the story of evolution is a story of multiple species. In fact, it is the story of all species. Coinciding in the West with the Biblical worldview, the historical definition of species was of an unchanging category of living beings: a lion and all its forebears and descendants were lions, since the creator has created these beings in their present, fixed form. Therefore, it came as a puzzle to naturalists when they first started beginning to see animals that were closely related but did not form interbreeding groups. Including that famous trip to the Galápagos Islands, Charles Darwin's voyage aboard the *Beagle*, coupled with his keen observation of animal husbandry, enabled him to first come up with a coherent account of how animals change shape over time around the same time Alfred Russell Wallace came to a similar conclusion. The world-shaking ramifications of that discovery still rankle many today, both because the new story did not need a divine author and because it has connected all species into one big family tree of relations, which makes humankind just another animal who shares a common primate ancestor with today's apes.

Briefly stated, the tree of life metaphor envisions the relationships between species as a branching trunk spanning millions and millions of years of evolutionary history. Because it tracks the birth of species rather than individuals, it is called a "phylogenetic tree," and because it groups species according to their clades, it is also a kind of a cladogram. However, a phylogenetic tree is more detailed and shows temporal relationships between different clades, whereas a cladogram only represents group affiliation. On a phylogenetic tree, distances between species represent both temporal and genetic distance. Unlike that other iconic representation of evolutionary history, the illustration "The Road to Homo Sapiens," recognized as the "monkey-to-man" image, the phylogenetic tree of life represents then-current scientific knowledge about species kinship, going even further than Donna Haraway's use of the term "cross-species kinship" by collecting all known species in one family tree.[5]

Representations of the tree of life are found in every media. In this article, I provide examples from only a few of them, including nonfiction works, such as the television documentary *Charles Darwin and the Tree of Life*, the website *OneZoom*, Richard Dawkins's *The Ancestor's Tale*, and fictional works, like Stephen Baxter's *Evolution* and the computer game *Birthdays: The Beginning*.[6] The purpose of this

<hr>

5   Donna Haraway, *Primate Visions: Gender, Race, and Nature in the World of Modern Science* (New York: Routledge, 2015).

6   Sacha Mirzoeff, *Charles Darwin and the Tree of Life*, aired 1 February 2009, BBC One; Richard Dawkins and Yan Wong, *The Ancestor's Tale: A Pilgrimage to the Dawn of Life* (London: Weidenfeld & Nicholson, 2016); Stephen Baxter, Evolu-

selection was to provide a spread of available media for analysis and to focus on examples from the twenty-first century for whose authors up-to-date scientific results were available. With the exception of Baxter's novel, all were published after the sesquicentennial anniversary of the publication *of On the Origin of Species,* during which time the popular imagination has turned toward Darwinian ideas again.[7] I have also sought high-profile examples of their respective media, reaching wide audiences. But first and foremost, all media products extensively featured the tree of life as an overarching master narrative of making sense of evolution.

As scholarly observers, we ought to note that not all representations of the tree of life surveyed here are created equal. Some are rigorously accurate, others have whimsical additions and some are exhaustive, while others are simplified to highlight key arguments. Nonetheless, they all manage to convey the grandeur of nature, the importance of biodiversity, and the fundamental interconnectedness of all life on earth. Unravelling how they do so and what their specific media contribute to that meaning, is the modest goal of this paper.

No Country for Old Stories?: The Trouble with Evolution Narratives

The theory of biological evolution by natural selection rests on three pillars: first, the variation between members of an interbreeding group of organisms, second, the heritability of variable traits, and third, the differential reproduction of those traits in the population. Note that Darwin did not need to know the precise mechanisms of inheritance, now known as the science of genetics — although a Czech monk in Brno, Gregor Mendel, has already been conducting experiments of inheritance at the time; nor did he realize the actual timescales involved in the process, even if then-recent advances in geology had already hinted at the vast timescales required, for example in Charles Lyell's or William Thompson, Lord Kelvin's work. Known today in geology and evolutionary biology as "deep time," coined as an analogy with "deep space, is a phrase used to convey a sense of sublimity on the millions and millions of years necessary for evolutionary change to occur.[8] For Darwin, deep time was incommensurable with shallow time, and "he hinted that this incommensurability perhaps resulted from human perceptual and cognitive weaknesses: the phenomenon of the gradual shading of varieties into separate species ought to lead us to be surprised that we do not find more examples of this 'occasional blending by intermedial forms'; he attributed our actual lack of surprise at this fact to 'our restricted notions of the lapse of time.'"[9] Hence, deep time always carries a connotation of challenging the limits of our representational capacities.

tion (New York: Del Rey/Ballantine Books, 2003); Yasuhiro Wada, Toybox Inc., and Arc System Works, *Birthdays: The Beginning* (NIS America, 2017).

7   Indeed, some of Baxter's representational choices, notably, with regard to mental time travel, can be questioned now with access to new scientific data.

8   Henry Gee, *In Search of Deep Time: Beyond the Fossil Record to a New History of Life* (Ithaca: Cornell University Press, 2001).

9   Note that Darwin's use of the word "intermedial" is best rendered today as "intermediary," and not to be confused with its current usage in media and inter-art studies, which describes the relationships between different media. Peter Dear, "Darwin and Deep Time: Temporal Scales and the Naturalist's Imagination," *History of Science* 54, no. 1 (March 2016): 3–18.

In fact, there is a major challenge to the then-contemporary imagination in the very title of Darwin's *On the Origin of Species,* namely, that there isn't just one origin of species as such. Species come about as a result of small modifications, and all species share a number of common ancestors from which they have descended. The term "speciation" refers to the process by which new species arise. This can come about in a number of ways; for example, by the separation of an interbreeding population onto two different, spatially isolated areas (i.e., "allopatric speciation"), or by the multiplication of their chromosome pairs resulting in a state (i.e., "polyploidy") that enables species to separate even when they are living in the same area (i.e., "sympatric speciation"). Common to all mechanisms of speciation is the requirement that there be some form of reproductive isolation, so that the two gene pools can deviate further from each other. Since Darwin's time, biologists have posited several definitions of what a species is, sometimes in contrasting if not mutually exclusive definitions. In the philosophy of biology, this is called the species problem: according to different definitions, we can identify a dozen species concepts. Some authors even question the reality of species altogether.[10]

It appears that insofar as we treat groups of animals as belonging to a species, we are creating evidence-based stories of their shared history and relationships in deep time. That storytelling is, crucially, not an anthropocentric venture because they focus on animals other than humans. In David Herman's working definition that best suits conventional forms of storytelling, a narrative is "a mode of representation that [...] focuses on a structured time-course of particularized events. [... T]he events represented [...] introduce some sort of disruption or disequilibrium into a storyworld [...]. The representation also conveys what it is like to live through this storyworld-in-flux, highlighting the pressure of events on real or imagined consciousnesses undergoing the disruptive experience at issue."[11] That disruption or disequilibrium can be something as mundane as not having anything to eat or as existential as not having any reason to live. Implicit in the phrase "what it is like to live through" is the notion that stories have protagonists, mostly human or sufficiently human-like agents with feelings and thoughts, intentions, and desires. In other words, protagonists have biological and mental lives, they interpret themselves and the world surrounding them, and act upon the world. Of particular interest to us is that characters of a story are "role-bearing or position-occupying individuals sometimes acting at cross-purposes with their own interests and goals or those of other such individuals."[12] In simpler terms, narrative

---

10 Marc Ereshefsky, "Revisiting the Conceptual Basis of Species" (2012); Jerry A. Coyne and H. Allen Orr, *Speciation* (Sunderland: Sinauer Associates, 2004), 9–54; *Stanford Encyclopedia of Philosophy,* s.v. "Species," https://plato.stanford.edu/entries/species/; Douglas J. Futuyma, *Evolutionary Biology,* 3rd edn. (Sunderland: Sinauer Associates, 1998); Massimo Pigliucci, "Species as Family Resemblance Concepts: The (Dis-)Solution of the Species Problem?" *BioEssays* 25, no. 6 (2003): 596–602; Matthew H. Slater, *Are Species Real? An Essay on the Metaphysics of Species* (Basingstoke: Palgrave Macmillan, 2013); Phillip Sloan, "Originating Species: Darwin on the Species Problem, in *The Cambridge Companion to the "Origin of Species,"* eds. Michael Ruse and Robert J. Richards (Cambridge: Cambridge University Press, 2009), 67–86.

11 David Herman, *Basic Elements of Narrative* (Chichester: Wiley-Blackwell, 2009), 9.

12 Ibid., 96–97.

thrives on conflict, whether internal or external. Conflicts are resolved by capable protagonists, who eliminate perceived threats to their individual and communal selves. Following Boyd, I insist that stories transmit behavioral and attitudinal information about how such personal and social challenges can be overcome by the protagonists into whose life-world the audience is admitted, gaining privileged mental access to their thoughts and feelings so that they may identify with them.[13]

Measured against conventional human yardsticks of narrative epitomized by Herman's prototypical definition, the tale of evolution might look pale in comparison. For starters, there is no clearly defined protagonist of evolution: every living being is on an equal footing, struggling to survive. While some fail and others succeed, neither is more important or meaningful than any other. It has terrible pacing, too. While it is temporally ordered, the hypothesized plot of the evolution of life is highly speculative when it comes to the exact time course of events. Not to mention the fact that it is enormous in spatiotemporal scope, with no well-defined narrative thread. It branches off and creates vast canopies of parallel stories.

The difficulties of telling the story of evolution have not eluded narratologists. As H. Porter Abbott so evocatively describes it, "species ooze. They ooze, moreover, in no particular direction. In fact, they ooze in many directions at once," and speciation "is a silent, hidden event that takes place unheralded within the still ongoing ooze of species."[14] What decides the fate of species is not the victory of one animal or plant over another; rather, it is innumerable victories or deaths. What's worse, for living fossils, evolution is not the story of change but of dogged conservativism. For animals like the platypus or the horseshoe crab, and plants like the ginkgo, the song has remained the same for millions of years.

The acceptance of evolution is much hindered by "the immense difficulty of narrativizing natural selection," and that it is the reason why evolution "has been subjected to so many narrative re-workings that *invariably distort* to the degree that they seek a clear narrative rendering."[15] In his diagnosis, this is a manifestation of a more deeply rooted problem, namely, that "neither *natural selection* nor *species,* as they were conceptualized by Darwin, are entities with agency. Worse, they do not seem to be narrative entities at all."[16] Furthermore, the story told about species effectively eliminates the original entity it is meant to explain. By showing that species transmute into each other, the earlier conception of a fixed species is obliterated, and what we call species in the post-Darwinian world are radically temporary entities. In the evolutionary stories I study, authors try to circumvent such theoretical problems of narration by picking individual members as a token of a species, by showcasing adaptive problems typical of that particular species, and by using behaviorist and mental narration.[17] This study contrasts media with a greater emphasis on narrativization and those with less narrative to bring their differing strategies of representation into clearer focus.

<hr>

13   Ibid., 188–99.

14   H. Porter Abbott, "Unnarratable Knowledge: The Difficulty of Understanding Evolution by Natural Selection," in *Narrative Theory and the Cognitive Sciences,* ed. David Herman (Stanford: CSLI Publications, 2003), 143–62.

15   Ibid., 143–44, emphasis added.

16   Ibid., 144.

17   Alan Palmer, *Fictional Minds* (Lincoln: University of Nebraska Press, 2004), 205–207.

In what follows, I want to focus my study on several different media types to convince readers that all mediations of the tree of life metaphor are working toward the same purpose: articulating the evolutionary sublime — that daunting yet majestic feeling when one encounters deep time — which "at once lifts individuals outside of time (because the vastness of its scale is beyond comprehension) while also placing them profoundly within time (as a minute blip within a vast and meandering trajectory)."[18]

An Infinite Tree: The Fractal View of Species in <u>OneZoom</u>

How do you envision every species in one giant drawing? That is the design challenge of visualizing a body of taxonomic knowledge that grows from year to year. As Theodore Pietsch's visual history of phylogenetic trees suggests, capturing biodiversity in just one image is a herculean task. Even its latest illustration, David Mark Hillis's universal tree of life only represents a square root of all species that were identified, "about 0.18 percent of the 1.9 million species that have been formally described and named."[19] How then, can we possibly transcend the limited space of the printed page, and see the tree of life in full bloom?

The answer, according to the OneZoom organization, is to take taxonomic data from physical space to cyberspace. As the creators of the *OneZoom* Tree of Life Explorer argue, "trees with millions of tips may require a page of paper larger than the observable universe to be printed: they break the paper paradigm, but on screen, users can still easily zoom in through the tree to any point of interest."[20] The *OneZoom* Tree of Life Explorer is a webpage that allows an expandable view of every species ever identified.

The visual representation follows the template of a continuously bifurcating and spiraling set of branches, where the bifurcation points distribute species according to how they have diverged from their ancestors, and the leaves left of the branch represent an extant species with a binomial name. Branches further down get thinner as fewer and fewer species sharing a common ancestor are piped through them until one branch segment can visualize the remaining handful of species. I encourage the reader to visit the website, as the tree itself is far more intuitive than its description would suggest. However, as competing representations pop up, some representational weaknesses emerge: "[t]he main limitation of OneZoom that makes it inappropriate for visualizing the complete ToL is that the fractal representation it uses prevents the presence of multifurcations in the trees (one node connected to more than two descendants), which is very common."[21]

The technology that allows endless zooming is the power of the computer to endlessly redraw smaller and smaller sections of the tree of life using the same

---

18   Cynthia Sugars, "The Evolutionary Sublime: Deep Time and the Historical Novel in Joan Thomas's 'Curiosity'," *Mosaic: An Interdisciplinary Critical Journal* 51, no. 3 (2018): 200.

19   Pietsch, *Trees of Life*, 313.

20   James Rosindell and L.J. Harmon, "OneZoom: A Fractal Explorer for the Tree of Life," *PLoS Biology* 10, no. 10 (2012): e1001406.

21   Damien M. de Vienne, "Lifemap: Exploring the Entire Tree of Life," *PLoS Biology* 14, no. 12 (2016): e2001624.

mathematical principles, known as fractals. In other words, it is a re-scalable set of images with different resolutions, similar to Google Earth's use of zooming and the short film *The Powers of Ten*'s earlier representations of scale and orders of magnitude.[22] In his study of different ways of writing universal or big history, Nasser Zakariya identifies such representations as expressions of the "scalar genre of synthesis," which constructs accounts "via a diagramming of space and/or time, often involving the expansion and contraction of spatial scales, or scales of both space and time."[23] Indeed, as visitors zoom from branch to branch, time and space are visually contracted in a very literal sense, since navigating in any directions involves shifts in represented time, and zooming out toward the big picture shrinks branches into leaves.

OneZoom and similar approaches to representing biodiversity demonstrate that digital technology breaks down the constraints of old media and allows for a finer grained and, one might even say, more exhaustive representation of relationships between organisms past and present. In terms of mediality, the website is unique among other representations discussed here because it is customizable to the user's needs and is fully searchable. Furthermore, it is not narrative at all but rather a pure visualization of a database. This symbolic form challenges the dominance of narrative constructions of knowledge, but due to its spatiotemporal arrangement of the relationships between species, it can be considered a form of protostory that needs a canny author to breathe it into life.[24] The next two case studies, David Attenborough's *Charles Darwin and the Tree of Life* and Richard Dawkins's *The Ancestor's Tale* are examples of two different attempts to narrativize a traversal of the tree of life.

Two Commentators Climbing the Same Tree: David Attenborough and Charles Darwin

Created for the 200th anniversary of his birth and the 150th anniversary of his most well-known work, the BBC's documentary film *Charles Darwin and the Tree of Life* is a breath-taking journey that follows the creation and elucidation of biology's single most important theory.[25] Taking the viewer on this tour is an august personage with a reassuring tone that generations of Britons grew up with and associate with quality television narration, Sir David Attenborough.

The documentary takes viewers through a canonical account of the status quo of naturalists' knowledge at the time, Charles Darwin's role in shaking up the consensus and the establishment of the theory, and gaps in his knowledge and

22   Eames Office, "Powers of Ten (1977)," *YouTube*, August 26, 2010, https://www.youtube.com/watch?v=ofKBhvDjuyo.
23   Besides the scalar genre of writing universal histories, Zakariya also identifies fabulaic, foundational, and historic forms of storytelling in big history. See Nasser Zakariya, *A Final Story: Science, Myth, and Beginnings* (Chicago: University of Chicago Press, 2018), 181–210; Ibid., 3.
24   Lev Manovich, "Database as Symbolic Form," *Convergence* 5, no. 2 (June 1999): 80–99; Yiannis Gabriel, *Storytelling in Organizations: Facts, Fictions, and Fantasies* (Oxford: Oxford University Press, 2000).
25   Mirzoeff, *Charles Darwin and the Tree of Life*, 2009.

later additions to his theory—edited and narrated with the benefit of hindsight. In many respects, the 2009 version of the story is standard documentary practice: a recognizable figurehead travelling across the land to find key points of interest with many scenes shot on location (e.g., Down House, the Natural History Museum, and so on) that showcase traces of historical events (e.g., specimens, fossils, and letters), interspersed with archival footage from Attenborough's other documentaries dealing with nature and Darwin. But, starting forty-eight minutes into this journey, we find a five-minute segment, a CGI animation designed by Shadow Industries, that charts the development of life as an evolutionary tree and highlights twenty-eight milestone species that help to explain the current view of evolutionary history.

Underscored by the rousing and curiosity-inspiring composition of Dan Jones, the segment begins with the appearance of hazy unicellular organisms fluorescing in blue as Sir David gently fades into the background, while his narration continues. Describing them as "seeds from which the tree of life developed," a straight, luminescent thread shoots upwards, zooming past a cell dividing in two, then it bifurcates swiftly into two threads, then four. Some strands ascend further, while other branches end abruptly, signaling their extinction. Time and again, the tree is occluded completely by organisms, gradually becoming more complex and hover into view. Attenborough narrates, "as more variations appeared, the tree of life grew and became more diverse," and viewers see the bifurcating prongs growing upwards but also becoming distinctively three-dimensional and far more arboreal. An early invertebrate even hugs one of the branches and crawls toward another divergence point.

The virtual camera follows this dizzying ascent to reach a shimmering underwater scene, while in the background the branches continue to grow, chordates and arthropods scurry about, and an *Acanthostega* crawls out to land. The focus shifts back to the fleet of branching lights against a carmine aurora, signifying the conquering of land and the birth of reptiles and inspects. A flock of dragonflies take to the air with the camera in tow, then we shift to the next odyssey out onto land, this time with a vertebrate, the *Tiktaalik*. A massive jump in time is condensed into a sweep of the camera over the dark landscape, and spectral dinosaurs appear, clad in a blue haze that is contrasted with the foreboding orange in the background toward which the camera travels: the cataclysm of meteors that killed off the dinosaurs. The light generated by the last impact halts the ascent of orange threads on the tree of life to signal the mass extinction event. A single comet trailing upward hails the coming of the birds, with a sunset-orange *Archaeopteryx* flying into the shot. The camera then lands on a pallid blue landscape, where a shrew-like mammal, a *Purgatorius* skitters hither and thither. A ninety-degree turn and zoom-out of the camera reveals its ground to be yet another branch that soon bifurcates to accommodate rodents, bats, elephants, bears, whales, and primates. The final shot is of a bioluminescent, eerie, blue-pink panorama, a glowing canopy that crowns Shadow Industries's vision of the tree of life.

Having basked in the glory of biodiversity, the inquisitive scholar can now discern some key meaning-making processes that make this representation fit the medium of the television documentary. The general trajectory of the animated segment is upwards and toward the horizon, pulling the viewer into the boughs of the tree. Thus, it is a technique of immersion that persuades its audience. Shifts from cold to warm tints along the orange-blue spectrum signpost whether we are in the sea, on the land, or above it, as well as marking the passage of the geological epochs, notably after the extinction of dinosaurs. The dinosaur portion is also the loudest on the string-dominated soundtrack, as menacing violins act as harbingers of doom and a few quick strokes of the bow finish the beasts off, then fade into silence. Other times, music plays second fiddle to Attenborough's hushed, eager recital, beckoning the audience to continue on the journey of discovery. His voice guides the viewers like a companion — an inspired choice, since, like Darwin, he stands among the greatest commentators of life's intricate web. Here, his narration interprets the main star of the segment: the animation.

Without the computer-generated imagery, the documentary would fall apart — the animated tree of life is the visualization of the conceptual significance of evolutionary theory. It comes as the culmination of the hour-long documentary, taking center stage at the end of the second act, after the discovery of the DNA molecule. Because, unlike *OneZoom*, the TV documentary has a temporally constrained, linear presentational format; CGI artists have to use camera movement and animation to give direction to evolution while emphasizing its arboreal and directionless character. To meet that challenge, the fossil record is arranged in a branching structure that the documentary must arrange into a single temporal plotline so that it can be narrated with a forward momentum. Without CGI, fossil fish, invertebrates of yore and the extinction of the dinosaurs — whose material traces we have seen in the preceding forty-five minutes — would not be vividly brought to life. This tree is a fully-fledged embodiment of Darwin's insight, fleshed out by later discoveries. In the original video on the Wellcome Trust's webpage, we see one final shot of the whole tree from the bottom, in whose shadow stands the only human being in the entire segment, Attenborough, whose tall stature is made diminutive by the widening canopy of the great Tree. This shot is the final decentering of the human being, emphasizing our small but significant role as discoverers, witnesses, nurturers, and pruners of life.

So Say We All: Collective, Multispecies Storytelling in The Ancestor's Tale

Through the ages, Darwin had many champions against the significant imaginative resistance to his ideas, but not one of these commands the attention with his opinions today more than Richard Dawkins. As a writer of popular scientific writings on evolutionary biology, Dawkins follows in the footsteps of Darwin, since, as Daniel Helsing explains, "Charles Darwin's *On the Origin of Species* (1859) resist[s] classification as either science or popularization or literature; [it is] everything at once."[26]

Dawkins and Yan Wong's *The Ancestor's Tale: A Pilgrimage to the Dawn of Life* is notable for a unique graphical motif, leaping off from the cover: it is OneZoom's tree of life discussed above. Of the fifty-eight arboreal illustrations found in the book, forty are fractal trees, and the other eighteen are cladograms and phylo-

---

26   Daniel Helsing, "The Literary Construction of the Universe: Narratives of Truth, Transcendence, and Triumph in Contemporary Anglo-American Popularizations of Physics and Astronomy," PhD thesis, Centre for Languages and Literature, Lund University, 2019, 17.

grams, which show lines of descent and genetic distance between fewer species, respectively. There is only one illustration of the tree of life that is a historical drawing, a detail of Ernst Haeckel's 1866 tree of life that shows the relationship between hippos and whales.[27] Compared to Zakariya's concept of the scalar genres of synthesis, these trees of life are fabulaic in nature because they illustrate "quasi-fictional narratives that employ storytelling devices such as a journey taken through different domains,"[28] of which Dawkins's pilgrimage narrative along the Tree of Life is a wonderful example. The *OneZoom* trees of life at the beginning of the chapter are at once the road map of the journey and the template of its major plot points.

Early on in *The Ancestor's Tale*, Dawkins and Wong betray a sense of unease of adapting biological data to the very human genre of storytelling: "[t]he historian must beware of stringing together a narrative that seems, even to the smallest degree, to be homing in on a human climax."[29] After all, the human experience of time is not only linear but unidirectional, and narrative generally serves the purpose of temporal ordering with a forward momentum. To remedy that, *The Ancestor's Tale* tells the story of evolution by proceeding backwards in time, from modern humans to the earliest forms of life, archaea. The backwards march is told in a series of "rendezvous," where the pilgrims are joined by their earlier common ancestors.

Intriguingly, the authors have consciously used a familiar literary template to guide this crab canon of a narrative: "[a]fter each meeting, we continue together on the high road back to our shared archaean goal, our 'Canterbury.' There are other literary allusions, of course, and I almost made Bunyan my model and Pilgrim's Regress my title. But [the *Canterbury Tales*] seemed increasingly natural" to think of as the master narrative of the book.[30] The choice of Chaucer is quite inspired; albeit integrated in the frame story, the *Canterbury Tales* is a series of loosely connected tales, and the structure of Dawkins's book, where chapters are divided by millions of years, lends itself well to this template. Each chapter is therefore titled after this fashion as "The Hippo's Tale," "The Orangutan's Tale," and so on.

As a rule, Dawkins does not engage in literary narration, opting for expository prose as the primary tone of the book. On one occasion midway through the book, however, readers might feel for a moment that they have wandered into another text entirely:

> [t]he star-nosed mole, who had joined the pilgrimage along with the other laurasiatheres at Rendezvous 12, listened to the Duckbill's Tale with close attention, and with growing recognition in what was left of his vestigial, pinprick eyes. "Yes!" he squeaked, too high for some of the larger pilgrims to hear, and he clapped his spades with excitement. "That's just the way it is for me… well, sort of." No, it won't do, I wanted to follow Chaucer in having at least one section devoted to what one pilgrim said to another, but I'll limit

---

27   Dawkins and Wong, *The Ancestor's Tale*, 239.
28   Zakariya, *A Final Story*, 3.
29   Dawkins and Wong, *The Ancestor's Tale*, 4.
30   Ibid., 9.

it to the heading and first paragrap, and now revert to my practice of telling the tale itself in my own words.[31]

This small narrative break is the only time in the whole of the 700-page book when the storytelling voice mimics the conventions of fiction, as if answering the unspoken question of the reader as to why Dawkins did not take further measures in adopting the Chaucerian template. It establishes the author as a scientist rather than an artist and reinforces the book's status as definitely belonging on the nonfiction shelf, despite its pretensions of literary structure.

In her study of *The Ancestor's Tale,* Janine Rogers affirms that the Chaucer analogy is not "mere literary window dressing"[32] and that the ethical core of Dawkins's decentering of the human race is linked up with Chaucer's "ethical framework for understanding the complex relations between parts and wholes."[33] She argues that Dawkins senses Chaucer's "implicit social commentary on the diversity of human life within the medieval estate system that divided humanity into discrete and non-continuous categories"[34] and adapts it to his evolutionary message, which celebrates the diversity of life and the dissolution of discrete and non-contiguous categories of species. But note that in "Dawkins's rendezvous format the pattern of interactions between the pilgrims is quite different from Chaucer's group, who mostly all start out the journey together."[35] And, not to put too fine a point on it, despite its inspired influence, the strength of Dawkins's prose does not come from the emulation of Chaucer's text. The idea of a straightforward message might find its home more readily in popular scientific texts, where genre conventions allow for a direct address of the audience, compared to a literary work of art.

Compounding that problem in a way that should be resonant with my discussion above about the narrative problems of evolution is Dawkins's admission that Chaucer had it easy because "[h]is cast list was a set of individuals. Mine is a set of groupings"[36]– although the animal species that "tell their story" in *The Ancestor's Tale* are always in the singular just as the eponymous Ancestor is, they are stand-ins for the porous group of the species. Instead of species, Dawkins places the onus of driving the story on another, unlikely protagonist, a "singular hero [that] has recurred in the minor, like a Wagnerian leitmotiv: DNA. It is our DNA that links us to the rest of the natural world, whose ancestral journey [...] we have been following all the while."[37] Taking the DNA as the hero of the story is of course all good and well, but it is a covert protagonification (if such a word exists), which never gets to be overtly declared in the narrative until the final pages. Feminist narratologist Venla Oikkonen states that crowning the DNA as the protagonist shifts the attention to the micro-narrative level, and Dawkins "succeeds in this by associating itself with the longevity and teleology commonly attributed to the species-

31 Ibid., 291.
32 Janine Rogers, "A Compaignye of Sondry Folk: Mereology, Medieval Poetics and Contemporary Evolutionary Narrative in Richard Dawkins' 'The Ancestor's Tale,'" *Interdisciplinary Science Reviews* 39, no. 1 (2014): 48.
33 Ibid., 47.
34 Ibid., 51.
35 Ibid.
36 Dawkins and Wong, *The Ancestor's Tale,* 25.
37 Ibid., 699.

level evolutionary narrative [...] and with anthropomorphic agency present in the organism-level evolutionary narrative."[38] In this narrative contest between the species and the gene's story, the outcome is decided at the start and is reinforced time and again by the scientist-narrator: "[t]he gene's eye view of evolution keeps forcing itself upon our attention," Dawkins writes, eliding his own status as the compiler of the story and adopting the perspective of the gene.[39] By the middle of the narrative, it would not be a mistake to call it a point-of-view character, in spite of having no chapter with the title "The Gene's Tale," for it would give the game away. For that, one should consult Siddhartha Mukherjee's entertaining but technical *The Gene: An Intimate History.*[40]

The Ancestor's Tale also situates the narrative temporalities of evolution vis-a-vis the literary conception of time, evoking the concept of the *evolutionary sublime*: "[t]he sweep of geological time is normally so far beyond the ken of poets and archaeologists it is daunting. But geological time is large not only in comparison to the familiar timescales of human life and human history. It is large on the timescale of evolution itself. [...] There has been too much time!"[41] The problem for popular science writers such as Dawkins and Wong, now, is how to fill the vast periods of time with a satisfying narrative that would make a convincing case for evolution.

Among the design affordances of narrative, the linear sequencing of events can prove to be a hurdle. Other than a direct line of descent, which would emphasize the genealogical, this-after-that narrative, there is information exchange between germ lines, that is, horizontal gene transfer, which complicates a straight story. Biologists now conceptualize time as "the biggest pattern" in natural history, and evolutionary biologists now spend more time investigating "how non-linear events outside the genealogical descent line disrupt an otherwise linear sequence of descent, by potentially adding new information that can causally influence future generations"; for example in "research on ecological inheritance, epigenetic inheritance, hereditary symbiosis, or lateral gene transfer [which] seek causation in the interactions between organisms, and these interactions in turn, provide yet another way to time change in natural history."[42] These aspects get the short shrift in *The Ancestor's Tale,* and most canonical stories of evolution in fact, as the authors seem adamant at containing the disruptive power of, say, epigenetics (e.g., in the epilogue to "The Mouse's Tale") in the story of evolution.

In Dawkins's defense, one of the reasons why the strict chronological ordering of the story cannot happen is due to the provisory nature of biological discovery, especially the further back in time we go. A lucid example is Dawkins and Wong's construction of the Great Historical Rendezvous, the endosymbiotic meeting of several bacteria to form the first eukaryotes. Honest and revealing, Dawkins writes, "I have referred to the Great Historic Rendezvous as a single event, because of what now appears to be its single momentous consequence, but it was actually

---

38   Venla Oikkonen, "Narrating Descent: Popular Science, Evolutionary Theory and Gender Politics," *Science as Culture* 18, no. 1 (2009): 18.

39   Ibid., 414.

40   Siddhartha Mukherjee, *The Gene: An Intimate History* (London: Vintage, 2017).

41   Sugars, "The Evolutionary Sublime," 309.

42   Nathalie Gontier, "Time: The Biggest Pattern in Natural History Research," *Evolutionary Biology* 43, no. 4 (2016): 632.

two or three events, perhaps widely spaced in time."[43] This is a direct acknowledgement of the narrator's authorial powers, which lays bare the device of synthesizing events for purposes of meaning-making. The complexities of deep time mediated by human narrative sometimes warrant such condensations of disparate events into a single, storied moment.

To close this discussion of Dawkins's management of his narratorial position as a historian of biological life by navigating the boundary between fact and fiction and genres of scientific and speculative storytelling, I turn to the last page, which summarizes the journey by exhorting the reader to:

> reflect on the fact that although this book has been written from a human point of view, another book could have been written in parallel for any of 10 million starting pilgrims. Not only is life on this planet amazing, and deeply satisfying, to all whose senses have not become dulled by familiarity: the very fact that we have evolved the brain power to understand our evolutionary genesis redoubles the amazement and compounds the satisfaction. [...] I feel I have returned from a true pilgrimage.[44]

A crucial form of a decentering is at the heart of Dawkins's message — humans are but one species among many, and all surviving forms of life are equally successful. Thus, in Dawkins's telling, the epic story of evolution is a fabulaic genre of synthesis, in which the authors use both science and artistic forms of expression to defamiliarize the human condition, which strengthens our ties of kinship with other lifeforms. Like Attenborough's documentary *Charles Darwin and the Tree of Life,* charting a single temporal course through the tangled tree of evolution, this time backward, constrains narrative complexity but, at the same time, endows our journey with emotional and ethical salience, something the tree of life — in its visualized database format — lacks. That story is our shared, collective fate, and we all tell it, one species at a time.

In the Minds of All That Live: Adaptive Decision-making and Mind-hopping from Species to Species in Stephen Baxter's <u>Evolution</u>

Stephen Baxter's Evolution is a book that takes a mind-bogglingly long view of history: beginning 65 million years ago at the beginning of the K-Pg (Cretaceous-Paleogene) extinction event and ending 500 million years in the future, it is a series of short stories that form a continuing narrative of life on earth, in which humanity plays a small but not insignificant part. The narrative is anthropocentric inasmuch as it only explores one branch of the tree of life, but it is a dazzling ascent through time. Like Dawkins's work, this fictional synthesis of life is fabulaic as it is "related to and told along a path of a science adventure story."[45] The framing story involves two scientists, Joan Useb and Alyce Sigurdardottir travelling to Darwin, Australia, to a conference which is being held on the climate catastrophe that threatens the future existence of human life. At the conference, they state, "[w]

---

43 Dawkins and Wong, *The Ancestor's Tale,* 615.
44 Ibid., 700.
45 Zakariya, *A Final Story,* 4.

e want to tell the story of humankind. Because now we have to decide how we are going to deal with the future. Our theme is the globalization of empathy," which could plausibly describe the mission statement of the book itself.[46]

In Baxter's work, the science behind evolution is a defining optic that structures the narrative in a way that challenges our conventions of storytelling. In a narratological view, "[h]uman evolution is [...] something fundamentally problematic, [because] the spatio-temporal scale of evolutionary processes resists straightforward capture in narrative form, because [...] narrative is not just a human practice, but a practice geared toward the spatio-temporal parameters of human societies."[47] In science fiction narratives, sometimes what comes after us will be unrecognizable as human: life will continue to exist even after our narrative patterns become exhausted. Deep time can only become narrative time by making prolepsis its primary figure, the dark matter to the matter of narrated events.

Soon after Alyce and Joan find a remarkable specimen, the narrative descends to the perspective of the animal whose teeth they have unearthed, Purga. She is a member of the shrew-like *Purgatorius* species, an extinct eutherian and the ancestor of mammalians living today. (Naming for the prehistoric animal cast usually follows similar conventions, with the binomial Latin names shortened.) Purga and his descendants, from Plesi to Noth, get chapters where the reader is introduced to the lifeworld of the species as if we were inside the mind of these ancient beasts before the story turns toward humankind and the future. For me, the prehistoric scenes are the ones worth discussing in terms of how they create narrative progression through thought representation.

To give the reader an idea of the style and level of narration Baxter at which presents our protagonists, here is how we zoom into Purga's mind as she surveys the environment:

> To Purga the world was a plain picked out in black, white, and blue, lit up by the uneasy light of the comet, which shone behind high scattered clouds. Her huge eyes were not as sensitive to color as the best dinosaur designs — some raptors could make out colors beyond anything that would be visible to humans, somber infrareds and sparkling ultraviolets — but Purga's vision worked well in the low light of night. And besides she had her whiskers, which fanned out before her like a tactile radar sweep.[48]

Much of the sensory information the reader gains would not be accessible to a human, and yet the narration mediates between the sensory life-world of the proto-mammal and the reader to convey, for example, how whiskers might be an organ of touch. Furthermore, the comparison between dinosaurs and Purgatoriuses are meaningful to the readers but not to the animals, and the comparison bifurcates the narratorial voice between the concerns of the animal we follow and the human trying to imagine what life must have been like to distant ancestors.

Despite the heightened sense of arousal that a small shrew-like creature under constant threat experiences, there is room for joy even in her busy days of survival:

46   Baxter, *Evolution*, 6.
47   Marco Caracciolo, "A Walk through Deep History: Narrative, Embodied Strategies, and Human Evolution," *Costellazioni* 2, no. 5 (2018): 131.
48   Baxter, *Evolution*, 12.

"[i]t was pleasing to climb, to feel her muscles work smoothly as they hauled her high above the dangerous ground, to use the delicate balance afforded by her long tail."[49] I would identify the narratorial style of thought representation here as a form of "free indirect perception," which is defined as descriptions that can be read as both a factual statement and "as the character's perception of the physical event and, even more importantly, by extension, the character's experience of the psychological implications of the event."[50] By describing the ground as "dangerous" and the upward movement as "pleasing," Baxter infuses his narration with the evolutionary coloring that makes a particular life-world qualitative. One of the major principles behind *Evolution*'s brand of narration is that without adaptive instincts, no features of the environment would be meaningful. Both the pleasures and the pains of life are shaped by the instincts natural selection has instilled in all living creatures.

The narrative voice describing Purga's thought processes is at times much more reminiscent of wildlife-documentary narration than what an animal could possibly know: "there was not enough food, the family, pent up in this burrow, might turn on one another. The imperatives slid through her mind, and a new decision was reached."[51] The lack of food is a factual, perceptual claim, one that animals can act upon, but the indirect presentation of the future, focused through Purga, stretches the willing suspension of disbelief. Although she might be aware of a lack of food for her conspecifics, no prehistoric animal would have been able to predict that an in-group squabbling would directly result from claustrophobia and nutritional scarcity. Note that the narrative agency does not belong to the individual animal here but instead to the genetic imperatives that govern her. Purga does not decide, the decision is made for her by instincts. The passive voice further underlines that genetic predispositions translate to algorithmic decision-making.

On other occasions, the small-scale, minute-to-minute life-world of Purga expands to a view much wider, almost supernatural insight into the conditions of life. When a predator attacks her, she is shown contemplating her fate: "[a]nd while Purga trembled in the remains of her burrow, a world trembled with her. If she submitted now, she would leave no living descendants: The molecular river of inheritance would be blocked, here, forever. Others of her kind would breed, of course; other lines would go on into far distant futurity, to grow, to evolve, but not Purga's line, not her genes."[52] There is a disturbing complexity of insight attributed to Purga here in free indirect thought, and contemplation is not at all a misnomer here. It is one of the peculiarities of Baxter's storytelling that many of the "decisions" that the genetic programming an animal "makes" are proleptically laid out, even though only humans can envision the future.[53]

---

49 Ibid., 14.

50 Palmer, *Fictional Minds,* 49.

51 Ibid., 44–45.

52 Ibid., 20.

53 At least, scientific consensus at the time of Baxter's writing was unanimous on asserting that mental time travel was a skill unique to humankind. The scientific premises have been challenged in recent years, as reported by *Nature*. See Michael Balter, "Can Animals Envision the Future? Scientists Spar Over New Data," *Science* 340, no. 6135 (2013): 909, but caution must still be exercised so as not to unduly anthropomorphize real-life animals.

Yet, this is narration with a hindsight bias, only because we, human readers of the story, know that *Purgatorius* is an ancestor species of modern mammals, do we get this level of far-futurity narration, which would be unnatural or impossible to gauge from the perspective of any protagonist, even people living in the twenty-first century. As Allan A. Debus remarks, despite its lowly status as a prehistoric proto-primate, Purga is "humanity itself personified."[54] The point here is that the narration oscillates between two perspectives, that of the animal, and those of her genes. Baxter evokes the Dawkinsian image of the *River Out of Eden* in his mention of the molecular river of inheritance, which, as Dawkins clarifies, "is a river of DNA, and it flows through time, not space. It is a river of information, not a river of bones and tissues: a river of abstract instructions for building bodies, not a river of solid bodies themselves."[55]

The chapters that detail the travails of prehistoric animals are almost exclusively descriptive, action upon action. For example, what rudimentary "speech" Purga might have is conveyed in piss. Fleeing from her attacker, she "helplessly squirted urine and musk, leaving a scent warning: *Beware! Mammal hunter about!*"[56] The exclamatory voice is undoubtedly Purga's, but it is not heard but smelt; yet its meaning is immediately translated for the human reader as if she were another fellow Purgatorius. Later, when we meet Stego, a Stegosaurus, "genuine" dialogue begins to emerge, albeit one that is mediated not by vocalizations but by nonverbal gestures: "[a] silent conversation passed in subtle movements, nods, eye contacts. That one, said Stego. Yes. Weak. Young. I will run at the herd. I will use the whip. Try to spook them. Separate the runt. Agreed. I will make the first run… It should have been routine. But as the orniths approached, coelurosaurs scuttled away and pterosaurs flapped awkwardly into the air."[57] It does not follow the formal conventions of human dialogue. Instead, it is reported speech. Other times, the narrator is a bit more explicit about how information passes between these dinosaurs and why vocalizations take the backseat in conversation: "[h]unting carnivores were accustomed to working silently. So their language was a composite of soft clicks, hand signals, and a ducking body posture."[58] These, and other instances of animal communication are powerful tools of defamiliarization, of decentering the human expectations of conversational storytelling, which the author puts to good use in presenting the reader with a unique perceptual environment for each species he narrates.

As the grand story of human ancestors proceeds, other species with more complex thinking are introduced in subsequent chapters. An odd example is a flashback halfway through Purga's tale of survival, from the Cretaceous to the Jurassic — a jump of about 80 million years. In it, we meet Listener, an *Ornitholestes* dinosaur who is capable of a far more sophisticated form of thinking than Purga. When she is separated from her group and meets a new tribe of her conspecifics, her shift of allegiance to the new group is "[s]omething hardened, a dark core, in

---

54   Allen A. Debus, *Dinosaurs in Fantastic Fiction: A Thematic Survey* (Jefferson: McFarland, 2013), 161.

55   Richard Dawkins, *River Out of Eden: A Darwinian View of Life* (New York: Basic Books, 1995), 4.

56   Baxter, *Evolution*, 8, italics in original.

57   Ibid., 53.

58   Ibid., 49.

Listener's mind. She knew she would spend the rest of her life with this herd."[59] That dark-core hardening is a poetic rendering of what we could feasibly call a "concept," forming as it does in the mind of a dinosaur that would have been the great-great-great-niece of the *Tyrannosaurus rex*. The author, not content to endow dinosaurs with sophisticated speech and abstract thinking, also gives them the gift of tool-making and myth-making: "their rudimentary mythos was dominated by the hunt, by legends of a kind of ornitholestes Valhalla. They were hunters who could make tools: that was all they would ever be, until there was nothing left to hunt."[60] At times like these, the imagination is not so much stretched as hung, drawn, and quartered.

Baxter is very keen on tiptoeing the fine line between anthropomorphism and doing justice to the uniquely animal traits of his host of characters. If Dawkins was negotiating the boundary between the fictive and nonfictive aspects of storytelling, Baxter is mediating between the human psyche and the animal psyche. With the growing complexity of social life and brain volume growth comes more forms of social cognition. One of the hallmarks of human cognitive development is our understanding that, just like us, fellow human beings have an inner life, thoughts, beliefs, and desires, and we know that people can hold erroneous beliefs or be mistaken about the state of affairs. The human privilege of intentional lying is explored in *Evolution* when another species ambassador, so to speak, Noth finds a cache of honey but intentionally does not call out to the others to notify them of the food. The narrator comments: "[i]t looked as if he had lied about the honey. But Noth was incapable of telling genuine lies — planting a false belief in the minds of others — for he had no real understanding that others had beliefs at all, let alone that their beliefs could be different from his, or that his actions could shape those beliefs."[61] Here Baxter is using arguments of evolutionary cognitive development to draw species boundaries, while at the same time generating empathy for a different way of life beyond the human.

Still, I want to emphasize that such an anthropomorphization of prehistoric animals is made almost necessary by the choice of medium, the prose of fictional narrative. Because narrative is a uniquely human form of structuring information, anthropomorphization is built into its very foundation. Even the most behaviorist forms of narration need some degree of mindfulness which enables the perception of stimuli in the storyworld and their evaluation by an agent who has goals, intentions, or desires. Granted, experimentations with non-human storytelling have been a facet of modern literature, but even the more conventional animal stories, which are internally focused, have to make recourse to some kind of cognitive "upgrading" to be pleasurable to read. Spatial constraints prohibit following Baxter's majestic traversal of the tree of life through humans to their future descendants, but the narrative strategies for representing animal minds are worth investigating, because fictional storytelling grants readers the ability to feel with animals deep in our evolutionary pasts, who have given their lives to birth us.

Although both Dawkins and Baxter testify to "the power of narrative to reframe the cultural models or ontologies that undergird hierarchical understandings of humans' place in the larger biotic communities of which they are mem-

---

59 Ibid., 56.
60 Ibid., 62.
61 Ibid., 113.

bers," they are still bound by the medial expectations of the reading public, and therefore have to resort to storytelling strategies that shall sweeten the sour pill of what Herman calls a "biocentric message" — that humans are but one chapter in the grand narrative of life.[62] The power of the genre of science fiction is that it has honed what Darko Suvin calls "cognitive estrangement," and although he originally used it to mean the realistic presentation of the alternative worlds of science fiction, it can also be fruitfully applied to the estrangement of cognition, since Baxter's *Evolution* portrays animal cognition in ways that are both familiar (anthropomorphized) and strange (spelling out evolutionary decision-making).[63] This form of mind-presentation is something that remains unique to science fiction narratives.

Where Species are Born: Constructing Habitats in Birthdays: The Beginning

Unlike any of the other representations of the tree of life metaphor analyzed here, *Birthdays: The Beginning* lets you not only observe evolutionary relations, but tinker with the very tools of Creation itself. To categorize it by genre, *Birthdays* is a fine example of what is called the "god game." In this genre, the player is granted extraordinary powers over a large swathe of land and can observe the algorithmic progress of a fine-tuned microcosm over periods of time, which range from historical eras to geological epochs. Usually, players are tasked with guiding a group of autonomous agents (e.g., AI-controlled non-player characters, whether represented as animals, humans, or specific historic civilizations) through a process of resource gathering, manufacturing, research, and demographic development while withstanding attacks from rival factions. The lack of direct control over your "units" is one of the key distinguishing features of the genre from other empire-building strategy titles. The other is a mythological theme, whereby your powers represent the abilities of omnipotent deities, such as shaping the earth, controlling the elements, and influencing your believers.

Birthdays strikes out in a different direction by marrying modern, accessible design with the gameplay promise of earlier life simulation games, like Maxis's *SimEarth* and *SimLife* that introduced complex and engaging game mechanics for simulating ecosystems.[64] The premise of *Birthdays* is that you are given dominion over cubic "planets" that can sustain life, only if you shape its terrain to create the right ecological variables. You are granted the power to raise or lower terrain on a tile grid, which determines how warm or cold your cube is; for instance, higher elevations lead to colder climes, while lowlands are warmer, and below ground level, ravines are filled with water to form rivers as larger plots become seas and oceans. In fact, close to the bedrock, the game's Mariana Trenches can become as hot as

62   David Herman, *Narratology beyond the Human Storytelling and Animal Life* (Oxford: Oxford University Press, 2018), 4.

63   Darko Suvin, *Metamorphoses of Science Fiction: On the Poetics and History of a Literary Genre,* exp. edn. by Gerry Canavan (Bern: Peter Lang, 2016).

64   Will Wright and Maxis, *SimEarth,* MS-DOS, Windows by Maxis, 1990, and Ken Karakotsios and Maxis, *SimLife: The Genetic Playground,* MS-DOS, Windows by Maxis, 1992.

70°C. Tiles that lie closer to water tiles are more humid than tiles further out, and different levels of humidity shape what kind of creatures may live there. Together, the tiles' altitude, temperature, and humidity give rise to various biomes, such as deserts, jungles, forests, snowy highlands, and swamps.

The gameplay alternates between the two modes of the simulation, Micro View and Macro View. In Micro View, the world slows down, and you make adjustments to the terrain until you run out of action points (even godly powers have their limitations), then you zoom out to Macro View, where you regenerate your points and see time pass as the world's events unfold in fast forward, millennia whooshing by. This is the mode where the game calculates the effects of the changes you made, most importantly, the creation of new biomes and species. This oscillation between micro and macro defines the primary gameplay loop — the major aesthetic charm of the game is seeing a barren cube turn into a lush biosphere teeming with life as a result of your actions.

The point of *Birthdays* is to create the necessary conditions for various organisms to come into existence. As lead designer Wada Yasuhiro explains, all species have three main conditions of emergence: "[t]he first is temperature, the second is terrain, and the third is 'what existed previously.'"[65] For example, Stromatolites only emerge underwater, in Shallows tiles, at temperatures between 38 and 55 degrees Celsius, but they also have a tolerance or Adaptation Range between –2 and 60 degrees Celsius, while later creatures are more finicky. Wada's "what existed previously" is actually an off-hand reference to the game's phylogenetic system. For example, even though the tile conditions for the emergence of modern humans are listed as having land tiles between 13 and 23 degrees Celsius and between 10 and 64 percent humidity, in fact, the player would have to meet all the conditions for prerequisite organisms on the game's dependency charts beforehand. So, they would also need to have birthed, in reverse order, *Homo erectus, Dryopithecus,* earlier primates and rodents, and land-dwelling organisms first.

Note that mutations in the game occur without direct intervention from the player. Just like life, speciation events are random possibilities rather than givens. The game also accurately depicts that changes in the biosphere lead to changes in the flora and fauna that inhabit each biome. The designer points out that "if an organism has primate ancestry, and its numbers increase, then it will evolve into the next form. Or, if it goes extinct, an organism *more suited to the environment* may be born."[66] *Birthdays* is unique among evolutionary god games for featuring over 280 organisms that are arranged into the game's evolutionary tree of life. This closely follows the lines of descent from microbiota to plants, fish, birds, or mammals, which the player can unlock by the careful micromanagement of the various biomes of the cube. Granted, the designers have also included some reality-challenged organisms on the phylogenetic chart for added whimsy, such as the Yeti and Nessie, supposedly originating from Australopithecine and Plesiosaurid ancestors, respectively.

Taking the analytical view, the game is a playful simulation of what is known in biology as "niche construction." By shaping the land, you create habitats for certain

---

65   PlayStation. "Birthdays the Beginning — Gameplay and Developer Interview — Part 2/3 'Nurture' | PS4," *YouTube,* February 16, 2017, https://www.youtube.com/watch?v=7wCAxGzb9Iw, 0:45.

66   Ibid., 1:15–1:30, emphasis added.

species. Another feather in the cap for the game is that it focuses on simulating animal populations rather than individual animals. The growth and shrinking of biomass shake up the previous balance of the ecosystem, and in the black box of the simulation, plant matter, herbivores, and carnivores are woven into a food chain you must sustain. Take away any cog, and the whole ecosystem suffers, and species may go extinct regularly. As Wada explains, "[b]ringing back something that went extinct is really hard work, [...] but it is very possible."[67] This allows for a more sophisticated simulation, compared to rivals in this admittedly niche genre of games. However, as one reviewer noted, "although the animal populations rise and fall in relation to one another on the [M]acro [V]iew where they're listed in a table on the right hand side, they don't actually interact in the [M]icro [V]iew. [...] It's a world filled with automata not life."[68] Thus it could be argued that the game makes for a more faithful simulation of evolution behind the scenes while being less accurate on the representational level.

The video game medium utilizes the powerful computing capacity of processors and graphics cards to not only show how organisms are related to each other but also to illustrate the process of how changes in the biological environment create selection pressures and enable speciation to occur. Still, the game does not simulate the effects of mating, sexual selection, reproductive isolation, genetics proper, and many other features we would associate with a wholly accurate representation of evolutionary development. Even so, *Birthdays* arranges many iconic prehistoric and still extant species into a working tree of life the player can unlock and explore the interactions between land and life at their leisure.

Coda

In this piece, I have compared fictional and nonfictive media to analyze how their design can highlight different approaches to the representation of evolutionary complexity of phylogenetic trees. Our first stop was *Charles Darwin and the Tree of Life,* which used the TV documentary format to retrace Darwin's steps and reconstruct his thinking. The CGI animation that crowned the film at once showed how the abstract spaces of the computer could be used to suggest the infinity of life and its powers to recapture lost moments of evolutionary history in a condensed format. These strengths were further exploited by the website *OneZoom,* which uses an innovative visual technique, namely, fractal imagery, to illustrate the relationship between all living species, a feat which would not be possible on paper. Then, in a close reading of *The Ancestor's Tale,* I highlighted the authors' intermedial strategies for meaning-making, such as a narrative patterning of the book that follows a literary template, and the personification of the gene as the covert protagonist for telling a coherent tale backwards. Stephen Baxter's *Evolution* took readers on another journey from the grim days of 65 million years ago

---

67   PlayStation, "Birthdays the Beginning — Create: Part 1 — Gameplay and Developer Interview | PS4," *YouTube,* January 18, 2017, https://www.youtube.com/watch?v=OTOfjv46mVE/, 4:45–5:00.

68   Philippa Warr, "Wot I Think: Birthdays the Beginning," *Rock Paper Shotgun,* May 5, 2017, https://www.rockpapershotgun.com/2017/05/05/birthdays-the-beginning-review/.

to ascend the phylogenetic tree. Baxter used the science fiction novel's propensity for portraying nonhuman or alien minds to great effect by putting the reader into the shoes of prehistoric animals whose thought processes and evolutionary decision-making the reader could follow, which resulted in a narrative style that is equally experimental and empathetic. Finally, I brought *Birthdays: The Beginning* in to show how the digital medium can shift the players' focus from narrative to systems thinking, drawing attention to the biological niches that give birth to new species, and what the interactive format's strengths are in representing biological complexity.

There is a lot that remains to be said about how different media capture evolution as a subject for multispecies storytelling. The present article is but a brief sketch — a much more modest contribution, but similarly reductive in scope as Darwin's "I think…" image when compared to his magisterial volume, the *Origin*. Here, I have tried to select a few illustrations that stay relatively close to current biological knowledge, but other outliers to be included, such as the Tree of Life at Disney's Animal Kingdom, or Terence Malick's 2011 film *The Tree of Life* come to mind, and other oddball examples could be easily found. At the same time, further theoretical synthesis is required for illuminating still hidden depths of intermedial theory and praxis, a thorny problem that asks for more space here and more time than I benefitted from during my stay as Crafoord Postdoctoral Fellow in Intermedial and Multimodal Studies at Linnaeus University in Växjö, Sweden. My time in Essen as a KWI Fellow at the Kulturwissenschaftliches Institut further allowed me to nuance the arguments made in this chapter, and to prepare it for publication. Without these two institutions, I would have been, like an extinct fish, be dead in the water. This study is a proof of concept that is part of an ongoing research agenda that investigates popular representations of complex scientific knowledge in various media. Like the various species that have rendezvoused on the pages of *The Ancestor's Tale*, I invite the reader to reach out and intertwine their thoughts with this contribution in the hope that joined forces can gallop faster toward new discoveries of origins.

References

Abbott, H. Porter. "Unnarratable Knowledge: The Difficulty of Understanding Evolution by Natural Selection." In *Narrative Theory and the Cognitive Sciences,* edited by David Herman, 143–62. Stanford: CSLI Publications, 2003.

Balter, Michael. "Can Animals Envision the Future? Scientists Spar over New Data." *Science* 340, no. 6135 (2013): 909. DOI: 10.1126/science.340.6135.909.

Baxter, Stephen. *Evolution.* New York: Del Rey/Ballantine Books, 2004.

Boyd, Brian. *On the Origin of Stories: Evolution, Cognition, and Fiction.* Cambridge: Belknap Press of Harvard University Press, 2009.

Caracciolo, Marco. "A Walk through Deep History: Narrative, Embodied Strategies, and Human Evolution." *Costellazioni* 2, no. 5 (2018): 123–46.

Coyne, Jerry A., and H. Allen Orr. *Speciation.* Sunderland: Sinauer Associates, 2004.

Darwin, Charles. *On the Origin of Species by Means of Natural Selection: Or, The Preservation of Favoured Races in the Struggle for Life.* London: J. Murray, 1859.

Dawkins, Richard, and Yan Wong. *The Ancestor's Tale: A Pilgrimage to the Dawn of Life.* London: Weidenfeld & Nicholson, 2016.

Dawkins, Richard. *River Out of Eden: A Darwinian View of Life.* New York: Basic Books, 1995.

de Vienne, Damien M. 2016. "Lifemap: Exploring the Entire Tree of Life." *PLOS Biology* 14, no. 12 (2016): e2001624. DOI: 10.1371/journal.pbio.2001624.

Dear, Peter. "Darwin and Deep Time: Temporal Scales and the Naturalist's Imagination." *History of Science* 54, no. 1 (2016): 3–18. DOI: 10.1177/0073275315625407.

Debus, Allen A. *Dinosaurs in Fantastic Fiction: A Thematic Survey.* Jefferson: McFarland, 2013.

Eames Office. "Powers of Ten (1977)." *YouTube,* August 26, 2010. https://www.youtube.com/watch?v=ofKBhvDjuyo.

Ereshefsky, Marc. "Revisiting the Conceptual Basis of Species." 2012. https://mallet.oeb.harvard.edu/files/malletlab/files/ereshefsky_in_boenigk_2012.pdf.

Estes, Douglas, ed. *The Tree of Life.* Leiden: Brill, 2020. DOI: 10.1163/9789004423756.

Fisler, Marie, Cédric Crémière, Pierre Darlu, and Guillaume Lecointre. 2020. "The Treeness of the Tree of Historical Trees of Life." *PLoS One* 15, no. 1: e0226567. DOI: 10.1371/journal.pone.0226567.

Futuyma, Douglas J. *Evolutionary Biology.* 3rd edn. Sunderland: Sinauer Associates, 1998.

Gabriel, Yiannis. *Storytelling in Organizations: Facts, Fictions, and Fantasies.* Oxford: Oxford University Press, 2000.

Gontier, Nathalie. "Time: The Biggest Pattern in Natural History Research." *Evolutionary Biology* 43, no. 4 (2016): 604–37. DOI: 10.1007/s11692-016-9394-3.

Helsing, Daniel. "The Literary Construction of the Universe: Narratives of Truth, Transcendence, and Triumph in Contemporary Anglo-American Popularizations of Physics and Astronomy." PhD diss., Centre for Languages and Literature, Lund University, 2019.

Herman, David. *Basic Elements of Narrative.* Chichester: Wiley-Blackwell, 2009.

———. *Narratology beyond the Human Storytelling and Animal Life.* Oxford: Oxford University Press, 2018.

Karakotsios, Ken, and Maxis. *SimLife: The Genetic Playground*. MS-DOS, Windows by Maxis, 1992.

Malick, Terence, dir. *The Tree of Life*. Fox Searchlight Pictures, 2011.

Manovich, Lev. "Database as Symbolic Form." *Convergence* 5, no. 2 (1999): 80–99. DOI: 10.1177/135485659900500206.

Mirzoeff, Sacha, dir. *Charles Darwin and the Tree of Life*. BBC, 2009.

Mukherjee, Siddhartha. *The Gene: An Intimate History*. London: Vintage, 2017.

Oikkonen, Venla. "Narrating Descent: Popular Science, Evolutionary Theory and Gender Politics." *Science as Culture* 18, no. 1 (2009): 1–21. DOI: 10.1080/09505430802668632.

OneZoom Core Team. *OneZoom Tree of Life Explorer Version 3.4*. 2019. http://www.onezoom.org/

Palmer, Alan. *Fictional Minds*. Lincoln: University of Nebraska Press, 2004.

Pietsch, Theodore W., and University of Washington. *Trees of Life: A Visual History of Evolution*. Baltimore: Johns Hopkins University Press, 2012.

Pigliucci, Massimo. "Species as Family Resemblance Concepts: The (Dis-) Solution of the Species Problem?" *BioEssays* 25, no. 6 (2003): 596–602. DOI: 10.1002/bies.10284.

PlayStation. "Birthdays the Beginning — Create: Part 1 — Gameplay and Developer Interview | PS4." *YouTube*, January 18, 2017. https://www.youtube.com/watch?v=cO5QmUw4fkk.

PlayStation, "Birthdays the Beginning — Gameplay and Developer Interview — Part 2/3 "Nurture" | PS4." *YouTube*, February 16, 2017. https://www.youtube.com/watch?v=7wCAxGzb9Iw.

Rogers, Janine. "A Compaignye of Sondry Folk: Mereology, Medieval Poetics and Contemporary Evolutionary Narrative in Richard Dawkins' 'The Ancestor's Tale." *Interdisciplinary Science Reviews* 39, no. 1 (2014): 47–61. DOI: 10.1179/030 8018813Z.00000000066.

Rosindell, J, and L.J. Harmon. "OneZoom: A Fractal Explorer for the Tree of Life." *PLoS Biology* 10, no. 10 (2012): e1001406. DOI: 10.1371/journal.pbio.1001406.

Slater, Matthew H. *Are Species Real? An Essay on the Metaphysics of Species*. Basingstoke: Palgrave Macmillan, 2013.

Sloan, Phillip. "Originating Species: Darwin on the Species Problem." In *The Cambridge Companion to the 'Origin of Species'*, edited by Michael Ruse and Robert J. Richards, 67–86. Cambridge: Cambridge University Press, 2009.

Sugars, Cynthia. "The Evolutionary Sublime: Deep Time and the Historical Novel in Joan Thomas's 'Curiosity." *Mosaic: An Interdisciplinary Critical Journal* 51, no. 3 (2018): 199–221. https://www.jstor.org/stable/26974118.

Suvin, Darko. *Metamorphoses of Science Fiction: On the Poetics and History of a Literary Genre*. Expanded edition by Gerry Canavan. Berlin: Peter Lang, 2016.

Wada, Yasuhiro, Inc. Toybox, and Arc System Works. 2017. *Birthdays: The Beginning*. NIS America.

Warr, Philippa. "Wot I Think: Birthdays the Beginning." *Rock Paper Shotgun*, May 5, 2017. https://www.rockpapershotgun.com/2017/05/05/birthdays-the-beginning-review/.

Wright, Will, and Maxis. *SimEarth*. MS-DOS, Windows by Maxis, 1990.

Zakariya, Nasser. *A Final Story: Science, Myth, and Beginnings*. Chicago: University of Chicago Press, 2018.

The Plant-story? Listening and Multispecies Storytelling

Fröydi Laszlo

As a visual artist working with several animal and plant species, I should have some experience with multispecies storytelling. But this issue has been very difficult to structure. I have wrestled with questions about the concepts that I base my thinking on, about human and nonhuman stories, about perspective and power, about thresholds, translation, technology, and many more. Most of my art is done in some kind of collaboration with or inspiration from animals, plants, algae, fungi, microscopic life forms like rotoferia, or forests, the latter that I consider multispecies life forms. This essay will not be about the artistic qualities of my work or from within a context of contemporary art. I will rather choose a few examples to show how my critical thinking and the creative art-process are mutually important practices to what may be called my own multispecies storytelling.

My first question concerns the concept of species. The species concept is founded in a system of classification that the western science of biology builds upon, and where one of the most essential divides goes between animals and plants. Do I really approach the plants, algae, animals as representations of this system? The answer is no, I don't, even if biology and ecology are very helpful tools when learning more about them. But it is also possible to make contact without focusing on evolution, biology, or classification. There are so many ways to tell a story within the myriad of human cultures, and even between human cultures we have difficulties understanding and translating. The life sciences, art, and humanities may tell their stories in different ways, and fundamental differences in approach may go even deeper in cultural formations like myth, religion, or situated practices. I'm aware that the ability to experience oneself as taking part in a multispecies network to a large extent is funded in childhood experiences, and I ask myself about the role of multispecies storytelling in the culture that I belong to.

Researching for this essay, I recently found the texts and ideas of former Waldorf school biology teacher Craig Holdrege and the Nature Institute homepage.[1] And, I think that if I had been taught biology according to the pedagogy that he presents, I would perhaps have felt more grounded in exploring the natural world and perhaps even chosen to study biology over painting. With roots in Goethean science, many of the pedagogical texts that Holdrege presents are deeply emotional and respectful to the wonder and overflowing variety of life on earth. It is

---

1   Craig Holdrege, "Goethe and the Evolution of Science," *In Context* 31 (2014): 10–23. https://www.natureinstitute.org/article/craig-holdrege/goethe-and-the-evolution-of-science/.

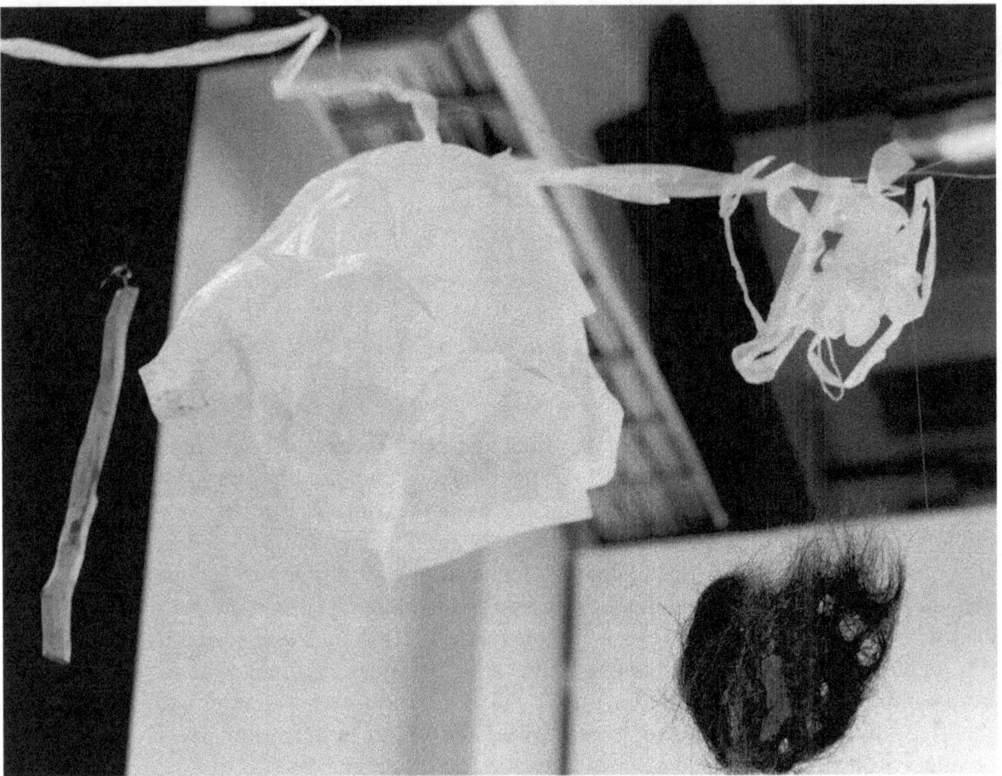

Fig. 6.1. Stick gnawed by rabbit, hair shed by Icelandic horse. Detail from installation at Gallery Huuto, March 2020. Photograph by the author.

interesting to think that a non-reductionist, soft empiricism was presented as a scientific method as early as in the 1790s. Although I have myself chosen another direction as pedagogue — I'm a Reggio Emilia atelierista — I think the inspiration from Johann Wolfgang von Goethe that Holdrege presents is still very relevant:

> An organic being is externally so many-sided and internally so manifold and inexhaustible that we cannot choose enough points of view to behold it, and we cannot develop enough organs in ourselves in order to examine it without killing it.[2]

What this means to me is that my fascination, emotional response, and feeling of overflowing information could all be part of a scientific research, according to Goethe and the Waldorf pedagogy, and even assist a necessary personal transformation.

But I chose to be an artist and started out drawing and painting. I still like to work outdoors and at the stables and to draw, paint, or photograph my own or wild plants and animals. Sometimes the inspiration would be to try to really see what is in front of me, other times it could be an exchange process between my object, the

---

2   E. Steiger, *Der Briefwechsel zwischen Schiller und Goethe,* Bd. I (Frankfurt: Insel Verlag, 1977), 12.

art media's materiality, and fantasy. I have even incorporated small works made by animals in art exhibitions and installations.

My experience is that engaging in art practices may even produce very accurate responses to mixed signals, as it develops both perception and the transformation of the senses. To me, as to the philosopher Ernst Cassirer, to whom I will refer later in this essay, art is in itself a way both *of* knowledge and *toward* knowledge. In the Reggio pedagogy, aesthetic elements are integrated in all kinds of education, and it is not about producing art. Rather, it is a method to explore the world and to gain the sensitivity and confidence that you need to engage with both nature and human society.

In these days, as we discuss the catastrophic effects of the Anthropocene, there are of course big hopes that we may change our lifestyles and technologies to reduce human impact. Undeniably, developing and advancing science and monitoring are vital, but to me it sounds like sheer hubris to think that the human species will ever know it all or manage the planet. It will always be information that we cannot access, translate, or apply to any structure.

To me, it seems like a personal transformation aimed at becoming in better resonance with this network could be possible even as part of an art process, as well as from many different perspectives of intense observation and listening. Yes, why should I believe that the world was just some kind of unspeaking materiality, when there are obviously so many processes, wills, and utterances all going on and intertwining?

From Footprint to Myth

The question about multispecies storytelling in combination with intermedial practices is intriguing. Many stories are based on traces of something that has actually happened to the media that preserve them, the signs are indexes. Reading the tracks of an animal in the sand and putting what you read into a human context as a hunting story is very foundational multispecies storytelling. And the physical track may be integrated in a shared memory through the formation of symbolic stories, and these stories again may be just as true and just as important for human understanding as recognizing the track itself. It is never just about observing, but it is even of structuring information into patterns, meanings, and stories.

I recently saw the film *The Great Dance: A Hunter's Story* from 2002, directed by the brothers Craig and Damon Foster. The film was made in collaboration with the !Xo of the San people. We meet a !Xo group that live as hunters and gatherers in the harsh environment of the Kalahari Desert. !Nqate Xqamxebe, a traditional hunter and tracker, shows us that his dancing, reading signs, praying, overcoming physical struggles, knowledge of utilizing plants and animals to make objects, food and medicine, and actually becoming the animal itself through tracking and hunting are all connected and necessary.

> When you track an animal, you must become the animal. Tracking is like dancing, because your body is happy — you can feel it in the dance and then

you know that the hunting will be good. When you are doing these things you are talking with God.[3]

Reading signs to understand exactly what has happened with an animal at a certain time and place is an empirical scientific practice, and for the !Xo hunters, it is connected to other practices like art and religion. In few but powerful words !Nqate Xqamxebe tells us about being a traditional hunter, he cannot be himself without being grounded in interspecies communication on many different levels. His being is depending on the plants and animals that live on their ancestral lands, his knowledge is situated and so is his feeling of self. In the end of the film, we are told that the San people's greatest struggles are about regaining hunting and gathering rights on their ancestral lands. I believe that one thing I can do, writing an essay like this, is to show respect to the people like the San that still live within multispecies networks and to the struggles and injustices that they are facing. And, the San are not all hunters and gatherers; rather they as a people represent a complex variety of lifestyles.

I have just said that very exact observation may be preserved and shared through the structure of myths. The !Xo hunters are reading footprints and other traces in the sand and the order of the signs are reconstructed in the form of hunters stories. Both the sand and the dance become media for storytelling.

But I could even say that for instance Darwin's theory of evolution is an example of a similar migration of signs. The media in which his story is written is not only the printed paper of *The Origin of Species*. It is even the bodies of the biological life forms where transformations become indexical signs of evolution. Darwin is at the same time a storyteller, a forensic, and a tracker, searching for traces of the unfolding history of evolution.

In my opinion, human development both in individuals and collectives depend on integrating many different practices, and mythological thinking is also a very "true" knowledge anchoring and stimulating the psyche, intuition, empathy, and fantasy, and it creates shared values, which of course may be both for good and bad. I will return to the issues of perception, ritual action, and myth when I refer to Cassirer, who has engaged deeply in the questions of human perception and cultural formations. I hope that Cassirer's thinking may be helpful to sort out some of the structures that puzzle me, even if it may be a bit strange to use a philosopher that was not really interested in communicating with animals or plants. I could instead have chosen some contemporary thinkers like Donna Haraway or Anna Lowenhaupt Tsing who have so greatly inspired multispecies storytelling, as I have benefited enormously from reading them both. I don't think my work criticizes their thinking, so I would probably say something most followers had already heard. Instead, I chose to share some of my questioning and struggles, even if I have not reached any clear conclusions, and to show you some of the tools I use. It will be up to the reader to ponder if I do my intellectual digging with a spade, a pointing trowel, or a teapot.

---

3   These are the words of hunter !Nqate Xqamxebe spoken in 1998 in the film *The Great Dance,* https://www.cultureunplugged.com/documentary/watch-online/filmedia/play/2419/The-Great-Dance.

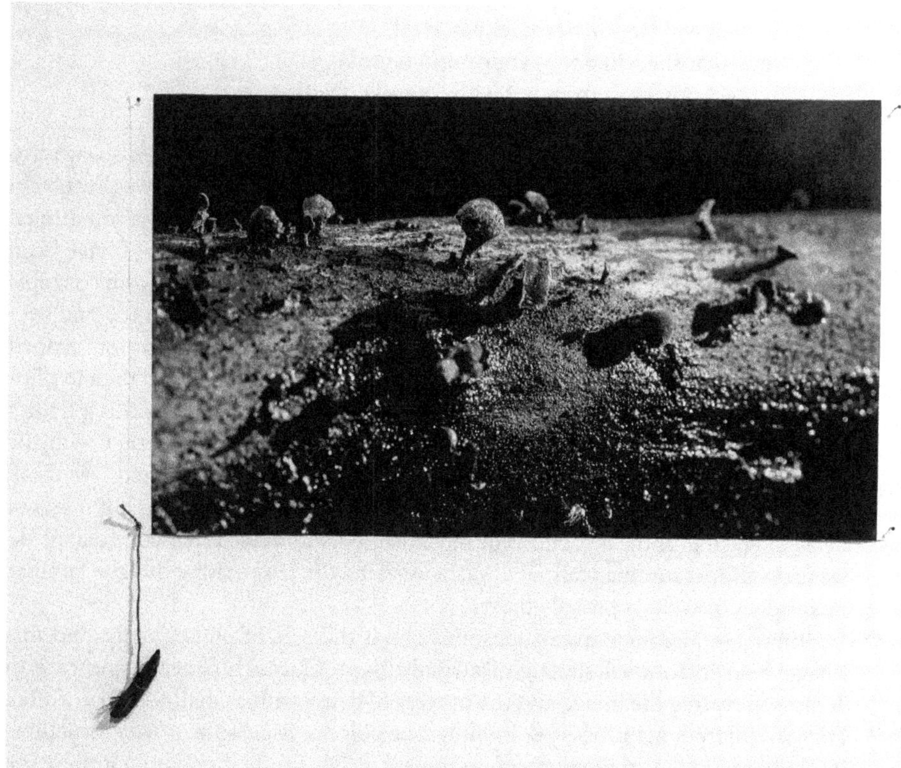

Fig. 6.2. A macro-photography of the fungi´s fruiting bodies is exhibited together with a small piece of wood containing the species bluegreen mycelium. Galleri Huuto, March 2020. Photograph by the author.

A Veil of Nature?

I ground my curiosity in nature at a captivating feeling of standing in front of a wonder, something unknown and even quite mystical. As I do not know what I experience, my search is both outward, as I strive to sense what captivates me, and inward, as I don't know how I experience the unknown. My art becomes a process log as does my waiting and becoming still. My intuition, paired with my trained techniques, mediate a processual dialogue between signs sent by my object of attention and the materiality of the media I work with paired with my motoric, emotional, and associative responses.

As a scientist, Goethe was strict on the stringency of the empirical observation itself. The scientist should not rush to any conclusion even if he or she intuitively grasped a pattern or a story. The delight of making patterns and coherence may just be rooted in our humanness and not in the object of study. The goal was to be able to see more and more of what was really happening with the studied object, and even if a personal response was necessary, it was as necessary to separate the signs themselves from it. Would it be possible to communicate with a specific animal or plant according to Goethe? No, to him as far as I understand it, believing in spirits would be to abandon science, but at the same time he lets Faust utter these words:

> Her veil will Nature never let you steal,
> And what she will not to your mind reveal,
> You will not wrest from her with levers and with screws.[4]

To insist that nature had to be listened to, and that reductionism would always create phenomena out of context was very radical at Goethe's time. He was even very early at seeing life as ecological entanglement and foregrounding transformational processes researching both development and specific species. While I have been trying to relate my investigations of nature to Goethe, I see that I do form concepts or images after certain patterns. One example is my difficult, but in the end successful, attempt to grow fruiting-bodies of a saprobic species of mushroom named Chlorociboria aeruginascens (or Green Woodcup) (see Fig. 6.2), and then to photograph them. The image sure looked like an alien landscape, the fruiting bodies had a resemblance to trees and the curving of the small stick together with the black "sky" made me think of going in for landing on a small asteroid. We think a lot about how different cultures create structures of understanding but may not be as interested in the structures of our misunderstanding. What conclusions do we draw almost automatically? How can we avoid the overwriting that the familiar image does to what is actually there?

There are of course many questions about the role of photography, and this image is an intentional staging of a result that took much patience and care to achieve. Creating the image and the process of living with a small world on a stick are two different art processes. I will not be able to discuss the power structures in photographic technology much in this essay, but I only mention that there are aspects that should be considered. First of all, it is photography's many similarities with hunting. The object is captured by the photographer,[5] and the subject's hidden position enables both predatory and voyeuristic passions to the gaze of both photographer and audience.[6]

Another question is that the repressive structure of photography is not only about the photograph or film. As there is a common belief in photography's ability to recreate the footprint in the sand as if the viewer should have seen the trace itself (i.e., its indexicality), images are easily taken as evidence of what has happened. But, as the image of the fungi shows, we do not always see what is really there; rather we see our own habits of structuring and making sense from images.

Art historian John Tagg writes that photographing is a practice that produces multiple framings by capturing and holding a moment, impression, or evidence.[7] This is a disciplinary process, and what is let out is as important as what is shown. If looking at the world through the lens of the camera is to become one-eyed, ac-

4   Johan Wolfgang von Goethe, *Faust, Part 1* (Tübingen, 1808), par. 657.

5   John Berger, "Why Look at Animals," in *About Looking* (London: Pantheon Books, 1980), 3–28.

6   Laura Mulvey, "Visual and Other Pleasures," in *Visual Pleasure and Narrative Cinema* (London: Palgrave Macmillan, 1986), 14–31.

7   See John Tagg, The Disciplinary Frame: Photographic Truths and the Capture of Meaning (Minneapolis: University of Minnesota Press, 2009); and the interview with Tagg by Ilija T. Tomanić, "Governmentality and the Image: An Interview with John Tagg," *Membrana* 1, no. 1 (2016), https://www.membrana.org/interview/governmentality-and-the-image-an-interview-with-john-tagg/.

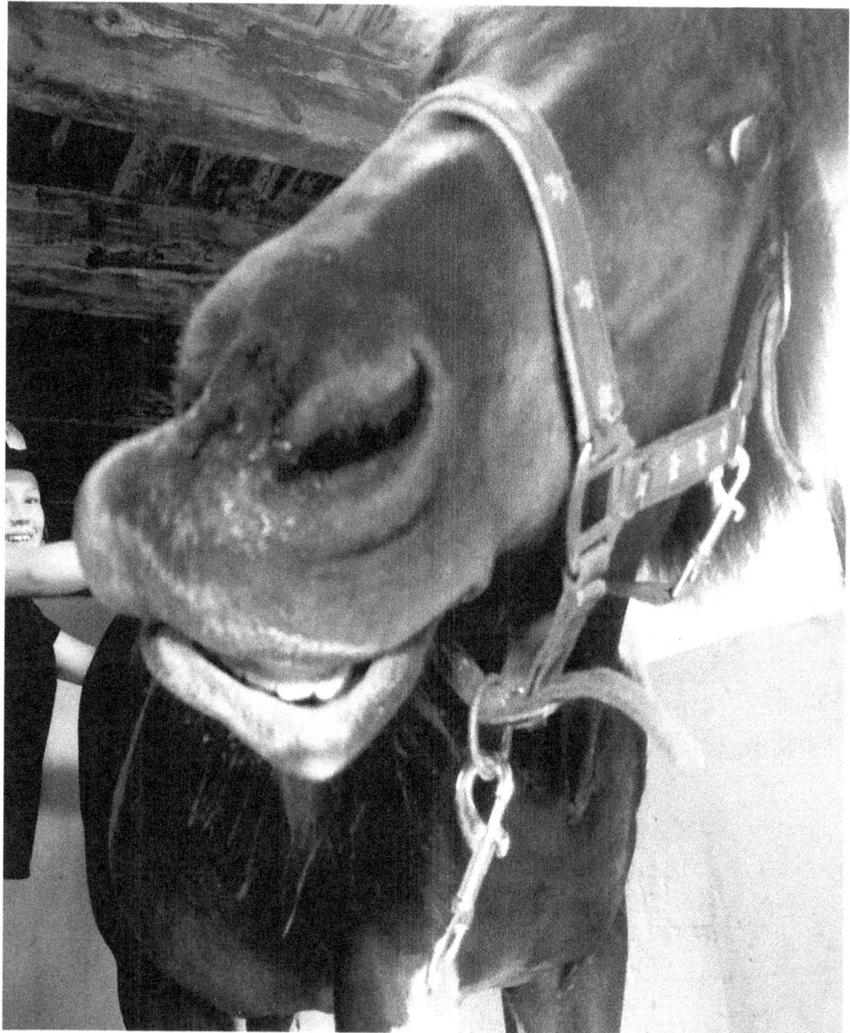

Fig. 6.3. Dear Trú tries to return the favor. Photograph by the author.

cording to Tagg, the practice of filing photographs in archives is a one-armed dis-cipline and the framing keeps both image and viewer in place. In that way I think that the afterlife of the evidence (as, for example, the filming of the hunting skills of the !Xo) is as important as the film itself considering paying justice to the object. One question is always who holds the camera and with what intentions.

Compassion and Interspecies Communication

The family pet rabbit, Ludde, and the Icelandic mare, Trú, have shown me the role of sign-systems in interspecies communication. The humans in our family started to hold pieces of dried carrot or apple over Ludde's head, this leading him to stand up whenever he wanted a treat. If he got something he did not really want, he would temporarily discard it to stand up again until we got him something satisfying. In time he would even go to the door and stand up to be let out or stand up as a general sign that he wanted attention.

In a similar way, Trú and I have agreed on some sign systems, as for example about how to groom (see Fig. 6.3). There are some parts of the grooming that are necessary but not pleasant (e.g., between the forelegs) and some that she really enjoys, mainly being rubbed and scratched at the neck and shoulders. When I come with the right brush, she will turn her neck toward it and exaggerate and almost mimic the signs that I take to be pleasure (e.g,. curling the upper lip) even before I have started. In this way she can, to a great extent, choose how to be groomed. If she signals go on, I'll take my time, and if she signals irritation I'll be as brief as possible.

If you care for a horse or a rabbit, I'm sure you have experienced something similar. Of course, it is a question if humans should teach animals to do tricks; isn't this just degrading to them? At the same time, providing an intra-species sign system may even give the animal a better chance to be listened to. Haraway writes interestingly about her relation to her dog Cayenne and how living with a companion animal is changing what it means to be both animal and human.[8] Together with our animals, and even our companion plants, we become something different. When humans and animals live together over generations, the ability to understand and communicate with humans becomes a selective advantage for the animal, and so does not complaining or internalizing stress reactions. In the same way, humans select edible, decorative, or other features possible to domesticate in plants. So, how close can we get to animals, plants, bacteria, fungus, algae, or viruses before we start to mix, interbreed and change?

My habit of living with plants is, at the moment, slowly turning my small and modern apartment into a witch cottage, as some plants, such as my aloe vera, are very pleased with this kind of habitat. I have to ask myself what I experience as I let my space be filled by plants, why I try to encourage their growth, and why I try to sharpen my own senses and intuition to register any early sign of wellbeing or distress. These beings that I care for, my "companion" plants, algae, and fungi all express themselves to me by either growing, flowering, fruiting bodies, or by breaking up into new individuals. I try to tune into their growth-patterns. Do they enjoy their soil? Is the light sufficient? Do they want more moisture, or will this cause wilt? Are they behaving in a way that resembles their natural growth, or do they change their ways under my influence? In time they seem to balance each other and turn into some indoor biotope, a potted jungle.

One problem is that I end up surrounded, trying to live in a giving and mutual relationships with all these expanding beings. I don't even know which one of these perhaps genetically identical bodies is the "original plant" that I initially bonded with.

Plant-shaped Perspectives?

If we let our storytelling be inspired by being surrounded by plants, there will not always be a fixed center of attention. Instead, we would find a subject stretching

---

8   Donna J. Haraway, *When Species Meet* (Minneapolis: University of Minnesota Press, 2007).

out into a kaleidoscopic plurality of perspectives, and even though the story could be told using a recognizable rhythm or method it would still be one of constant transformation.

I have felt a bit like this when reading the German philosopher Ernst Cassirer.

He always makes a collection of thoughts from the ancient Greeks to his contemporaries, and he is interested in so many different issues. In his writings, it seems like he is more interested in the process of thinking than of rushing to conclusions. To me, reading him is a rather slow but still fertilizing process where I feel my thoughts meandering.

Environmental philosopher Irene J. Klaver has some interesting views on meandering as a natural process, one that has also gained a lot of cultural connotations.[9] The factual river Meander, now called "Büyük Menderes" located in Anatolia, was mentioned two thousand years ago as so winding that the word "meander" came to mean riverine sinuosity and came to stand for anything twisting and curving.[10] Meandering is a time-consuming process and one that covers a broad area. We do not know exactly how and why rivers meander; the process is unpredictable, and meandering makes the course of the river come and go in a complex and entangled process. It is tempting to see this unpredictability as chaotic, but chaos is not the same as randomness. Rather, it signals that the changes involved in the process produce so complex effects that it is impossible to measure them all. Klaver says that linearity has become the privileged paradigm of progress and efficiency, while meandering has taken on a negative connotation of aimless wandering, undirectedness, longwinded argumentation, or simply being in the way of efficiency. But, at the same time the ecological understanding of the varied ecosystem functions that meandering may enhance may open for a revaluation of meandering and facilitate both acceptance for complexity in a cultural imagination and a different way of thinking about efficiency. Could this be an inspiration to perhaps adapt narrative structures better to focus on and with plants?

It is common to force thinking of plants into straight narratives. A flower lives for a summer to be pollinated and produce seeds that will live again next spring. But it is not that simple at all. This generic narrative fits well when we want to compare with human life stories, but plants are so diverse and they live through different states of being, connected and unconnected to what we call "body." They are in constant metamorphoses and exist in multiple temporalities where the difference between life and death are more gradual than with animals. It shows that the idea about individual bodies does not really apply to plants, even if human plant-storytelling tends to foreground the plant-as-body.

From my position as artist, I have been thinking much about how to tell a multispecies story, and I have come up with some alternatives, but they all struggle with problems of power, framing, and translation, if the ambition is to include a somewhat nonhuman perspective.

A history told by and about humans focusing on natural and cultural entanglement in a multispecies network demands respect and knowledge of ecology, history, and specific, situated, experiences. A history told from the perspective

9   Irene J. Kalver, "Reclaiming Rivers from Homogenization: Meandering and Riverspheres," in *From Biocultural Homogenization to Biocultural Conservation*, eds. Ricardo Rossi et al. (Cham: Springer, 2018), 49–69.
10   Strabo, *Geographica*, ed. A. Meineke (Leipzig: Teubner, 1877).

of one or more nonhuman species voiced by a human storyteller, as is the case in many myths, may contain deep knowledge and respect for the importance of the nonhuman but is still anthropomorphizing. Attempts to decipher and translate (into a for-humans understandable form) nonhuman species own expressions and trying to conceptualize these expressions into stories are equally difficult, as we will not know what kinds of value-systems apply to the nonhuman. Listening to nonhuman stories may even be dependent on adapting human technology to it and retelling the story could be impossible without human mediation.

One of my favorite writers, Ursula Le Guin, has written masterpieces about vegetal storytelling. The novel *The Word for World Is Forest,* which must have been very influential to the makers of the film *Avatar,* tells about a people that connect through their ritual dreaming to a forest-mind.[11] In the short story "Vaster than Empires," the planetary, vegetative intelligence of the alien World 4470 is described as "one big green thought."[12] In the very interesting short story, "The Author of the Acacia Seeds and Other Extracts from the Journal of the Association of Therolinguistics," Le Guin addresses the problems of translating between animal languages as each language is founded on the experience of being specific bodies in the world — and so metaphors and value-systems are, too.[13] One Therolinguist also addresses the lack of plant perspectives. In all these stories, Le Guin points to the fact that all experience is experience of being some kind of lifeform, even when speaking about a planet. Perhaps with some exception for cnidarians like siphonophores, man-o- wars and hydrozoan, most animals have distinct bodies that may or may not function similarly to the human. But plants? forests? the undifferenced algae or the moving slime mold— do they have bodies? And if stories are always told by bodies, what human experience could prepare us to think as plants?

Engaging with the science of plants, it is hard not to notice that classification, collection, and educational display of plants are deeply inscribed in a visual culture. In visual art and literature, the plant may be decorative, wild, symbolic, but more often, it is a green "backdrop" around which a character of a story evolves. Even if we are used to look at plants, we may still be blind to their importance and agency.

The concept "plant-blindness" describes how the Western culture I belong to mostly approaches *plantness* as inferior to animalness and as, assumedly, passive and insentient.[14] Even Goethe protested this.16 Breaking the zoocentric habit of

<hr>

11   Ursula K. Le Guin, *The Word for World Is Forest* (New York City: Berkley Books, 1976).

12   Ursula K. Le Guin, "Vaster Than Empires and More Slow," in *New Dimensions 1: Fourteen Original Science Fiction Stories,* ed. Robert Silverberg (New York City: Doubleday Books, 1971), 87–123.

13   Ursula K. Le Guin, "The Author of the Acacia Seeds and Other Extracts from the Journal of the Association of Therolinguistics," in *Fellowship of the Stars,* ed. Terry Carr (New York City: Simon & Schuster, 1974), 170–78.

14   J.H. Wandersee and E.E. Schussler, "Preventing Plant Blindness," *The American Biology Teacher* 61 (1999): 82–86. Wandersee and Schussler coined the term "plant blindness" to highlight the preference in American education for animals over plants amongst biology students. They built their theory on a body of work from psychology that showed human preference for images of vertebrate animals with forward-facing eyes over flowering plants.

ignoring plants could be encouraged through meaningful, multimodal, and aesthetic human-plant experiences, or even by questioning habitual conceptualizations of plants. When we conceptualize animal stories, commonly in the form of constructing animal narratives or by the help of different media following or siding with the animals' perspective, we often talk of this as being "let in to" specific animal worlds. These specific worlds are limited by what each kind of animal may experience through its senses, but as we use our human technology, we may at the same time gain the outside perspective of an "all-seeing eye."

Another important issue is that our thinking with the nonhuman species is relative to the diversities of human cultures and the ways these relate to issues like differences between people (for example race, class, and gender). This again influences both scientific and cultural practices. This is especially evident when we start to think with plant species and plant bodies. According to Elaine P. Miller, the vegetal has in the Western tradition been associated with the feminine and even to a dark and passive state, mentally and physically, inferior to the brightly glowing animal energy.[15]

The Danish writer and dramaturge Ulla Ryum talks of the linear conceptualization of time in what she calls a traditional, "Aristotelian" storytelling as a forward moving stream or force driving the listener to stay in a controlled suspense.[16] As the story revolves around a singular event and centered on a main character, the audience is told to accept the conditions for the plot instead of investigating them. Ryum says that the linear temporality works at the expense of the cyclical and material conditions of our lives by letting one position exclude and displace the other. Both Ryum and Le Guin have made similar theories of a special, feminine, interspecies or inclusive storytelling, which I find useful. The theories of dramaturgy and non-linear storytelling and *The Carrier Bag Theory of Fiction* have some striking similarities.[17] Instead of focusing chronologically on a plot where a specific problem must be overcome by heroic effort, they want the story to evolve around a center in a spiraling or networking fashion. Tsing's *The Mushroom at the End of the World* is another example that this way of entangled storytelling may be valid not only in prose and playwriting but even in scientific research.[18] These spiraling or networking methods make it possible to let the story meander through different temporalities, to intertwine specific, situated, or mythological perspectives, and to link the fragments together in ways that are inclusive of multiple and often divergent experiences.

My work with the freshwater algae *Aegagrophila Linnaei* (Lakeballs, *Marimo* or *Kúluskítur* in Icelandic) has been an example of circling — a spiral action that I will

---

15   Elaine P. Miller, *The Vegetative Soul: From Philosophy of Nature to Subjectivity in the Feminine* (Albany: SUNY Press, 2002).

16   Ulla Ryum, "Om den ikke-aristoteliske fortælleteknik," NTK seminary report from *Dramatikern i dialog med sin samtid*, 2nd part, Reykyavik, June 4–11, 1982. See also Lisa Rosendahl and Kajsa Dahlberg, "Non-linear Narrative Structures: The Dramaturgy of the Spiral," lecture at the Oslo National Academy of the Arts, February 20, 2019, https://khio.no/events/817/.

17   Ursula K. Le Guin, "The Carrier Bag Theory of Fiction," in *Dancing at the End of the World: Thoughts on Words, Women, Places* (New York City: Grove Press, 1989), 165–70.

18   Anna Lowenhaupt Tsing, *The Mushroom at the End of the World: On the Possibility of Life in Capitalist Ruins* (Princeton: Princeton University Press, 2015).

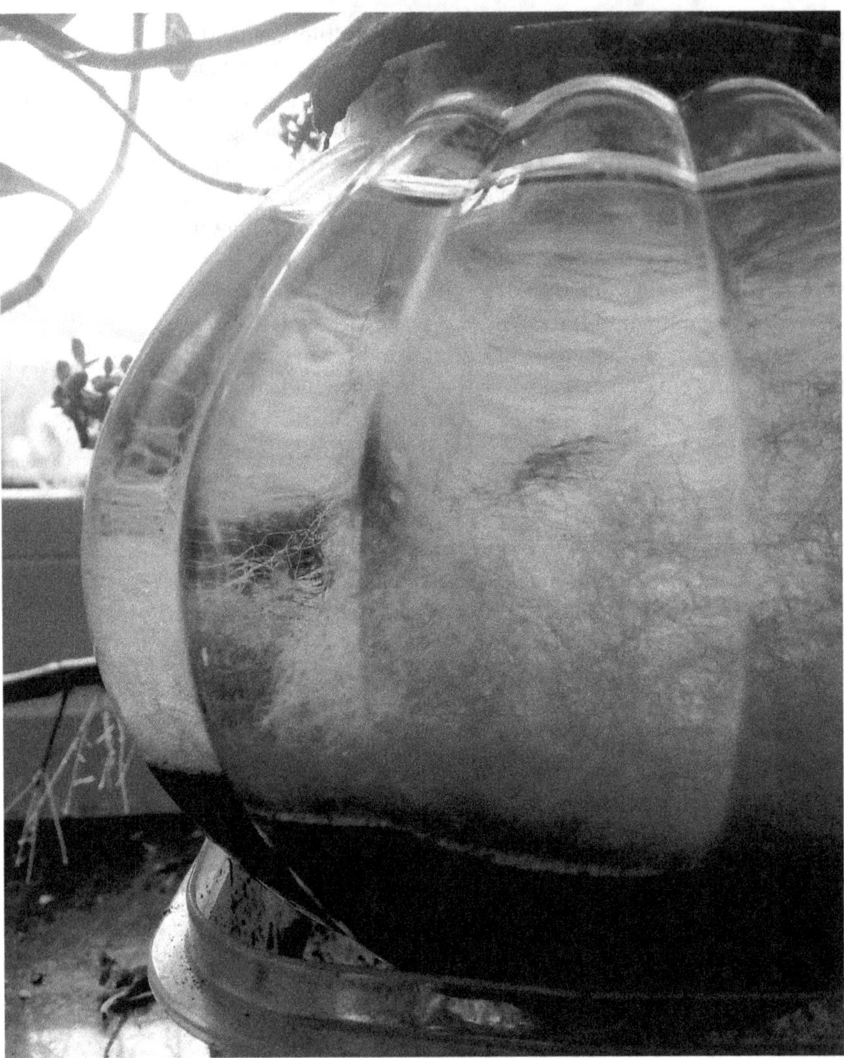

Fig. 6.4. Marimo, Spirogyra, Daphnia and Pondsnails create a small ecosystem. Photograph by the author.

probably continue for as long as my algae agrees to live with me. The daily listening to them inspires me to always keep my radar out for any new information concerning their species. At the same time, I now have three jars of bright-green balls that I have grown from just some small filaments from Icelandic "*Kúluskítur.*" I try to understand and assist their growing through using my senses, intuition, and experience. I have collected a lot of different kinds of interesting information about them, historical, cultural, and botanical. I have made paintings of them and filmed the microscopic life forms grazing on their branches. I've made research trips to Mývatn in Iceland and research-workshops to certain Swedish lakes where they could still be found in the 1960s. I have documented and experimented, but I will just present some images of them here. One thing that I had considered to do with my Marimo was to photograph them in similar settings every day, and then make

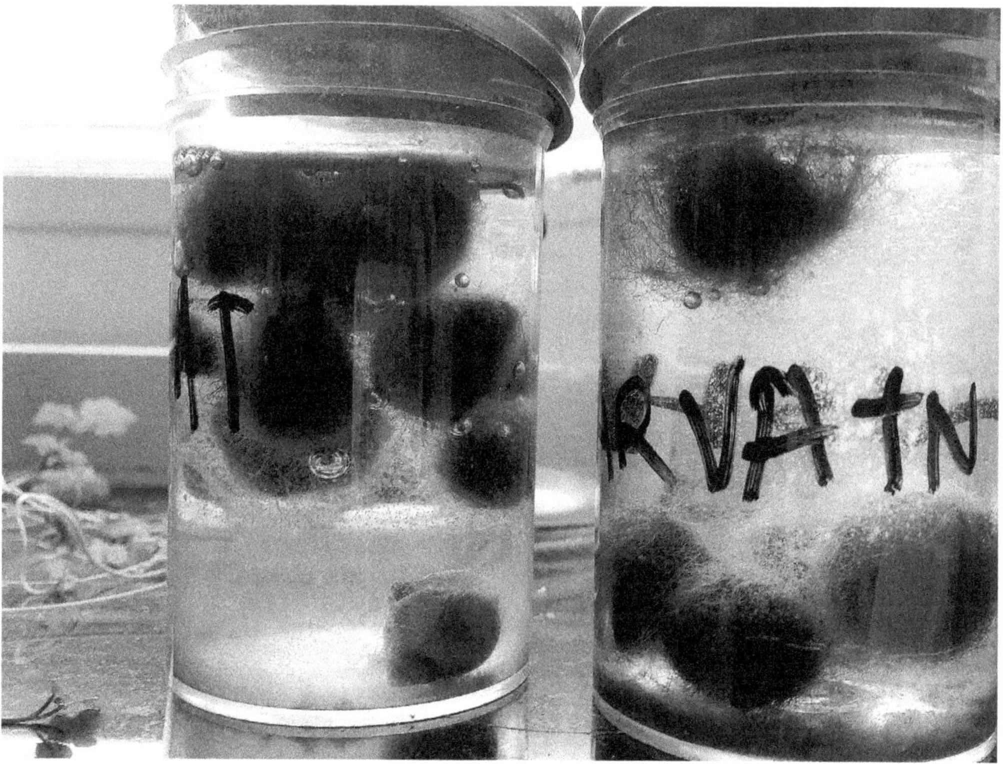

Fig. 6.5. Kúluskítur is the Icelandic name , I grow samples from Mývatn and Vatnshlíðar-vatn respectively. Photograph by the author.

a series to show their growth process. I would either show all these photographs, where apparently very little is happening, on the walls of a gallery space or make an animated film based on the images. But I found that this didn't really fit with the way I wanted to relate to my algae; it felt a bit too aggressive to photograph them this much and so scheduled. So, I just photograph them every now and then, when I feel that they express something. (See Figures 6.4, 6.5, and 6.6)

For my work with Marimo, I think the most important thing is that I recognize that the small containers are like worlds where a lot of different processes are going on. I may tap into these processes, but I do not run them. By following them, interacting with them, and by projecting my vision into them with photography, a microscope, or expressive painting, I want most of all to open my senses for the wonders of transformation and to take part in it.

As Elaine Miller writes about Goethe's investigation of metamorphoses of plants, it consists of an interplay between careful observation and expectant waiting.[19] And Goethe is aware that nature is not independent of the way in which it is approached by the human observer, that we structure nature in turning our thought to it. His scientific ideal does not presume a distant and neutral position;

---

19   Miller, *The Vegetative Soul,* 73. I personally think the ideal of the transformation of the observer may be due to, or at least inspired by, Goethe being a practicing alchemist.

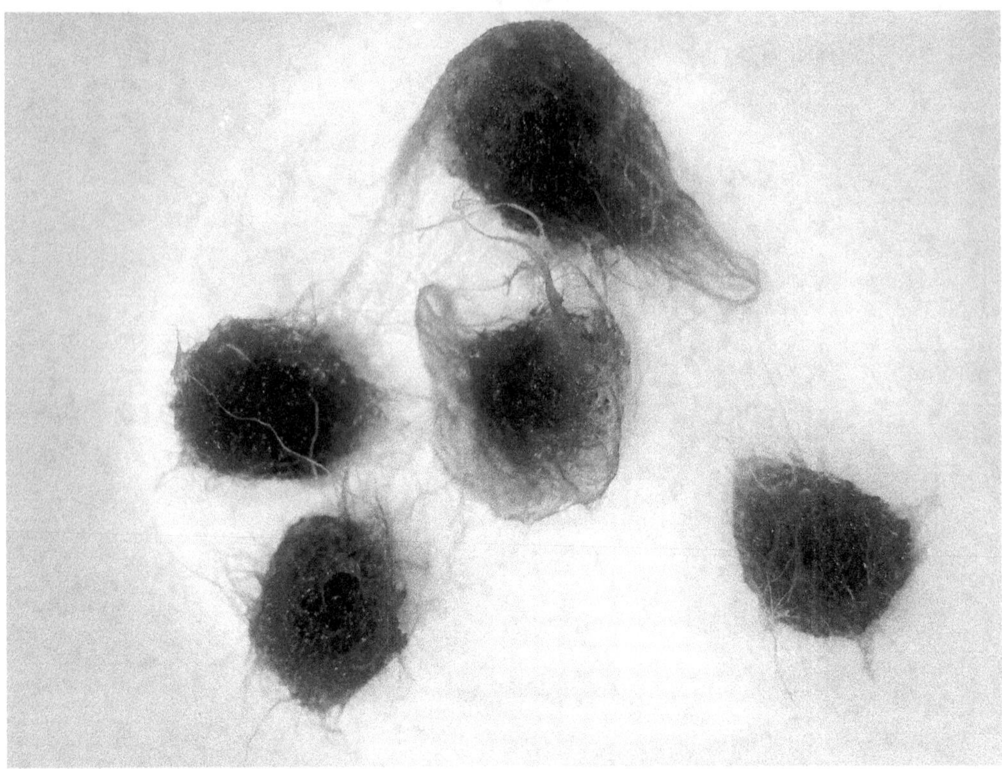

Fig. 6.6. Spring growth-burst. Photograph by the author.

rather, you should allow yourself to be transformed through following the transformation of the phenomena.

I'm not sure that it would help me to make a visualization of my Marimo's growth process by framing their expression in a linear way and a capture that in many ways align the plant temporality to a human's pace. I think that my attempt at making Marimo-inspired paintings is closer to my experience of living with it. In painting I find a media where time can be layered, like in a geological formation, and where sensuality, mysticism, and intuition may occur when my mood and will to express my experience meets with movement and materiality. Here, the expression of singular events that may have their root in different temporalities may coexist and be expressed as simultaneous and entangled, and it is obvious that my own mood and experience is part of the expressed.

Struggling with Nature Documentaries

The kind of narrative used in presenting animals lives even suggests how we can relate and interact with them. Species protection and reproduction is often foregrounded, and the species are in danger of being aestheticized or objectified as jewels in nature's collection. The underwater epic *My Octopus Teacher* is an example of a much more intuitive and process-oriented way of presenting the animal

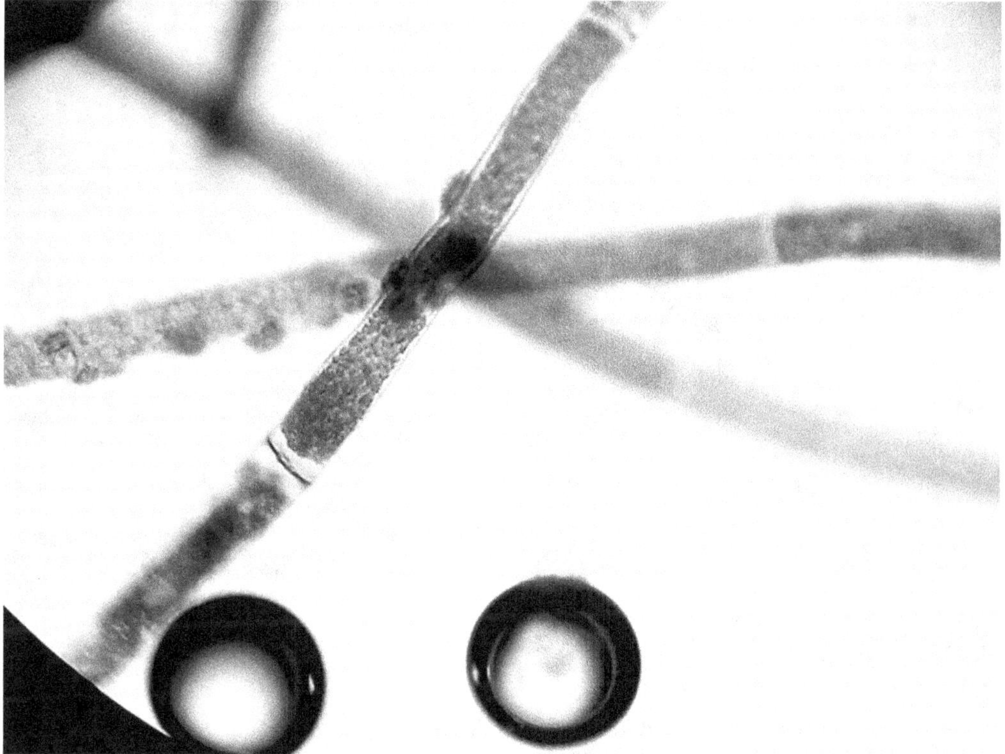

Fig. 6.7. The diatom species *Cymbella* abundantly "grazing" on the branches of my wild-caught *Aegrophila linnaei*. I have not been able to sustain *Cymbella* in my small tanks, though. Photograph by the author.

world to a human public.[20] In the 2020 documentary film, diver and filmmaker Craig Foster (yes, him again, from the *Great Dance*) tells us about how, during one year, through daily dives in the kelp-belt lining the South African shore, he managed to get very close to the animals living there. At one point, he finally felt that he was a part of the ecosystem, and that he belonged there. This film is as much about Foster's growing sensitivity and compassion as it is documenting animal behavior. At the same time, Foster tells us how much time, patience, and sensitivity to tracks and traces, which he started learning from the !Xo hunters, is necessary to get close enough to the animals' natural behavior to really understand the complexity of interaction in the "sea forest," as he calls it. When you start to reach this level of interspecies learning, the complexity of the ecological pattern is perceived in a very deep and mind-transforming respect for an intelligence in nature, which he calls the "forest mind." In this way, it is as much a story about his experience of kelp and kelp society as it is about the species that live in it.

In *My Octopus Teacher,* Foster decides to visit a certain shy octopus every day for a year. We see how she gradually starts to reach out to him, touch him, and explore him. She becomes a significant other to Foster, a teacher and a friend. And I think what makes this film special is that, although it's double narrative (one about the lifecycle of an octopus and a human while finding spiritual meaning in nature

20   Pippa Ehrlich and James Reed, dir., *My Octopus Teacher* (Netflix, 2020).

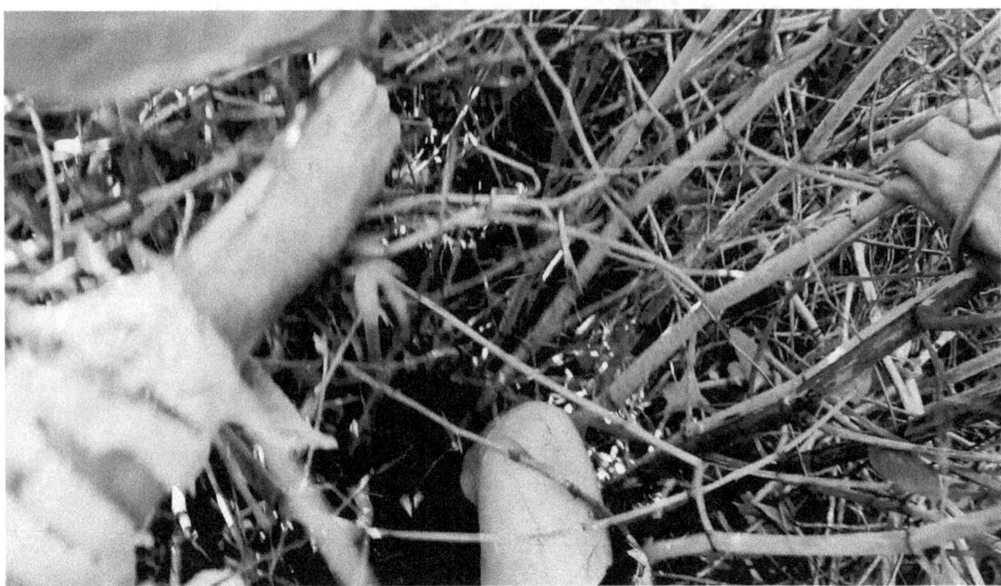

Fig. 6.8. The man's perspective at the second scene in the thicket, as his clothes are starting to tear. Film still by Nils Agdler/Fröydi Laszlo.

and the other about healing from depression) is told in a quite traditional way, it evolves around the fact that all encounters between humans, animals, algae, or plants, may change lives — both human and nonhuman.

My own experience is that there is a gap between my understanding of myself and the relation to the other species. It seems to be impossible to build understanding without some use of metaphor and construction of models. When I consider some animals and plants friends and family members, I register that I'm making projections. But, being projections of love, how could I do otherwise? These beings are significant personalities to me, and the closest I come is to model my feelings on what I feel for humans. I can't feel love in a totally abstract way, even if it would perhaps be more honest to do so. It seems to be common in most human cultures to construct concepts and models for all kinds of thinking, and doing so from a base in the senses, emotions, and the orientation of the human body in space and time. We must suppose that even other species construct some kind of meaning on a similar basis.

The octopus lady has indeed been a good ambassador for octopus intelligence, resourcefulness, and spirit.

What is perhaps most important when it comes to the issue of ethics in a multispecies context is a question on what ground we may build a deep respect and understanding of life on earth as something always overflowing the limitations of our concepts and ideas. Deborah Bird Rose and Thom van Dooren make several very good suggestions in their essay "Lively Ethography: Storying Animist Worlds," where they focus on ethos as a qualitative and sensorial way of being in the world, relating to it and to other beings.[21] The sensitivity to the ethos of other

21   Thom van Dooren and Deborah Bird Rose, "Lively Ethnography: Storying Animist Worlds," *Environmental Humanities* 8, no. 1 (2016): 77–94.

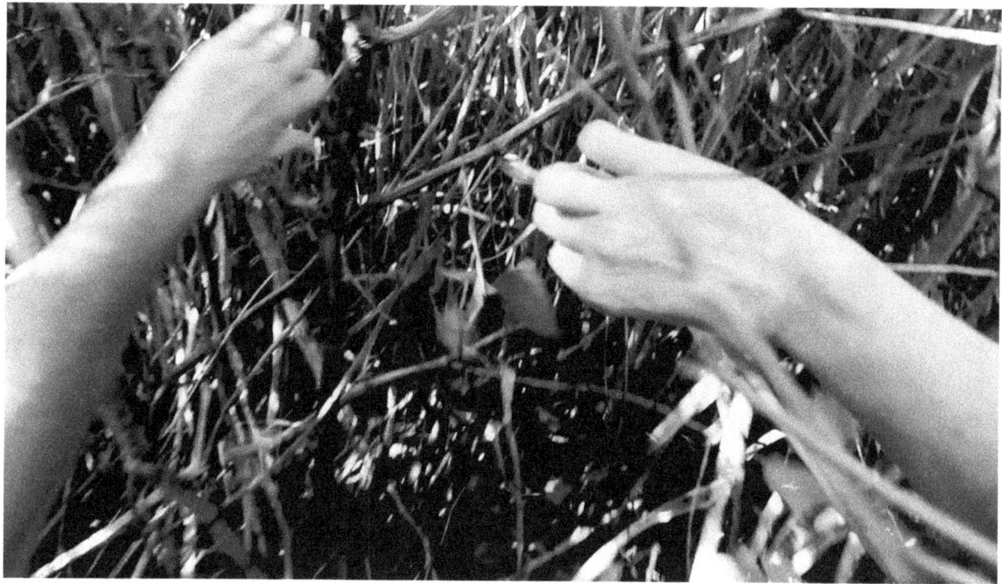

Fig. 6.9. The woman's perspective. Film still by Nils Agdler/Fröydi Laszlo.

species may in this way be both foundational to any ethics and something possible to share across species borders.

At the same time, as it becomes evident through films like *My Octopus Teacher,* different populations may share different ways of life. This is not just a question about species but of individual lives. Although perhaps genetically similar, different populations may represent different cultures and ethos.

Making Our Own Nature Documentary

In summer 2019, my artist colleague and friend Nils Agdler and I, along with a knotweed thicket, made a short film or filmed performance called "The Pest." After thinking for weeks about how difficult it is to be totally respectful, I tend to get frustrated and to do something rather playful and risk being a bit incoherent to relieve my stress. This time, I needed to confront my feelings toward the knotweed, as this plant-species had just some years ago cost me the chance of living in a house with a garden instead of having to cramp all my plants on a small balcony.

I could not have asked any actors to do the roles of this short film, as part of it was that I had to confront the knotweed myself and to test how it feels to be vulnerable and exposed while getting close to the plant. I wanted to show some naked, exposed humans, both attracted to and repelled by the plant, and even a sex scene without the pornographic sensibility. (The fact that Nils and I are two not-that-fit, middle-aged persons kind of helped out with that issue.)

My perspective has really changed several times during the process. First, knotweed is a pest getting in the way of human hopes and ambitions, but isn't it our own fault? If European botanists in the 1860s hadn't engaged in its dispersion it would probably still live a quiet and noninvasive life on some Japanese volcano

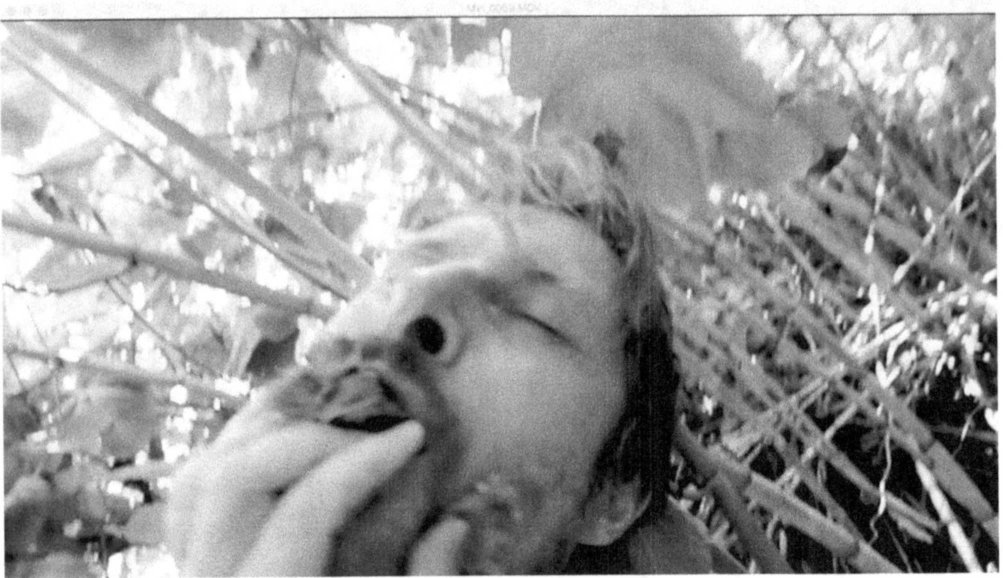

Fig. 6.10. Knotweed tastes ok but the foliage is quite rough. Film still by Nils Agdler/
Fröydi Laszlo.

slopes. Another shift in my perspective was the recognition that participating in a rather egoistical and consuming culture, I'm quite an invasive species myself. Nils and I did put a warning text in the beginning of our film, as the knotweed is an invasive species that should not be spread, but we even wanted to show it some love. We wanted to raise some questions about the harsh language often used when confronting the problems of invasive species — their being pests that have to be totally eradicated. Could we ever allow a language that so resembles racist rants against any being? Isn't the warlike metaphor always aimed at causing aggression and conflict instead of understanding the complexity of the problem, and trying to solve it using compassion and responsibility?[22]

"The Pest" has a linear and very classical structure but plays with different perspectives to raise questions about both human and nonhuman agency. The film begins when first a male and, later, a female reluctantly enter a dense and large knotweed boscage behind a bicycle path, as if escaping from the rather drab and noisy suburban landscape surrounding them. In fact, to enter the grove was challenging. Not only was it very dense but the stems would scratch and cut our bodies as we tore through them. In addition, we were soon infested by bloodsucking tics. Inside the thicket, portable cameras fastened on the man and the woman's head film the story, and the first-person perspective changes regularly between them. (See Figures 6.8 and 6.9).

The main characters set out on a mission to conquer nature only to find themselves trapped and their clothes torn by the plant. This is not only about a human subject being overcome by a plant, but even about how the camera may degrade

22   Thomas Michael Bach and Brendon M.H. Larson, "Speaking about Weeds: Indigenous Elders' Metaphors for Invasive Species and Their Management," *Environmental Values* 26, no. 5 (2017): 561–81.

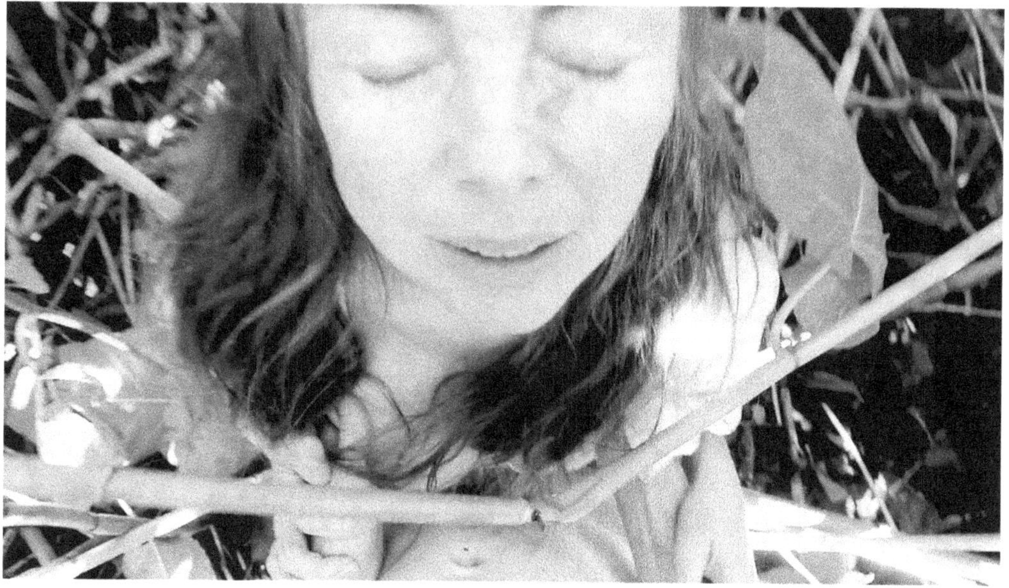

Fig. 6.11. This scene has a quite convincing soundtrack. Film still by Nils Agdler/Fröydi Laszlo.

and consume its object. The first-person perspective, and the more and more na-ked bodies, could just as well suggest a nature documentary done by the help of "critter-cam." The man and woman both strive straight forward through snapping branches and rough foliage to end up together at the hearth of the labyrinth. Here they find a sheltered and paradisiac clearing where they end up in each other's arms. As they are simultaneously eating the knotweed leaves and passionately en-joying their partner (see Figs. 6.10 and 6.11), even the story reaches a climax with their mutual orgasm. The camera's perspective changes after the climax, we now see the naked couple from a still camera and through some knotweed foliage. Even the humans are standing totally still embracing, and slowly they turn green (see Fig. 6.12). As we leave our Adam and Eve in their womblike paradise, the last im-age shows a newborn, green-skinned baby creeping out from the thicket.

We have seen the struggle to be "one with nature" transform the humans, first by becoming more animal and in the end by merging with the plant. But "The Pest" could even be seen from the perspective of an anthropomorphized plant being the brain behind it all. Then, the film could be read as a story of how two humans are lured into symbioses with a cunning plant. The plant will shelter them and feed them, but as they eat its leaves, they slowly turn green. In the end the humans seem to have lost all ambition to ever leave their small Eden again. It is as though they are being eaten by or incorporated in the plant, and they are now as sessile as it. The exception is the baby, the seed, which in the last scene crawls out to conquer or infest new terrain.

But is this a story about *Reynoutria japonica,* the knotweed? No, it is not about the plant itself. It is about humans brushing with it. But that is not exceptional. Does any human-made narrative really allow for an authentic nonhuman story? Do we really catch a glimpse of the animal's own world by using tracking equip-ment like GPS or cameras strapped to their bodies? Or plant stories by speeding up

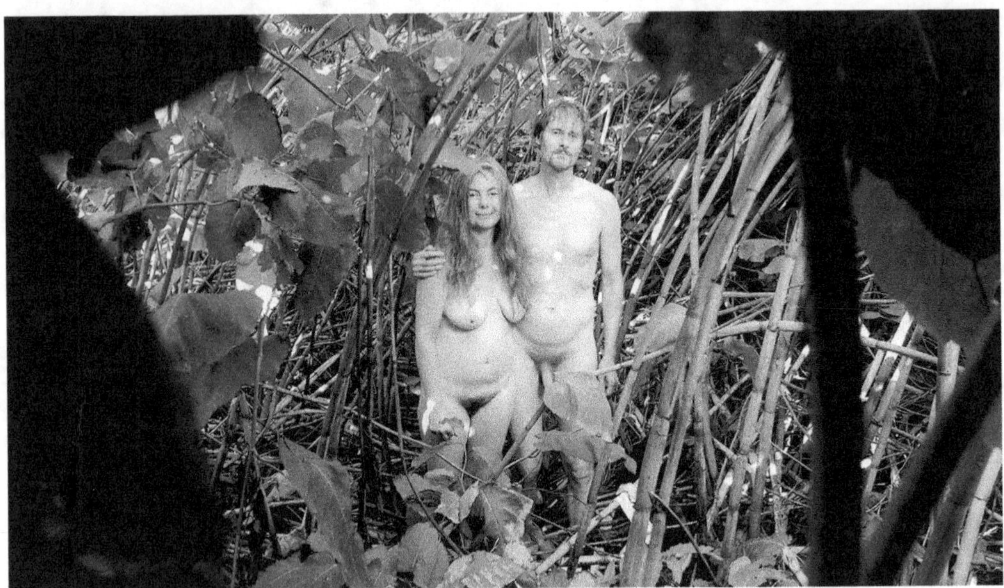

Fig. 6.12. The forest-dwellers about to turn green. Film still by Nils Agdler/Fröydi Laszlo.

their movements by time-lapse photography? I do not deny that these technologies may be vital to gathering important ecological information, but it has some disadvantages. Even if you call it a nature documentary, the story told is never neutral. We tell it from a human, cultural, and gendered perspective. Photography is no neutral technique, especially not when it comes to photographing the nonhuman. And, if it fails to create an empathic perspective, it is even a danger that the viewer's gaze may turn more predatory or voyeuristic than usual, as we get closer to the action.

Could Some Philosophy Help Me Sort Out My Questions?

In the beginning of this essay, I wrote that some foundational aspects of Ernst Cassirer's philosophy could be helpful regarding my art and thinking. One reason why I'm especially interested in Cassirer is that I had an uncle, a sociologist and philosopher, named Dag Østerberg who, in the 1980s, argued that Cassirer's philosophy could be more educational to present-day readers than Heidegger's work.[23] At my uncle's time, Cassirer was not much discussed, but today his thinking seems to have a renaissance. I have read Cassirer to and fro for some years, but I am no expert at all. I think that as I write from the position of being an artist and not a philosopher, I can be quite free in my speculations, which could add some original perspectives.

Cassirer's philosophy is often called neo-Kantian, but he is not trying to re-launch Kant's philosophy. In his thinking, which contains a wide and interdisciplinary spectrum of both historical and contemporary thinking, he combines

23   Dag Østerberg, *Metasosiologisk Essay* (Oslo: Universitetsforlaget, 1971).

elements from Kant, Goethe, and Husserl into a foundation for a philosophy that unites cultural critique and history with theory of science and embodied cognition.[24] His philosophy does not presuppose a transcendental and idealistic base for cognition, as is the case with Kant. Neither does Cassirer's philosophy create any dualism between mind and body. In his writing, he rather tries to analyze the entangled experience of being human as a both natural and social being, at the same time living in and creating its natural and cultural world.

Cassirer was one of the first thinkers outside the field of biology to relate to the theories of Jakob von Uexküll.[25] Both Cassirer and Uexküll were inspired by Kant's idea that *the thing in itself* is never really presented to us but only filtered through our sensorial impression of it. Uexküll widens this perspective to include even nonhuman animals and their different perceptual worlds. This changes the perspective (at his and Cassirer's time) of the world as an ordered system, where each species has a specific place, to the perception of an only partly perceptible myriad of worlds where the different species may have a multitude of entangled connections. These beings may be both subjects creating their own species-specific world of meaning, and objects in other species' *Umwelt*. Each being will include to it meaningful aspects of, and relations to, other beings and entities, while excluding irrelevant information. We may read Uexküll's turn as an early opening for a multispecies perspective, which from its base in biology, helped by philosophers like Cassirer, has spread through a variety of disciplines.

To Cassirer, the human cannot just simply receive a meaningful world based on signs filtered by the senses. Cassirer says that to be human is never just an individual experience, as the base of the human cognition is a triadic structure. He says that all our experience of being rests on or resonates with what he calls the "basic phenomena." This triadic structure may be explained as the human experiencing being a body (i.e., *I*) that relates to other bodies (i.e., *you*), which in turn involves the world (i.e., *it*). The basic phenomena are prior to all thought and inference and are the basis of both, Cassirer asserts.[26] In this way every action has and is experienced from within this structure.

I think that Cassirer approaches the concept of perception in an interesting way when he describes human reality as a network of different strategies of creating meaning in a shared world. Meaning is not just given; it is created in a dynamic field. He calls the human the *animal symbolicum*, which means that we are animals that create both ourselves and our reality when we are using different sets of symbols. Rather direct, emotionally laden expressions may in time be more and more

24 See John Michael Krois, "Philosophical Anthropology and the Embodied Cognition Paradigm: On the Convergence of Two Research Programs," in *Embodiment in Cognition and Culture*, ed. John Michael Krois et al. (London: John Benjamins Publishing Company, 2007), 273–89.

25 Jakob Johann von Uexküll (1864–1944), Baltic German biologist. His most notable achievement is the notion of *Umwelt*, meaning the environment that a species of animal perceives according to its unique cognitive apparatus. Animal behavior can thus be best explained if the environment is understood as a sphere subjectively constituted by an animal species. Uexküll is considered as one of the pioneers of biosemiotics.

26 Ernst Cassirer, *The Philosophy of Symbolic Forms*, Vol. 4: *Metaphysics of Symbolic Forms*, eds. John Michael Krois and Donald Phillip Verene, trans. John Michael Krois (New Haven: Yale University Press, 1998).

structured into different cultures, based on methods of knowledge and communication. The *animal symbolicum* possess symbolic systems that gives it access to symbolized worlds. By means of symbolic thought, humans were from their early states able to gain access to new perspectives and alter their surroundings, a fact which could lead to the co-evolutionary interaction between culture and nature.[27]

That mythology, as a way to systematically approach the world, derives from symbolic thought may not be a surprise. But to Cassirer, even language, art, history, and the natural sciences are seen as what he calls "symbolic forms." For me as an artist, the inclusion of art as foundational to human reality and society is very important. This means that art not only illustrates the world but it also produces new and important meaning and knowledge and opens the world to us. Just what a symbolic form is, or how many of these "methods of creating reality" there are or should be, is not the most important question for Cassirer. What is opened is the thought that any experience of reality, for us or any other life form, is related not only to the presence of perceptible information but even in how it is structured. This is partly limited by the body's senses, but then again the senses are trained and developed during interaction in an environment. It is typical for the human to create symbolic structures as a part of comprehending or taking in information. This could be seen as some kind of constant need for storytelling that appear spontaneously in an individual, but even has a collective impact when it becomes a cultural formation. Underlying stories from disparate fields like botany, logics, religion, music, or painting are all as "true" or as "real" as the other, it is of little use to search for absolutes. Cassirer asks us to look for the context of each "truth" to understand and analyze it. He uses the illustration of a curved line on a flat plane to demonstrate the method with which we approach what we want to define will likely limit what we find. To the geometer, the line could mean a quantitative relation between the two dimensions of the plane; to the physicist, the line perhaps shows a relation of energy to mass; to the painter a relation between light and darkness, shape, and contour. But of course, the line in itself may be all or none of these at the same time.[28]

In many ways we could see Cassirer as a media-philosopher before his time. Marshall McLuhan, the first to be named "media-philosopher," wrote that "all media are active metaphors in their power to translate experience into new forms."[29] His way of seeing media as an extension of the human body — changing both hu-

---

27   See Ernst Cassirer, *The Philosophy of Symbolic Forms,* Vol. 1: *Language,* intr. Charles W. Hendel, trans. Ralph Manheim (New Haven: Yale University Press, 1955); *The Philosophy of Symbolic Forms,* Vol. 2: *Mythical Thought,* eds. E.W. Orth and J.M. Krois, trans. Ralph Manheim (New Haven: Yale University Press, 1955); *The Philosophy of Symbolic Forms,* Vol. 3: *Phenomenology of Cognition,* eds. E.W. Orth and J.M. Krois, trans. Ralph Manheim (New Haven: Yale University Press, 1998), but the idea of the animal symbolicum is even summarized in Ernst Cassirer, *An Essay on Man* (New Haven: Yale University Press, 1944).

28   Cassirer, *The Philosophy of Symbolic Forms,* Vol. 3, 200–201. The same example appears in Cassirer's 1927 essay "Das Symbolproblem und seine Stellung in der Philosophie," in *Symbol, Technik, Sprache,* eds. E.W. Orth and J.M. Krois (Hamburg: Meiner, 1985), 1–22.

29   Marshall McLuhan, *Understanding Media: The Extensions of Man* (New York City: McGraw-Hill, 1965), 56.

man self-experience and the human world — echoes Cassirer's writing.[30] These two philosophers share the belief that the very construction of metaphor is rooted in a physical experience of being human bodies situated in time and space. I don't know if McLuhan was inspired by Cassirer or if the similarities in their thinking have other causes.

When Cassirer begun writing his philosophy of the symbolic forms, he took inspiration from the art historian Aby Warburg who put emphasis on the myths being founded in ritual action. Warburg said that prior to any mythical narrative, the ritual action served as containers for and expressions of emotions. Warburg regarded this as the basis of culture and gave special attention to the study of the representation of emotional expression in gesture, rituals, and depiction. This is another interesting aspect for me, being a visual artist and dealing with different media's ability to contain and translate emotional expressions. Cassirer agreed with Warburg that ritualized action is more elementary than language. The narratives we call "myths" offer explications of what people do; humans first engage in ritual actions and then interpret them verbally.[31]

In the 1980 book *Metaphors We Live By*, by cognitive linguist Georg Lakoff and philosopher Mark Johnson, they argue that our conceptualization of being in the world has its base in the human body and is expressed in the use of metaphor.[32] Some of these metaphors are foundational; for example orientational metaphors as "up" and "down." Even to something as "neutral" as orientation we design value; as "up" tends to go together with positive evaluation, while downward orientation goes with a negative one.

When Cassirer says "[t]he human body and its particular parts offer a kind of 'preferred system of relationships,' upon the basis of which the differentiation of space as a whole, and everything within it, can be referred to."[33] He is in line with Lakoff and Johnson's theory of concepts and the claim that concept formation depends upon metaphorical thought. It is even important that taking the body as the source of the "preferred system of relationships" includes emotional as well as cognitive aspects of understanding. This thinking of an original conceptual base in the body, its orientation in time and space and linked to emotional responses, foregoes a later formation of a system of values and strategies, which develops at the intersection of biology and learned or symbolic behavior. This is foundational for human ethics and narrative both, and I believe that this may even relate to our understanding of nonhuman species.

To Cassirer, bodily orientation in time and space is foundational to all the knowledge, myths, narratives, methods, and technology we develop. In his *Philosophy of Symbolic Forms*, Cassirer says that human technology, both scientific equipment and media, have a tendency to resemble and make more powerful

30   Cassirer, *The Philosophy of Symbolic Forms,* Vol. 2.
31   See Krois, "Philosophical Anthropology and the Embodied Cognition Paradigm."
32   Georg Lakoff and Mark Johnson, *Metaphors We Live By* (Chicago: University of Chicago Press, 1980).
33   Ernst Cassirer, *Die Begriffsform im mythischen Denken* (1922; Hamburg: Felix Meiner Verlag, 2009), 45, translated in Krois, "Philosophical Anthropology and the Embodied Cognition Paradigm," 285.

our own bodies.[34] Cassirer elaborates on the concept "organ-projection" by Ernest Kapp.[35] In short, the theory is that the *Homo sapiens* is learning about itself by making tools that expand its own body (e.g., hand-held tools like hammers, saws or drills expands the hand, all our optics expands our eye, and so on), this does not only work outward, helping *Homo sapiens* to expand its influence over its world, but even inwards, changing what it means to be a human. By creating new possibilities for bodily experience, we become something new both mentally and physically. We even understand our organs through our technology, as we say the eye works like a lens or perhaps that the brain is like a computer network.[36]

However, even the beaver building a dam or the knotweed, invading urban infrastructure are adaptable bodies that change what it means to live as respective species, by acting on and with new opportunities of their own making. As an artist, I don't see a foundational difference between creating a technological apparatus and the technics of utilization of animals or plants. These are both technological strategies and may even include media strategies, such as printing on plants in the form of paper.

I think it is something in the old alchemist Paracelsus's saying that all *Arcanum*, active ingredients, in any substance will be a poison in some dose even if it may be beneficial in another. Thus, unwrapping the agency of plants in my thinking sounds in tune with what Cassirer thinks about technology.

To Cassirer, the human animal is exceptional, so it is not so obvious that his thinking should lend itself to overbridging a gap between the human and the nonhuman species. But just as Cassirer departs from Kant, I will try to do a departure from his human-centeredness where I see that there is a chance to do so. Cassirer says that at some point in evolution, signal routines (which as I see it exist in both animals and plants) became rituals, and natural signals became cultural symbols. And, unlike most philosophy before him, Cassirer does not draw the demarcation between the human and the nonhuman animals on the ability to reason but instead by the ability for mythological thought. To Cassirer "[s]ymbolism makes rationality possible, but much more as well," and Cassirer even credits animals with some degree of mythical or ritual abilities.[37] He is very early at writing about neurological function in a philosophical context when he draws parallels between a spider that needs to follow a symbolic routine before it may recognize what has been trapped in its net as prey and the experiences of a neurological patient named Schneider who is only able to follow his doctor's instruction to knock on the door if it is followed with a sentence like "to see if somebody is in."[38] And it is clear that many nonhuman species make use of what we call rituals and symbolic actions to participate in and structure their perceptual worlds. The question is at what stage we may call this a culture.

34   Cassirer, *The Philosophy of Symbolic Forms*, 2:215–18.
35   Ernest Kapp, "Grundlinien einer Philosophic der Technik" (Braunschweig: G. Westermann, 1877).
36   See McLuhan on electricity and the nervous system in *Understanding Media*, 57, 68.
37   Krois, *Philosophical Anthropology*, 283.
38   Ibid., 281.

Conclusion

My departure has been in the argument that different species live in different kinds of worlds, depending on their physiology and needs. Both Cassirer and Uexküll thought that animals have access to a much more direct and instinctive experience of the shared world than humans, but none of them say much about how and why it should be so.

Even if a view of existence as composed of simultaneous "perceptual bubbles" may give a process-oriented and open view of the environment, there are some issues that should not be ignored, such as discussing perceptual world and cultural projections. If we go with the model of the bubble, each being is hidden behind and make use of a perceptual screen, which in many ways lights its existence as a more or less solo performance, where the actor at death returns to darkness. The trope of darkness even exists in the metaphor of perceptual blind spots and even in imagining the perception of time as a rhythmic procession of frames. Even if Uexküll's *Umwelt* concept builds heavily on sight, sensorial blindness could just as well be to the olfactory, infrared, audible, or other. Each being in this way becomes a player on a separated perceptual stage, in a world that is mostly imperceptible.

However, perception does not equal agency nor does it participation. If we want to move our story closer to the ecological functions on earth, there will be no lit stages or silenced audiences, and no big changes when it comes to playing a role between living and nonliving material. It is a general question if alien agency needs analytic capture and translation to be recognizable, or if we as Merleau-Ponty has suggested may at any moment surrender to a mode of existence that is neither a personal perception from within the "bubble" of the self, nor the world brought to the senses through the "screen" of carnality.[39] Merleau Ponty likens the preconceptual perception of immersion in existence with tapping into a dynamic silence.[40]

I have foregrounded that the perceptual world of any species is something created in an active process, including interplay between action, signaling, response procession (in many cases, we could call this learning), and biological factors. Some responses and action patterns may be translatable over species borders, others not. To understand this, Karen Barad may be of help when she talks of "intra-action."[41] Here she opens the perspective on action from focusing on an agency motivated by the will or need of the individual to the more complex interrelations involving both other life forms and material factors that may follow any change.

My conclusion is that we, as humans, are always resonating and developing within a web of intra-action, shared with other humans, nonhumans, and the

---

39 Maurice Merleau-Ponty, *The Visible and the Invisible*, ed. Claude Lefort, trans. Alphonso Lingis (Evanston: Northwestern University Press, 1968).

40 Ted Toadvine, "The Reconversion of Silence and Speech," *Tijdschrift voor filosofie* 70, no. 3 (2008): 457–77.

41 Karen Barad, *Meeting the Universe Halfway: Quantum Physics and the Entanglement of Matter and Meaning* (Durham: Duke University Press, 2007). Here Karen Barad's concept "intra-action" makes a replacement for the term "interaction"—which necessitates pre-established bodies that then participate in action with each other—which may be of help. Intra-action understands agency as not an inherent property of an individual or human to be exercised, but as a dynamism of forces (141).

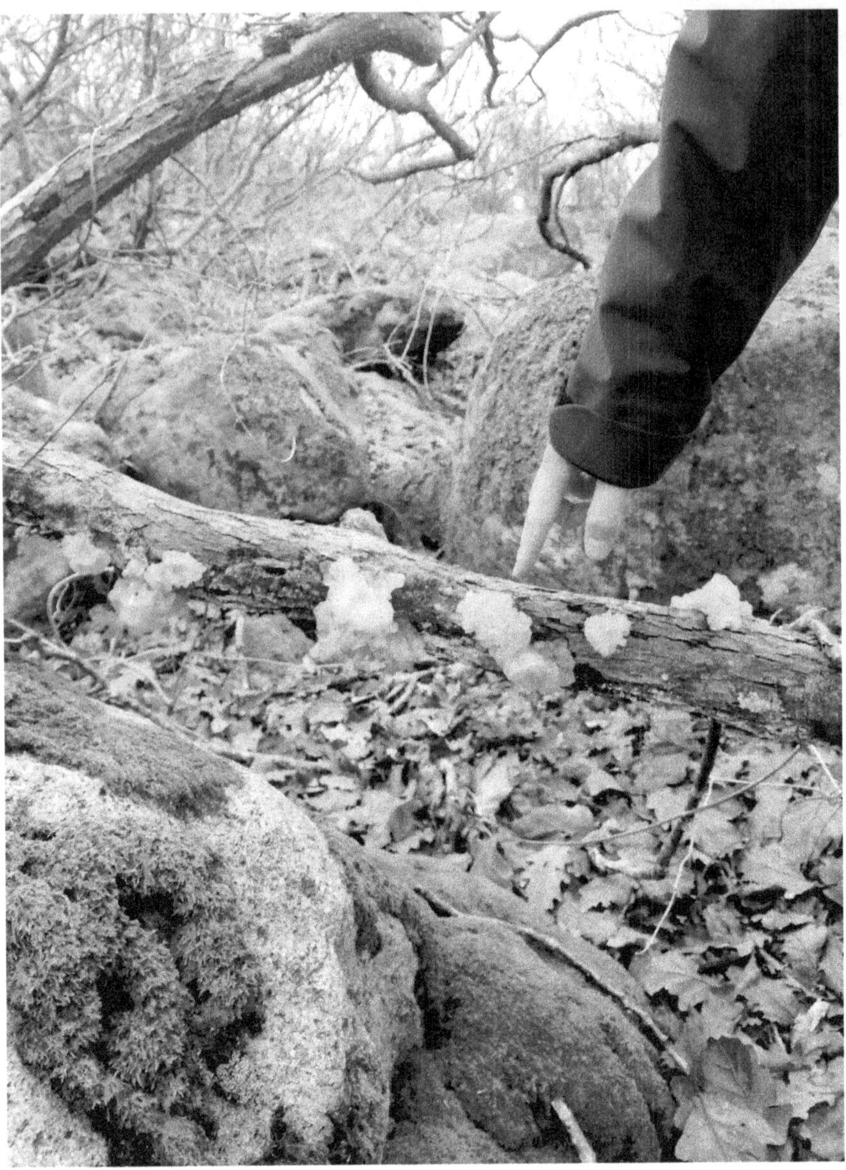

Fig. 6.13. Art project/field trip to see how local slime moulds may relocate themselves during a week. Photograph by the author.

physical and material conditions at both smaller and larger scales. We are always involved in complex natural and cultural processes of learning. All our different storytelling from science to poetry, myth to religion, work from different angles to make us integrate the understanding of being an "I" in a constant and unavoidable relation to both a "you" and an "it."

An important multispecies perspective seems to open if we put the foundation of an integrated self, a symbolic capability and even the possibility to be an ethical subject at a preconceptual level. For a philosopher like Cassirer, the individuality of the "I" does not go before the "you" or the "it," our experience of being human is tripartite. The entwining and integration of these three modes or perspectives are equally necessary to create any form of meaning; the basic phenomena are foundational to and forego any thought.

The ritualized action of Cassirer and Warburg is also preconceptual, it is a way of sharing emotions which in time may bring these emotions into systems that create shared values, and the beginning of a culture. As I see it, this obviously happens in some animal populations and even in many interspecies relations. In time we may learn to recognize what we may call cultural formations in more and more animal, plant, and even others, sometimes called "lower" species. As an example, French biologist Audrey Dussutour has researched learning and memory in varieties of the slime mold, *Physarum polycephalum* (see Fig. 6.13), and found that varieties from different continents have different "specialties." For instance, the Japanese slime mold was the fastest to grow toward and reach its food source; the Australian one was the most exact, and the American the fastest and most "greedy" consumer. As an anecdote Dussutour tells that when the food source was ecological oatmeal, the Australian and Japanese slime molds were both eager to consume it, but the American one did not want to touch it. This slime mold instead preferred a well-known American brand. Perhaps even behavior like this could be described as cultural differences within the species?[42]

It is obvious that there is always signaling present, some signs are shared between species that have the perception to register and to make meaning from it, or not. As humans, we are always creating and taking part in stories that have different effect on different species, even without us noticing. The body may both be the sender of a message and an inscribed media, and what may be considered both media and message is very different from species to species. As an example, plants communicate chemically, often at trans-species level, both through earth and air, and in ways that is still known rather little about.

Each being has unique experiences, and very different ways of expressing this. Language and expression are relative to body and physical factors, so if we speak of multispecies storytelling in a more-than-human context, the varying media that may possibly carry and transmit the different stories relate to anatomy, morphology, and translation. Listening to other species may be done with the help of technology or as mystical experiences and will never be a waste of time even if we may not understand much initially. And, the story is never just about the storytelling, but even the sensitivity of the good listeners and the potential for learning and transformation.

The initial state of multispecies entanglement on earth is still one of uncontrollable overflow and abundance, which may bring forth both joy, wonder, and a will to take an ethical and responsible consequence.

---

42 Jacques Mitch, dir., *Le blob, un génie sans cerveau* (ARTE France - Hauteville Productions - CNRS Images / Avec la participation de Planète+, 2019).

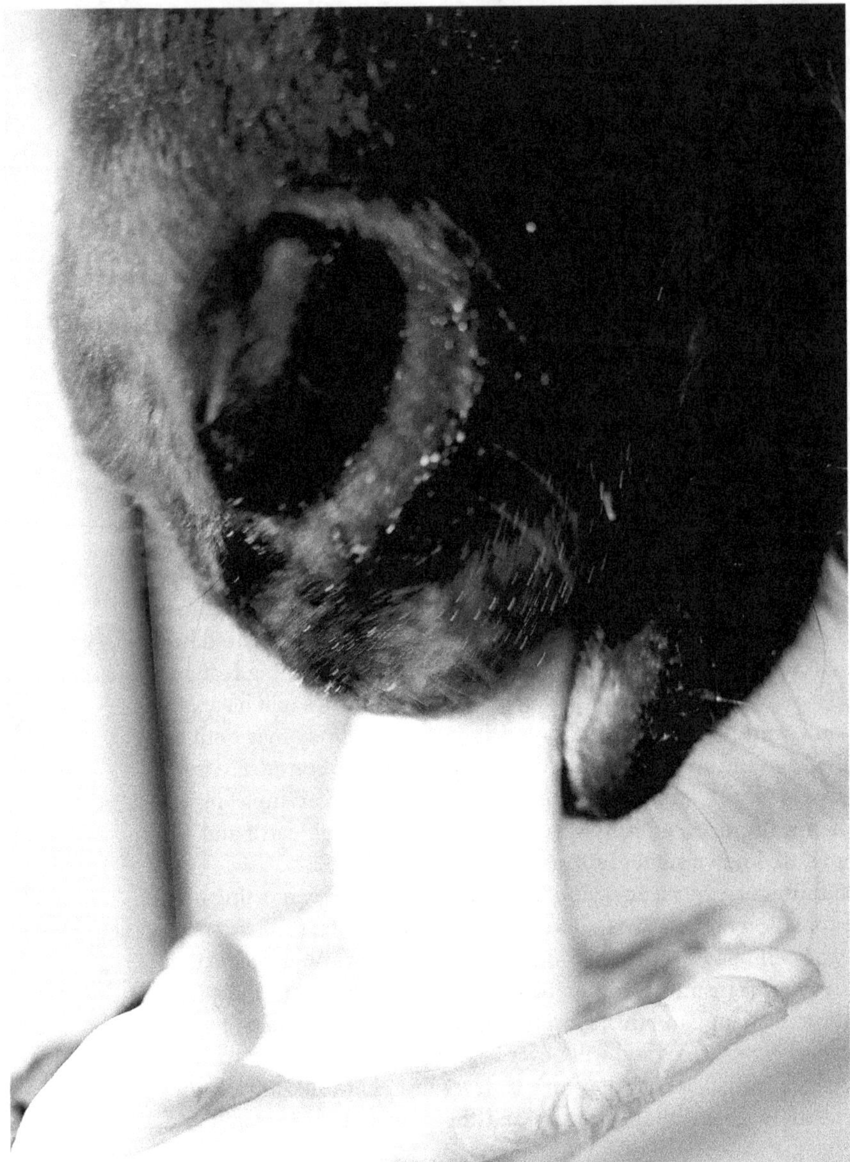

Fig. 6.14. Thank you for sharing your time with me. Photograph by the author.

References

Bach, Thomas Michael, and Brendon M.H. Larson. "Speaking about Weeds: Indigenous Elders' Metaphors for Invasive Species and Their Management." *Environmental Values* 26, no. 5 (2017): 561–81. DOI: 10.3197/096327117X15002190708119.

Barad, Karen. *Meeting the Universe Halfway: Quantum Physics and the Entanglement of Matter and Meaning.* Durham: Duke University Press, 2007.

Berger, John. "Why Look at Animals." In *About Looking,* 3–28. London: Pantheon Books, 1980.

Cassirer, Ernst. *An Essay on Man.* New Haven: Yale University Press, 1944.

———. "Das Symbolproblem und seine Stellung in der Philosophie." In *Symbol, Technik, Sprache,* edited by E.W. Orth and J.M. Krois, 1–22. Hamburg: Meiner, 1985.

———. *Die Begriffsform im mythischen Denken.* Hamburg: Felix Meiner Verlag, 2009.

———. *The Philosophy of Symbolic Forms,* Vol. 1: *Language.* Introductory note by Charles W. Hendel. Translated by Ralph Manheim. New Haven: Yale University Press, 1955.

———. *The Philosophy of Symbolic Forms,* Vol. 2: *Mythical Thought.* Edited by E.W. Orth and J.M. Krois. Translated by Ralph Manheim. New Haven: Yale University Press, 1955.

———. *The Philosophy of Symbolic Forms,* Vol. 3: *Phenomenology of Cognition.* Edited by E.W. Orth and J.M. Krois. Translated by Ralph Manheim. New Haven: Yale University Press, 1998.

———. *The Philosophy of Symbolic Forms,* Vol. 4: *Metaphysics of Symbolic Forms Including the Text of Cassirer's Manuscript on Basis Phenomena.* Edited by John Michael Krois and Donald Phillip Verene. Translated by John Michael Krois. New Haven: Yale University Press, 1998.

Ehrlich, Pippa, and James Reed, dir. *My Octopus Teacher.* Netflix, 2020.

Haraway, Donna J. *When Species Meet.* Minneapolis: University of Minnesota Press, 2007.

Holdrege, Craig. "Goethe and the Evolution of Science." *In Context* 31 (2014): 10–23. https://www.natureinstitute.org/article/craig-holdrege/goethe-and-the-evolution-of-science/.

Kalver, Irene. "Reclaiming Rivers from Homogenization: Meandering and Riverspheres." In *From Biocultural Homogenization to Biocultural Conservation,* edited by Ricardo Rossi, Roy H. May Jr., F. Stuart Chaplin III, Francisca Massardo, Michael C. Gavin, Irene J. Klaver, Aníbal Pauchard, Martin A. Nuñez, and Daniel Simberloff, 49–69. Cham: Springer, 2018.

Kapp, Ernest. *Grundlinien einer Philosophie der Technik.* Braunschweig: G. Westermann Verlag, 1877.

Krois, John Michael. "Philosophical Anthropology and the Embodied Cognition Paradigm: On the Convergence of Two Research Programs." In *Embodiment in Cognition and Culture,* edited by John Michael Krois, Mats Rosengren, Angela Steidele, and Dirk Westerkamp, 273–89. Amsterdam: John Benjamins Publishing Company, 2007.

Lakoff, George, and Mark Johnson. *Metaphors We Live By.* Chicago: University of Chicago Press, 1980.

Le Guin, Ursula K. "The Author of the Acacia Seeds and Other Extracts from the Journal of the Association of Therolinguistics." In *Fellowship of the Stars,* edited by Terry Carr, 170–78. New York: Simon & Schuster, 1974.

———. "The Carrier Bag Theory of Fiction." In *Dancing at the End of the World: Thoughts on Words, Women, Places,* 165–70. New York: Grove Press, 1989.

———. *The Word for World Is Forest.* New York City: Berkley Books, 1976.

———. "Vaster Than Empires and More Slow." In *New Dimensions 1: Fourteen Original Science Fiction Stories,* edited by Robert Silverberg, 87-123. New York City: Doubleday, 1971.

Lowenhaupt Tsing, Anna. *The Mushroom at the End of the World: On the Possibility of Life in Capitalist Ruins.* Princeton: Princeton University Press, 2015.

Merleau-Ponty, Maurice. *The Visible and the Invisible.* Edited by Claude Lefort. Translated by Alphonso Lingis. Evanston: Northwestern University Press, 1968.

McLuhan, Marshall. *Understanding Media: The Extensions of Man.* New York City: McGraw-Hill, 1965.

Miller, Elaine P. *The Vegetative Soul: From Philosophy of Nature to Subjectivity in the Feminine.* Albany: SUNY Press, 2002.

Mitch, Jacques, dir. *Le blob, un génie sans cerveau.* ARTE France - Hauteville Productions - CNRS Images / Avec la participation de Planète+, 2019.

Mulvey, Laura. "Visual and Other Pleasures." In *Visual Pleasure and Narrative Cinema,* 14–31. London: Palgrave Macmillan, 1986.

Østerberg, Dag. *Metasosiologisk Essay.* Oslo: Universitetsforlaget, 1971.

Rosendahl, Lisa, and Kajsa Dahlberg "Non-linear Narrative Structures: The Dramaturgy of the Spiral," lecture at the Oslo National Academy of the Arts, February 20, 2019, https://khio.no/events/817/.

Ryum, Ulla. "Om den ikke-aristoteliske fortælleteknik," NTK seminary report from *Dramatikern i dialog med sin samtid,* 2nd part, Reykjavik, June 4–11, 1982.

Steiger, E. *Der Briefwechsel zwischen Schiller und Goethe,* Bd. I. Frankfurt: Insel Verlag, 1977.

Strabo. *Geographica.* Edited by A. Meineke. Leipzig: Teubner, 1877.

Tagg, John. *The Disciplinary Frame: Photographic Truths and the Capture of Meaning.* Minneapolis: University of Minnesota Press, 2009.

Tomaníc, Ilija T., and John Tagg. "Governmentality and the Image." *Membrana* 1, no. 1 (2016). https://www.membrana.org/interview/governmentality-and-the-image-an-interview-with-john-tagg/. DOI: 10.47659/m1.024.int.

Toadvine, Ted. "The Reconversion of Silence and Speech." *Tijdschrift voor filosofie* 70, no. 3 (2008): 457–77. https://www.jstor.org/stable/40890443/.

van Dooren, Thom, and Deborah Bird Rose. "Lively Ethnography: Storying Animist Worlds." *Environmental Humanities* 8, no. 1 (2016): 77–94. DOI: 10.1215/22011919-3527731.

von Goethe, Johan Wolfgang. *Faust, Part 1.* Tübingen, 1808.

Wandersee, J.H., and E.E. Schussler. "Preventing Plant Blindness." *The American Biology Teacher* 61 (1999): 82–86. DOI: 10.2307/4450624.

CHAPTER 7

Arrangements for an African Anthropocene: Multispecies Storytelling at the Adderley Street Flower Market in Cape Town

Melanie Boehi

On a spring day in September in 2018, an exhibition of flower arrangements took place at the Adderley Street flower market in Cape Town, South Africa. Among the displays were a pyramid of fynbos shrubbery and arum lilies, spray-painted in metallic blue and orange; a vase full of white arum lilies, orange strelitzias, and green leaves; and a round, compact design with a pink protea flower at its center, surrounded by yellow pincushions, red Barberton daisies, and wild olive leaves. These flower arrangements told stories about history and life in an "African Anthropocene."[1] They were stories about their makers' relationships to the flora, the land, and the environment of the Cape region, personal and intergenerational histories of migration, contemplations of nostalgia, and aspirations for the future. They were stories told by people together with plants, by plants together with people, and by human-vegetal assemblages.

The flower arrangements were displayed during an installation of *Storytelling in the Language of Flowers* during the Institute for Creative Arts Live Art Festival as part of curator Cornelia Knoll's public art program "In the Time of the Anthropocene."[2] *Storytelling in the Language of Flowers* is a multidisciplinary project by Nowseum with the aim to research and document stories about life in an African Anthropocene.[3] Inspired by the use of flowers as a means of communication by both plants and people, it playfully references the idea of floriography, a coded language of flowers that is practiced through the exchange of floral gifts. The festival installation included four connected segments: a flower show with flower arrangements made by flower sellers; a public floristry workshop; the dis-

---

1   The term of an African Anthropocene was introduced by Gabrielle Hecht, "Interscalar Vehicles for an African Anthropocene: On Waste, Temporality, and Violence," *Cultural Anthropology* 33, no. 1 (2018): 109–41, and Gabrielle Hecht, "The African Anthropocene," *Aeon*, February 6, 2018, https://aeon.co/essays/if-we-talk-about-hurting-our-planet-who-exactly-is-the-we.

2   "ICA's Celebration of Live Art," *University of Cape Town News*, August 27, 2018, https://www.news.uct.ac.za/article/-2018–08–27-icas-celebration-of-live-art/.

3   Melanie Boehi, "Storytelling in the Language of Flowers," *Nowseum*, https://nowseum.com/2018/09/18/storytelling-in-the-language-of-flowers/.

tribution of a series of flower-wrapping papers which could be recycled into a newspaper, called *Cape Town Floriography Papers*; and a sound installation with the title *arrangement for new flowers*.

This chapter explores how multispecies storytelling evolved in *Storytelling in the Language of Flowers* as a narrative strategy to bring together epistemologies, people, and places that have been segregated by histories of colonialism and apartheid. Following Donna Haraway, it approaches flowers as constitutive to worlds of "material-semiotic nodes or knots in which diverse bodies and meanings coshape one another."[4] The chapter asks how in the art project's storytelling activities, flowers and plants functioned not merely as passive vehicles for symbolisms and metaphors deployed by humans but how they actively participated in storytelling with an "ontologically entangled authorship."[5] The chapter suggests that because *Storytelling in the Language of Flowers* evolved as locally rooted, arrangement — an activity and aesthetic form that has throughout its history been inherent to human-plant encounters at the Adderley Street flower market — became central to the project's multispecies storytelling.

A dictionary defines arrangement as "something arranged such as: a preliminary measure; a piece of music that has been changed so that it can be performed by particular types of voices or instruments; an informal arrangement or settlement especially on personal, social, or political matters."[6] In *Storytelling in the Language of Flowers,* flowers were arranged as stories in activities not fully controlled by the human arrangers, which in turn rearranged human positionalities and subjectivities. Connecting the plants at the flower market to plants documented in archival records allowed for a rearranging of archives. The arrangement of music in the sound installation expressed hope for better future arrangements. These arrangements functioned as intermedia that inhabited spaces between conventional forms of media and were flexible and therefore suitable for not only marking but also transcending disciplinary boundaries.

1. Locating the Anthropocene at the Adderley Street flower market

Ever since the concept of the Anthropocene gained traction, it has been criticized for its ambiguous politics. Numerous alternative terms, such as the Capitalocene, Plantationocene, or Chthulucene, have been suggested to bring the politics of anthropogenic processes of climate change into focus.[7] Gabrielle Hecht proposed a further addition: an African Anthropocene.[8] Hecht argued that the framing of hu-

---

4   Donna Haraway, *When Species Meet* (Minneapolis: University of Minnesota Press, 2008), 4.

5   Donna Haraway and Thyrza Nichols Goodeve, "Nothing Comes without Its World: Donna J. Haraway in Conversation with Thyrza Nichols Goodeve," in Donna Haraway, *Modest-Witness@Second-Millennium.FemaleMan-Meets-Onco-Mouse: Feminism and Technoscience* (New York: Routledge, 2018), xix.

6   *Merriam-Webster Dictionary,* s.v. "arrangement," https://www.merriam-webster.com/dictionary/arrangement/.

7   Donna Haraway, "Anthropocene, Capitalocene, Plantationocene, Chthulucene: Making Kin," *Environmental Humanities* 6, no. 1 (2015): 159–65.

8   Hecht, "Interscalar Vehicles for an African Anthropocene," 109–41. Hecht, "The African Anthropocene."

manity as the culprit of environmental degradation neglects unequal distributions of responsibility and vulnerability. Africa is particularly affected by this. Despite much of the resource extraction at the core of anthropogenic developments having occurred in Africa, the continent is underrepresented in Anthropocene research. Hecht suggested the term "African Anthropocene" not as "continental essentialism" but as a strategy of "putting the Anthropocene in place" and as "a means of holding *the planet* and *a place on the planet* on the same analytic plane."[9] Rather than zooming into a place, she suggests using "that place as a point of departure for thinking about the Anthropocene and its multiple forms of violence."[10] *Storytelling in the Language of Flowers* takes up this call by locating the Anthropocene at the Adderley Street flower market.

The Adderley Street flower market is situated in the inner city of Cape Town, at Trafalgar Place, between the disused Standard Bank building and the Golden Acre shopping mall.[11] It is Cape Town's biggest flower market, consisting of thirteen stalls employing approximately thirty people. The flower market operates seven days a week, twenty-four hours a day, with a guard selling flowers at night. Most of the flower sellers are related to each other and belong to families who have been in the trade for several generations. Most vendors are women and identify as "Coloured"; a racial category introduced by the apartheid state to describe mixed-race people, many of whom were descendants of the enslaved people who were brought to the Cape from Southeast Asia and southern Africa during the rule of the Dutch East India Company.[12]

Stories about the origins of flower-selling in Adderley Street abound. Many of today's flower sellers can trace their ancestors' activities back to the early twentieth century. Some historians suggested that flower-selling began in the eighteenth century, possibly with enslaved people hawking flowers on behalf of their owners.[13] More likely, flower-selling began in the mid-1880s by vendors, some of whom were descendants of enslaved people, who were working independently.[14] This makes the Adderley Street flower market the oldest site in Cape Town where Black people have traded continuously to this day. Records concerning flower sellers initially entered archives when white settlers perceived their activities as a problem. In

9   Hecht, "Interscalar Vehicles for an African Anthropocene," 112. Original emphasis.

10   Ibid.

11   Melanie Boehi, "The Flower Sellers of Cape Town," *Veld & Flora* 99, no. 3 (2013): 132–35.

12   In this chapter I use the term "Coloured" to refer to people's self-identification and the process of racializing the bodies of flower sellers. The South African English spelling rather than the American English spelling is deliberately used for the term. I use the term "Black" in an inclusive way to refer to refer to all people whom the apartheid government had oppressed on racial grounds. When people use the term "Black" in a different way, such as to refer in a narrow sense to Africans, I highlight this in the text.

13   Barbara Campbell Tait, *Cape Cameos: The Story of Cape Town in a New Way* (Cape Town: Stewart, 1948), 113, and Lawrence George Green, *Tavern of the Seas* (Cape Town: Rustica Press Limited, 1947), 76.

14   Lance Van Sittert, "From 'Mere Weeds' and 'Bosjes' to a Cape Floral Kingdom: The Re-Imagining of Indigenous Flora at the Cape, c.1890–1939," *Kronos* 28 (November 2008): 110.

1893, the Forestry Department introduced permits for flower sellers to limit the harvesting of wild flowers, and in 1897 all flower-picking on Table Mountain was prohibited, forcing the vendors to travel further away to source flowers.[15] Protection of the flora was bound up with limiting poor, Black people's access to land and natural resources. The regulation of flower-selling was strongly connected to the wider colonial politics of conservation which justified the forced removal of people living in areas that were declared as parks or game reserves and whose subsistence activities were framed as poaching and then criminalized.[16] Critics pointed out the double standards of targeting flower sellers while allowing wealthy, white citizens to continue picking flowers undisturbed or to buy illegally harvested flowers.

Parallel to the vilification of the flower sellers as threats to the flora, a different process of stereotyping emerged that turned them into urban icons. In the early twentieth century, photographs of flower sellers were frequently reproduced on postcards, in local newspapers, and tourist guidebooks.[17] The latter listed the Adderley Street flower market as one of Cape Town's main tourist destinations and presented both the flowers and flower sellers as attractive sights.[18] The images and description of the flower sellers characterized them as female, poor, and Coloured or Malay. Portraits of flower sellers usually featured one or several women, dressed simply, wearing a headscarf, holding a bunch of flowers, and smiling at the camera. The vendors were imagined as happily serving middle- and upper-class customers, being well integrated into a colonial and postcolonial urban economy in which Black people cater to white people's needs. These gendered, racialized, and classed stereotypes have persisted throughout the twentieth and into the twenty-first century. A recent example of this is a large wall display at the domestic departure terminal of the Cape Town International Airport that depicts a woman flower seller at the Adderley Street flower market and bears the caption "*Sien djulle wee!* See you again!" with the colloquial, Afrikaans section printed in a larger font size to mark the vendor's racialized identity as a person classified as Coloured.

The images and imaginations about flower sellers say more about their producers than about the people working in the cut-flower trade who have always been a more diverse group than the stereotypes about them suggested. Contrary to the clichés, both women and men were involved in the trade, and their economic status ranged from working poor to middle class. The prominence of flower sellers in urban images and literature is not unique to Cape Town. Elizabeth Huneault analyzed how, in the nineteenth century, "flower girls" evolved as a popular discursive figure in European cities.[19] In spite of the fact that only a small percentage

15   Ibid., 119.

16   Maano Ramutsindela, *Parks and People in Postcolonial Societies: Experiences in Southern Africa* (Dordrecht: Kluwer Academic Publishers, 2004).

17   Cf. postcard collection in the National Library of South Africa, Cape Town Campus, PHA, CT. Composites; PHA, CT. Flower Sellers.

18   Cf. Josiah Robert Finch, *The Cape of Good Hope: Being the Official Handbook of the City of Cape Town* (Cape Town: Sid. P. Cowen, 1909), 127; Cape Peninsula Publicity Association, ed., *Cape Town and the Cape Peninsula: A Holiday Guide* (Cape Town: Cape Peninsula Publicity Association, 1940); John Muir, *Guide to Cape Town and the Western Cape* (Cape Town: Howard Timmins, 1976), 25; Peter Joyce, Jill Johnson, and Ashley Joyce, *Weekends in and around Cape Town* (Cape Town: Struik Timmins Publishers, 1991), 10–11.

19   Kristina Huneault, *Difficult Subjects: Working Women and Visual Culture, Britain*

of the urban working population was employed in the trade, flower vendors were depicted more often than any other occupational group. They were stereotyped as female, poor, and amenable to educational interventions by gentlemen or missionaries.[20] The discursive figure of the Cape Town flower seller can be traced back to that of the European flower girl. It was further shaped by the local, colonial context that racialized and exoticized the flower seller as Coloured and Malay and linked them to the history of slavery at the Cape.

Although flower sellers were highly visible, little attention has been paid to what has been going on beyond the images and imaginations. Like other colonized people, many narrators relegated them to the sphere of tradition rather than history. Yet, contrary to the perception of flower-selling being an old tradition that has always been there, the flower sellers have actively made their presence possible. At various moments throughout the twentieth and twenty-first century, the future of the Adderley Street flower market was put at risk. In the late-nineteenth and early twentieth century, sellers countered adverse conservation laws by sourcing flowers from further away and replacing wild flowers with cultivated ones. In 1965 the apartheid authorities proclaimed central Cape Town a White Group Area and announced that the flower market would be removed.[21] This triggered heated debates in the local press about whether the removal of a well-known tourist destination would negatively impact South Africa's international reputation. The flower sellers were allowed to continue to trade in the city, probably as a result of the reputational concerns, and also because they catered to white customers. In 1978, closure of the market was once more discussed when the municipality identified the presence of unhoused people as a problem.[22] As had happened before, the flower sellers' iconic status was deployed as an argument for allowing them to remain. In the early twenty-first century, the vendors faced new challenges in the form of infrastructure developments in Adderley Street for which they were not consulted, and increased competition from department stores. To gain leverage, they often referred to their status as the original flower sellers and thus inserted themselves into the city's heritage narrative that has continued to marginalize them — to this day, no official information board marks the flower market as a historical site. The flower sellers refused to be completely victimized by the racial, gender, and class stereotypes about them, but have instead used them as a resource for negotiating access to trading space and opportunities.

The discursive figure of the flower seller has not only been entangled with the lives of real people but also of real plants. The plants were not just passive objects that added color to the flower sellers' pictures but actively contributed to shaping the history of flower-selling, and the trade in turn influenced their biographies. The flower sellers' harvesting in the wild put pressure on some plant populations. From the early twentieth century, the vendors gradually replaced wild flowers with cultivated ones, which they either grew themselves or bought from farms. Many flower sellers lived in Constantia, which was a semi-rural, Black community until

    1880–1914 (Aldershot: Ashgate, 2002).

20 Jack Goody, *The Culture of Flowers* (Cambridge: Cambridge University Press, 1993), 224.

21 "No Flowers, by Order," *The Cape Argus,* June 22, 1965.

22 Keri Swift, "Blooming Trouble," *The Cape Argus,* June 23,1978, and "Flower Sellers to Get Council Support," *The Cape Argus,* June 22, 1978.

its designation as an exclusively white area under the apartheid Group Areas Act. As a consequence, its Black residents were forcibly removed, and it has since become one of Cape Town's most exclusive residential areas. Following the forced removals, most flower sellers lost the ability to cultivate their own plants. These developments made the cut-flower trade more capital-intensive and led to a concentration of fewer sellers with bigger stalls. Today, flowers of fynbos species are acquired locally, but exotic flowers are mostly imported, from greenhouses in the Gauteng region or further away, in East Africa. The cut-flower industry is infamous for its exploitative labor relations and adverse impacts on the environment, and it cannot be ruled out that some of the flowers in Adderley Street are embedded in these practices.[23]

Despite being cultivated and harvested on farms, flowers of indigenous plant species that are sold at the flower market are framed as representatives of wild plants. Cape Town is situated in the Cape Floristic Region, an area of about 90,000 km2 that is characterized by high levels of plant diversity (9,030 species) and endemism (69 percent).[24] In 2004, UNESCO acknowledged the "outstanding universal value" of the region when it placed the Cape Floral Region Protected Areas on the World Heritage List.[25] Many plants in the Cape Floristic Region are endangered or of conservation concern, for which climate change is a driving factor. As Deborah Bird Rose, Thom van Dooren, and Matthew Chrulew wrote, extinction not only affects a single species but "is an inherently and inextricably *biocultural* phenomenon."[26] In Cape Town, threats to the flora are threats to the larger social fabric, and the flower sellers are particularly affected by this. Due to the common perception of the cultivated indigenous plants as wild, the flower market, similar to a botanical garden, functions as a space for thinking about the future of multispecies relationships in the city.

The impact of the climate crisis on the Adderley Street flower market became particularly obvious during a drought which began in 2015.[27] The drought worsened to the extent that, in 2018, Cape Town announced the prospect of a "Day Zero" when the city would run out of water.[28] Water consumption was limited to fifty liters per person and day, and access to springs became an issue of heated

23   Cf. Gerda Kuiper and Andreas Gemählich, "Sustainability and Depoliticisation: Certifications in the Cut-Flower Industry at Lake Naivasha, Kenya," *Africa Spectrum* 52, no. 3 (2017): 31–53.

24   Peter Goldblatt and John Manning, *Cape Plants: A Conspectus of the Cape Flora of South Africa* (Cape Town: National Botanical Institute, 2000), 7.

25   UNESCO World Heritage Committee, "Decisions Adopted at the 28th Session of the World Heritage Committee (Suzhou, 2004)" (Paris: UNESCO World Heritage Centre, 2004).

26   Deborah Bird Rose, Thom van Dooren, and Matthew Chrulew, "Introduction: Telling Extinction Stories," in *Extinction Studies: Stories of Time, Death, and Generations,* eds. Deborah Bird Rose, Thom van Dooren, and Matthew Chrulew (New York: Columbia University Press, 2017), 5.

27   Piotr Wolski, "Was the Water Shortage Caused by Farmers, City Dwellers or Drought?" *GroundUp,* July 19, 2018, https://www.groundup.org.za/article/was-water-shortage-caused-farmers-city-dwellers-or-drought/.

28   Jonathan Watts, "Cape Town Faces Day Zero: What Happens When the City Turns Off the Taps?" *The Guardian,* February 3, 2018, https://www.theguardian.com/cities/2018/feb/03/day-zero-cape-town-turns-off-taps/.

debates that further highlighted the legacy of apartheid spatial planning.[29] The restrictions meant that the flower sellers had to reduce the amount of fresh water in which they kept their flowers, which increased the risk of spoilage. The drought also caused a price increase for flowers. Some vendors observed that demand shrank because customers didn't want to use their water quota on luxury items like watering flowers. Climate change will continue to have profound impacts on the multispecies community at the Adderley Street flower market.

The complex entanglements of human and plant lives make the Adderley Street flower market a suitable site for examining life in an African Anthropocene. Thinking from and with the flower market requires scrutiny of political, social, and environmental histories, on a local as well as a global scale. It demands considering the flower sellers, their family histories, and the history of forced removals; the plants that have become extinct as a result of the cut-flower trade; the laborers who are exploited in the production of cut flowers; and the environmental impacts of the cut-flower industry. Holding flowers at the Adderley Street flower market means holding together multiple histories of violence and entering a net of complex connections across time and space.

2. Arranging Flowers

Flower arrangements appear in many different forms at the Adderley Street flower market. Always on offer are "mixed bunches," the composition of which changes according to season and availability of the flowers. Customers often select flowers from buckets containing single species and ask flower sellers to arrange them. The vendors also regularly make arrangements for special occasions like weddings, funerals, corporate functions and religious holidays. Most vendors keep portfolios of past work in the form of a photo album or a collection of photographs on a mobile phone, in case customers need inspiration. Clients also bring images of arrangements and ask flower sellers to recreate them. Flower arranging is influenced by the human participants' knowledge, experiences, memories, senses, and imaginations. It is also shaped by plants. Some plants flower seasonally and are only available for limited periods. Plants' bodily forms influence the type of arrangement done with them because human arrangers take properties like their size, colors, vase life, or dried look into consideration. Flower arranging is further shaped by an agency which is neither fully located with the human or vegetal participants but with the human-vegetal assemblage that emerges in the process of flower arranging. Flower arranging is not merely an expression of human mastery over nature but of multispecies interactions.

Storytelling in the Language of Flowers positioned multispecies communication at the center of its activities. For the festival installation, each market stall was asked to contribute a flower arrangement for a once-off flower show. Since the 1870s, flower shows have been popular social events in the Western Cape.[30] The show at the flower market was one with twists and turns. Conventionally, exhibitors display flowers and arrangements made of plants gathered in the wild

---

29   C.A. Davids, "The Water Point," *Africa Is a Country,* August 8, 2018. https://africasacountry.com/2018/02/the-water-point/.

30   Julia Wood, "Spring Wildflower Shows," *Veld & Flora* 78, no. 2 (1992): 38–43.

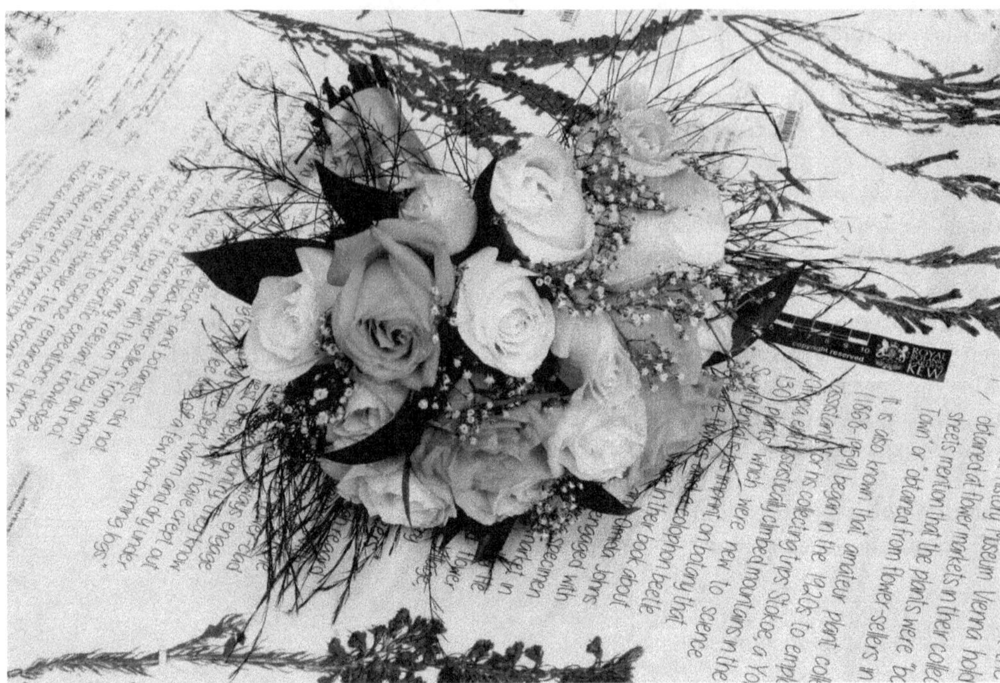

Fig. 7.1. Bridal bouquet made by Alison Snyders. Photograph by the author.

or which they have grown and compete for prizes. Most flower shows were predominantly attended by white exhibitors and visitors. For the show at the flower market, the arrangements were made of market flowers with the aim to tell stories about history, place, and belonging. It suggested that flower shows were not only spectacles of beauty and biodiversity but also sites of knowledge production that could bring forth complex stories.

The flower sellers were invited to respond to the theme however they wanted; the only restriction was a budget allocated to each stall. Some flower sellers made arrangements which told tales of their biographies and family histories. One of them, Sandra "Millie" Solomons, made an arrangement of proteas. She explained that she was "born in the proteas" because her family had for decades specialized in trading fynbos species.[31] Her mother would leave Cape Town on a Monday for the Grabouw area, pay local farmers to harvest on their properties, sleep over in a barn, and come back to the market on Tuesday. Following in their mother's footsteps, Millie and her sister Joan have worked at the flower market for decades. Today they no longer harvest flowers themselves but buy them through intermediaries. The proteas in Solomons's arrangement were entangled with biography and family history; they were a link through time to the generations that came before them, and through space, because they connected the market and the land where the plants grow. Alison Snyders recreated a bridal bouquet and explained that it

---

31　All quoted conversations with flower sellers or floristry workshop participants took place during the installation of *Storytelling in the Language of Flowers* on September 12, 2018, or during follow up interviews on September 13, 2018, at the Adderley Street flower market in Cape Town.

represented the joy of participating in customers' celebrating their love, as well as her own love for flowers and the flower market (see Fig. 7.1).

Several vendors made arrangements with a focus on plants that are classified as indigenous to South Africa to express pride in the nation's biodiversity. Gairoeniesa Oliver made a bouquet of flowers that are local to the lakesides of Cape Town, including arum lilies and reeds, and explained that "local is lekke" (*lekke* is colloquial Afrikaans for nice). The Cape's indigenous flora have for a long time been loaded with meaning in the context of settler colonialism. Van Sittert analyzed how, since the 1890s, appreciation of the Cape flora has evolved as a marker of white settler identity.[32] Jean and John Comaroff further analyzed how the discursive figures of indigenous and exotic plants became entangled with nationalism and xenophobia.[33] Yet settlers and white nationalists did not have a monopoly on ascribing meaning to plants. In Zoë Wicomb's *You Can't Get Lost in Cape Town*, settler narratives about indigenous plants wilt when one of the protagonists compares them with longer indigenous histories.[34] The flower sellers' arrangements also claimed more complex narratives through which the arrangers positioned themselves in the South African landscape.

One display directly connected the country's plants to its politics. Faiza "Poppy" Saliem made a bouquet of arum lilies, proteas, and strelitzias, and explained that it reminded her of the old South African flag (see Fig. 7.2). Because of its association with the apartheid regime, the display of the old flag, which was the country's official flag from 1928 to 1994, has in the post-apartheid era been regarded as inappropriate.[35] In August 2019, the South African Equality Court ruled that the "gratuitous display" of the flag constituted hate speech, unless it was for "genuine artistic, academic, or journalistic expression in the public interest."[36] Saliem's bouquet connected to the old flag through the plants' colors. Unlike hoisting the flag, the flower arrangement conveyed an ambiguous message. It could be read as a political statement, an expression of nostalgia, or a meditation on what Ann Laura Stoler describes as "colonial presence"; as that which is "past but not over."[37] Death is never far from a flower arrangement. Flowers wilt and rot, and from their organic matter new life can grow. Artist Kapwani Kiwanga demonstrates the power of flower arrangements as political comment in her work *Flowers for Africa,* for which she recreates flower decorations of African independence celebrations.[38] Kiwanga invites reflections on plants as witnesses of past moments and "alternative

32   Van Sittert, "From 'Mere Weeds' and 'Bosjes' to a Cape Floral Kingdom," 113–29.

33   Jean Comaroff and John L. Comaroff, "Naturing the Nation: Aliens, Apocalypse, and the Postcolonial State," *Social Identities* 27, no. 3 (2001): 233–65.

34   Zoë Wicomb, *You Can't Get Lost in Cape Town* (London: Virago 1987), 188–89.

35   John Hogg, "Flagged a Hate Crime," *New Frame,* August 23, 2019, https://www.newframe.com/light-reading-flagged-a-hate-crime/.

36   Ohene Yaw Ampofo-Anti, "Equality Court Prohibits Display of Old South African Flag," *GroundUp,* August 22, 2019, https://www.groundup.org.za/article/old-south-african-flag-constitutes-hate-speech-says-equality-court/.

37   Ann Laura Stoler, *Duress: Imperial Durabilities in Our Times* (Durham: Duke University Press, 2016); on nostalgia in post-apartheid South Africa, see Jacob Dlamini, *Native Nostalgia* (Auckland Park: Jacana Media, 2009).

38   Carina Bukuts, "Kapwani Kiwanga's Afrofuturist Garden," *Frieze,* October 27, 2020, https://www.frieze.com/article/kapwani-kiwangas-afrofuturist-garden.

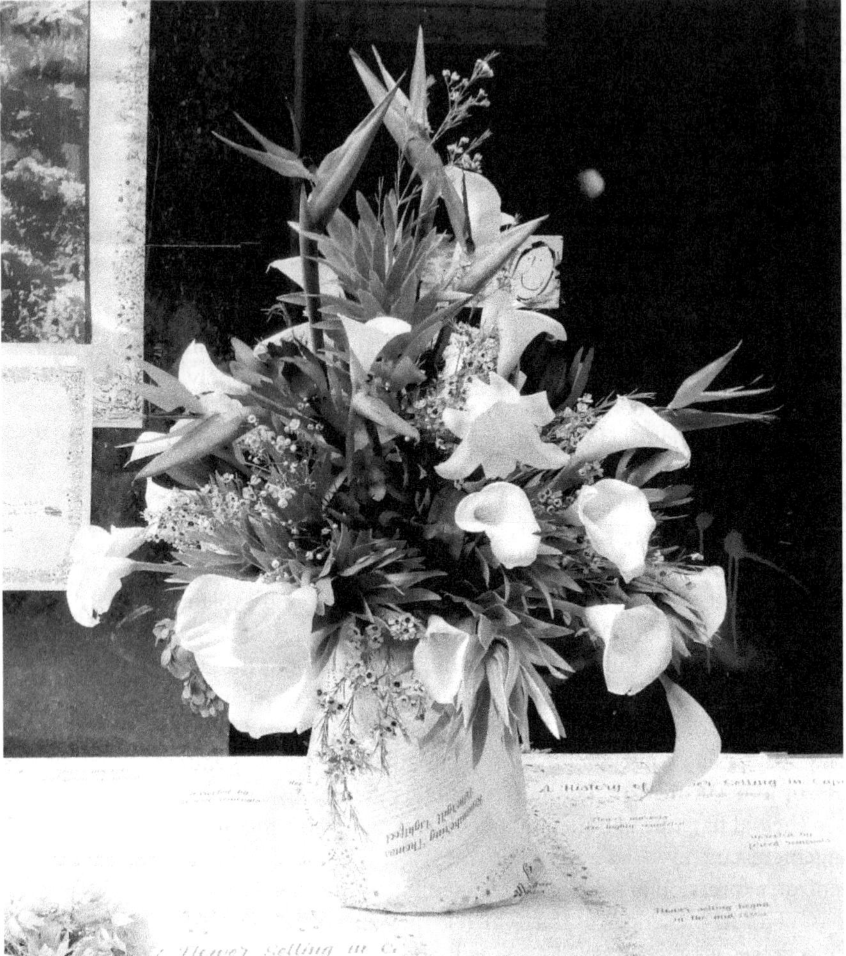

Fig. 7.2. Flower arrangement in the colours of the old South African flag made by Faiza "Poppy" Saliem. Photograph by the author.

lenses to look at history."[39] Saliem's flower arrangement offered one such alternative lens through which a multitude of stories could be seen.

Besides the flower sellers, *Storytelling in the Language of Flowers* also invited the public to make flower arrangements. On the morning of the event, about fifteen participants, some with in-depth knowledge of botany and some complete novices, gathered around a long table on the pavement in Adderley Street. Karin Bachmann, a flower seller, who for the occasion took on the role of floristry teacher, opened the session with an introduction to the flower market. This was followed by a comment by a participant, Phakamani m'Afrika Xaba, a horticultural scientist working at the Kirstenbosch National Botanical Garden, about the historically tense relationship between the botanical garden and the flower market, which he hoped to improve with time. As a gesture of goodwill, Xaba and a group of students and interns had brought two crates of plants from the botanical garden

39   Melanie Boehi, "The Silent Ambassadors," *Chimurenga Chronic* (April 2018): 13.

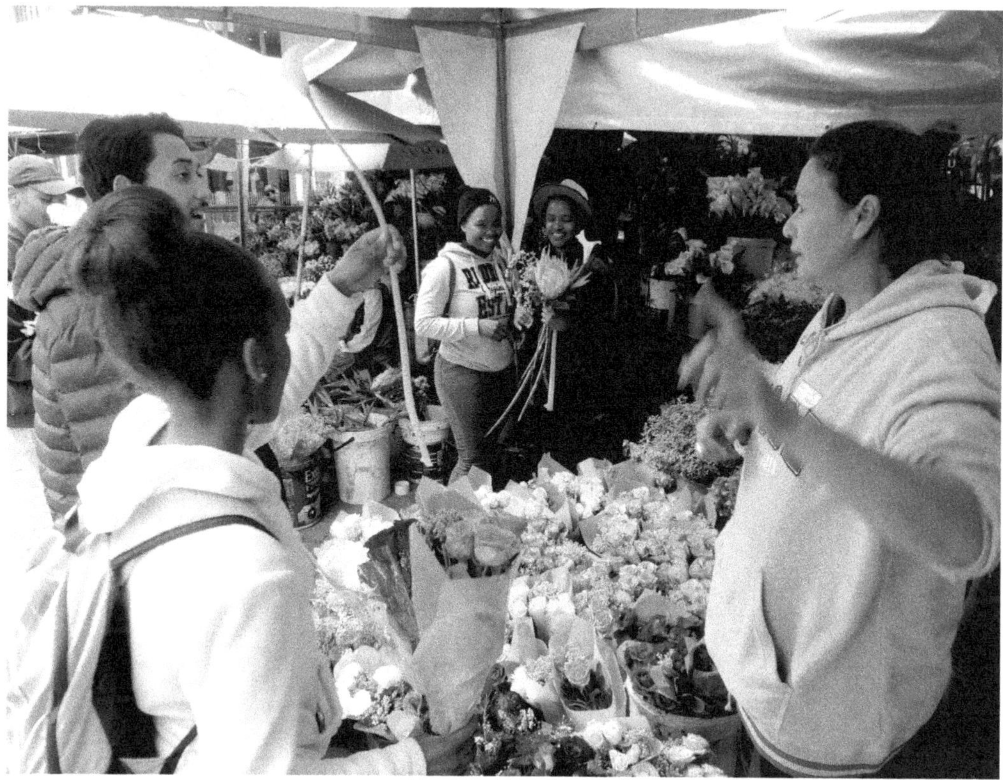

Fig. 7.3. Workshop participants select flowers under guidance of Karin Bachmann (right). Photograph by the author.

that they had selected to tell "a brief story about Cape Town," which they explained was "a lot of stories in one."

Bachmann instructed participants to think about stories they wanted to tell and to select flowers accordingly. She then guided her students through the process of arranging the plants, using a piece of floral foam as basis. "Take your biggest flower and put it [at] the center," she instructed them. "Whichever flowers you choose, you take three at the time. No twos, that doesn't make a statement." As they were busy selecting, cutting, and placing flowers, the participants occasionally asked Bachmann for advice, but they mostly worked in silent concentration. Nobody worried about the three-not-two rule; the participants worked in a flow that suggested that the plants were guiding their hands as much as their hands were guiding the plants (see Figs. 7.4–7.5). Once completed, members of the group were invited to share their stories (see Figs. 7.6–7.7).

Several participants made flower arrangements as self-portraits. One participant explained she was thinking of the complicated relationships with the different women in her life, and that she "was choosing different flowers and trying to bring it all together." She commented that the process allowed her to think carefully. Another participant focused on roses she identified with because they were both soft and thorny, and she selected different colors to represent various aspects of her personality. Two participants combined memories of the past and goals for the future in their arrangement: they included a strelitzia as an homage to the Eastern Cape where they grew up and the plants grow naturally and to their wealth aspi-

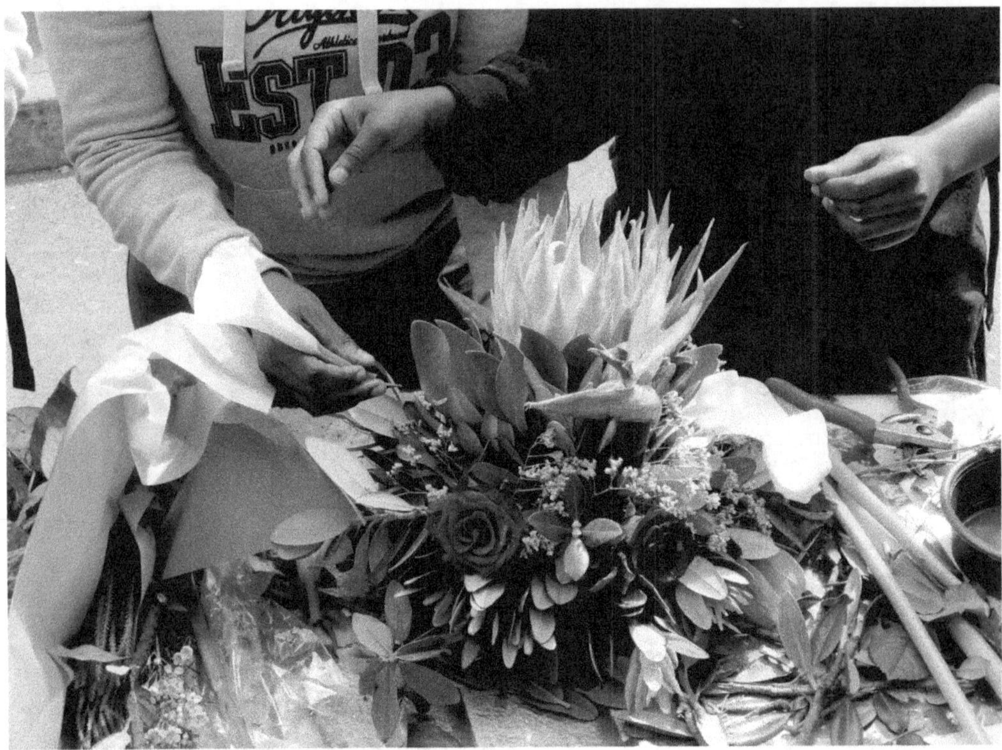

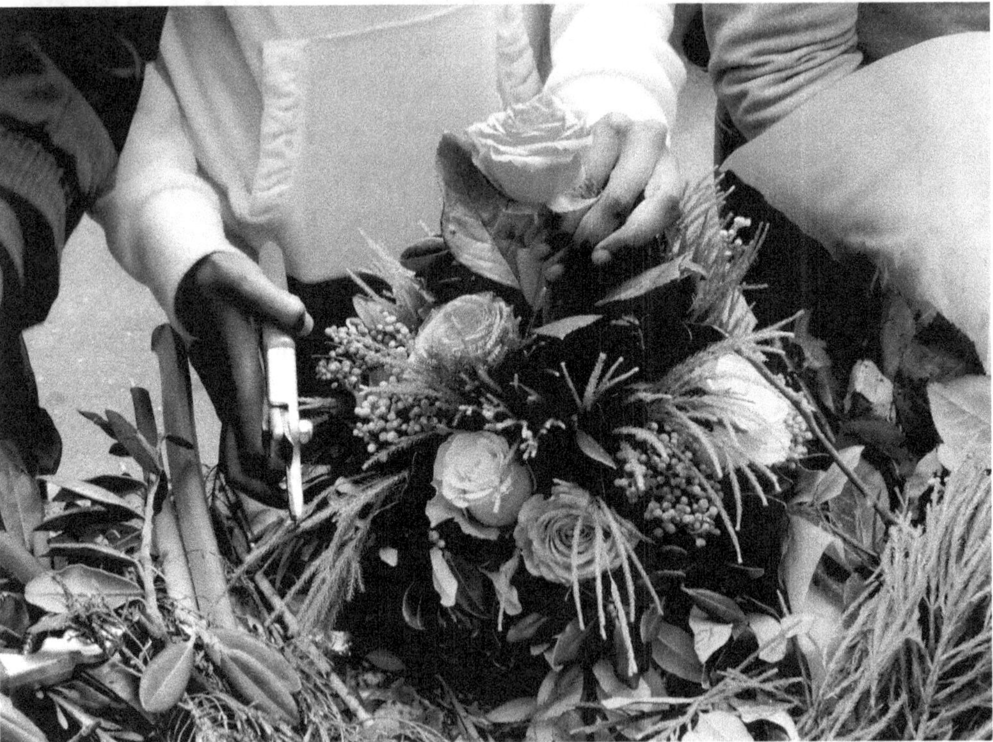

Figs. 7.4, 7.5. Workshop participants arrange flowers. Photograph by the author.

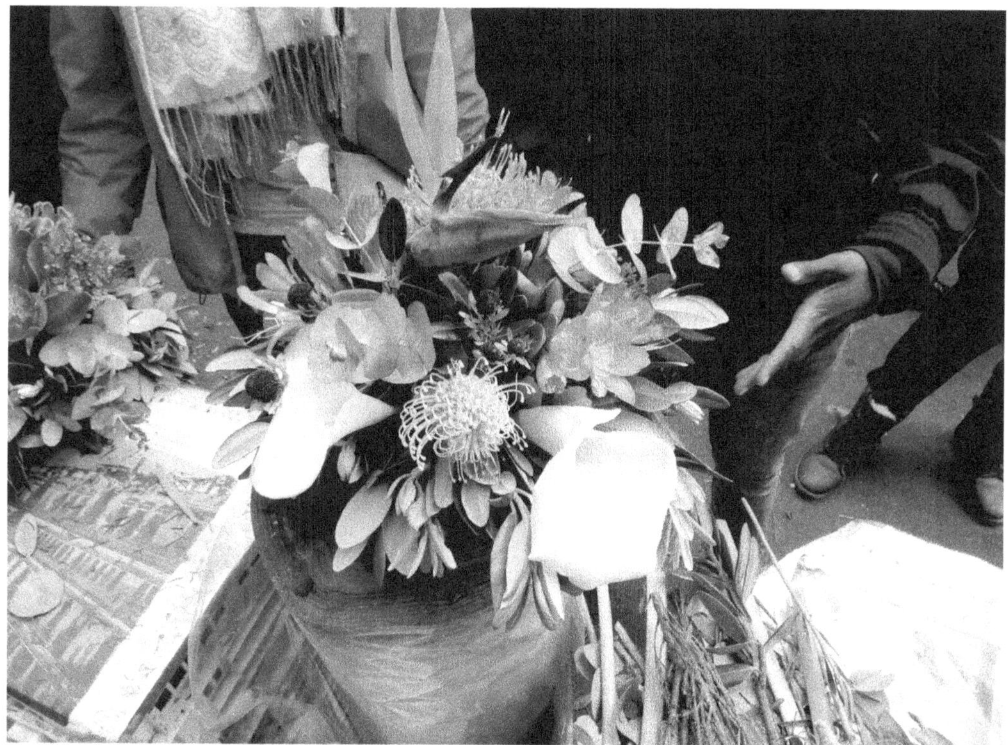

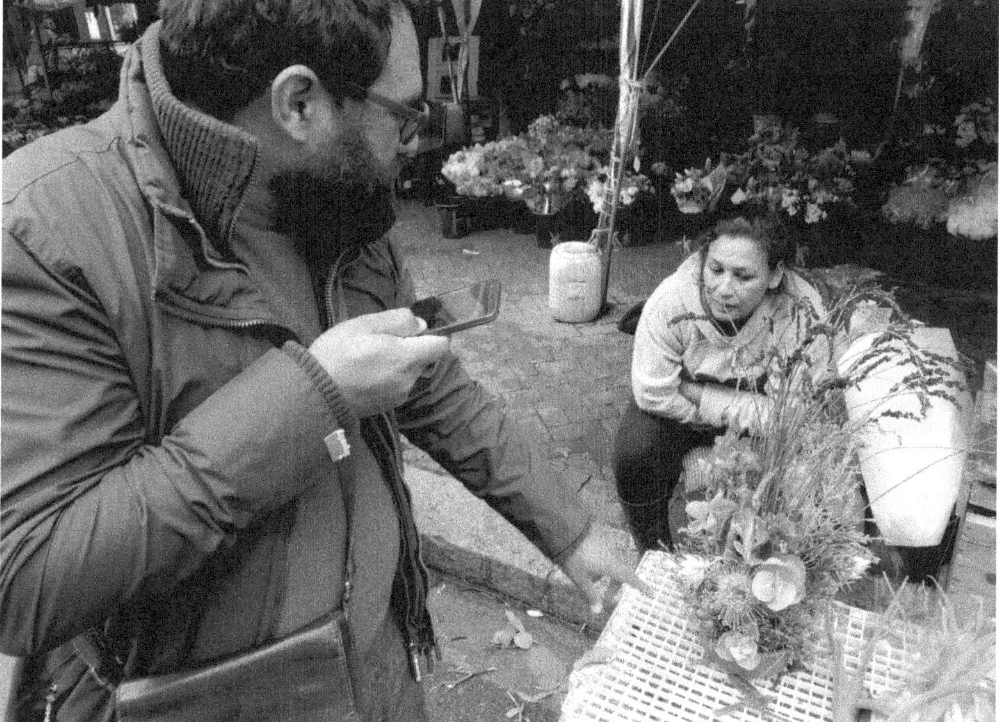

Figs. 7.6, 7.7. Workshop participants share the stories that their flower arrangements tell. Photograph by the author.

rations—the flower is included on a South African coin. Several arrangements evoked stories of family and migration. One participant made a flower arrangement that included a strelitzia, pincushions, and arum lilies. He included the strelitzia to represent Matatiele in the Eastern Cape and arum lilies to represent Grabouw in the Western Cape, the places where he grew up. Not having visited the Eastern Cape for three years, and Grabouw for a month, he said the flower arranging took him home. He explained that the colorful arrangement represented his personality: "I am Black of course, right, but I grew up in a Coloured community [and] I know five official [South African] languages."[40] Another participant made an arrangement including a protea, pincushions, and Barberton daisies. Growing up as the child of a South African mother living in Europe, her family used to buy proteas at the airport at the end of vacations and then treasure the dried flowers for years, until the next visit. Reflecting on making the flower arrangement, she said that it "felt nice to experiment with mixing it all up" and being open to "just let[ting] it all emerge."

In their introduction to *The Language of Plants,* Monica Gagliano, John C. Ryan, and Patrícia Vieira distinguish between plants' "*extrinsic* and *intrinsic* language."[41] They describe extrinsic language as the language humans used to "express what is 'peculiar' [...] about plant being," while intrinsic language comprises "the modes of communication and articulation used by vegetal species to negotiate ecologically with their biotic and abiotic environments."[42] When describing their stories, flower sellers and floristry workshop participants primarily related to plants' extrinsic language. They invoked and mixed various epistemologies, ranging from plant science and its modes of classification to the popular genre of the language of flowers and its association with emotional expressions.[43] Plants' intrinsic language was also present in the flower arrangements. Michael Marder characterized the language of plants as "an articulation without saying."[44] Plants, he explained, articulated themselves through their growth, which in turn articulated nature as a growing whole and the elements in which they were rooted. The flower arrangements did not include entire plants but only cut flowers and branches of leaves. Yet, as part of plants, they had emerged as articulations of their environments, ranging from farms dedicated to sustainable harvesting to industrialized greenhouse production. Cut flowers and stems also articulate a space between life and death; they are able to absorb water and minerals but are ultimately destined to wilt, dry, and decompose.

40   The speaker here uses the term "Black" in the sense of African.

41   Monica Gagliano, John C. Ryan, and Patrícia Vieira, "Introduction," in *The Language of Plants: Science, Philosophy, Literature,* eds. Monica Gagliano, John C. Ryan, and Patrícia Vieira (Minneapolis: University of Minnesota Press, 2017), xvii. Original emphasis.

42   Ibid., xvii–xviii.

43   On floriography see Isabel Kranz, Alexander Schwan, and Eike Wittrock, eds., *Floriographie: Die Sprachen der Blumen* (Paderborn: Wilhelm Fink, 2016); Beverly Seaton, *The Language of Flowers: A History* (Charlottesville: University Press of Virginia, 1995); Goody, *The Culture of Flowers,* 232–53.

44   Michael Marder, "To Hear Plants Speak," in *The Language of Plants: Science, Philosophy, Literature,* eds. Monica Gagliano, John C. Ryan, and Patrícia Vieira (Minneapolis: University of Minnesota Press, 2017), 119–20.

Arranging flowers as a form of storytelling allows humans to make arrangements together with plants and be themselves arranged by plants. Not quite fitting into the binary of extrinsic and intrinsic language is therefore a third mode of communication which can be described as an assembled language: the language of the assemblage of human and vegetal flower arrangers. This assembled language is an expression of what Jane Bennett described as "onto-sympathy."[45] Onto-sympathy is a mode of communication and cross-species affiliation between animal and vegetable bodies. According to Bennett, sympathy occurs in processes of gravitation (when a human body leans toward or is drawn to a plant body), corporation (when the human body and the plant body form a corporation, through activities like eating and smelling), and annunciation (when the human person becomes aware of the affinity between the human and vegetal body). In the flower arranging activities, gravitation occurred when flower arrangers were drawn to a plant, selected it, prepared it, and placed it in the arrangement. Nobody included edible plants, but corporation happened when arrangers smelled plants' scents. Snyders's bridal bouquet also came close to being incorporated into a person's body. Annunciation took place when participants reflected on the good feelings they experienced during the activity and reached a stage of "just let[ting] it all emerge."

The flower market is usually a place where people come to consume products of nature. Inviting people to arrange flowers and share stories potentially rearranged understandings of nature as resource. When harvested sustainably, the plants on which the flowers and branches grew could continue to flourish; thus the flowers in the arrangements remained connected to life elsewhere. Luce Irigaray reminds us that flowers and fruits "are not the end of a plant, but a moment of its growth, which cannot be separated from the complete motion without removing the plant from its life."[46] Reflecting on breathing and how, in breath, the vegetal world is a partner for human existence, Irigaray suggests that it requires that humans find ways of appropriate engagement, because "it is not fitting to take advantage of the environment in which we live without making our contribution to it."[47] Storytelling can be one way of finding out how to make responsible contributions. In *Storytelling in the Language of Flowers,* the flowers enabled a diverse group of participants to share intimate stories. In particular, the meeting of flower sellers and delegates from the botanical garden established a new link between two historically segregated places and communities. Telling stories with flower arrangements pushed participants out of their comfort zones because it did not grant expert status to any participant and broke down professional hierarchies and disciplinary boundaries. This allowed human participants to rearrange their

---

45 Jane Bennett, "Vegetal Life and Onto-Sympathy," in *Entangled Worlds: Religion, Science, and New Materialisms,* eds. Catherine Keller and Mary-Jane Rubenstein (New York: Fordham University Press, 2017), 89–110. Another approach to assembled language is Tihana Nathen's concept of "herb-I-graphies" with which she describes sharing authority in the context of ethnographic writing about human-plant interactions. Tihana Nathen, "'Being Attentive': Exploring Other-than-human Agency in Medicinal Plants Through Everyday Rastafari Plant Practices," *Anthropology Southern Africa* 41, no. 2 (2018): 115–26.

46 Luce Irigaray, "What the Vegetal World Says to Us," in *The Language of Plants: Science, Philosophy, Literature,* eds. Monica Gagliano, John C. Ryan, and Patrícia Vieira (Minneapolis: University of Minnesota Press, 2017), 129.

47 Ibid., 128.

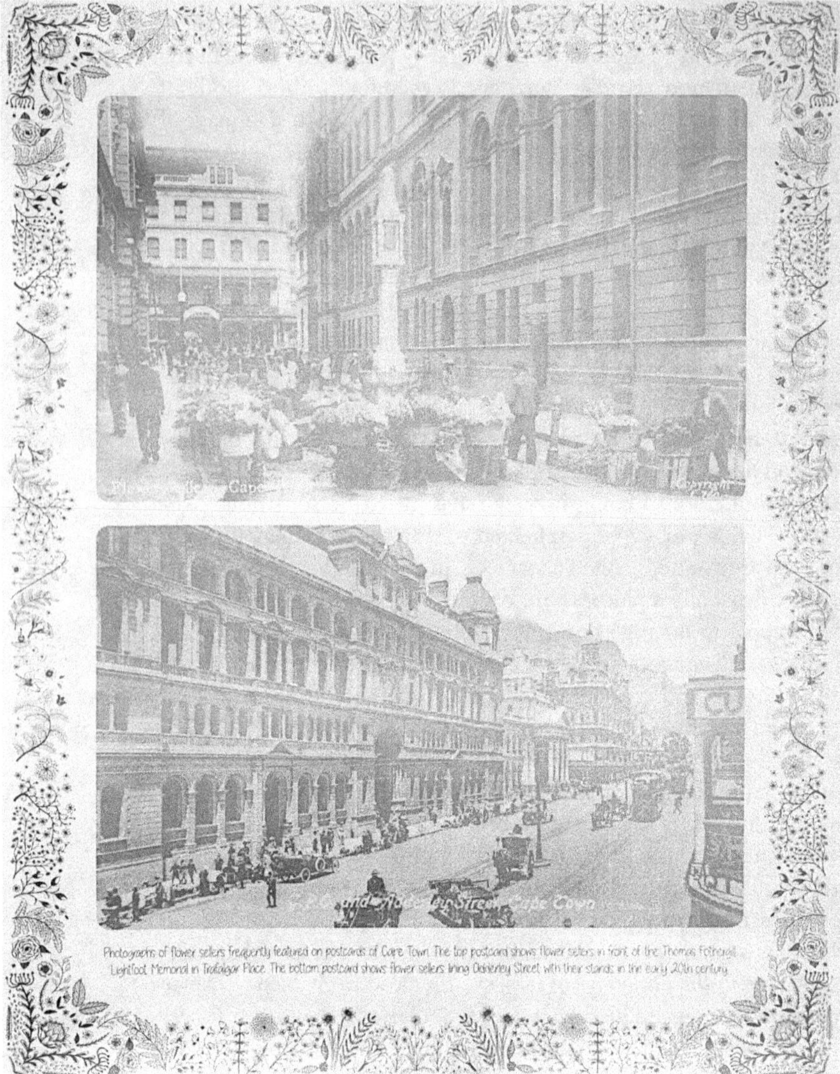

Fig. 7.8. A flower wrapping paper from the *Cape Town Floriography Papers* brings historical postcards back into circulation.

knowledge and their position in a multispecies community that gives hope about the possibilities for future cohabiting in an African Anthropocene.

3. Rearranging Archives

For a long time, the Adderley Street flower sellers have wrapped flowers in stories. Not only have they arranged flowers as stories and used stories as resources, but they have also used old newspapers to pack flowers for customers. Inspired by this practice, *Storytelling in the Language of Flowers* distributed the *Cape Town Floriography Papers,* a series of six flower wrapping papers that could be used to wrap up flowers and then be recycled into a newspaper. Each of the six papers provided a vantage point on the history of flower-selling in Cape Town.

Several flower wrapping papers featured photographs and addressed connections across time and space. One paper featured postcards that depicted the flower market in the early twentieth century (see Fig. 7.8). The postcards that had once delivered floral greetings from Cape Town into the world had recently been bought in international, online auctions. By bringing them back to the flower market, the wrapping paper closed the circle of the images' journeys. Two papers showed photographs of flower sellers from the 1940s that are kept in the Iziko Museums of South Africa's Social History Centre. Unlike the images on the postcards, these photographs were more documentary than ethnographic. Although nobody recognized the depicted individuals, several current vendors remarked they looked alike themselves and could be relatives. Another paper featured a collage of an archival photograph of the flower market in the 1930s, kept in the National Library of South Africa, and portraits of current vendors, each posing with a bunch of flowers. The collage meditates on disruptions and continuities. None of the contemporary sellers managed to identify the persons depicted in the archival photograph, but they nonetheless acknowledged possible kinship. Some of the plant species in the 1930s photograph are still sold today, but most of the flowers with which the current vendors posed were not available then; whereas the flower market remained in Adderley Street over the years, the routes that flower sellers and plants travelled changed dramatically over time.

Two flower wrapping papers were concerned with historical narratives. One included an essay about the history of flower-selling based on oral history interviews with flower sellers and archival research conducted in the National Library of South Africa and the collections of the Western Cape Archives and Records Service. Another paper addressed how, in the early twentieth century, botanists and plant collectors "discovered" several plant species at the flower market. They prepared herbarium specimens from them and described and named them. These herbarium sheets are today kept in the Bolus Herbarium at the University of Cape Town, the herbarium at the Royal Botanic Gardens, Kew, and the Natural History Museum, Vienna. Their labels mentioned that the plants were "bought fresh in the streets of Cape Town" or "obtained from flower sellers in the streets of Cape Town" but did not formally acknowledge the interactions between plant collectors and flower sellers.[48] With the exception of T.P. Stokoe, who in the 1920s befriended some flower sellers and held their expertise in high regard, plant collectors did not acknowledge their interactions with flower sellers.[49] Yet the herbarium sheets demonstrate that flower sellers contributed knowledge to botany.

Each of the flower wrapping papers featured a floral border designed by artist and graphic designer Salma Price-Nell. The border included flowers that are common at the Adderley Street flower market, as well as flowers that defy existing tax-

---

48 The three herbarium sheets featured on the flower wrapping paper were: "Erica macowanii Cufino," *Royal Botanic Gardens, Kew,* http://specimens.kew.org/herbarium/K000314030/; "Erica fervida L. Bolus," *Royal Botanic Gardens, Kew,* http://specimens.kew.org/herbarium/K000225286/; and "Erica latiflora L. Bolus," *Royal Botanic Gardens, Kew,* http://specimens.kew.org/herbarium/K000225239/.

49 Peter Slingsby and Amida Johns, *T.P. Stokoe: The Man, the Myths, the Flowers* (Muizenberg: Baardskeerder, 2009).

onomies. Price-Nell described these as "hybrid and fantasy flowers."[50] These flowers invite thinking about the flowers that will exist in a future marked by higher temperatures, water scarcity, and accompanying political, economic, and social conflicts. The hybrid and fantasy flowers are a warning as well as a sign of hope. They stand for genetically modified plants that are designed to blossom in ruins for the sake of maximizing profits, but also for plants that might evolve and flourish in future "emergent ecologies."[51]

Together, the *Cape Town Floriography Papers* not only provided a historical overview but also mapped out, circulated, and connected archival records kept in various collecting institutions. Most of the archives and libraries where archival records concerned with flower-selling are kept are located close to the flower market. Yet they are also worlds apart. Despite having an interest in the collections, the flower sellers were rarely aware that they are open to the public. That "the status and power of the archive derive from [the] entanglement of building and documents" might have influenced this.[52] The buildings in which some of the collections are situated emerged as sites of state power: the National Library of South Africa is housed in a prominent colonial building at the edge of the Dutch East India Company's Garden, while the Western Cape Archives and Records Service is located in the former Roeland Street Prison. The collecting institutions were not only set apart from the flower sellers but also from each other, with a firm line drawn between natural and social history collections. Yet, as the herbarium sheets of the plants collected in Adderley Street show, natural history records are also social history records, and the stories learned from them blur the disciplinary borders that their holding institutions work to uphold.

Joela Jacobs proposed the term "phytopoetics" to describe the role of plants in the creation of texts and language. She suggested that phytopoetics bring into focus "both a poetic engagement with plants in literature and moments in which plants take on literary and cultural agency themselves."[53] Phytopoetics manifested in the *Cape Town Floriography Papers* in several ways. The featured essays and images addressed narratives about plants, and choices concerning paper type, size, and layout were made to accommodate plants. Plants, together with flower sellers, inspired the papers' content; they hold them together and allow for cross-referencing among various collecting institution. The papers were not numbered and could be arranged in whatever way readers preferred. Flower sellers also put them up as posters along the walls of the Golden Acre shopping mall where they came to function as substitutes for official information boards. As a phytopoetics publication, *Cape Town Floriography Papers* enabled a rearrangement of archives, as if to prepare ground in which new multispecies stories about life in an African Anthropocene can grow.

<hr>

50   Salma Price-Nell, "Cape Town Floriography," *The Salsa,* December 6, 2016, https://www.thesalsacreative.com/single-post/2016/12/06/Cape-Town-Floriography/.

51   Eben Kirksey, *Emergent Ecologies* (Durham: Duke University Press, 2015).

52   Achille Mbembe, "The Power of the Archive and Its Limits," in *Refiguring the Archive,* eds. Carolyn Hamilton et al. (Dordrecht: Kluwer Academic Publishers, 2002), 19.

53   Joela Jacobs, "Phytopoetics: Upending the Passive Paradigm with Vegetal Violence and Eroticism," *Catalyst: Feminism, Theory, Technoscience* 5, no. 2 (2019): 1.

4. Arrangements for the Future

If plants performed a protest song, would humans listen? During the installation of *Storytelling in the Language of Flowers,* music filled a section of the Adderley Street flower market. The music was not performed by plants but emanated from a loudspeaker hidden behind flower buckets. Yet, if we follow Bernie Krause's thesis that the origin of music is in "wild places," all musical compositions are to some degree phytopoetic expressions.[54] The sound installation with the title *arrangement for new flowers* invoked a vegetal future that grows out of histories of violence and resistance.[55] Its composer, Neo Muyanga, described it as a remix of "samples of palesa, plantation workers, water [and] soil shuffles, extra: unit of slave strings." The composition referenced gendered ideas of beauty and love. "Palesa," which means "flower" in seSotho, is a common name among South African women and is also the title of a popular love song. The composition alluded to the struggles of enslaved people and plantation workers, as well as to the struggles of the natural environment. Being played into Adderley Street's everyday soundscape that is characterized by busy street life — the running of car engines, hooting minibus taxis, chatting pedestrians, flower sellers loudly advertising their wares — it drew listeners into a world that is chaotic and violent but also resilient and beautiful. Through the sampling of sounds from various archives, Muyanga grounded the composition firmly in the past. By framing it as an arrangement for new flowers, he also projected it into the future. As an arrangement in the sense of "a piece of music that has been changed so that it can be performed by particular types of voices or instruments," the composition was an attempt to accommodate the flowers that will come in the future and extended an invitation to potential participants to join the performance and be rearranged by it into new formations.

Like the flower arrangements made for the flower show and during the floristry storytelling workshop, *arrangement for new flowers* invoked both the extrinsic and intrinsic language of plants. The extrinsic language, introduced through palesa, is connected to music referencing flowers. The components of the composition invoking plantation workers and enslaved people's music referred to the violence inflicted on both people and plants by slavery and colonial agriculture. The intrinsic language of plants was involved in references to the sounds and compositions that plants make together with their multispecies communities in soil and water. For long, researchers were interested in whether plants make and respond to music in ways that are beneficial to them rather than merely resulting from colliding molecules.[56] Recent studies suggested that seeds and seedlings react to ultrasound exposure and that some plants release defensive chemicals upon being exposed to the sound of herbivores feeding.[57] Scientists have also observed that the pho-

---

54   Bernie Krause, *The Great Animal Orchestra: Finding the Origins of Music in the World's Wild Places* (London: Profile Books, 2013), 10.

55   Neo Muyanga, arrangement for new flowers, sound installation, 05'39".

56   Richard Karban, "The Language of Plant Communication (and How It Compares to Animal Communication)," in *The Language of Plants: Science, Philosophy, Literature,* eds. Monica Gagliano, John C. Ryan, and Patrícia Vieira (Minneapolis: University of Minnesota Press, 2017), 10.

57   Monica Gagliano, Stefano Mancuso, and Daniel Robert, "Towards Understanding Plant Bioacoustics," *Trends in Plant Science* 17, no. 6 (2012): 232–96, and

tosynthesis by marine algae produces sound.[58] It is all these various sounds that *arrangement for new flowers* encourages us to listen to and to accommodate in future arrangements.

5. Conclusion

In *Storytelling in the Language of Flowers,* multispecies storytelling evolved as a narrative strategy to bring together epistemologies, people, and places that have in the past been segregated. Conventionally, the Adderley Street flower market has been framed as a site of ethnography with marginal interest to botany; a site where nature and culture meet and where the boundaries between these two spheres are being constantly redrawn. *Storytelling in the Language of Flowers* moved beyond these frameworks by embracing a practice that is rooted in the forms and aesthetic practices which have evolved in Adderley Street ever since flower sellers started their business there. Bringing together a wide range of disciplines, including history, botany, floristry, and music, the project developed a storytelling practice that is not only interdisciplinary but works toward a new mix-and-match storytelling methodology.

Arrangement evolved as a common theme in all activities of *Storytelling in the Language of Flowers.* Arrangement here is an inherently intermediate practice because its main media — flower arrangements, flower wrapping papers, and sound — inhabit a space between conventional forms of media and are constantly evolving from one form to another: Flower arrangements turn into stories; flower wrapping papers are recycled into newspapers; and a music composition becomes a flower arrangement. It is this fluidity and flexibility which allows for an openness to change, and which makes multispecies storytelling a powerful strategy for researching, documenting, and thinking about life in an African Anthropocene.

Heidi M. Appel and R.B. Cocroft, "Plants Respond to Leaf Vibrations Caused by Insect Herbivore Chewing," *Oecologia* 175, no. 4 (2014): 1257–66.

58   Simon E. Freeman et al., "Photosynthesis by Marine Algae Produces Sound, Contributing to the Daytime Soundscape on Coral Reefs," *PLoS One* 13, no. 10 (2018): 1–14.

Acknowledgments

I would like to thank all participants of Storytelling in the Language of Flowers, especially Karin Bachmann, Chrischené Julius, Cornelia Knoll, Rupert Koopman, Neo Muyanga, Ayesha Price, Salma Price-Nell, Tim Rüdiger, and Phakamani m'Afrika Xaba. I thank Pro Helvetia Johannesburg for project funding. I presented a first draft of this chapter at the "Multispecies Storytelling in Intermedial Practice" conference, and I am grateful for the comments that I received there. I am also very thankful to Ida Bencke, Jørgen Bruhn, and the two anonymous reviewers for their valuable comments and encouragement.

References

Appel, Heidi M., and R.B. Cocroft. "Plants Respond to Leaf Vibrations Caused by Insect Herbivore Chewing." *Oecologia* 175, no. 4 (2014): 1257–66. DOI: 10.1007/s00442–014–2995–6.

Bennett, Jane. "Vegetal Life and Onto-Sympathy." In *Entangled Worlds: Religion, Science, and New Materialisms,* edited by Catherine Keller and Mary-Jane Rubenstein, 89–110. New York City: Fordham University Press, 2017.

Boehi, Melanie. "The Flower Sellers of Cape Town." *Veld & Flora* 99, no. 3 (2013): 132–35. https://hdl.handle.net/10520/EJC143279.

———. "Storytelling in the Language of Flowers." *Nowseum,* September 18, 2018. https://nowseum.com/2018/09/18/storytelling-in-the-language-of-flowers.

———. "The Silent Ambassadors." *Chimurenga Chronic* (2018): 10–13.

Bukuts, Carina. "Kapwani Kiwanga's Afrofuturist Garden." *Frieze,* October 27, 2020. https://www.frieze.com/article/kapwani-kiwangas-afrofuturist-garden.

Campbell Tait, Barbara. *Cape Cameos: The Story of Cape Town in a New Way.* Cape Town: Stewart, 1948.

Cape Peninsula Publicity Association, ed. *Cape Town and the Cape Peninsula: A Holiday Guide.* Cape Town: Cape Peninsula Publicity Association, 1940.

Comaroff Jean, and John L. Comaroff. "Naturing the Nation: Aliens, Apocalypse, and the Postcolonial State." *Social Identities* 27, no. 3 (2001): 233–65. DOI: 10.1080/13632430120074626.

Davids, C.A. "The Water Point." *Africa Is a Country,* August 8, 2018. https://africasacountry.com/2018/02/the-water-point.

Dlamini, Jacob. *Native Nostalgia.* Auckland Park: Jacana Media, 2009.

Finch, Josiah Robert. *The Cape of Good Hope: Being the Official Handbook of the City of Cape Town.* Cape Town: Sid. P. Cowen, 1909.

"Flower Sellers to Get Council Support." *The Cape Argus,* June 22, 1978.

Freeman, Simon E., Lauren A. Freeman, Giacomo Giorli, and Andreas F. Haas. "Photosynthesis by Marine Algae Produces Sound, Contributing to the Daytime Soundscape on Coral Reefs." *PLoS One* 13, no. 10 (2018): 1–14. DOI: 10.1371/journal.pone.0201766.

Gagliano, Monica, Stefano Mancuso, and Daniel Robert. "Towards Understanding Plant Bioacoustics." *Trends in Plant Science* 17, no. 6 (2012): 232–96. DOI: 10.1016/j.tplants.2012.03.002.

Gagliano, Monica, John C. Ryan, and Patrícia Vieira. "Introduction." In *The Language of Plants: Science, Philosophy, Literature,* edited by Monica Gagliano,

John C. Ryan, and Patrícia Vieira, vii–xxxiii. Minneapolis: University of Minnesota Press, 2017.

Goldblatt, Peter, and John Manning. *Cape Plants: A Conspectus of the Cape Flora of South Africa.* Cape Town: National Botanical Institute, 2000.

Goody, Jack. *The Culture of Flowers.* Cambridge: Cambridge University Press, 1993.

Green, Lawrence George. *Tavern of the Seas.* Cape Town: Rustica Press Limited, 1947.

Haraway, Donna. "Anthropocene, Capitalocene, Plantationocene, Chthulucene: Making Kin." *Environmental Humanities* 6, no. 1 (2015): 159–65. DOI: 10.1215/22011919–3615934.

———. *When Species Meet.* Minneapolis: University of Minnesota Press, 2008.

Haraway, Donna, and Thyrza Nichols Goodeve. "Nothing Comes without Its World: Donna J. Haraway in Conversation with Thyrza Nichols Goodeve." In Donna Haraway, *Modest-Witness@Second-Millennium.FemaleMan-Meets-OncoMouse: Feminism and Technoscience,* xiii–xlvii. New York: Routledge, 2018.

Hecht, Gabrielle. "Interscalar Vehicles for an African Anthropocene: On Waste, Temporality, and Violence." *Cultural Anthropology* 33, no. 1 (2018): 109–41. DOI: 10.14506/ca33.1.05.

———. "The African Anthropocene." *Aeon,* February 6, 2018. https://aeon.co/essays/if-we-talk-about-hurting-our-planet-who-exactly-is-the-we.

Hogg, John. "Flagged a Hate Crime." *New Frame,* August 23, 2019. https://www.newframe.com/light-reading-flagged-a-hate-crime.

Huneault, Kristina. *Difficult Subjects: Working Women and Visual Culture, Britain 1880–1914.* Aldershot: Ashgate, 2002.

"ICA's Celebration of Live Art." *University of Cape Town News,* August 27, 2018. https://www.news.uct.ac.za/article/-2018–08–27-icas-celebration-of-live-art.

Irigaray, Luce. "What the Vegetal World Says to Us." In *The Language of Plants: Science, Philosophy, Literature,* edited by Monica Gagliano, John C. Ryan, and Patrícia Vieira, 126–35. Minneapolis: University of Minnesota Press, 2017.

Jacobs, Joela. "Phytopoetics: Upending the Passive Paradigm with Vegetal Violence and Eroticism." *Catalyst: Feminism, Theory, Technoscience* 5, no. 2 (2019): 1–18. DOI: 10.28968/cftt.v5i2.30027.

Joyce, Peter, Jill Johnson, and Ashley Joyce. *Weekends in and around Cape Town.* Cape Town: Struik Timmins Publishers, 1991.

Karban, Richard. "The Language of Plant Communication (and How It Compares to Animal Communication)." In *The Language of Plants: Science, Philosophy, Literature,* edited by Monica Gagliano, John C. Ryan, and Patrícia Vieira, 3–26. Minneapolis: University of Minnesota Press, 2017.

Kirksey, Eben. *Emergent Ecologies.* Durham: Duke University Press, 2015.

Kuiper, Gerda, and Andreas Gemählich. "Sustainability and Depoliticisation: Certifications in the Cut-Flower Industry at Lake Naivasha, Kenya." *Africa Spectrum* 52, no. 3 (2017): 31–53. DOI: 10.1177/000203971705200302.

Kranz, Isabel, Alexander Schwan, and Eike Wittrock, eds. *Floriographie: Die Sprachen der Blumen.* Paderborn: Wilhelm Fink, 2016.

Krause, Bernie. *The Great Animal Orchestra: Finding the Origins of Music in the World's Wild Places.* London: Profile Books, 2013.

Marder, Michael. "To Hear Plants Speak." In *The Language of Plants: Science, Philosophy, Literature,* edited by Monica Gagliano, John C. Ryan, and Patrícia Vieira, 103–25. Minneapolis: University of Minnesota Press, 2017.

Mbembe, Achille. "The Power of the Archive and Its Limits." In *Refiguring the Archive,* edited by Carolyn Hamilton, Verne Harris, Jane Taylor, Michele Pickover, Graeme Reid, and Razia Saleh, 19–26. Dordrecht: Kluwer Academic Publishers, 2002.

Muir, John. *Guide to Cape Town and the Western Cape.* Cape Town: Howard Timmins, 1976.

Nathen, Tihana. "'Being Attentive': Exploring Other-than-human Agency in Medicinal Plants Through Everyday Rastafari Plant Practices." *Anthropology Southern Africa* 41, no. 2 (2018): 115–26. DOI: 10.1080/23323256.2018.1468720.

"No Flowers, by Order." *The Cape Argus,* June 22, 1965.

Price-Nell, Salma. "Cape Town Floriography." *The Salsa,* December 6, 2016. https://www.thesalsacreative.com/single-post/2016/12/06/Cape-Town-Flori-ography.

Ramutsindela, Maano. *Parks and People in Postcolonial Societies: Experiences in Southern Africa.* Dordrecht: Kluwer Academic Publishers, 2004.

Rose, Deborah Bird, Thom van Dooren, and Matthew Chrulew. "Introduction: Telling Extinction Stories." In *Extinction Studies: Stories of Time, Death, and Generations,* edited by Deborah Bird Rose, Thom van Dooren, and Matthew Chrulew, 1–17. New York Columbia University Press, 2017.

Seaton, Beverly. *The Language of Flowers: A History.* Charlottesville: University Press of Virginia, 1995.

Slingsby, Peter, and Amida Johns. *T.P. Stokoe: The Man, the Myths, the Flowers.* Muizenberg: Baardskeerder, 2009.

Stoler, Ann Laura. *Duress: Imperial Durabilities in Our Times.* Durham: Duke University Press, 2016.

Swift, Keri. "Blooming Trouble." *The Cape Argus,* June 23, 1978.

UNESCO World Heritage Committee. "Decisions Adopted at the 28th Session of the World Heritage Committee (Suzhou, 2004)." Paris: UNESCO World Herit-age Centre, 2004.

Van Sittert, Lance. "From 'Mere Weeds' and 'Bosjes' to a Cape Floral Kingdom: The Re-Imagining of Indigenous Flora at the Cape, c.1890–1939." *Kronos* 28 (November 2008): 102–26. https://www.jstor.org/stable/41056484.

Watts, Jonathan. "Cape Town Faces Day Zero: What Happens When the City Turns Off the Taps?" *The Guardian,* February 3, 2018. https://www.theguard-ian.com/cities/2018/feb/03/day-zero-cape-town-turns-off-taps.

Wicomb, Zoë. *You Can't Get Lost in Cape Town.* London: Virago, 1987.

Wolski, Piotr. "Was the Water Shortage Caused by Farmers, City Dwellers or Drought?" *GroundUp,* July 19, 2018. https://www.groundup.org.za/article/was-water-shortage-caused-farmers-city-dwellers-or-drought.

Wood, Julia. "Spring Wildflower Shows." *Veld & Flora* 78, no. 2 (June 1992): 38–43. https://hdl.handle.net/10520/AJA00423203_2528.

Yaw Ampofo-Anti, Ohene. "Equality Court Prohibits Display of Old South Afri-can Flag," *GroundUp,* August 22, 2019. https://www.groundup.org.za/article/old-south-african-flag-constitutes-hate-speech-says-equality-court.

CHAPTER 8

"You have to learn the language of how to communicate with the plants" and Other Selva Stories

Kristina Van Dexter

The War on Forests

Climbing foothills of endless pasto. Its rasping of rubber boots resounds into the silence. The silence of birdsong, of the cantos of taitas whose rezos protect the selva. Silence extends like dallis toward the horizon. Dallis, the common name for pasto introduced to conquer the forest. The living past. The luster of the glaring sun, the gloria of their golden pursuit, scorching foothills of endless pasto. No, not the golden pinta of the taitas, whose songs conquer the darkness; cattle. A few cattle gather in the shade of a lone tree. In this forest with no trees, the cattle-trodden spirit world, even the taitas tend cattle.[1]

The word "cattle" in English is related to "capital." Cattle in Spanish is *ganado*, the root of which, *ganar*, is "to gain," to "conquer." Cattle enabled the colonization of Colombia's forests and the Indigenous life-worlds intertwined with them. Colonial conquest found legitimacy in imaginaries of "wild" forests and their Indigenous inhabitants tied to the church.

This was Indigenous land. It was colonized by the church. The church was a cattle system. How did they produce this system? They invented a saint. Ganaderos bow to San Isidro. They give cattle as offerings. It's sorcery.[2]

Cattle legitimized the consolidation of large tracts of land in order to defend incursions from campesinos. The origin of war in Colombia is traced to these land conflicts in the twentieth century which followed with the displacement of campesinos to the forest frontier, precipitating its colonization. Campesinos were given titles to tracts of "empty forests"—a categorical negation of the existence of Indigenous life-worlds—conditioned on their conversion to pasture. Once entitlements ceased though, these "colonization" fronts were taken over with the production of coca for narco-trafficking that provided financing for a growing in-

---

1   Translation of Spanish words: *pasto* is "cattle grass"; *taitas* are "elders"; *cantos* are "songs"; *rezos* are "prayers and conjurings."

2   Field Notes (2017). Campesino, Putumayo, Colombia.

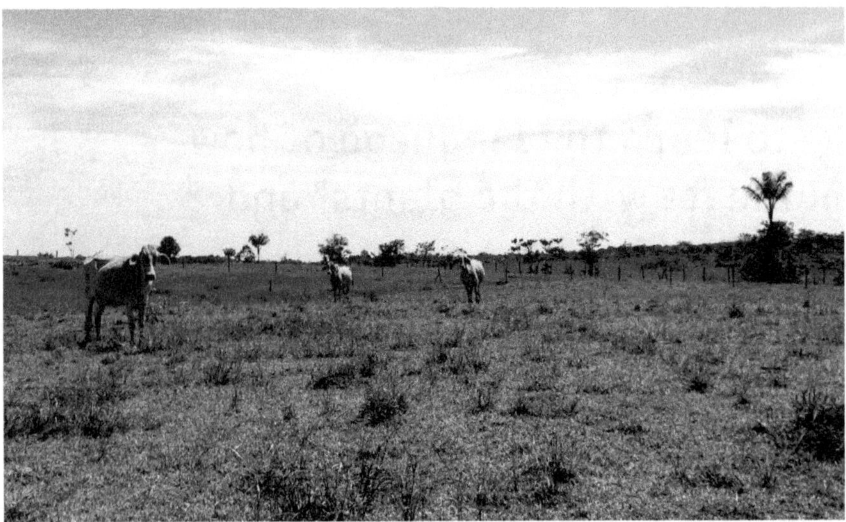

Fig. 8.1. The War on Forests, Putumayo, Colombia. Putumayo is where the Andean foothills fold into the Amazon lowlands. This important ecological corridor is threatened with the ongoing war on forests. Photograph by the author.

surgent war. Putumayo, which at the turn of the century produced most of the world's coca for narco-trafficking, was the focus of a counterinsurgent war carried out through Plan Colombia. This Cold War militarization of forests involved their defoliation with fumigations of glyphosate that covered forests to eradicate them of coca crops and the FARC (Fuerzas Armadas Revolucionarias de Colombia, The Revolutionary Armed Forces of Colombia), opening the way for capital investments. The fumigations of coca crops were indiscriminate, causing displacement, soil degradation, and deforestation as coca extended further into the forest.

> *The problem is that they did not spray only the coca plant. When the planes passed over here, the crops and pastures were sprayed. The fumigation poisoned the soils, killing the earth, killing the campesino. In some places the earth is so destroyed that it still does not give.*[3]

Coca plantations for narco-trafficking were often consolidated and converted into cattle pasture following fumigations and paramilitary interventions, often carried out in complicity with the military, that displaced campesinos from their farms. Cattle were instrumental to the consolidation of former FARC-controlled forests and for the investment of narco-profits.

Implicated in Colombia's war and colonization of its forests, cattle also represent "peace" for those navigating life in the frontier. In times of peace, cattle ranching is often the only "licit" option for coca growers — a transition that followed on fumigations of coca crops and that which is increasingly problematic within the context of the country's transition to peace.

3   Ibid.

> *Cattle ranching is the boom we have now, we are coming out of a transition,*
> *those of us who have coca crops. The farmers lived from coca, and now they live*
> *on cattle. The coca gave them everything, now the cattle give them everything.*
> *We are in a transition from coca to cattle, but this requires clearing forest and*
> *is now unstoppable. Cattle are destroying more forests than coca. Soils used for*
> *cattle ranching are also impacted and recovery is difficult.[4]*

The initiation of peace with the FARC in 2016 incited devastating forest loss which continues to rise. Forests that were off-limits during the war and due to the FARC's control over colonization and forest clearing are increasingly converted to pasture through narco-profits.

"Peace" in Colombia is what a campesino in Putumayo called *otra guerra* — a "war" waged on the forests and their diverse life-worlds. This war involves the rending of human and other-than-human life-worlds intertwined with the forest and the disruption of their life-generating relations. This war of ecocidal destruction is a "crime against peace."[5] The ecocidal destruction of forests is an enactment and extension of ongoing colonization and its capitalist extensions. This war extends to the forests of the world, taking claims on life to come. The word "forest" itself is implicated in this war, the ecocidal destruction of forests and their diverse life-worlds. Forests were and remain instrumental to ongoing colonization and the ecocidal destruction it engenders. The forest is connected to colonial conquest, Cold War counterinsurgencies, and the conversion of forests into capitalist commodities. The ecocidal destruction of forests and their life-worlds is intertwined with the destabilization of the climate. The forest continues to condition how we think about forests and our responses to their destruction. This carries important implications for our global climate crisis, responses to which depend on forests and the Indigenous and other communities whose life-worlds are co-constitutive of them.

Our global climate crisis is exposing the limitations of how we think of forests. This requires that we "de-forest" our thinking in recognition of how the forest is implicated in its ongoing colonization and destruction. To think differently is to consider our relentless relational contingencies with forests.[6] To think differently is to "think with and like forests."[7] Our global climate crisis and the ecocidal destruction of forests is grounded in "thinking fragmentation, thinking discontinuity."[8] It takes a forest to think the "long term connectivities" that enable life's ongoingness.[9] In the face of our global climate crisis, this calls for thinking like a forest toward thinking with connectivity in consideration of the relational contingencies of hu-

---

4   Ibid.

5   Sailesh Mehta and Prisca Merz, "Ecocide — A New Crime Against Peace?" *Environmental Law Review* 17, no. 1 (2015): 3–7.

6   Val Plumwood, "Nature in the Active Voice," *Australian Humanities Review* 46 (2009), http://australianhumanitiesreview.org/2009/05/01/nature-in-the-active-voice/.

7   Eduardo Kohn, *How Forests Think: Toward an Anthropology Beyond the Human* (Berkeley: University of California Press, 2013).

8   Deborah Bird Rose, "Slowly Writing into the Anthropocene," *Text Journal* 20 (2013): 1–14.

9   Ibid.

mans and the other-than-human life-worlds of the forest.[10] In thinking with and like forests, I trouble the notion of what a forest is — that which is implicated in its ongoing colonization and destruction — with the possibilities of forests otherwise — forests and the diverse life-worlds with whom they are relationally co-constituted, and that which are increasingly colonized and lost to deforestation.[11] Possibilities for forests otherwise emerge through the worlding relations of living forests. This essay foregrounds the relational condition of living forests to trouble the notion of forests with the possibilities of forests otherwise, and to open the possibilities for responses to forest destruction. Throughout this essay, I ground my thinking within those living forests. I think with Indigenous and other communities whose life-worlds are embedded within and co-constitutive of them. This relational notion of living forests, I contend, offers orientation for our global climate crisis.

The Possibilities of Inheritance

In reflecting on what we have inherited in times of "peace" within a context of ongoing war, this essay looks to forests and the communities who live with and defend them for guidance on how to inherit destruction in a way that opens the possibilities for differential forest futures. The campesinos and Indigenous communities in Putumayo, Colombia, whom I followed through forests and farms, describe the forest in terms of its relationality. Their forest farms are often indistinguishable from the forest. The forests they revealed to me form living entanglements of diverse life-worlds decomposing each other and the forest itself through temporal relations of death folding into life. This relationality is what they call the "selva." [12] These communities, whose life-worlds are entangled with the selva, are embedded within the "ecological relations in that world as communicative relations."[13] In the selva, the dead nourish the living through temporal relations of communication that link the past with possibilities. The ecocidal destruction of forests entails the loss of these connectivities, rending entangled human and nonhuman life-worlds and disrupting their communicative relations, threatening life's ongoingness.

The ongoing ecocidal destruction of the forest with whom our pasts and possible futures are entangled is a call to responsibility for ethical response or dialogue.[14] Dialogue involves witness to humans' and nonhumans' collective inheritances of war and ethical response to ecocidal destruction that engenders possibilities for peace.[15] Dialogue demands coming face-to-face with the inheritances of the ongoing war on forests — it is a way of responding to ecocide that turns into

<hr>

10   Ibid.

11   Eduardo Kohn, "Ecopolitics," *Society for Cultural Anthropology,* January 21, 2016, https://culanth.org/fieldsights/ecopolitics/.

12   Kristina Lyons, "Decomposition as Life Politics: Soils, Selva, and Small Farmers under the Gun of the U.S.–Colombia War on Drugs," *Cultural Anthropology* 31, no. 1 (2016): 56–81.

13   Eduardo Kohn, "Beyond Language," pca-*Stream,* November 2018, https://www.pca-stream.com/en/articles/eduardo-kohn-beyond-language-100.

14   Deborah Bird Rose, *Reports from a Wild Country: Ethics for Decolonisation* (Sydney: University of New South Wales Press, 2004).

15   Rose, "Slowly Writing into the Anthropocene."

ethnical involvement.[16] This involves witness to ecocidal destruction to open the possibilities for differential forest futures. To witness this is to come face-to-face with the inheritances of the ongoing war on the forest and its ecocidal destruction. It involves listening to the forest in its diverse registers of communication: to the earthy redolence of decay and decomposition; to the germination of seeds; to lunar rhythms and the temporalities of rain; to the flowering of trees; to the comings and goings of pollinators and seed dispersers; and to the silences. The silence of foothills covered in extensive cattle grass, of rows of coca plants, and of dead soils and desiccated crops on farms fumigated with glyphosate. Listening to the forest is to witness the loss of connectivity of death nourishing life.

Face-to-face with the inheritances of ongoing war, I am called to responsibility through writing. This is writing called forth in encounters with the death and destruction of the selva. It emerges through dialogue with the selva, entangling stories of the selva drawn from ethnographic fieldwork and the selva's poetics.[17] Dialogue emerges through the poetics of the selva — its rhythms and diverse temporalities embodied in ethical time — the communicative relations of forest spirits, soils, plants, seeds, pollinators, and humans that link the past with the future.[18] This poetics of the selva is connected to the communicative relations, rhythms, and diverse temporalities of Indigenous relations with the selva itself.[19] It emerges from a resistance to ongoing colonization and war that replace the selva's diverse relationalities with "disarticulated fragments."[20] It is no coincidence that for Indigenous communities, this "sacred poetry" is composed of a language of earthly communication that is not intended for humans only but rather for the "revitalization of the earth."[21]

What I am interested in exploring here are the possibilities of ethical responses were we to relate not only the data on deforestation but the endangered liveliness of the forest itself. This requires learning to listen to forests in their diverse registers of communication that tell of the temporal relations that draw together humans and nonhumans relations of response to their collective, inherited pasts and responsibilities toward the possibilities of life's ongoingness.

Entangled in <u>Rastrojo</u>

In front of a wood-planked house, there is a hand-painted sign nailed to a tree, it reads, "en el interior del ser humano se ha talado el bosque de su sensibilidad, por esto es preciso ¡reforestar el corazón!?[22] Displaced in the midst of war, these

---

16   Rose, *Reports from a Wild Country.*
17   A collection of the author's insurgent poetics in defense of the selva, including sound poetry, on which this essay follows is published on pazconlaselva.net/.
18   Deborah Bird Rose, "Multispecies Knots of Ethical Time," *Environmental Philosophy* 9, no. 1 (2012): 127–40.
19   Deborah Bird Rose, "To Dance with Time: A Victoria River Aboriginal Study," *The Australian Journal of Anthropology* 11, no. 2 (2000): 287–96.
20   Rose, "Slowly Writing into the Anthropocene," 7.
21   Stuart Cooke, "Indigenous Poetics and Transcultural Ecologies," *Interdisciplinary Literary Studies* 20, no. 1 (2018): 24.
22   "Within the human, the forest of the mind has been cut down, for this reason it is necessary to reforest the heart!"

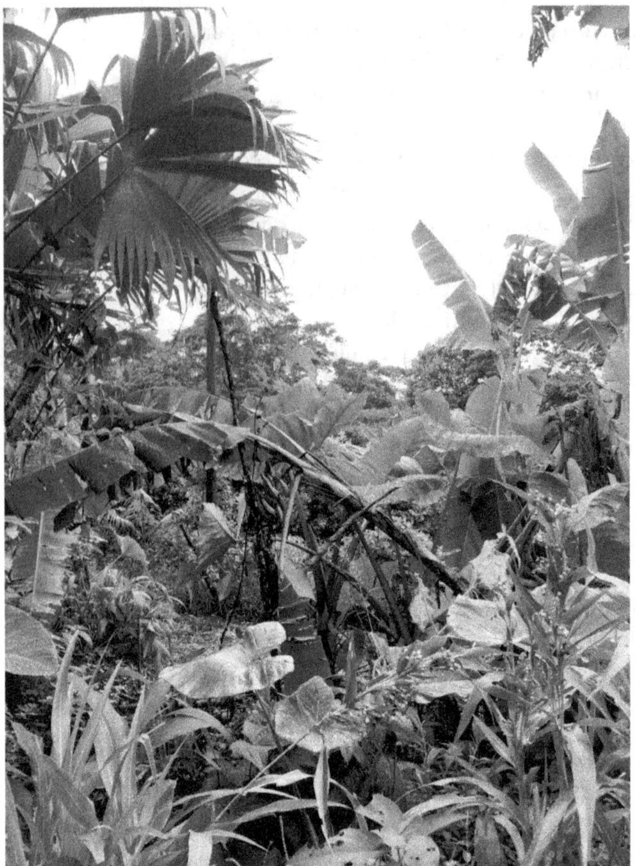

Fig. 8.2. Selva Farm, Putumayo, Colombia. Photograph by the author.

farmers found themselves "entangled in *rastrojo*" with cattle grass that remains rooted in desiccated soils, rendered lifeless from ongoing war. In these soils, they planted seeds gathered from the forest and carried from farm to farm. Germinating the midst of destruction are the possibilities for life's ongoingness. The earthy redolence of decay and decomposition indicates the force of the life of the forest to regenerate in the face of destruction. For communities negotiating life on the edge of the frontier, rastrojo re-grounds them with the continuum of the life of the forest. It draws them into relations with the forest itself: germinating seeds, fungi, dead plants and leaf litter, soils, roots, fermenting cacao del monte, copoazú, and maraca, and the comings and goings of pollinators and other seed dispersers. Grounded in the life-generating relations and temporalities of the forest in which the dead nourish the living, farmers cultivate rastrojo in response to the war on forests. Rastrojo indicates forest destruction and the possibilities for frontier livability.

The relational condition of living forests and their diverse life-worlds is embodied in rastrojo. Rastrojo is the forest growth following disturbance. It indicates destruction, and also the possibilities for life's ongoingness. Rastrojo is integral to the forest cultivation of Indigenous and other communities. It constitutes the continuum of Indigenous communities' forest-fallow cultivation characteristic of forests. For other communities navigating life on the edge of the frontier, rastrojo is the recolonization of the farm with the forest, constituting a form of resistance to the ongoing colonization and destruction of forests grounded in a reparative relationality with the forest on which their lives depend. Rastrojo indicates the force of the life of the forest to resist destruction and recolonize disturbed patches, engendering the conditions for life's ongoingness, including through collaborations with Indigenous and other communities. Rastrojo opens the possibilities to think differently. I look to rastrojo for thinking with the forest and thinking through its destruction toward the cultivation of responses grounded in a reparative relationality. Thinking with those communities and thinking with forests in rastrojo can transform our thinking of forests toward learning to think relationally and therefore opening the possibilities of responding to forest destruction.[23]

Amid devastated, denuded soils, campesinos in Putumayo are cultivating peace with the selva. These campesinos calls themselves "selvasinos" referring to their relation to the selva. Selva-farming is a response to the ongoing colonization — coca cultivation, cattle ranching, and the imposition of capitalist-oriented farming — that is driving the destruction of the Amazon. On one selva farm, clusters of cattle grasses were tangled with copoazú, maraca and cacao del monte. There Álvaro and Alba cultivate life on their selva-farming, working to recuperate the soils and their connection with the selva, a response to their displacement during paramilitary occupation of Putumayo that of the ongoing destruction of the Amazon. On their selva farm, once dedicated to cattle, they plant cacao del monte, camu camu, copoazú, maraca, and arazá. Selva-farming is what Álvaro described as "recolonizing the farm with the selva."[24] Recolonizing the farm with the selva involves the nourishing and reconfiguring campesinos' relations with the selva from inheritances of war, colonization, displacement, coca cultivation, and fumigations toward responsibility. Alba told how

> the people who live here who come from other parts, they do not know these soils. The campesino works to produce food. The tendency is to plant for profit and to do this the campesino clears forests. The point is that campesinos here do not know what our soils are like, they do not know that these soils are composed of and depend on the relations of different organisms and plants of the Amazon. When the forest is cleared the diversity of the soils is lost. The campesino here clears forests to sow, those soils no longer produce life, and so the campesino goes on clearing forests looking for productive soils.[25]

The recolonization of farms involves the collection of seeds and soils from the selva for nourishing soils degraded from fumigations and cattle. "The soils do not produce due to the fumigations and here we learn how to care for them. We collect soils and seeds from the forest to recuperate the soil communities. We planted trees and the birds and other creatures returned, those who left when the coca and cattle came. They collect and disperse seeds, working with us to return life to these

---

23 Plumwood, "Nature in the Active Voice"; Lyons, "Decomposition as Life Politics."
24 Field Notes (2018). Campesino, Putumayo, Colombia.
25 Ibid.

soils once again."[26] Campesinos depend on these soils which in turn depend on the relationships of decomposition, of death folding into life. Selva-farming is to "give back to the selva," which in turn nurtures the campesino.

On the ground, fermenting half-eaten arazá fruits give off the earthy redolence of decay and decomposition. Here, the dead nourish the living. The possibilities for life and peace emerge through the temporal relations of germinating seeds, soils, fungi, dead plants, leaf litter, and the comings and goings of pollinators and other seed dispersers. Selva-farming involves "learning from the selva," told Álvaro. This requires a posture of openness to its diverse temporalities of the selva: to decay and decomposition, the productive relations of fungi and soils, dead plants and leaf litter, fermenting cacao del monte, copoazú, and maraca, to the germination of seeds, to lunar rhythms and the patterns of rain. Through selva-farming, campesinos learn to listen and dialogue with the selva. Selva-farming emerges from the communicative relations of campesinos, soils, seeds, plants trees, birds, and pollinators embedded within the selva's diverse temporalities and relations of life, death, germination, and decomposition. It involves learning from the selva, learning to listen to its diverse registers of communication. Álvaro paused from cutting the encroaching cattle grass and dug the point of his machete into the soil around a banana plant to expose its roots. Through the discoloration of its leaves, Álvaro explained, the banana plant is communicating that it is not receiving enough nutrients. "You have to learn how to communicate with the plants, with the soils — with the selva," told Álvaro. Communicating with the selva entangles campesinos' relations of responsibility embedded within the selva's diverse temporalities and rhythms. "This does not exist in capitalism. It has another rhythm, to harvest for plata." Álvaro described how the failed rural development implemented with Plan Colombia is reproduced within the context of peace which introduces licit crops and orients the relations of campesinos, soils, seeds, plants, and pollinators toward capital investments. Selva-farming is a response to this colonization and destruction.

Selvas within the selva

The origin of the force is searching
so, as if to say, "what is the true word of strength?"
He is looking for
so he who works prepares his strength
that strength is in the ambil
the strength is in mountain salt, it is in the coca.[27]

Singing in the night, the *payé*, or Muruí elder, communicates with the selva through the spirits of the coca and tobacco — a dialogue through which the cultivation of the *chagra* is negotiated. For the Muruí of the Lagartococha Resguardo

26   Ibid.
27   A chant by Hipólito Candre, Uitoto elder. Juan Álvaro Echeverri and Hipólito Candre-Kinerai, *Tabaco frío, coca dulce: Palabras del anciano Kinerai de la Tribu Cananguchal para sanar y alegrar el corazón de sus huérfanos = Jírue diona riérue jíibina: Jikofo Kinéreni éirue jito Kinerai ie jaiéniki komeki zuitaja ie jiyóitaja úai yoina* (Leticia: Universidad Nacional de Colombia, Sede Amazonia, 2008).

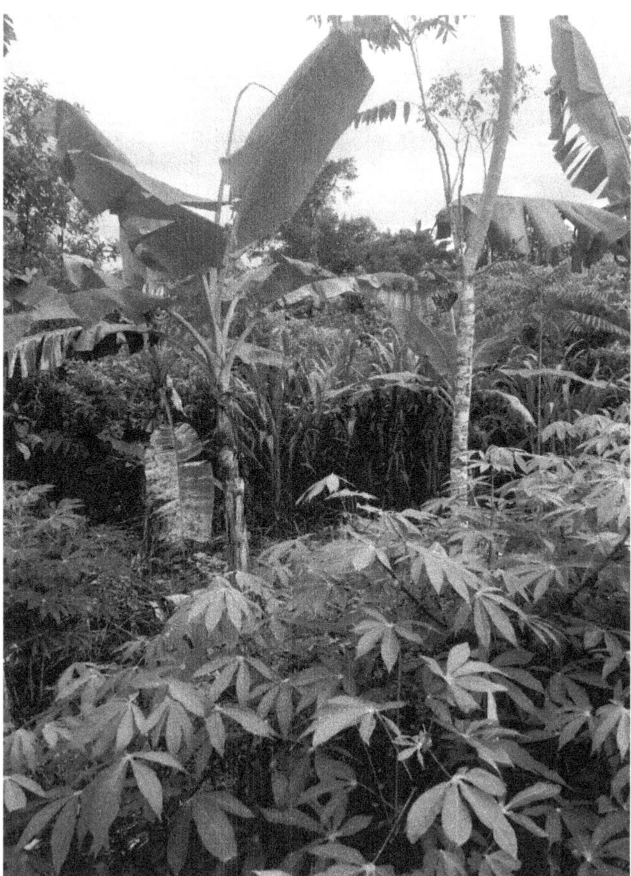

Fig. 8.3. Recolonizing the farm with the selva. Putumayo, Colombia. Photograph by the author.

in Puerto Leguízamo, Putumayo, the chagra is "the center of life." The chagra is a traditional cultivation plot that nourishes the connections of the community with the forest. It is embedded within the temporalities and relations of the forest itself. Its cultivation involves communication with the forest which is transmitted from generation to generation through songs and stories. At the center of the chagra is coca and tobacco. With coca and tobacco, the payé enters into communication with the spirits of the selva in the *mambeadero*. The mambeadero is to dialogue with the selva. On this night, the dialogue consisted of negotiating the location of the chagra and permission to clear forest for its cultivation.[28]

The opening of the forest and cultivation of the chagra depends on communication with the forest that originates in the mambeadero. The mambeadero is "a place of dialogue" with the forest.[29] The mambeadero constitutes the center of

28 Field Notes (2018). Muruí Resguardo Lagartococha Resguardo. Putumayo, Colombia.

29 Juan Álvaro Echeverri and Edmundo Pereira, "'Mambear Coca No Es Pintarse De Verde La Boca': Notas Sobre El Uso Ritual De La Coca Amazónica," in *Perspectivas Antropológicas Sobre La Amazonía Contemporánea*, eds. Margarita.

the chagra where the story of its origin is inherited and transmitted from generation to generation. In the mambeadero, the payé enters a dialogue with the forest through communication with the spirits of coca and tobacco. With coca and tobacco, the payé chants until nightfall, negotiating with these spirits to define the location of the chagra and to obtain permission to cut down the forest for its cultivation. Communication with the forest enables the payé to enter "negotiation and participation in the dialogic relationship" with the forest.[30] This dialogic relationship is embodied in the chagra itself, embedded within and co-constitutive of the temporal diversity and relationality of the forest. Once the location of the chagra is determined, the community organizes a minga to clear the forest and prepare the soils for cultivation. The chagra is later left fallow to return to the selva and regenerate forest. In rastrojo, nutrients return the soil through decomposition generating forest regrowth, including through the dispersal of seeds from birds and different species of pollinators.[31]

The chagra embodies the temporalities and communicative relations that draw these communities together with the forest. It constitutes a form of defense to its continuous destruction. Following decades of conflict, coca cultivation for narco-trafficking and the invasion of cattle ranching, the chagra is increasingly lost. The erosion of this ethical time and relations these communities with the forest is directly related to the destruction of the forest. The selva is comprised of spirits that protect it. These entities are the owners of the selva. The owners are the trees, the spirits of the selva. The defense of the selva is the defense of life. Its protection has to do with the spiritual connection among human and spirit worlds. It is the loss of spiritual connection that causes deforestation.[32]

It is certain that the selva still exists despite ongoing colonization, conflict, and forest destruction through the communication and ongoing dialogue of Indigenous *taitas* (elders) with the spirits of the selva. To the Cofán, the selva is the "spirit world," comprised of invisible beings, forest spirits, trees who are persons, and persons who are also jaguars. Dialogue with the selva, or spirit world, is enabled through yajé, a sacred plant through which the Cofán enter communication with the selva.

> *Chiga ("the Taita Tigre," or master of the spirits) and Yajé is the entrance to the world of the spirits; it is the spirit of the Tigre (jaguar, the Taita Tigre), through which the abuelos mayores relate to all the other spirits. The spirit of yajé governs all other spirits. Mayores (elders) are able to come into contact with the spirits of the selva, through the yajé. The yajé is the one who indicates where to plant and where or how to cut trees. In this way, they can ask for*

Chaves and CarlosL. del Cairo (Bogotá: Instituto Colombiano de Antropología e Historia ICANH & Universidad Javeriana, 2010).

30 Val Plumwood, "Nature in the Active Voice," *Australian Humanities Review* 46 (2009): 188–89.

31 Field Notes (2018). Muruí Resguardo Lagartococha Resguardo. Putumayo, Colombia.

32 Field notes (2018). Representative of La Asociación de Mujeres Indígenas "La Chagra de la Vida" (ASOMI), Putumayo, Colombia.

> *protection for the selva, which is carried out through attacks on invaders (like jaguar attacks).[33]*

Yajé enables the Cofán taitas to communicate with the spirit world — the plant spirits, who are considered persons, or with invisible persons who inhabit the selva, those who teach what each plant is for. The yajé also reveals to the taitas the spirits of the forest. In communication with these spirits, the taitas enter negotiations with them. This includes cultivation of the chagra in the selva. The spirits, through yajé, indicate where to clear forest for cultivation: "the yajé is the one who indicates where to sow and where or how to cut trees."[34] These negotiations also imply protection of the selva:

> *As every settler brings pure cows, I also wanted to put pure cattle. I already wanted to knock down those sides to put pure cattle. But like this, taking yagesito one day, it introduced me to some mountain spirituals, and they scolded me. All that forest must be preserved because if not, the food is going to run out. So, I thought about it there, and now I know that the forest has to conserve. The Indian knows that you don't mess with those spirituals.[35]*

For the Cofán, whose life-worlds are continually negotiated in dialogue with the selva, the defense of the selva essential to life's ongoingness. The role of the taita in these communities is necessary for negotiating life in the selva. Their rezos for communicating with the spirits of the selva are essential to its protection:

> The colonist does not know how to protect the selva because he has no rezos, does not take yajé and therefore does not have communication with the spirits of the selva. When the colonists come to clear the selva, to plant coca or pasto for cattle, they are killing people — the trees are people.[36]

For this Cofán community in Guamuez Santa Rosa, a resguardo in Valle de Guamuez, Putumayo, the negotiation of life in the selva depends on this these communicative relations, though these relations remain threatened with ongoing war and colonization that introduced coca for narco-trafficking and cattle into this community. With the destruction of the selva that is occurring from ongoing colonization, the spirits of the forest are disappearing. The destruction of the selva is the destruction of the spirit world. The Cofán, in negotiation with the forest spirits, lived from the forest though they are increasingly dependent on the food in town. In the context of these transformations, the transmission of stories and learning about how to communicate with the selva is interrupted, especially given that new generations is recruited to cultivate coca. The disruption of these relations is the death of ethical time, which carries grave consequences for the protection of the forest.

---

33 Field Notes (2018). Cofán taita, Putumayo, Colombia.
34 Ibid.
35 O. Conteras, personal correspondence. 2019.
36 Field Notes (2018). Cofán taita, Putumayo, Colombia.

Toward a Dialogue with the Selva

The way to enter the world of forests is to listen. To listen is to open oneself to thinking differently — to think with and like forests. In Muruí Indigenous communities, this living forest thought is inherited and transmitted from generation to generation through stories told within the context of the mambeadero, which constitutes a ceremonial context for thinking and communicating with the forest. The location of the chagra and permission for forest clearing is granted through communication with forest spirits in the mambeadero. For the Cofán, the cultivation of the chagra and life with the forest is oriented through communication with the "spirit world." Through yajé, the Cofán develop a dialogical relationship with the forest spirit world. The orientation of life with the forest depends on this dialogic relationship that involves thinking with and learning from the forest spirits who indicate, for example, where to clear forest for cultivation. This communication essential for orienting and cultivating life with the forest. The following citation from a Cofán in Putumayo, Colombia further illustrates this relationship: "we know how to preserve things. If it were not for us, this forest would no longer be here. The yajesito shows us the spirituals that we must preserve. If one does not respect those spirituals, everything ends there."[37] For campesino communities navigating life on the frontier amid ongoing war, dialogue consists of learning how to communicate with the soils and plants and listening to their diverse registers of communication. It constitutes their re-grounding within the continuum of the life of those living forests. Thinking with and like forests and their relational life worlds demands re-grounded thinking within forests themselves toward thinking relationally with their diverse relations, narratives, and temporalities. This is necessary for orienting ethical response to our global climate crisis. The ethical relations in which our fragmented thinking of forests is embedded is what's driving their destruction and our global climate crisis. Learning to listen to forests in their diverse registers of communication is necessary for cultivating responses to their ecocidal destruction.

> *past the horizon*
> *the silence is ruptured*
> *with cantos*
> *the language of the ceaseless humming, vibrating, stirring*
> *the songs that conquer the darkness*
> *their rhythm folds the roots of trees, the spirits and the forest together*
> *a ritual response*
> *rezos para proteger la selva*[38]

---

37   O. Conteras, personal correspondence, 2019.
38   Rezos are the prayers of taitas to protect the selva.

References

Bird Rose, Deborah. "Multispecies Knots of Ethical Time." *Environmental Philosophy* 9, no. 1 (2012): 127–40. https://www.jstor.org/stable/26169399.

———. *Reports from a Wild Country: Ethics for Decolonisation* (Sydney: University of New South Wales Press, 2004).

———. "Slowly Writing into the Anthropocene." *Text Journal* 20 (2013): 1–4.

———. "To Dance with Time: A Victoria River Aboriginal Study." *The Australian Journal of Anthropology* 11, no. 2 (2000): 287–96. DOI: 10.1111/j.1835-9310.2000.tb00044.x.

Cooke, Stuart. "Indigenous Poetics and Transcultural Ecologies." *Interdisciplinary Literary Studies* 20, no. 1 (2018): 1–32. DOI: 10.5325/intelitestud.20.1.0001.

Echeverri, Juan Álvaro, and Hipólito Candre-Kinerai. *Tabaco frío, coca dulce: Palabras del anciano Kinerai de la Tribu Cananguchal para sanar y alegrar el corazón de sus huérfanos = Jírue diona riérue jííbina: Jikofo Kinéreni éirue jito Kinerai ie jaiéniki komeki zuitaja ie jiyóitaja úai yoina.* Leticia: Universidad Nacional de Colombia, Sede Amazonia, 2008. https://repositorio.unal.edu.co/handle/unal/70116.

Echeverri, Juan Álvaro, and Edmundo Pereira. "'Mambear Coca No Es Pintarse De Verde La Boca': Notas Sobre El Uso Ritual De La Coca Amazónica." In *Perspectivas Antropológicas Sobre La Amazonía Contemporánea*, edited by Margarita Chaves and Carlos Del Cairo, 565–594. Bogotá: Instituto Colombiano de Antropología e Historia ICANH & Universidad Javeriana, 2010.

Kohn, Eduardo. "Beyond Language." *PCA-Stream*, November 2017. https://www.pca-stream.com/en/articles/eduardo-kohn-beyond-language-100.

———. "Ecopolitics." *Society for Culture Anthropology*, January 21, 2016. https://culanth.org/fieldsights/ecopolitics/.

———. *How Forests Think: Toward an Anthropology Beyond the Human.* Berkeley: University of California Press, 2013.

Lyons, Kristina. "Decomposition as Life Politics: Soils, Selva, and Small Farmers under the Gun of the U.S.–Colombia War on Drugs." *Cultural Anthropology* 31, no. 1 (2016): 56–81. DOI: 10.14506/ca31.1.04.

Mehta, Sailesh, and Prisca Merz. "Ecocide — A New Crime Against Peace?" *Environmental Law Review* 17, no. 1 (2015): 3–7. DOI: 10.1177/1461452914564730/.

Plumwood, Val. "Nature in the Active Voice." *Australian Humanities Review* 46 (2009). http://australianhumanitiesreview.org/2009/05/01/nature-in-the-active-voice/.

CHAPTER 9

The Anti Menagerie: Fictions for Interrogating the Supremacy of World-shaping Violence

Cassandra Troyan and Helen V. Pritchard

The First Giraffe

At the opening to the Multispecies Storytelling Conference, Gunlög Fur, the dean of the Faculty of Arts and Humanities at Linnaeus University and professor of history, is making an address on the "First Giraffe in Paris." The audience of artists, academics, and students listen while seated comfortably in the lecture theater. Behind the dean a lithograph news-plate is projected and depicts an encounter between a harnessed giraffe and a human figure in "Jardin des Plantes," the botanical garden of Charles X in Paris. The plate is titled, "[d]iscourse from the Giraffe to the Chief of the Six Osages, delivered on the day of their visit to the King's Garden, translated from the Arabic by Alibassan, the Giraffe's interpreter."[1] The fictional news story depicts a scene in which the two celebrity-spectacle figures of the nineteenth century — a giraffe gifted to Charles X and a member of the Osage Nation delegation — engage in a conversation in Arabic about the king. The pamphlet was used to mediate satire to give voice to criticisms of Charles X. The giraffe on her journey through France became a ventriloquist, a multispecies figure that could critique the sovereign, even though the animal was under the domain and control of humans. The giraffe is given permission to do and say, through her charismatic animation, that which humans cannot.[2] The colonial ordering of their positions is clear, for the purposes of racial capitalism — the Osage people are placed in the same hierarchical position as the giraffe. Fur tells the story of the giraffe and the four men and two women from the Osage Nation who were brought to Paris in 1827 on the premise of a diplomatic visit by French beaver fur traders, portrayed through the daily newspaper coverage and pamphlet production as the last chance to see these representatives of a vanishing people.[3]

---

1   Gunlög Fur, "First Giraffe in Paris," welcome address presented at "Multispecies Storytelling in Intermedial Practices," Linnæus University, Växjö, Sweden, January 23–25, 2019.

2   Heather J. Sharkey, "'La Belle Africaine': The Sudanese Giraffe Who Went to France," *Canadian Journal of African Studies/Revue canadienne des études africaines* 49, no. 1 (2015): 53.

3   Jean Deannison, *Colonial Entanglement: Constituting a Twenty-First-Century*

Through this inscription, one of intertwined colonial and racial violence, the giraffe became renowned across Europe, and even after her death, the giraffe's skeleton was held in the museum of natural history in La Rochelle until very recently.[4] From her sexualization as a spectacle and commodity-driven life to her use in anatomical narratives after her death, the giraffe became kin of the primates described by Donna Haraway in *Primate Visions,* whose living and dead bodies become "part of the system of unequal exchange of extractive colonialism."[5] Indeed, through the practices of multispecies storytelling the shifting and unsteady terrains of who or what can be captured and who or what is animate enough to tell a story emerges. Fur's story created a necessary intervention that framed our experience of the conference through this historical and politically situated multispecies encounter.

However, the encounter between the giraffe and the Osage is more than a novel meeting, in which nonhuman animals and humans might communicate freely and without bounds. Instead, what it unfolds are the hardened entanglements of consumption, exploitation, labor, and the racially organizing capacities of multispecies storytelling that can be imploded as a mode for structuring the racist, Western imaginary of imperialist fantasy, if not countered otherwise. We believe that this story of the "First Giraffe in Paris" is a multispecies storytelling of an epic scale, one in which the giraffe and the Osage are all coerced, to become assumed, to be open as figures for narrative to take place, to become the figurations of the stories that colonialism or capitalism wants to tell. This is not so much the animal as the extractable resource to "think with" or "think like," but the commodification of the animal as site that can be inscribed with the "story." In this chapter, we seek to form new bonds of what we call "multispecies solidarity" that are sensitive to these histories of exploitation, and actively work to challenge them through collaborative speculative multispecies storytelling. This chapter is comprised of the theoretical framing and questions that ground our practice along with the three fictive scenarios that help give shape in their content and form, as to how these new bonds could be.

Introduction

The story of the giraffe and the Osage demonstrates that these multispecies histories are already existing as records of imperial violence and capture, although through our own investigations, we do not wish to make these moments merely visible through historical reanimation. Fur's analysis as a historian is greatly appreciated and crucial in contextualizing this moment but we believe the work of fiction provides a critical intervention by calling into question the relations between fact, fiction, and narration and who is given the voice and authority to be able to make claims to the category of history. History as we know it is *human* history, a "we" that claims dominion over nonhuman realms through a homogenous

Osage Nation (Chapel Hill: University of North Carolina Press, 2012); Tracy Neal Leavelle, "Religion, Encounter, and Community in French and Indian North America," PhD diss., Arizona State University, 2001.

4   Sharkey, "'La Belle Africaine.'"

5   Donna J. Haraway, *Primate Visions: Gender, Race, and Nature in the World of Modern Science* (New York City: Routledge, 2013), 20.

purview that both erases and marks their exclusion; meaning a significant inquiry should not only shift from the perspective of the historian but on the level of the species too, which ultimately challenges the notion of species itself. In order to interrogate the narrative of this collective "we," in relation to histories of colonial, imperial, and capitalist violence, we must address the anthropocentricism of the Anthropocene and its reinscribing of the category of species.

In our current geological epoch of the Anthropocene, the destruction of the planet has been assigned to the collective mythos of *Homo sapiens* as the dominant driving force of this violence. Important interventions and studies in decolonial, anti-racist, Indigenous, Black, and Marxist scholarship have complicated the narrative of the Anthropocene to acknowledge the roles that empire, capital, and racial terror have played within its formation both conceptually and geologically.[6] As discussed by Kathryn Yusoff, "[a]s the Anthropocene proclaims the language of species life — *Anthropos* — through a universalist geologic commons, it neatly erases histories of racism that were incubated through the regulatory structure of geologic relations."[7] The racialized narrative lurking beneath this Earth Science framework demonstrates that the ecological ruin we face as a species has not been perpetuated by humans on this planet as a cohesive totality.

What underpins our writing practices in this chapter is a commitment to calling into question the latent colonial violence at the heart of the issues of environmental destruction while also challenging the notion of universality within

---

6   See Kathryn Yusoff, *A Billion Black Anthropocenes or None* (Minneapolis: University of Minnesota Press, 2019); Kathryn Yusoff, "Geologic Life: Prehistory, Climate, Futures in the Anthropocene," *Environment and Planning D: Society and Space* 31, no. 5 (2013): 779–95; Andreas Malm, "In Wildness Is the Liberation of the World: On Maroon Ecology and Partisan Nature," *Historical Materialism* 26, no. 3 (2018): 3–37; Andreas Malm, *The Progress of This Storm: Nature and Society in a Warming World* (New York: Verso Books, 2018); Andreas Malm, *Fossil Capital: The Rise of Steam Power and the Roots of Global Warming* (New York: Verso Books, 2016); Andreas Malm and Alf Hornborg, "The Geology of Mankind? A Critique of the Anthropocene Narrative," *The Anthropocene Review* 1, no. 1 (2014): 62–69; Jason W. Moore, *Capitalism in the Web of Life: Ecology and the Accumulation of Capital* (New York City: Verso Books, 2015); Axelle Karera, "Blackness and the Pitfalls of Anthropocene Ethics," *Critical Philosophy of Race* 7, no. 1 (2019): 32–56; Tiffany Lethabo King, *The Black Shoals: Offshore Formations of Black and Native Studies* (Durham: Duke University Press, 2019); Romy Opperman, "A Permanent Struggle Against an Omnipresent Death: Revisiting Environmental Racism with Frantz Fanon," *Critical Philosophy of Race* 7, no. 1 (2019): 57–80; Zoe Todd, "Indigenizing the Anthropocene," in *Art in the Anthropocene: Encounters among Aesthetics, Politics, Environments and Epistemologies,* eds. Heather Davis and Etienne Turpin (London: Open Humanities Press, 2015); Arun Saldanha, "A Date with Destiny: Racial Capitalism and the Beginnings of the Anthropocene," *Environment and Planning D: Society and Space* 38, no. 1 (2020): 12–34; Dipesh Chakrabarty, "The Climate of History: Four Theses," *Critical Inquiry* 35, no. 2 (Winter 2009): 197–222; Dipesh Chakrabarty, "Anthropocene Time," *History and Theory* 57, no. 1 (March 2018): 5–32; Dipesh Chakrabarty, "The Planet: An Emergent Humanist Category," *Critical Inquiry* 46, no. 1 (Autumn 2019): 1–31; Nancy Tuana, "Climate Apartheid: The Forgetting of Race in the Anthropocene," *Critical Philosophy of Race* 7, no. 1 (2019): 1–31.

7   Yusoff, *A Billion Black Anthropocenes or None,* 2.

discussions of accountability and climate change — interrogating "who" is the responsible "we." In the words of Andreas Malm and Alf Hornborg, "[i]f climate change represents a form of apocalypse, it is not universal, but uneven and combined: the species is as much an abstraction at the end of the line as at the source."[8]

For Dipesh Chakrabarty, this abstraction manifests in the uneven terrain of history due to our inability to contend with these apocalyptic consequences, ascribable to the unfeasible task of experiencing *mankind* as a species:

> We can only intellectually comprehend or infer the existence of the human species but never experience it as such. There could be no phenomenology of us as a species. Even if we were to emotionally identify with a word like mankind, we would not know what being a species is for, in species history, humans are only an instance of the concept species as indeed would be any other life form. But one never experiences being a concept.[9]

Consequently, world history as the relation of all species taken as its totality or as a shift from an anthropocentric worldview still suffers from transhistorical or ahistorical abstraction, which ultimately undoes blame for the timely material effects of a select percentage of humans' destruction of the planet. Yet the uneven atrocity for who is the human "we" responsible is one aspect that affects and crosses both human and nonhuman species lines. The articulation of this "we" through discourses of the Anthropocene is an inherently anthropocentric framing that must be addressed in relation to multispecies storytelling as it reinscribes and reproduces the category of "species" in of itself. Thus, for our project, we are not interested in redefining the Anthropocene; instead we look to go beyond the limitations embedded within the framework it presents. The ability then to attend to those differences while seeking to escape the limitations of the category of species would mean the abolition of the classification of species in of itself to build a true multispecies or transspecies solidarity. As Elaine Gan outlines in her work on widening from human action to multispecies coordinations, to tell multispecies stories is to approach the "we" as emergent and contingent, assembled from entities who might generally be studied separately.[10]

As a form of practice-based research in this chapter we have written fictions in order to understand and attune to ways in which multispecies survival is inextricably connected to our own. One of the key commitments in multispecies storytelling has been the attempt to displace the human as the center of the stories told about world-making practices or to queer the boundary between human and nonhuman to undo the categories that hold them in place.[11] However, despite the critters, tubers, and composters without "ontological starting or stopping point,"[12]

---

8   Malm and Hornborg, "The Geology of Mankind?" 5–6.

9   Chakrabarty, "The Climate of History: Four Theses," 220.

10   Elaine Gan, "Time Machines: Making and Unmaking Rice," PhD diss., University of California Santa Cruz, 2016, 133.

11   Donna J. Haraway, *Modest−Witness@Second−Millennium.FemaleMan−Meets−OncoMouse: Feminism and Technoscience* (Hove: Psychology Press, 1997), 50; Noreen Giffney and Myra J. Hird, eds. *Queering the Non/human* (New York City: Routledge, 2016).

12   Haraway, *Modest−Witness@Second−Millennium.FemaleMan−Meets−Onco-*

we argue that for many theorists and writers who have flocked to the sites of multispecies practice there is little engagement with what Miriyam Aouragh and Paula Chakravartty describe as the contested backdrop of racial and colonial violence and anti-colonial struggle against which these theories were waged.[13] Therefore, much multispecies storytelling has struggled to displace the ways in which species is held in place. Although many accounts have opened spaces of alterity beyond humanist concerns, as we have written about elsewhere, their search for positive engagements with nonhumans has often attended to the liberatory potential of multispecies storytelling as a given.[14] This has led to perspectives that often obscure how speciesism is based in earlier colonial encounters and affected by the fractures of capitalism. Instead, we propose that multispecies solidarity stories must address the role of colonial rule in actively constructing a narrative of dominance and subjugation to all living organisms under its purview.

Through the following three fictions of multispecies storytelling, we explore the shifting and unsteady terrains that emerge from who or what can be captured and de/con/tained and who or what is animate enough to tell a story. "Act Naturally" is set during the present COVID-19 pandemic, a global crisis that has caused many aquariums and zoos to close for unforeseen amounts of time, even leading some to bankruptcy. When the animals' engagement with an audience moves entirely to social media platforms, it returns us to the questions of what the purpose of the zoo is and how is it different from a circus or a prison for the caged performers. The story "Act Naturally" is influenced by *Shirokuma Café,* the Japanese manga where animals live and work alongside humans and their caged cohabitants, and the role of animals who are captive versus those who live in the human world unfolds the interlocking relations between borders, nations, enclosures, and containment.[15]

In the following fiction, "They Say It Is Love," we enter the barn of choreographer Luc Petton and the violent practice of imprinting and domesticating signets to female dancers. Through the internal dialogue of the dancer, we witness how choreographic imaginaries become deeply entangled with the history of eugenics and eroticized labor to reproduce multispecies storytelling. However, as the dancer and the swans perform on Luc Petton's inhospitable stage, we imagine a revolt and uplifting riot, which produces a discourse of multispecies solidarity and possibility. The multispecies resistance continues as we meet beavers attempting to survive and thrive in the constantly hostile urban context of contemporary Stockholm.

The third and final text "The Crisis of Culling," is a para-fictional tale that draws upon the historical plight of the beaver being hunted into near extinction and their current resurgence as a species, marking them as destructive pests. The role of the beaver in society is taken up by the transhistorical character Lewis Henry Morgan — a nineteenth century American anthropologist and author of *The American Beaver and His Works* (1868) whose writings on kinship were extremely

    Mouse, 51.

13   Miriyam Aouragh and Paula Chakravartty, "Infrastructures of Empire: Towards a Critical Geopolitics of Media and Information Studies," *Media, Culture & Society* 38, no. 4 (2016): 559–75.

14   Helen Pritchard, "The Animal Hacker," PhD diss., Queen Mary University of London, 2018.

15   Mitsuyuki Masuhara, dir., *Shirokuma Café* (Shogakukan, 2012).

influential for Karl Marx and Friedrich Engels — as he facilitates public discourse, including the question of who owns land and who gets to lay claims to it. Culminating in multispecies solidarity that centers an Indigenous understanding of creating accomplices rather than allies, the struggles of the beaver are aligned with Indigenous Sámi and anarchist forest protectors who discover the possibility for resilient, intergenerational resistance.

The weaving of complicated and complicit narratives unfolds a map of complex histories and multispecies violences between corporations, the state, academia, and intermedia. By detangling the multiple narratives of this imploded knot — that ruby-wearing giraffe, the Osage people, eco-terrorist, beaver, the Sámi people, captive penguin, a barista, polar bear, fucking pandas, imprinted signet, orca, multispecies ensemble — we reconstruct and destabilize histories of colonialism, contemporary art, geopolitics, and environmental crisis.

Act Naturally

The zoo caretaker penguin is watching the captive penguin, Wellington, watch the whales, and the whales watch him as they record this for the aquarium's Twitter account. "Wellington, meet the belugas! This weekend, Wellington visited Kayavak, Mauyak, and baby Annik, who were very curious about this little rockhopper. Belugas are northern-hemisphere animals, so they would likely never see a penguin!"[16] Their thinking wanders from Wellington to the orca who returned an iPhone to someone after they dropped it in the water, or the time that white family was surrounded by a pod of whales and the mother called the police. "Officer, officer, we have an emergency, we're surrounded by three gray whales." "They're very intelligent! Oh my God, Oh my God!" The father said repeatedly in joyful disbelief as his family cried in horror. "Oh my God it's rolling! Oh my God look at that!"[17]

Confusing whales for sharks, or the encountering of a mammal so large you appreciate and fear the realization of your smallness. The greatest misunderstanding is the human family's misinterpretation of their intentions and how failing is never benign but always political. A horizon where instead of calling the police, you look out and see a fleet of communist dolphins dancing in the sunset.[18] The dolphins have been protected by the communist state workers all dressed in matching Adidas tracksuits. The workers cared for the dolphins, preparing them to be airlifted by helicopters to safety. A fleet of workers in solidarity with a fleet of dolphins on a political mission.[19]

16   @shedd_aquarium, *Twitter,* March 30, 2020, https://twitter.com/shedd_aquarium/status/1244743245588021250?lang=en/.

17   TIME, "Woman on Family Boating Adventure Calls Cops About Whales," *YouTube,* October 9, 2018, https://www.youtube.com/watch?v=Q4iQrDuf1r8.

18   Blake Stilwell, "Iran May Have a Fleet of Communist Killer Dolphins," *Military.com,* n.d., https://www.military.com/off-duty/iran-may-have-fleet-communist-killer-dolphins.html.

19   Jeff Farrell, "Irma: Cuba Airlifts Dolphins to Safety from Deadly Hurricane," *The Independent,* September 9, 2017, https://www.independent.co.uk/news/world/americas/irma-hurricane-florida-cuba-dolphins-cayo-guillermo-island-cienfuegos-a7937596.html/.

Instead, here they are in the aquarium, empty of human visitors, taking penguins for a walk. They call this walk a date, with the chaperones documenting every move. All they can think of is a panda rolling in a tire saying "service, service" over and over.[20] A group of penguins investigate a statue of a penguin. Penguins walk down stairs. "Wait for the hop at the end!" They imagine the captive penguins running out of the frame and past the info center desk and never looking back as they walk out of the building into the world. They go to a cafe run by one of their friends and sit there all day drinking caffè mochas. They get their drivers licenses. They get drunk and talk about their crushes on other penguins. They go home to their studio apartment. What kind of life could the un-captive penguins make for themselves? And how the zoo caretaker penguin sits differently in theirs, the unmaking of nature, the natural world disintegrating, sloughing off itself, eating a newly shed coat; caught between a dream of a free world and its manufactured enclosure.

"Where's Wellington now?" hashtag. The zoo caretakers are forced to find a new form of animation in this crisis. They're told it is for the captive penguins' stimulation since they're without crowds and rely on the zoo caretakers. They are at work. They are suddenly essential workers and more visible than ever. They think: what is a circus without an audience, a prison without prisoners or walls, an institution constantly remaking itself in and around a function of the natural where only they can provide the boundaries and limitations? "Public aquariums, zoos and museums provide sources of inspiration, knowledge and enjoyment for millions of Americans."[21]

If a museum is dead culture, the zoo is its animated entertainment counterpart. They create games for the animals to find their food. They love to see them "act natural" in a way that only they can define through the created conditions. Part-time Panda asks the full-time Panda at the zoo what it means "to act natural" and how he can do it.[22] He does not understand what it means, but he understands what it means to be cute and uses his popularity to make sense of his time there. A polar bear at the zoo wearing a cap wants to see the other polar bears but is not allowed to. He cannot confuse the polar bears in captivity with his autonomy. In order to see the polar bears, he has to pretend to be a stuffed polar bear rug. "It is one of the most intimidating animals on the planet and one of the few animals that actually see us as food."[23] The polar bear cannot go see the seals because they will be traumatized by an encounter with their most feared predator. The polar bear is domesticated, and he is very benevolent and calm in his cap and cross body messenger bag that he wears on this outing; or in his apron while working or the way he polishes the glasses behind the bar or when making perfect cappuccinos. The polar bear is asked by the penguin how he feels when he sees the seals, and he says he is confused, that he does feel a bit excited, and a rush wells up inside of him that he hasn't felt before. He tries to hold onto this sensation but also wants to keep

20   Masuhara, dir., *Shirokuma Café*.
21   Aquarium Conservation Partnership, "We Need Your Help," *New Mode*, 2020, https://act.newmode.net/action/aquarium-conservation-partnership/we-need-your-help/.
22   Masuhara, dir., *Shirokuma Café*.
23   Animal Channel, "Wild Polar Bear Tries to Break In - BBC Earth," *YouTube*, August 4, 2019, https://www.youtube.com/watch?v=9G1aHkLHQ2I.

it at a distance. He ultimately likes to keep his emotions under control. Others admire him for his sensibility. "Like you, we are doing what we can to get through this crisis. We want to continue to serve as sources of inspiration, knowledge and enjoyment for you and millions of Americans, but we need your help."[24]

In between the photo-ops and live streams, they walk down long industrial corridors as the captive penguins shit on the linoleum floors. People want more videos, but zoo caretakers are working under pressure, as they've been cut down to a skeleton crew while being required to take care of more and different animals than they are accustomed to. Zoo caretaker penguin is now caring for most of the captive penguins, along with the pandas too. They're constantly threatened with this new encroaching reality that even when things return to "normal," many of them will not have jobs while the same number of animals will remain and still require their care day in and out. "At 32 years old, Wellington is no spring chicken and not just because he's a penguin! He is more than double the life expectancy of a rockhopper. Thanks to laser therapy and cataract surgeries, he's 'still got it' and can enjoy going on enriching adventures."[25]

But some of the animals don't have the privilege of enrichment or of leaving their enclosures. Rather, they are savoring this new silence and privacy—the tigers, gorillas, pandas. All constantly expected to perform, their every action worthy of attention and praise. To "act natural." It became quite bothersome to even know how to live, sleep, fuck, or breathe. The two full-time pandas have gotten exceptionally good at acting naturally but they are also really bored by it, rolling around in their enclosures, playing in snow, and chasing each other. They try to recreate what it's like being in the wild, being unfettered and unbothered, to live as if no one is watching, even though they're constantly aware of this fantasy they're cultivating. They've been talking about potentially fucking for years now but are always annoyed by all the on lookers.

The two full-time pandas finally fuck and wonder if one of them will get pregnant and then how another, much larger spectacle will eclipse the mundaneness of their lives.[26] The zoo caretakers feel excited as they watch the pandas fuck and think about the possibility of finally having baby pandas. The days are long and slow without visitors passing by and slipping into each other. They wonder how long this will go on.

As the pandemic continues without an end in sight, the zoo caretaker penguin accepts a temporary furlough to see their partner who they're in a long-distance relationship with. Without the zoo, they have nothing to keep them there. They came to the border with all the necessary paperwork, and they spoke to every consulate and embassy they could think of calling. They knew it might be tricky but decided it was worth the risk. When they arrive at the border everything goes wrong. They're deemed to be a risk and the border agents are incredibly angry at them for trying to come into the country. They say that they have nowhere else to go and consider the country they're trying to get into one place that they call home. They're deemed a tourist and fail at being one, so they're detained. They're

---

24   Aquarium Conservation Partnership, "We Need Your Help."

25   @shedd_aquarium, *Twitter,* March 18, 2020, https://twitter.com/shedd_aquarium/status/1240355895571251207?s=20/.

26   @hkfp, *Twitter,* April 6, 2020, https://twitter.com/HongKongFP/status/1247175409902342145/.

searched, questioned, and interviewed about why they would come here when everything is locked down. They realize they belong nowhere but know they cannot say this to the border agent.

Ultimately, the border agents care little about anyone that is detained, and they do not try to hide this. To them it is quite clear that they're paid to attend to the border. Instead, they have hired caretakers who watch and feed anyone who is put in detention. The zoo caretaker penguin is kept in custody and handled by the detention caretakers. They sign many different papers on clipboards. They are taken behind a curtain and their body is thoroughly searched. All their bags are taken into another room and secured with identity tags. They go into a holding cell. There is a large glass window that separates them from the detention caretakers. There is nothing that they can do except watch TV. They think about acting naturally, they think about enrichment. The detention caretakers come into the room and ask if they want any water or something to eat. They follow them to the main room and look at cupboards full of snacks. Fruit in a cup, crisps, cookies, and pasta. They think about hiding shellfish in a plastic ball, about making a cake out of yams for a turtle's birthday.[27] "If an animal isn't feeling well, it can't tell us what's wrong."[28]

They take a few packages of cookies and a bottle of water and go back into the holding cell. "For me, most of it is building the relationship. Once you've established a rapport, and there's a mutual trust, the program can progress. You also have to remember to maintain that rapport; some sessions should just be for fun and not always pushing for new behaviors."[29]

They think of continents, terrains, habitats. Of their dead friends and elderly animals. Of oil tankers full of fresh saltwater being transported to the aquarium because the microorganisms must be preserved and cannot be replicated. Of animals crossing the sea in massive ships and dying, traveling along the same transatlantic slave routes the boats had carried with humans held as cargo. Or when travelling along in regal caravans, the caretakers also enslaved, made to be admired along their epic journey. A giraffe wearing a bejeweled cloak, already owned by the king.

The zoo caretaker penguin is in the holding cell when a border agent is let into the space. They're sitting in a diner booth with bright-blue cushions eating cold pasta, as they are told they are not being let into the country. The border agent stands over them and has them sign several pages on a clipboard. They're still being held in the holding cell but are told they will be deported the following morning. They think about "acting natural." Should they cry and plead? Resist and make a scene? They think about what the border agent might be expecting them to do in this situation. The zoo caretaker penguin expresses their sadness and worries they might not be able to come into the country again later. The border agent reassures them that they know they're not a criminal, that this is a matter of immigration and safety, instead. Their career will not be affected.

They feel like they're floating, transporting themselves back to the other enclosures where they spend most of their time. They imagine putting back on the

<hr>

27   @shedd_aquarium, *Twitter,* March 14, 2020, https://twitter.com/shedd_aquarium/status/1238967660991393792?s=20/.
28   @shedd_aquarium, *Twitter,* March 30, 2020.
29   @shedd_aquarium, *Twitter,* March 24, 2020, https://twitter.com/shedd_aquarium/status/1242485466492010504?s=20/.

panda suit to interact with the pandas in the enclosure. How they will nurse one of the new-born babies in front of an ecstatic audience. At the end of their shift, they will leave the enclosure and instead of walking to the break room to clock out and going home to their studio apartment, they will go around and unlock every cage and post it to Twitter and wait for it to go viral.

They Say It Is Love

The dancer is cradling the cygnets in the front seat as Choreographer Luc Petton reverses sharply out from the zoo car park at the Jardin des Plantes in Paris, the zoo at which the last animals of the royal menagerie of Versailles lived out their days. On the back of the car seat lies the dancer's copy of *King Soloman's Ring* by ethologist and eugenicist Konrad Lorenz with underlined sections and paper bookmarks. As the car winds through the rural, French roads, the dancer goes over the passages on imprinting in Lorenz's book. She is one of the six female dancers, chosen by Petton who will repeat the movements from Lorenz's 1935 study to imprint the cygnets so that they can dance as Swans in Petton's production.[30] He tells her that together they will create "a new world where communication could [be] possible between living creatures."[31]

Over the next six weeks Petton watches from the side-lines as the dancer forms a deep attachment to the cygnets. Like Lorenz she becomes a goose-mother. No one mentions the other implications of the 1935 study in relation to the upcoming ballet, at least not publicly. And when Lorenz gets cited endlessly in artworks and academic papers about multispecies care, Human Computer Interaction and environmental humanities, everyone will forget the historical usage of his work or at least will not worry about engaging with that part.

The dancer was the first large moving object that the cygnets met when they broke through the speckled blueish-grey eggshells.[32] No matter how exhausted she is from sleeping on the zoo floor, her continuation as a dancer, as a cultural producer, will depend on the next stages of her reproductive labor disguised as productive labor at Petton's research studio. She will need to perform a care for captivity. She recalls the pages of the Lorenz's book that show the images of cygnets following him, the self-appointed foster mother to care for the captive swans. As they sit on the barn floor Petton tells her that if this is successful, he plans on expanding his market to the United States using locally bred swans. Petton tells her this is a project of love and care. The cygnets nip her ears and suck on her legs, and as her nose still stings from their continual attacks, she wonders about this care and who it's for. She wonders what it means for Petton to generate new markets from the shared captivity between her and Pollux and Lida — a practice Despret

---

30   Amy Serafin, "Some of These Performers are Really Typecast," *The New York Times,* June 3, 2012, https://www.nytimes.com/2012/06/03/arts/dance/choreography-with-real-swans.html/.

31   Lisa Mullins, "French Company Puts Real Swans on Stage," *The World,* June 12, 2012, https://www.pri.org/stories/2012-06-12/french-dance-company-puts-real-swans-stage-swan/.

32   Serafin, "Some of These Performers Are Really Typecast."

notes "has become a practice of caring" in the dance, impregnation, and research studio.[33]

It's 2010 in Orlando, Florida and families have spent their holiday budgets on "Dine with Shamu," a delicious all-you-can-eat buffet at a reserved poolside table for an unforgettable, up-close encounter with magnificent marine mammals. Reservations were made at the Dine with Orcas Check-In Station, the Reservation Center or Guest Services just inside the park — if space was available. As the families experience majestic orcas up-close from the poolside patio, they enjoy a one-of-a-kind dining experience. Orcas scrape their broken teeth along the glass walls and jump onto the platforms alongside the diners. During the dining experience there was nothing out of the ordinary observed.[34]

At the end of the show, the trainer had climbed out of the pool; the trainer was lying with her face next to the magnificent marine mammal. On learning of the whale's increasing aggression and previous killings, The Occupational Safety and Health Administration (OSHA) representative had told her on the call that, if possible, the trainer should bring the working conditions to her employer's attention. However, unlike the whale, she was replaceable and besides she hadn't felt convinced that her job would be protected. Now she was lying on the platform, with her blonde ponytail dangling in the water, interacting with the whale, giving people a bit more of a show, using fish to reward him. She was doing the trainer hug, the pat, throwing fish for him and things, she was lying on that platform and when he came up, she would hug him.[35]

The eyewitness could see that the whale was coming up to the blonde trainer to receive his treats and whatnot and that she was enjoying him coming up and doing his loops. Suddenly the eyewitnesses could see the trainer with the black and white uniform and the blonde ponytail was in the water with what looked like the largest male at the park and so the eyewitness believed it was the whale from "Dine with Shamu."[36]

At this point they hadn't sounded the alarm, but the trainer is spread eagle in the water; she was scrambling, reaching, and the whale approaches her to carry out his brutal act against his trusted captive companion. The eyewitness said at first it was like he was going to foot lift her, like they do in the "Believe Show," but instead he impacted her squarely in the chest. Then he came around again and he opened his mouth, only her legs remaining in view. The senior trainer at SeaWorld at the time of her death said, "[w]e'll never know why he made that choice to grab her and pull her into the pool. He had a great relationship with her, and she had a great relationship with him. I do believe that he loved her, and I know that she loved him."[37]

33   Vinciane Despret, "The Body We Care For: Figures of Anthropo-zoo-genesis," *Body & Society* 10, no. 2–3 (2004): 130.

34   Take Part, "Death at SeaWorld Eyewitness Interview with Jessica Wilder | The Cove | TakePart," *YouTube,* November 26, 2012, https://www.youtube.com/watch?v=sx8MQrdinTU.

35   Ibid.

36   Ibid.

37   Simon Worral, "Former Trainer Slams SeaWorld for Cruel Treatment of Orcas," *National Geographic,* March 29, 2015, https://www.nationalgeographic.com/news/2015/03/150329-orca-blackfish-seaworld-dolphins-killer-whales-ngbook-talk/.

Dragging her body through the straw the dancer reflected on how tired she felt. Today at Petton's barn had been particularly exhausting as Marie-Agnès Gillot, the principal dancer from the Paris Opera Ballet who had danced Odile-Odette in "Swan Lake," had been invited by Petton to join them all.[38] As Petton and Gillot instruct her to raise and lower her arms, repeatedly the dancer stares at the black curtains, no daylight view. Petton introduces the dancer to Gillot as the foster mother for Pollux and Lida. She is reminded that she is one of four young artists that benefit from the Talent Dance program. All of them are aged less than twenty-five and they were spotted by the agency who coproduced the first performances of Swan.[39]

As she raises and lowers her arms, Petton reminds her this is more than a job, this is love, this is care—and she has both for the cygnet. She immerses herself; this isn't a job now, but a passion. This is the third week, and the domestic device is at work. Pollux and Lida, have already began to mirror her, following her arm with their beaks as they stretch their necks to shadow her arms in *agence* with her.[40] She cares for the cygnet; she cares for their capacity to dance with her, their capacity to work alongside her.[41] As she rolls around on the floor, Pollux and Lida scratch at her back and tear at her ears and Petton directs her from the sidelines. She tells Gillot that it is becoming more "natural" to be in relation with the cygnet. As Pollux and Lida learn to walk like her, drink like her and caress her, the presence of Gillot reminds her of the days and nights that she has spent with the cygnets is a great gateway to the professional world.

As the imprinting has been successful, Pollux and Lida now panic when she is not near, so the dancer stays full time at the barn and together with the other talent-program dancers they share "new natural" conditions. The dancer lies awake during the long nights in the barn thinking of her body and Pollux's swan body dancing in Petton's opera. As the project recently received a large research council grant the dancer imagines the bodies of herself and cygnets as labor and capital investments of Petton and academia, selling the show like Gillot, their lives constituted by each other and the opera, "La Confidence des Oiseaux," a "multispecies reality of ruthless exploitation."[42]

The next morning, they are performing the movements once more. Dissociating, the dancer rolls across the straw and she considers her caring role. If this barn knowledge is caring, it demonstrates that both knowledge and caring itself is based on capitalist exploitation and accumulation. She considers how the knowledge and caring that emerges from this multispecies agence is not any exception to capitalist production but rather is propelled by her shared state of captivity with Pollux and Lida — indeed their shared captivity and capacity for storytelling opens new

38   Serafin, "Some of These Performers Are Really Typecast."

39   Luc Petton, "Luc Petton," *Le Guetteur,* n.d., https://www.lucpetton.com/fr/luc-petton-en/.

40   Brett Buchanan, Matthew Chrulew, and Jeffrey Bussolini, "On Asking the Right Questions: An Interview with Vinciane Despret," *Angelaki* 20, no. 2 (2015): 165–78.

41   Vinciane Despret, "Who Made Clever Hans Stupid?" *Angelaki* 20, no. 2 (2015): 77–85.

42   Brian Whitener, "Animal Accumulation," *Blindfield Journal,* August 4, 2018, https://blindfieldjournal.com/2018/08/04/animal-accumulation/.

markets for Petton. And as she wonders about jail breaking them all, Lida climbs onto her back leaving a road map of scratch marks as she slips off. Rolling one more time she makes a mental note that it will be the stories of the dancer's discipline and the disciplining of the baby swans, the cult-like rituals of the research studio, the injuries to her body, the removal of the eggs after the impregnation of the swan, told across media outlets and academic papers that will eroticize this capital. No longer just a goose-mother, her injured, scratched body will become a financial asset in the spectacle of selling the show. Her stinging back reminds her of the intertwining of affective and erotic capital, reminds her how each stage of the imprinting secures her place, increases her value within the company. Despite her rent arrears and containment in the barn she feels lucky — lucky that her capacity for love and care makes it possible to succeed under these conditions of making multispecies stories.

As the dancer and cygnets repeat the movements, Petton stands at the edge of the barn looking on from the sidelines at his progeny from the impregnation protocol. In the damp barn air, Petton considers the further implications of this imprinting, after all as Lorenz had shown, it is not only that the cygnet now recognizes the dancer as its parent but also there will be a powerful sexual connection between the dancer and the swan. Petton closes his eyes and envisions a multispecies spectacular, the dancer on stage with Pollux as the adolescent bird pursues a cross species fuck with her, the coy dancer swimming in a half sphere, reminiscent of a Dita von Teese martini glass burlesque routine, but instead of a giant olive, beside her is a swan. The commissioned music will interpret the intimacy of their unique connection and the audience will feel the frightened thrill at watching this risky liaison as water splashes off the stage. Later that day the dancer listens to Petton's plan as she pours surgical spirit onto cotton pads. The dancer dabs the cotton pads onto the backs of her bleeding ears, and for a moment she notices the implications of this "work." She asks herself what it means for an opera, based on the cocreated expression of human and swan, to carry with it the negative shape of captivity and her compliant affective labor? For a moment she remembers this is pregnancy as work, this is mothering as work, this is sex as work; she wonders what it would be to tell that story of the research studio in the opera "Swan." She imagines a scene on the stage in Paris in which six protesting swan parent-lover-dancers exhausted from the days and nights at the barn of preparing the cygnets for performance, demand safer working conditions. She imagines the parents and lovers in the audience acknowledging their unwaged labor is also generative of capital. The audiences rising from their seats and joining the dancers and swans on the stage forming alliances, the most radical confrontation of multispecies strength and solidarity.

The Crisis of Culling

Outside the window next to their kitchen table there was a park falling into a grandeur of decay. The rotting leaves left since there was no one to rake them, ponds overflowing with algae, fungi sprouting on the wet lawn. The sun barely reaches the horizon, partially blocked by the looming castle tilting further and further toward the sea. The ground on which the castle sits is slowly slipping back onto the sea floor through centuries of underwater excursions, maritime antique collectors looking for souvenirs and false promises of buried treasures. These mythologies lead one charlatan archaeologist to begin a covert midnight dig at the site with dynamite in an attempt to blast out the hidden fortune.

Yet, the biggest culprit considered responsible for the sinking of this heritage site and blocking access to further investigation, were the beavers and their massive burrows and dams that were almost greater than the castle walls. It was a vast network culminating in an enormous lodge, which had flooded and turned the otherwise pristine and manicured facade of the park back into a feral territory.

It was an eyesore according to residents, but there was an underlying current of fear that led many to voice their beliefs that the beavers were beginning to take too much. There were reports of beavers biting residents on river tours, attacking commuters trying to get on buses and anyone who found their presence to be a tourist worthy novelty.[43] In the capital city there was a great mass of cameras that had been smashed or snatched from curious onlookers' hands by the beavers. The cameras were now stacked on top of the largest lodge in the main harbor, as both a sign of victory and a warning. The incidents of beaver arson had perhaps caused the greatest amount of worry due to the destruction of private property and city infrastructure. Although some claimed this was unintentional, others began to suspect that there were greater motivations at stake.

"The beavers themselves would probably not claim they destroy society functions. But they often fell trees that fall on electricity wires. If I may offer a theory, without having any insight into the case, I think it's a tree that has fallen and caused sparks," beaver expert Lars Plahn at the county council's environmental department told SVT.[44] In response to these acts, a silent culling started to take place for the animals supposedly causing "too much harm."[45] The webbed-footed ringleaders of the beaver crime syndicate and those making general mischief were singled out and shot by the game warden, Tommy Tuvunger, in the capital city. In order to not cause alarm or distress to human citizens, they were shot with silenced weapons.

Despite the animal-control protocols that the local council had agreed upon, one especially graphic killing of a beaver mother and her kits was documented and went viral on social media, causing public outrage that created a space for societal discourse on the presence and nature of the beavers. *Are beavers intelligent, curious, and emotional creatures that should be protected, or are they destructive vermin, lowly rodents that should be exterminated like rats and mice? Are they a threat to society and order? And seemingly most important, are they cute, or ugly? Just* how *cute are the babies?* Special news segments were dedicated to these topics as reporters spoke to passers-by on the street.

Self-proclaimed "experts" began to step forward to share their unwanted opinions, with some even invited onto television for the supposed sake of unbiased reporting by presenting both sides of the issue. They came with diagrams of beavers' brains to show, following the work of Konrad Lorenz, that it had been shrinking

---

43   "Beaver Bites Bus Passenger in Sweden," *The Local Sweden*, March 31, 2015, https://www.thelocal.se/20150331/beaver-bites-swedish-bus-passenger/.

44   Ibid.

45   James Owen, "Beavers Returning to Sweden's Capital Can Be a Dam Nuisance," *National Geographic*, April 19, 2016, https://www.nationalgeographic.com/animals/article/160419-beavers-animals-science-sweden-world-wild-cities/.

through the process of its evolution and urban conditioning rather than growing larger, somehow proving the inferiority of the beaver and a case for their extermination. Although, through fact-checking, experts remarked that the results of this study were in fact in relation to the Mountain Beaver (*Aplodontia rufa*) native to the northwestern United States and parts of southern British Columbia, not the Eurasian or European beaver (*Castor fiber*), which was under discussion and living in the city limits. *Castor fiber* is just as intelligent in comparison to other rodents or mammals, in terms of its relative body weight to brain size, or the *encephalization quotient* (EQ). Yet according to Professor Emeritus Dietland Müller-Schwarze, from the Department of Environmental Biology at the State University of New York, "the EQ (0.8) of the Eurasian beaver is slightly lower than that of the North American beaver."[46]

In response to the phrenological discourse, Lewis Henry Morgan, nineteenth-century anthropologist, social theorist, and railroad lawyer, came forward via transhistorical hologram, as the most enthusiastic supporter of the beavers, although admittedly his expertise was in relation to the American beaver, of which he wrote a massive study called *The American Beaver and His Works* (1868). Rather than going on about the size of the beavers' brains, he mostly spoke to the public about how the beaver lived; the complex construction of their lodges and dams, their ways of changing and cultivating the landscape according to their needs. He saw first-hand how the development and expansion of the railroad in North America often threatened the beavers' habitats, along with the aggressive hunting and trapping of beavers for their pelts by non-Native, white settlers. He discovered the resilience of the beaver when stories from hunters told of beavers marked by trap wounds, some missing one, or two of their legs, yet still living on for years after these incidents. On the question of whether or not they felt pain during these executions, Morgan discussed the specific characteristics of the beavers — he often referred to them as "the mutes," which caused a conflict in the beaver and disability communities, but was ultimately resolved after mediation — in relation to our own human faculties by stating, "[w]hen, therefore, we find the phenomena of pleasure and pain displayed by individuals of every species, and to be essentially the same in kind among them all, it leads to the same general conclusion; namely, that all living creatures possess a similar mental principle. This leaves the question of difference in degree, which was rendered necessary by difference in species."[47]

In the city and beyond, a parallel conversation was happening, although around issues of sovereignty and land recognition for the Sámi people.[48] Despite fighting for the preservation of their customs and language for hundreds of years, only recently did these concerted efforts force an uncomfortable public discourse on the legacies of Swedish colonialism and lead to the Constitution of Sweden to be finally amended in 2011 to officially recognize the Sámi as a people.[49] Especially

46 Dietland Müller-Schwarze, *The Beaver: Its Life and Impact* (Ithaca: Cornell University Press, 2011), 12.

47 Lewis Henry Morgan, *The American Beaver and His Works* (Philadelphia: J.B. Lippincott & Co., 1868), 252.

48 Gabriel Kuhn, *Liberating Sápmi: Indigenous Resistance in Europe's Far North* (Oakland: PM Press, 2020).

49 "World Directory of Minorities and Indigenous Peoples — Sweden: Sámi," *Ref-World,* March 2018, https://www.refworld.org/docid/49749ca35.html.

for the Sámi in the present-day Stockholm region, as they're usually assumed to live in the far North, although originally their territories extended throughout the whole of Sweden, Finland, Norway, and Russia, without the existence or violence of border regimes limiting their once free movement.[50]

To make the best use of their newfound platform, the beavers brought attention to other organizations taking part in land occupations in the Finnish boreal forest, and those in solidarity with international, Indigenous communities for the protection of their own ancient growth forests, such as Cree First Nation of Waswanipi in Canada.[51] The beavers wanted to make a clear statement about their position, so they started to leave messages in arranged woodchips throughout the city that would later be broadcasted on the nightly news: "WHOSE LAND? OUR LAND" or "LAND BACK"

Morgan followed by reaffirming his stance on respecting Indigenous sovereignty, as he had spent an extensive amount of time with the Iroquois and learned greatly from their communal ways of living in shared longhouses. Unfortunately, due to his progressive positions that wished to challenge the hegemony of humans and white settler colonialism, he was labelled a "cultural Marxist" by the far-right media internationally and accused of being a communist. Whether or not this was his political position was never really addressed, instead the fact that Karl Marx wrote a précis on Morgan's ground-breaking work, *Ancient Society* (1877), which was later used by Friedrich Engels to write *The Origin of the Family, Private Property and the State* (1884), was taken as proof of his affiliation with their ideas. To the alt-right trolls, Engels's declaration at the forward to his book noting, "Morgan in his own way had discovered afresh in America the materialistic conception of history discovered by Marx forty years ago, and in his comparison of barbarism and civilization it had led him, in the main points, to the same conclusions as Marx," was enough of a damning association.[52]

Rather than an outright public condemnation of Morgan, there was an actual resurgence of general interest in the work of Engels and the early Humanist writings of Marx. A new edition of *The Ethnological Notebooks of Karl Marx (Studies of Morgan, Phear, Maine, Lubbock)* (1882) transcribed and edited, along with an introduction by Lawrence Krader, became an international bestseller, translated into thirty languages.[53] The unlikely success of this work caused several conflicts,

<hr>

50   Giuseppe Amatulli, "The Legal Position of the Sámi in the Exploitation of Mineral Resources in Finland, Norway and Sweden," PhD diss., Åbo Akademi University, 2014, and Anni-Kristiina Juuso, "Saamelaisten asioita koskeva sovintoprosessi Kuulemisraportti," *Valitoneuvosto, Julkaisuarkisto Valto*, November 26, 2018, http://urn.fi/URN:ISBN:978-952-287-673-7.

51   Phillipa Duchastel de Montrouge, "The Red Line — A Week in Solidarity with the Sámi People in Finland," *Greenpeace*, September 4, 2018, https://www.greenpeace.org/canada/en/story/4183/the-red-line-a-week-in-solidarity-with-the-sami-people-in-finland/.

52   Friedrich Engels, "Preface to the First Edition, 1884, 'The Origin of the Family, Private Property and the State,'" trans. Alick West, *Marxist Internet Archive*, 2000, https://www.marxists.org/archive/marx/works/1884/origin-family/preface.htm/.

53   Lawrence Krader, "The Ethnological Notebooks of Karl Marx: A Commentary," in *Towards a Marxist Anthropology: Problems and Perspectives* (Berlin: De Gruyter, 1979), 153–171.

fallouts, and crises in the far-right community, all bemoaning how they brought this upon themselves. Upon coming out of his eight-day medically induced coma in Russia to detox from benzodiazepines, Jordan B. Peterson responded with such wild rage and envy that he quickly became addicted to DMT and later fell to his death from an airplane while trying to investigate "chemtrails" from an Airbus A340's engines.

Despite this new international network of communist beaver advocates, the killings continued at home. The beavers tried to bring awareness to their plight by historicizing their struggle. Those who had avoided the slaughtering by the game warden and individuals protecting their "private property," referred to this purge as the "Second Great Culling," the "First Great Culling" being when they were hunted to near extinction, with the last beaver seen in Sweden by 1871. When they returned to their land it was only through the manufactured and human-led transportation of their species, were able to thrive again in the places they had been eradicated for their pelts. Despite their success in repopulating, through their destruction of so-called "private property," they found themselves at odds with the modern world that was rapidly building against them. Some humans responsible for the violence refused to take responsibility or to even acknowledge the killings. They claimed it wasn't their decision, their right to intervene. In an attempt to bring the public discourse back into the realm of science, Ola Jennersten, biologist at the non-profit World Wildlife Fund Sweden, claimed that "since landowners — in this case the city of Stockholm — own hunting rights to kill animals on their property, it's up to them to create their own management plans, he says. And sometimes their record keeping — for instance, how many animals they've shot — can be off. I didn't know [about the beaver cull]," he adds, "but I can imagine that you need to take away some individuals if they cause too much harm."[54]

Morgan found this sentiment to be unacceptable. *Should humans also be exterminated directly when they cause too much harm to private property?* He asked the public:

> Their acts, in innumerable instances, are seen to be acts of intelligence and knowledge, such as a man would perform under similar circumstances, and yet, there is an unwillingness to recognize in them the results of deliberate processes of reasoning, followed by an exercise of the will. A large class, it is true, acknowledge some reasoning powers in the mutes, but under such qualifications, limitations, and restrictions, that, in effect, it denies to them the possession of a free intelligence. The real question is practically evaded. Their acts should be tested by the same analysis which is applied to human acts, and full credence be given to the results. As we cannot place ourselves in personal connection with the animal mind and thus obtain their testimony concerning their mental processes, we are remitted to their personal acts. Upon these, however, a judgment can be formed as definitely as one man can pronounce upon the act of another man. While this method is not as irrefragable as an appeal to consciousness, it is one upon which mankind act implicitly in their own affairs.[55]

54 Owen, "Beavers Returning to Sweden's Capital Can Be a Dam Nuisance."
55 Morgan, *The American Beaver and His Works*, 259.

A number's game. A technicality against those who can be considered too plentiful. A pest, worthy of extermination or tolerable when kept under control. The Media and Publicity cadre of the Communist and Anarchist Beaver Allies League (CABAL) had taken to documenting the most affectionate moments in the beaver's lives in hopes of making them appear as cute as possible: when they participated in social grooming, the babies breast feeding, or cuddling with mom and dad. Due to their nocturnal nature, there was a livestream infrared camera set-up in a beaver lodge, called the "LodgeCam," to try to give a more intimate picture of their daily lives and how they lived cooperatively with other species during the winter months.

Yet, to state nature managers such as Tuvunger, his only concern was, "[t]he only plan I have is to keep the population in balance with what nature can handle."[56] In retribution, the beavers became more daring in their actions, purposefully leaving tracks and traces to and from their crimes, sometimes even spelling out in the remains of sawdust left at a gnawed-up tree stump "EYE FOR AN EYE" or "YOU'RE NEXT." Understandably, the game warden was genuinely concerned and vehemently stressed that these events must be hidden from the public eye. He chalked up these gestures, at best, as pranks by local "troubled youth" or Indigenous activists, and, at worst, anarchist eco-terrorist trying to claim the beavers' actions for their own causes. Although more serendipitous circumstances would bring the Sámi people and environmental rights "extremists" into an unwavering pact of solidarity with the beavers.

During a recent tree-sit to protect a tract of old growth forest against the extension of a highway, in the middle of the night, settler and Indigenous forest-protectors could hear a large tree falling in the distance. Believing it was another act of illegal logging practices by a private company, they ran toward the crashing expecting to find a group of workers, only to see a massive beaver beginning to drag away the felled trunk through a scattering of woodchips that read, "LIGHTS OUT."[57]

The bright headlamps of the forest protectors alarmed the beaver who at that moment obviously felt under attack. Silently the forest protectors looked around at each other, shut off their headlamps and sat on the ground. The beaver was confused and continued to thump his tail on the ground to ward off the intruders. After a while, he was still unsettled by the whole incident but started to drag the log to the river. Rather than sitting and passively watching him, the protectors carefully went and began to lift the log so it would be much easier for the beaver to carry. The beaver conveyed his frustration with this gesture, as he could obviously do this himself, and did not need them to come and make assumptions about what he could or could not do and what he might really want them to do. The settler forest protectors felt embarrassed by their comfort with their authority and wanted to unlearn their oppressive behavior. They asked what they could do to be good allies to the beaver and his community.

With this question, slowly many beavers began to appear from the surrounding forest and bank of the river in the darkness. The forest protectors now found themselves surrounded as the beavers huddled up to speak together. The beavers

---

56   Owen, "Beavers Returning to Sweden's Capital Can Be a Dam Nuisance."

57   Emma Löfgren, "Swedish Beaver Knocks out Power for Thousands," *The Local Sweden,* August 19, 2015, https://www.thelocal.se/20150819/beaver-knocks-out-power-to-thousands-in-sweden/.

spoke rapidly in impassioned tones, occasionally glancing back to look at the forest protectors, who stood silently waiting for the beavers to come to a consensus about what they could do. As the minutes turned to hours, some beavers began to go off as others continued to converse. The beavers who went off continued their work of felling trees and chewing bark. It became clear that the beavers were collecting woodchips and bark as they started to write a message to the forest protectors. With brilliant speed they quickly crafted a message that read: "ACCOMPLICES NOT ALLIES."

As the forest protectors began to talk together about the meaning of the message, a projection beam settled on the forest floor illuminating the holograph of Morgan, who also sat silently in reflection.

"What does that mean?" one of the settler forest protectors asked.

"Well," I think it means should we "desire to merely 'unlearn' oppression, or to smash it to fucking pieces and have its very existence gone?"[58]

"Instead of lifting a log, why don't we try picking up a hammer, a torch, or a chainsaw?"

The beavers sat waiting as dawn started to approach. In the faint light the forest protectors could now see that some of the beavers were missing toes, parts of their feet, whole legs severed at the shoulder but completely healed with thick fur covering the site of the absent limb. They remembered Morgan's accounts of beaver surviving several trapping attempts, losing their limbs to escape often aided by other beavers coming to their rescue. And Morgan's account of one beaver who had escaped three different traps and was finally caught by his one remaining fully intact leg. From the inner circle, this beaver appeared.

He appeared to be an elder of some sort, as the other beavers paid great attention to whenever he spoke, listening carefully and pausing all other chatter. Yet, the timeline didn't match up, how old could this beaver be? The forest protectors soon realized they were surrounded not only by elders, but by ancestors as well. They felt overcome with a new understanding of what they were struggling to articulate, what they were up against, the stories they thought and told themselves suddenly unravelling. A circuitous logic, a fiction that can never really approach the nature of the story, the storytelling form itself, because to do so, it would need to destroy the storytellers. From this, the forest protectors knew what they needed to do as they followed the beavers to their lodges, and recited the beaver tracts, tracing out their shared lineage and history.

> *"By his sagacity, his industry, and his artificial erections"* [59]
> *Yet never small or weak*
> *Dull eyed or mute*
> *Our resilience in practice*
> *Our tactics always changing*
> *Adapting, biting, fighting united*
> *By our "immortal principle"* [60]

---

58 "Accomplices Not Allies: Abolishing the Ally Industrial Complex," *Indigenous Action,* May 2, 2014, http://www.indigenousaction.org/accomplices-not-allies-abolishing-the-ally-industrial-complex/.

59 Morgan, *The American Beaver and His Works,* 267.

60 Ibid., 284.

Not traps can take us
No prisons can hold us
When you kill the cop in your head
When you live outside the law
As we raise our black flag over every lodge
With every sabotage, a new day's work
Into a better light.

In the full morning light, on the horizon where the castle usually sat, now was a sunken pile of collapsed towers and charred ruins. On the riverbank there was a message of warning and resolution that read "END OF AN EMPIRE" in woodchips, with the anarcho-communist flag flying high above the beavers' lodges. Their human comrades did not hide their solidarity as they floated on an adjacent platform, constructed with the help of the Beaver Lodge Construction Squad, as the humans sat armed and ready, with the silencers from their weapons removed.[61]

Coda: Towards a Multispecies Solidarity

If the abolition of the category of species itself is what is necessary for a multi or transspecies solidarity, then different forms of storying must include a shift in political action. Instead of being in collusion with colonial and imperial narratives, multispecies stories need to be accomplices and collaborators with our nonhuman comrades. We propose that through acts of refiguring and collapsing speciesist categories it might be possible to create a collective political imaginary — viewing it as part of the responsibility of the so-called "human species" to act in solidarity. The intersection of these solidarities coincides and expands out of current political struggles, as we see an increased visibility in occupations and blockages of infrastructures and supply chains along with struggles for land and liberation, from Sacred Stone Camp at the Standing Rock Indian Reservation in resistance to the Dakota Access Pipeline, to the Unist'ot'en Camp on the unceded territory of the Unist'ot'en clan of the Wet'suwet'en First Nation peoples in so-called northern British Columbia, Canada or Turtle Island and beyond, in solidarity with Indigenous communities.

Aligning with acts of autonomous exploration, this project seeks to work with forms of making knowledge and being in the world inspired by the Zapatismo practice of making the road while walking it. Only through beginning this work of resistance and resilience, can we seek other collaborators and accomplices looking for new ways of understanding political possibilities by articulating our existence on this planet outside of a speciesist paradigm.

In dialogue with these concerns, the three short stories in this chapter emerged through a process-based practice for developing writing and narratives for a multispecies storytelling that can take responsibility for its material histories while wanting to move beyond just acknowledging them. We do not wish to police or reestablish moralism around multispecies storytelling, but we do think it's time for the emerging field to reflect on itself. The fictions address how multispecies sto-

---

61   BBC Earth, "Beaver Lodge Construction Squad | Attenborough | BBC Earth," *YouTube*, May 18, 2009, https://www.youtube.com/watch?v=iyNA62FrKCE/.

rytelling often presents itself as a flourishing otherwise but can also become a site of harm and damage because of the histories it inherits in its attempts to decenter the human. The stories engage with this damage and harm through the practice of "multispecies solidarities" and the grounds of oppression within the field itself they need to unsettle.

The scenes chosen for the stories in this chapter focus on the modes in which multispecies storytelling often upholds enclosure, borders, and containment. As part of our practice, we go into these sites, to address those points intentionally as a way of explicating forms of violence happening both in the human and nonhuman realms. In particular, we deal with contemporaneous stories in which humans and animals are coproduced as commodities and productive of capital even in scenes of containment and lockdown, held in place by borders — psychic, physical, and legal.

Multispecies storytelling should not just focus on fiction or fictioning to open spaces of possibility. It must also mean a commitment to and through our writing to practices of the abolition of enclosure, capture and borders as forms of carceral violence and the industrial continuum of academia that are explicitly related to processes of dehumanization and objectification. A practice that must challenge the easy assumptions of liberating nature or assigning agency to animals as the way to counter Anthropocentric thinking.

We cannot just turn to the voice of the animal as a means of decentering colonial violence. Multispecies storytelling should not be about ventriloquizing animal subjectivities; instead we propose that multispecies storying can be a practice of getting close to and partially understanding the material relationships between histories produced through violence, as an act of solidarity. This is specifically why within the stories we give great attention to the forms of narration that take place to unsettle a desire to give human voices and normative intentions to animal actors. For example, as human writers, we have made the decision to not create spoken dialogue for the beavers, yet we have still chosen a mode of communication in the form of wood chips while using the English language. In these moments we attempt to bridge between human and nonhuman animal worlds in an acknowledged act of incommensurable exchange, the human characters are then required to reorient themselves to new forms of listening, learning, and cohabiting on the beavers' terms.

In acts of multispecies solidarity, we attempt to think through how we might dismantle the white supremacy inherent within institutions, scholarly study, and artistic practices. Yet, the context and application of this approach, also requires honesty and attention toward the formulation of this multispecies communism and what kinds of storytelling this would invent, according to its context, placement, and usage. As Audre Lorde called, to lay the groundwork for political action, academic feminists must deal with the differences between us and the resulting differences in our oppressions.[62] We acknowledge we are writing this from within the academy. As white queer antifascists and antiracists, we see it as part of our responsibility to cultivate an ethics of betrayal toward the institutions that reproduce systematic oppression by going beyond critiquing power, to instead seeking

---

62   Audre Lorde, "The Master's Tools Will Never Dismantle the Master's House," in *Sister Outsider: Essays and Speeches* (New York City: Crossing Press, 1984), 110–14.

to "smash it to fucking pieces" as an "intellectual accomplice would strategize with, not for and not be afraid to pick up a hammer."[63] We want to pick up and think of the hammer as a tool of building, repairing, and sabotaging in equal measures of its potentialities.

Read through the politics of the hammer, storytelling is the act of how material violence is made real, and anything outside of that narrative is treated as a pestilence, a virus, an anomaly, when that is actually the nature of resistance. Empire must erase these histories to create a clear, concise, logical narrative of the imperial domination that makes it seem as if it is natural. The subjugation of nature is a logical consequence and progression of human conquest told through fictioning and storytelling.

In smashing these supremacist modes, we look to question not only dominant historical narratives, but also the notion of storytelling as a form of truth-telling in of itself. By embracing a para-fictional approach, rather than giving primacy to a particular stylistic voice, we call for the need to open spaces for fictions and speculative tracks that engage with the beaver's resilience, the zoo caretakers' collusion, and the swan's disobedience, as methods for interrogating the supremacy of world-shaping violence.

63   "Accomplices Not Allies: Abolishing the Ally Industrial Complex."

References

"Accomplices Not Allies: Abolishing the Ally Industrial Complex." *Indigenous Action,* May 2, 2014. http://www.indigenousaction.org/accomplices-not-allies-abolishing-the-ally-industrial-complex/.

Amatulli, Giuseppe. "The Legal Position of the Sámi in the Exploitation of Mineral Resources in Finland, Norway, and Sweden." PhD diss., Åbo Akademi University, 2014.

Animal Channel, "Wild Polar Bear Tries to Break In - BBC Earth." *YouTube,* August 4, 2019. https://www.youtube.com/watch?v=9G1aHkLHQ2I.

Aouragh, Miriyam, and Paula Chakravartty. "Infrastructures of Empire: Towards a Critical Geopolitics of Media and Information Studies." *Media, Culture & Society* 38, no. 4 (2016): 559–75. DOI: 10.1177/0163443716643007.

Aquarium Conservation Partnership. "We Need Your Help." *New Mode,* 2020. https://act.newmode.net/action/aquarium-conservation-partnership/we-need-your-help/.

Baldwin, Andrew, and Bruce Erickson. "Introduction: Whiteness, Coloniality, and the Anthropocene." *Environment and Planning D: Society and Space* (2020): 3–11. DOI: 10.1177/0263775820904485.

BBC Earth. "Beaver Lodge Construction Squad | Attenborough | BBC Earth." *YouTube,* May 18, 2009. https://www.youtube.com/watch?v=iyNA62FrKCE.

"Beaver Bites Bus Passenger in Sweden." *The Local Sweden,* March 31, 2015. https://www.thelocal.se/20150331/beaver-bites-swedish-bus-passenger.

Buchanan, Brett, Matthew Chrulew, and Jeffrey Bussolini. "On Asking the Right Questions: An Interview with Vinciane Despret." *Angelaki* 20, no. 2 (2015): 165–78. DOI: 10.1080/0969725X.2015.1039821.

Chakrabarty, Dipesh. "The Climate of History: Four Theses." *Critical Inquiry* 35, no. 2 (Winter 2009): 197–222. DOI: 10.1086/596640.

Chakrabarty, Dipesh. "Anthropocene Time." *History and Theory* 57, no. 1 (March 2018): 5–32. DOI: 10.1111/hith.12044.

Chakrabarty, Dipesh. "The Planet: An Emergent Humanist Category." *Critical Inquiry* 46, no. 1 (Autumn 2019): 1–31. DOI: 10.1086/705298.

Clarke, Charles G. *The Men of the Lewis and Clark Expedition: A Biographical Roster of the Fifty-one Members and Composite Diary of Their Activities from All Known Sources.* Glendale: Arthur H. Clark, 1970.

Dennison, Jean. *Colonial Entanglement: Constituting a Twenty-first-century Osage Nation.* Chapel Hill: University of North Carolina Press, 2012.

Despret, Vinciane. "The Body We Care For: Figures of Anthropo-zoo-genesis." *Body & Society* 10, nos. 2–3 (2004): 111–34. DOI: 10.1177/1357034X04042938.—

———. "Who Made Clever Hans Stupid?" *Angelaki* 20, no. 2 (2015): 77–85. DOI: 10.1080/0969725X.2015.1039843.

Duchastel de Montrouge, Philippa. "The Red Line — A Week in Solidarity with the Sámi People in Finland." *Greenpeace,* September 4, 2018. https://www.greenpeace.org/canada/en/story/4183/the-red-line-a-week-in-solidarity-with-the-sami-people-in-finland/.

Engels, Friedrich. "Preface to the First Edition, 1884, 'The Origin of the Family, Private Property and the State." Translated by Alick West. *Marxist Internet Archive,* 2000. https://www.marxists.org/archive/marx/works/1884/origin-family/preface.htm/.

Farrell, Jeff. "Irma: Cuba Airlifts Dolphins to Safety from Deadly Hurricane." *The Independent,* September 9, 2017. https://www.independent.co.uk/news/world/americas/irma-hurricane-florida-cuba-dolphins-cayo-guillermo-island-cienfuegos-a7937596.html.

Fur, Gunlög. "First Giraffe in Paris." Welcome address presented at *Multispecies Storytelling in Intermedial Practices,* Linnæus University, Växjö, Sweden, January 23–25, 2019.

Gan, Elaine. "Time Machines: Making and Unmaking Rice." PhD diss., University of California Santa Cruz, 2016.

Haraway, Donna J. *Modest–Witness@Second–Millennium.FemaleMan–Meets–OncoMouse: Feminism and Technoscience.* Hove: Psychology Press, 1997.

———. *Primate Visions: Gender, Race, and Nature in the World of Modern Science.* New York City: Routledge, 2013.

———. *When Species Meet.* Minneapolis: University of Minnesota Press, 2013.

@hkfp. *Twitter,* April 6, 2020. https://twitter.com/HongKongFP/status/1247175409902342145/.

Giffney, Noreen, and Myra J. Hird, eds. *Queering the Non/human.* New York City: Routledge, 2016.

Juuso, Anni-Kristiina. "Saamelaisten asioita koskeva sovintoprosessi Kuulemisraportti." *Valitoneuvosto, Julkaisuarkisto Valto.* November 26, 2018. http://urn.fi/URN:ISBN:978-952-287-673-7.

Karera, Axelle. "Blackness and the Pitfalls of Anthropocene Ethics." *Critical Philosophy of Race 7,* no. 1 (2019): 32–56. DOI: 10.5325/critphilrace.7.1.0032.

King, Tiffany Lethabo. *The Black Shoals: Offshore Formations of Black and Native Studies.* Durham: Duke University Press, 2019.

Kuhn, Gabriel. *Liberating Sápmi: Indigenous Resistance in Europe's Far North.* Oakland: PM Press, 2020.

Krader, Lawrence. "The Ethnological Notebooks of Karl Marx: A Commentary." In *Towards a Marxist Anthropology: Problems and Perspectives,* edited by Stanley Diamond, 153–71. Berlin: De Guyter, 1979.

Leavelle, Tracy Neal. "Religion, Encounter, and Community in French and Indian North America." PhD diss., Arizona State University, 2001.

Löfgren, Emma. "Did a Beaver Burn Down a Swedish Family Home?" *The Local Sweden,* December 10, 2015. https://www.thelocal.se/20151210/did-a-beaver-arsonist-burn-down-swedish-home.

Löfgren, Emma. "Swedish Beaver Knocks Out Power for Thousands." *The Local Sweden,* August 19, 2015. https://www.thelocal.se/20150819/beaver-knocks-out-power-to-thousands-in-sweden.

Lorde, Audre. "The Master's Tools Will Never Dismantle the Master's House." In *Sister Outsider: Essays and Speeches,* 10–14. New York City: Crossings Press, 1984.

Masuhara, Mitsuyuki, dir. *Shirokuma Café.* Shogakukan, 2012.

McKittrick, Katherine. *Demonic Grounds: Black Women and the Cartographies of Struggle.* Minneapolis: University of Minnesota Press, 2006.

Malm, Andreas. *Fossil Capital: The Rise of Steam Power and the Roots of Global Warming.* New York: Verso Books, 2016.

———. "In Wildness Is the Liberation of the World: On Maroon Ecology and Partisan Nature." *Historical Materialism* 26, no. 3 (2018): 3–37. DOI: 10.1163/1569206X-26031610.

———. "The Origins of Fossil Capital: From Water to Steam in the British Cotton Industry." *Historical Materialism* 21, no. 1 (2013): 15–68. DOI: 10.1163/1569206X-12341279.

———. *The Progress of This Storm: Nature and Society in a Warming World.* New York: Verso Books, 2018.

Malm, Andreas, and Alf Hornborg. "The Geology of Mankind? A Critique of the Anthropocene Narrative." *The Anthropocene Review* 1, no. 1 (2014): 62–69. DOI: 10.1177/2053019613516291.

Malm, Andreas, and Shora Esmailian. "Doubly Dispossessed by Accumulation: Egyptian Fishing Communities between Enclosed Lakes and a Rising Sea." *Review of African Political Economy* 39, no. 133 (2012): 408–26. DOI: 10.1080/03056244.2012.710838.

Moore, Jason W. *Capitalism in the Web of Life: Ecology and the Accumulation of Capital.* New York City: Verso Books, 2015.

Morgan, Lewis Henry. *The American Beaver and His Works.* Philadelphia: J.B. Lippincott & Co., 1868.

Müller-Schwarze, Dietland. *The Beaver: Its Life and Impact.* Ithaca: Cornell University Press, 2011.

Mullins, Lisa. "French Company Puts Real Swans on Stage." *The World,* June 12. 2012. https://www.pri.org/stories/2012-06-12/french-dance-company-puts-real-swans-stage-swan.

Opperman, Romy. "A Permanent Struggle Against an Omnipresent Death: Revisiting Environmental Racism with Frantz Fanon." *Critical Philosophy of Race* 7, no. 1 (2019): 57–80. DOI: 10.5325/critphilrace.7.1.0057.

Owen, James. "Beavers Returning to Sweden's Capital Can Be a Dam Nuisance." *National Geographic,* April 19, 2016. https://www.nationalgeographic.com/animals/article/160419-beavers-animals-science-sweden-world-wild-cities.

Petton, Luc. "Swan." *Le Guetteur,* 2012. https://www.lucpetton.com/fr/repertoire/swan/swan-en/.

Petton. Luc. "Luc Petton." *Le Guetteur,* n.d. https://www.lucpetton.com/fr/luc-petton-en/.

Pritchard, Helen. "The Animal Hacker." PhD diss., Queen Mary University of London, 2018.

Saldanha, Arun. "A Date with Destiny: Racial Capitalism and the Beginnings of the Anthropocene." *Environment and Planning D: Society and Space* 38, no. 1 (2020): 12–34. DOI: 10.1177/0263775819871964.

Serafin, Amy. "Some of These Performers Are 'Really' Typecast." *The New York Times,* June 3, 2012. https://www.nytimes.com/2012/06/03/arts/dance/choreography-with-real-swans.html.

Sharkey, Heather J. "'La Belle Africaine': The Sudanese Giraffe Who Went to France." *Canadian Journal of African Studies/Revue canadienne des études africaines* 49, no. 1 (2015): 39–65. DOI: 10.1080/00083968.2015.1043712.

@shedd_aquarium. *Twitter,* March 14, 2020. https://twitter.com/shedd_aquarium/status/1238967660991393792?s=20/.

———. *Twitter,* March 18, 2020. https://twitter.com/shedd_aquarium/status/1240355895571251207?s=20/

———. *Twitter,* March 24, 2020. https://twitter.com/shedd_aquarium/status/1242485466492010504?s=20/.

———. *Twitter,* March 30, 2020. https://twitter.com/shedd_aquarium/status/124
4743245588021250?lang=en/.

Stilwell, Blake. "Iran May Have a Fleet of Communist Killer Dolphins." *Military.
com,* n.d. https://www.military.com/off-duty/iran-may-have-fleet-communist-
killer-dolphins.html.

Take Part. "Death at SeaWorld Eyewitness Interview with Jessica Wilder | The
Cove | TakePart." *YouTube,* November 26, 2012. https://www.youtube.com/
watch?v=sx8MQrdinTU.

"This Curious Animal Grew Larger over Time — But Its Brain Didn't Quite Keep
Up: Researchers Find the Mountain Beaver's Ancestor Had a Larger Relative
Brain Size." *ScienceDaily,* June 27, 2018. http://www.sciencedaily.com/releas-
es/2018/06/180627160227.htm.

TIME. "Woman on Family Boating Adventure Calls Cops About Whales." *Youtube,* October 9, 2018. https://www.youtube.com/watch?v=Q4iQrDufir8.

Todd, Zoe. "Indigenizing the Anthropocene." In *Art in the Anthropocene: Encounters among Aesthetics, Politics, Environments and Epistemologies,* edited by
Heather Davis and Etienne Turpin, 241–54. London: Open Humanities Press,
2015.

Tuana, Nancy. "Climate Apartheid: The Forgetting of Race in the Anthropocene." *Critical Philosophy of Race* 7, no. 1 (2019): 1–31. DOI: 10.5325/critphil-
race.7.1.0001.

Yusoff, Kathryn. *A Billion Black Anthropocenes or None.* Minneapolis: University
of Minnesota Press, 2019.

———. "Geologic Life: Prehistory, Climate, Futures in the Anthropocene."
Environment and Planning D: Society and Space 31, no. 5 (2013): 779–95. DOI:
10.1068/d11512.

Whitener, Brian. "Animal Accumulation." *Blindfield Journal,* August 4, 2018.
https://blindfieldjournal.com/2018/08/04/animal-accumulation/.

"World Directory of Minorities and Indigenous Peoples — Sweden: Sámi." *Ref-
World,* March 2018. https://www.refworld.org/docid/49749ca35.html.

Worral, Simon. "Former Trainer Slams SeaWorld for Cruel Treatment of Orcas."
National Geographic, March 29, 2015. https://www.nationalgeographic.com/
adventure/article/150329-orca-blackfish-seaworld-dolphins-killer-whales-ng-
booktalk.

CHAPTER 10

#FEELSWeoutheregettinthisbread

Gillian Wylde

Consider the Velociraptor paired with captions depicting giant chicken lizard as being deeply immersed in metaphysical digital inquiry #unravelling quirky paradoxes on the internets. Also, known as slippery worlds of screens and feels, emoji and mouths radiating tentacle, alimentary canal, blood, and swamp that we share. It is a messy repetition of loops, exterior intensities, and anaerobic encounter.

They write that we know that becoming is always becoming-with — in a contact zone where the outcome, where who is in the world, is at stake. Lol.

Consider the activity of a swarm, a network with no center to dictate order, populated by "a multitude of different creative agents" or "acquired knowledge" of lodge, dam, and canal building transmitted among beavers.

They research coral sex and reproduction as one focus and employ feminist and queer theory to think anew about how corals generate generations. They write of the sensuous interplay of optical groping and touch in their encounters with cup coral and jellyfish and they develop an analytic they call fingeryeyes to articulate the palpability of cross-species encounter with laptop servers, email programs, and LGBTQI+ nerve organs.

The girdle is ornamented with spicules, bristles, hairy tufts, spikes, or snake-like scales.

In this sense, it can be considered a "smell" or "taste" organ; food is sensed before each stroke of the radula grinding mouthparts. Cuckoo squeakers prolong bodily bodying. This is disruptive care. Think of "inverts" — the kind without backbones as well as the sort who transpose gender roles — interrupt heteronomativity. Heteronormativity is interrupted. Hashtag: Press Delete button.

Hey, Little Ham, do you know fellow Space pioneers Miss Able or Miss Baker? Hey, Little Bonobo, why not ask the gay rabbits to predict your future. This is very real feels, showing pleasure or contentment. An ocean of violets in bloom. Animals strike curious poses. This is what it sounds like. When doves cry.

FYI Mariah Carey isn't taking no gay rabbits on tour with her.
Just a few months ago, she downsized her arena tour to give fans a chance to see her in a more intimate environment.

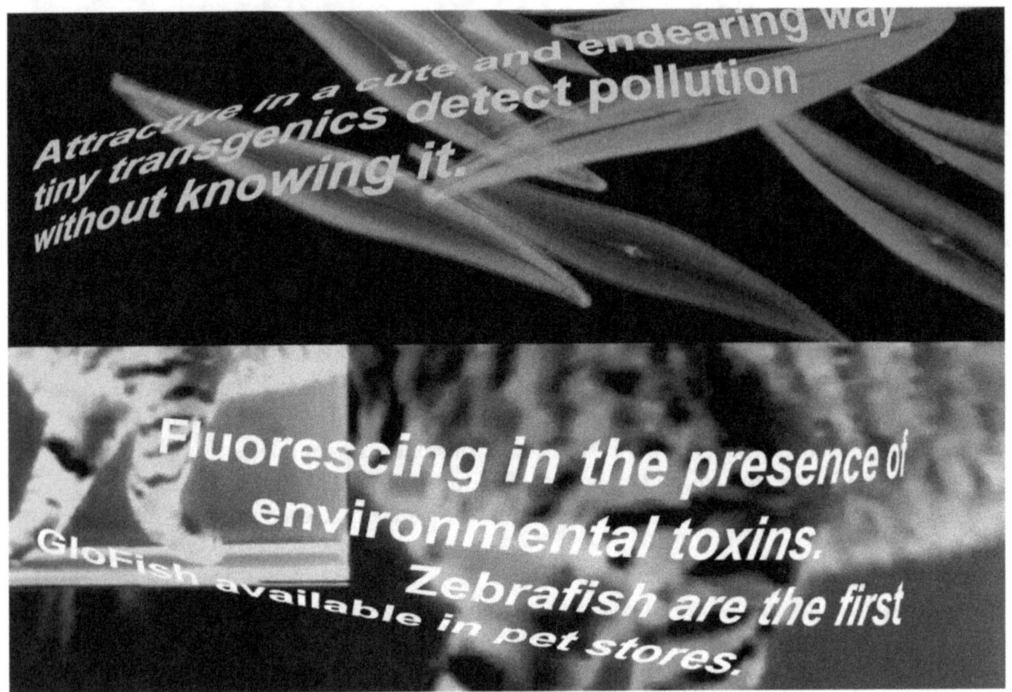

Oh — yeah, the gay rabbits, of course. What is this about gay rabbits? I heard about that. Somebody said I had gay rabbits with me somewhere or something? That's right.

Yeah, that would be not true. That would be one of those lies like I don't walk on carpeting. That would be not true.

The gay rabbits understand why being left out hurts so bad.

Rabbit Face is approved as part of Unicode 6.0 in 2010 and added to Emoji 1.0 in 2015.

By the way, What Would Animals Say If We Asked the Right Questions?

Hey, post internets paranoid pup cakes! (Muffled Autonomous Sensory Meridian Responses playing in the background.)

The best shit-kicker-Fibonacci-feminist manifestos are available via YouTube computational algorithms, browser referencing, and virally transmitted memes 4 sho!

Consider also: tick, donut, or water bear, invoking speculative fictional methods such as carriers, radiation, mental diseases, vectors, viruses, scientific accidents.

This is deep pizza, so animal. Otter has underarm pockets to keep small rocks for laters. They are talking about an algae takeover. This is Queer Revolt. Characterized by the soothing tones of Chakra indeterminacy. This is Haraway Donna Donna, wow wow. Many queer revolts undermining biological-determinist ideologies.

Or check how cells perceive other cells in municipal parks, public libraries, discotheques, academia, hotel lobbies, etc.

BTW the gay rabbits won't walk on carpeting.

Attractive in a pretty endearing way, tiny transgenics detect pollution without knowing it. Fluorescing in the presence of environmental toxins. The first GloFish are available in pet stores, sold in bright rave red, anonymous green, spirit whisper orange-yellow, phantom mist blue, and salty tear purple fluorescent colors. "Electric Green-," "Sunburst Orange-," "Moonrise Pink-," "Starfire Red-," "Cosmic Blue-," and "Galactic Purple-"colored tetra (an "Electric Green" tiger barb and a glo-Rainbow Shark) have been added to the lineup. The rights to GloFish are owned by Spectrum Brands, Inc., which purchase GloFish from Yorktown Technologies, the original developer of GloFish, in May 2017. This is cute, fluorescing petishism.

Fruit flies are launched into space aboard a US V-2 rocket in 1947. The rocket reaches 109 kilometers which technically makes the flies the first animals in space. They are all recovered alive.

This is a messy repetition of loops, bulbous intensities, and anaerobic fabulations.

Jeff Goldblum is an insect man. I'm an insect, I'm an insect, he says — who dreamt he was a man and loved it, but now that dream is over, and the insect is awake.

Rather than manipulating a physical environment, they are now, as they put it, "gardening" in someone's mind.

This is gay full story.

50,000 bluebottles trigger sensors, feeding into a "neural network" that changes the pace at which the images on the screens evolve.

The flies are fed sugar up in the rotunda, they congregate. The flies are unable to breed without the presence of protein.

Is not bitmap image formats. Is Mammoth.
Is not Care Bear Cousin with pink weight and red heart on it.
Is teenage elephant with an exquisite singing voice and severe stage fright.
Is not happy-go-lucky termite who tries to find the best in every situation.
Is possum with voice of Isaac Hayes.
Possum is common suburbia
Possum is shy small
Possum is here to clean up the world
Possum is high on cuteness
Possum is a squirrel
Critter is a rabbit and squirrel repellent
Critter is busy doing mathematical functions
Critter is addicted to pinball
Critter is all STS
Rabbit is an absolute gem
Rabbit is the best cat evr
Rabbit is so selfie thing//
Critter *is* thick knot *thing*

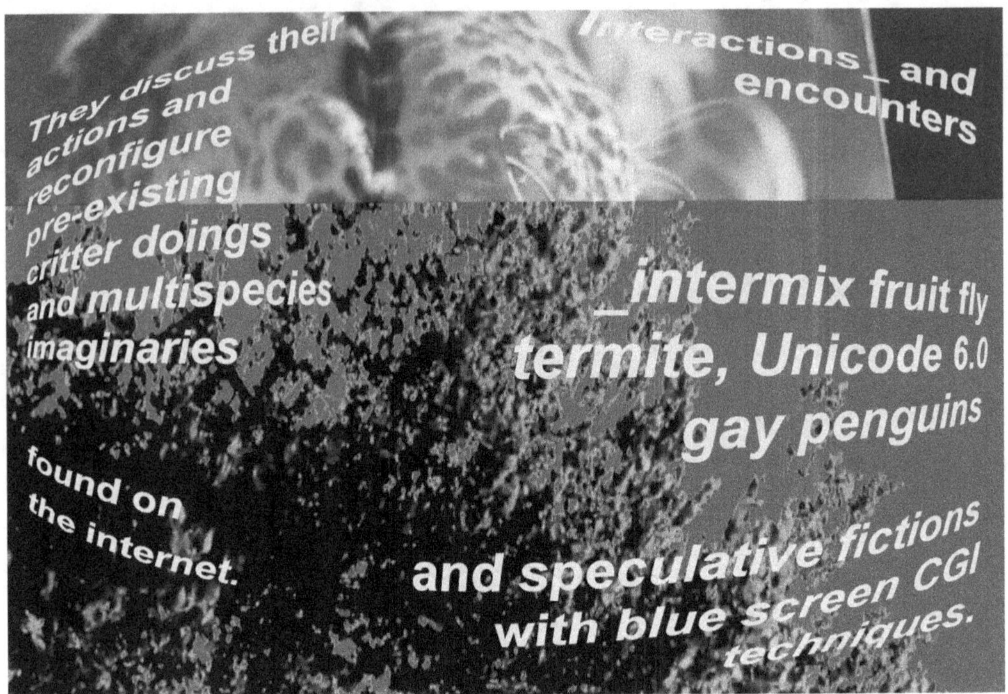

Critter is motion capture thing?
Critter is International Homo Penguin Conference, Genus Corvus helping small nocturnal Old World mammal across the highway.

International homo Penguin Conference itself turns down a lucrative sponsorship deal because of concerns about its use of wildlife selfies in promotional material.

AKA "bad wildlife selfies" — meaning someone hugging, holding, or inappropriately interacting with a wild animal.

A "good wildlife selfie" on the other hand is described as a picture where there is no contact between an animal and a human, and the animal is not being restrained or held in captivity to be a used as a photo prop.

Celebrities have contributed to the popularity of wildlife selfies, Roger Federer and Margo Robbie take up ferocious posing with quokkas in Australia, Justin Bieber assumes an attitude with large solitary tiger, Kim Kardashian hoses down elephant in parking lot and Taylor Swift is seen singing to a kangaroo wearing gloves. This is life wild.

Everyone knows that dogs are trying too hard.

Dogs, generally acknowledge the camera — sometimes even running straight into it — which makes for less intriguing or authentic footage funnies. What Kind of Cat Would Your Dog Be? Caring for this mouse is an unusual experience. Everyone knows cats rule the Internet. Grumpy Cat is now a bona fide business, with magazine covers, movie deals and merchandise, including an iced coffee line.

A is for cow chips, cat fur balls, horse apples; bristletails and springtails.
A is for any segmented invertebrate effectuated by frictions.
A as in things rubbing against each other, shadow theory-isms, and CAN YOU JUST NOT!
A is for parasitic arachnid living by feeding inside the cute ears of mammals.
A is for migrating birds that carry ticks with them on their journeys.
A is for ostrich drone guitar tuning — all the strings tuned to the same note like a cello getting up in the morning.
A is for misogyny, fear of aging, and an incuriosity about actual animals (2008: pages 28–30)
A is for Hayward, Eva. "Enfolded Vision: Refracting the Love Life of the Octopus." *Octopus: A Journal of Visual Studies* (2005): 29–44.

Naturally the cat is distracted.

It is an hour-long procedure the veterinary surgeon implants a microphone in the cat's ear canal, a small radio transmitter at the base of its skull and a thin wire into its fur. This will allow the cat to innocuously record and transmit sound from its surroundings. Due to problems with distraction, the cat's sense of hunger, the project is abandoned due to the difficulty of training the cat to behave as required, and the equipment is taken out of the cat; the cat is re-sewn for a second time; the cat will live a long and happy life.

Compare with happy soft-bodied mollusks or honest codfish and rabbits moon — filmed under a blue filter and set within a wooded glade during the night. Think of sucker-bearing flexible limbs, soft sac-like bodies, strong beak-like jaws, no internal shell, or any of the many clusters of bulbous nerve endings.

Consider the action of twisting or the state of being twisted, especially of one end of an object relative to the other. Whole bodies of many worms.

Now all of our new neighbors can enjoy an amazing home," say IKEA. "Even our furry, feathered, and flying friends."

IKEA works with UK artists and designers to create this series of animal habitats, repurposed from the company's used furniture.

Honey I'm Home! by artist Hattie Newman is a home for bees built from IKEA's Burvik side tables from the Tottenham IKEA store. The Bug Bud by Iain Talbot is an insect "hotel" made from cladding from Høvåg Pocket sprung mattress, medium firm, dark grey, standard double Greenwich IKEA store.

Bughattan by Adam Furman invites bees and wasps to rest made from IKEA's Kallax storage range. Ashton upon Mersey IKEA store. Dom by Supermundane is a colorful birdhouse made from IKEA's Flysta shelving units range from the Southampton IKEA store.

Helpful words:
— Pfeffa: Cat
— Vair: Defecate

Internets u sure is a knot in motion, lols.

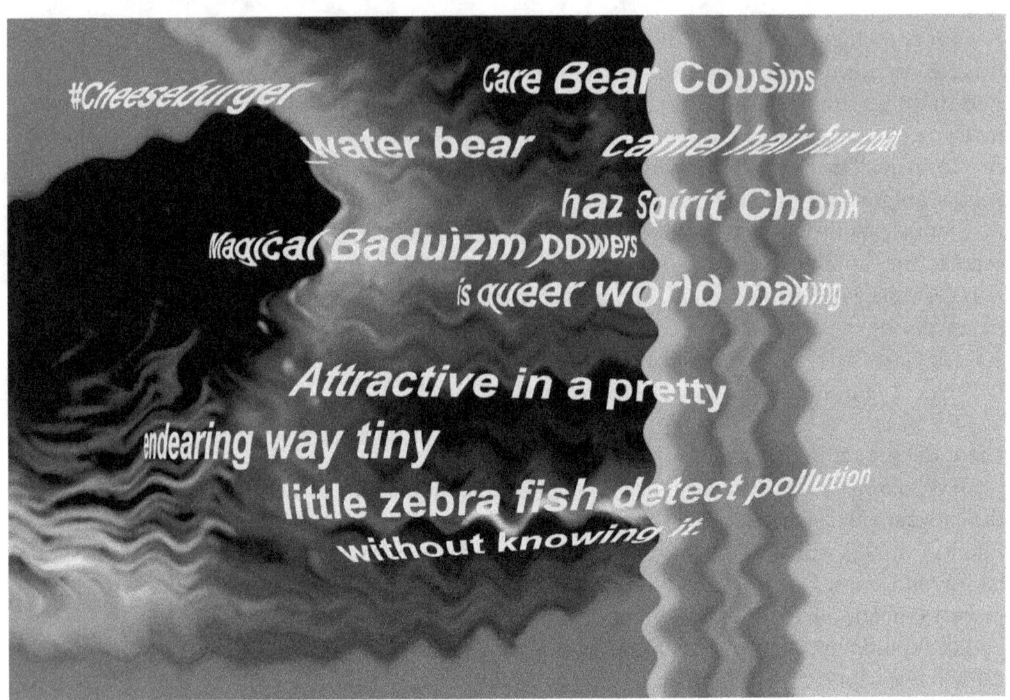

Very small Darwin is sad. Resplendent in a shearling coat.

It's definitely faux fur it's not a shearling it's a fake shearling double breasted jacket. Very small Darwin is found wandering around an IKEA car park in Canada, very small Darwin is agitated having escaped from the car only to be found on the Ontario branch of the store's car park. Some people think all the monkeys hang out together in a common area — that doesn't happen. Rude monkeys sitting down with tails curled up are, approved as part of Unicode 6.0 in 2010 and added to Emoji 1.0 in 2015.

Is Swedish IKEA for monkey?

All their molecular transformations are into living things. They have a "computer-like mind," quicker than Alpha's computer. AKA Eagle Flying in Brian The Brain. Calculate flight times in The A-B Chrysalis, analyze the raw data in The Immunity Syndrome. They attain the form of an animal by knowing its molecular structure. Additionally in The Rules Of Luton they cannot change directly from one form to another, although they can in The Metamorph (dog to gorilla), The Lambda Factor (chimp to caterpillar), A Matter Of Balance (monkey to Shermeen), The Rules Of Luton (kestrel to lion), and The Taybor (dog to ferret). They can change just parts of their self: their hairstyle in One Moment Of Humanity, their hand to a claw in The Taybor.

Physicists [...] take the vacuum as something substantial [...] the scene of wild activities.

The (female) cat being breaks the fruit bowl. The cubists spend their time hoping to glue it back together.

It's more likely the dog is trying to bury the fish rather than save it. World renowned animal expert Patricia McConnell, writes several books on animal behavior, weighs in on her Facebook page that this is "a perfect example of 'caching' behaviour." The dog buries something it interprets as food but doesn't want to eat right away. The "rescue" interpretation is a good example of why understanding the ethology of a species is important when making motivational attributions.

Everyone knows dogs are trying too hard.

Squid is making the most of your Internet Connection by optimizing a caching proxy for the Web supporting HTTP, HTTPS, FTP. Branches, coconut shells, and stones, IMacs, Gameboys simple wildlife habitats incorporate hidden cameras for capturing images of the animal visitors.

Kitty Cams emerge in 1996. Someone sticks the phrase "I can haz Cheezburger?" on a seemingly smiling short haired Scottish blue named Happy Cat. Things are really taking off.

The image's text is often idiosyncratic and intentionally grammatically incorrect. This is lolspeak.

For example, "Ceiling Cat," AKA Ceiling Cat is watching you.

Fail cat (a cat with a slice of processed cheese on its face), AKA fail cat is failing

Fatso is wearing a blue shirt and "playing" an upbeat rhythm on an electronic keyboard, AKA Fatso can haz rhythm.

Live bold and full of spirit. Raccoons have sensitive little taste bud hands. Naturally racoons engage in questions of multispecies environmental and reproductive justice and carrier bag theories of fiction manifestos.

They lack thumbs, so can't grasp objects with one hand. Forepaws extend cognition for search engine browsing, word to time calculation, and Imaginative pizza foraging.

"Cuteness gets really dark really fast."

Koko the Gorilla is dead at 46.

KOKO "touches the lives of millions as an ambassador for all gorillas and an icon for interspecies communication and empathy." Koko uses the kitten as a scapegoat when she is being bad this is not good. Koko rips a steel sink from a wall, and points at All Ball, and signs "cat did it."

"Koko understands that she's special because of all the attention she gets from professors, academics, caregivers, and the media."

Caregiver shows the 10-year-old Koko a photo of a bird in a magazine. THAT ME, Koko signs. "Is that really you?" KOKO GOOD BIRD, she responds. "I thought you were a gorilla." KOKO BIRD. The caregiver asks, "you sure?" Koko responds, pointing to the bird, KOKO GOOD THAT. "Okay, I must be a gorilla," the caregiver says. BIRD YOU, the gorilla signs. "We're both birds?" Koko responds by signing GOOD. "Show me," the caregiver prods. FAKE BIRD CLOWN. "You're teasing me. What are you really?" Finally, Koko gives in, with a laugh: GORILLA KOKO.

Caregiver: We're going to be on the phone with a lot of people who are going to ask us questions...

KOKO: Nipple.

Caregiver: She has vegetables for dinner… raw vegetables…
KOKO: Nipple.
RIP Koko, forever in our hearts. I'll think of you every time I see a nipple. We are doing you proud by our artwork of you.

What's wrong with cats? The cats come to be petted.

Consider this is something close to realism "digital fur technology" mysticism. In some scenes, hands and feet are forgotten by the effects team, most notably in the final song where Judi's non-furry hand, complete with her wedding ring, is front and center.
The trailer for *Cats* is truly the gift of the summer.

Urine-proud, tiny terrapin rides a dead fox down Regents Canal, London. London canals are home to many wild terrapins, who have been breeding there since the Teenage Mutant Ninja Turtle craze of the 90s, when parents bought them for kids but subsequently got rid of them because they're vicious little shits.

#basic #queerrevolt #morethanhuman #Dykea #MashUp #worms #compost #fatbergs #rubbing #naturalhorror #WetOrganicMatter #deadedontheinside #impure #JLO #taxons # If it died, I ride. If it fox, I docks, If it floats, I boat.

* * *

The art writing *#FEELSWeoutheregettingthisbread* considers multispecies interrelationships and stories that circulate rapidly and widely on the internet and how they replicate, mutate, and evolve. More-than-human, critter narratives kindle a speculative poetic essay involving supernatural, futuristic, and other digitally imagined elements. The text invokes more than real world intra-actions with critters, technologies, and microorganisms as a means to ask how the representation of digital multispecies and kin interrelatedness are shaped conceptually by mediated screen, keyboard, and the context of Web 2.0.
The work considers how multispecies imagery and narratives are adapted, mutated, and reformed to make or mean and do something otherwise. Writing playfully critiques and reconfigures preexisting critter doings and multispecies imaginaries found on the internet. Research seeks to investigate how together thinking with critters might, as Teresa Castro notes, present the opportunity "to queer ourselves-as-humans" and "make a step toward becoming other and to think otherly."[1]
Taking up with queer feminist practices and dynamics speculates on new relationalities, curious proximities, and colligations that that might bring into being something other than themselves. As David Getsy notes, when "queer" is used as transitive verb (to queer), it allows for strategies for the "undercutting of the stability of identity and of the dispensation of power that shadows the assignment of categories and taxonomies."[2]

---

1   Teresa Castro, "The Mediated Plant," *e-flux Journal,* September 2019, https://www.e-flux.com/journal/102/283819/the-mediated-plant/.
2   David J. Getsy, *Queer* (London: Whitechapel Gallery, 2016).

The essay is a performative assemblage of becoming other theories and queer creature imaginaries that critique heteronormative, binary systems and extensive taxonomic sampling online. Multispecies imagery, sounds, and words are sourced via search engine algorithm and digital browser foraging to consider how digital critters become entangled with viral meme or GIF and are copied and shared widely by internet users. Performative assemblages reimagine a multispecies takeover or intervention or hack where any sense of linearity or chronological space-time logic is bent and mutates.

This writing is a messy repetition of loops, superficial intensities, and wild anaerobic fabulations. Via the Internet, critters present themselves as the perfect image size for sharing via social media and "social distancing" protocol. We read that "animal webcams that can get you through social distancing have increased in popularly during the C-19 pandemic."[3] The critter is a live telematics apparition, both there and not there absorbing no light. Scattering light equally in all directions. As research tells us that "spending just twenty minutes a day immersed in an environment where we feel connected with the natural world can significantly lower our stress hormone levels."[4]

What does this mash up of critter doings, myth, and animal story gone viral tell us about anthropocentric dominant narratologies within internet screen time? Helen Pritchard notes that "what might be seen as anthropomorphizing could be understood differently as practices that are more about sharing possible imaginaries with nonhuman animals. These practices draw out proximity and intimacy as part of our contemporary imaginations of nonhumans and computation."[5]

The writing that shares these possible imaginaries with nonhuman animals is in order to consider queer storytelling as multiple types of vocalization and nonhuman sensory cues where overlaps flourish. "#FEELS We out here getting this bread" is arranged not as a single or sustained discursive argument but as a series of creature thought fragments. It is an attempt to highlight and consider, as much as possible, activities of accumulation, arrangement, movement, and emergence in order to challenge anthropocentric dominant narratives and short circuit heteronormative, sexist, and lazy antediluvian hierarchies.

3   Rebecca Ruiz, "Spending 20-minutes in Nature Could Make You Less Stressed Out," *Mashable,* April 4, 2018, https://mashable.com/article/nature-pill-stress-mental-health/?europe=true/.

4   Ruiz, "Spending 20 Minutes."

5   Helen Pritchard, "The Animal Hacker," PhD thesis, Queen Mary University of London, 2018.

References

Castro, Teresa. "The Mediated Plant." *e-flux Journal,* September 2019. https://www.e-flux.com/journal/102/283819/the-mediated-plant/.

Getsy, David J. *Queer.* London: Whitechapel Gallery, 2016.

Ruiz, Rebecca. "Spending 20-minutes in Nature Could Make You Less Stressed Out." *Mashable,* April 4, 2019. https://mashable.com/article/nature-pill-stress-mental-health/.

Pritchard, Helen. "The Animal Hacker." PhD Thesis. Queen Mary University of London, 2018.

CHAPTER 11

Learning from the Lake

Katie Lawson

The text that follows is comprised of excerpts from writing that accompanied an exhibition I curated in 2018 at the Art Museum, Toronto, *Learning from the Lake: Maggie Groat and Kelly Jazvac.*[1] This exhibition sought to question the possibility of developing ecofeminist curatorial methods or frameworks through aqueous thinking and determining guiding principles toward new logics, new ethics, new practices. Can curatorial work — as a kind of storytelling — be reshaped by aqueous thinking, by multispecies and more-than-human relationalities, by watery territories? In its abbreviated form, these meandering streams of thought look not explicitly to the artworks or the exhibition as material manifestation but rather to the theory and methodology that came to inform the practice from which it emerged.

This text is a representation of my own situated knowledge,[2] as a woman of settler descent who is grateful for the privilege to conduct research and cultural work which engages with Tkaronto, the gathering place. For thousands of years, it has been the traditional land of the Huron-Wendat, the Seneca, and most recently, the Mississaugas of the Credit River. The territory was the subject of the Dish With One Spoon Wampum Belt Covenant, an agreement between the Iroquois Confederacy and Confederacy of the Ojibwe and allied nations to peaceably share and care for the resources around the Great Lakes. Today, this meeting place is still home to many Indigenous people from across Turtle Island, and I carry forth a profound sense of response-ability and respect for all in a human and more-than-human world.

Shifting Shorelines: Does the Wave Belong to the Lake or the Land?

When I stand in the middle — and only the middle — of my sleepy residential intersection and look south, I can see the Lake. I can't quite smell it or feel the moisture of its air or hear the clambering of pebbles and waves over one another, but I can sense its state of being by the presence or absence of white caps, or the vibrancy of its blue-green hue. As a whole, it never freezes, but in the winter sun the surface becomes a sheet of gold. If I stay in this place: lifetimes ago I am un-

---

1   Maggie Groat and Kelly Jazvac, *Learning from the Lake: Maggie Groat and Kelly Jazvac,* June 14–July 7, 2018, Art Museum at the University of Toronto, Toronto, Canada.

2   Donna Haraway, "Situated Knowledges: The Science Question in Feminism and the Privilege of Partial Perspective," *Feminist Studies* 14, no. 3 (Autumn 1988): 575–99.

derwater. I am underwater when land was water; when Lake Ontario was Lake Iroquois and the shoreline still licked the edge of what is now Davenport Road, that high ridge that separates the north and south sides. Earlier still, before the melt, I am under ice, nearly four kilometers under the Laurentide Glacier of the Pleistocene. This sprawling sheet of glacial ice that covered most of the land mass still manages to hold me. What was here is now there, there now here. When the glacier melted in the St. Lawrence River valley, water from Lake Iroquois rushed out to the Atlantic Ocean.

I had lived in the city for a year before biking out to the Leslie Spit, the passive recreational zone of the city's harbor front. My mouth filled with gnats and my ankles gathered dust as I made my way across the slender, manmade headland, considering the surface that carried me: this compilation or congregation of decades worth of displaced excavation and construction waste from the urban core subways and office towers. Fingers reaching out into the body of the Lake, nearly grazing Ward's Island, leaning over to whisper to the south shores of Ontario. What was here is now there, there now here — 6,500,000 cubic meters of sand and silt were dredged from the Outer Harbour, the Inner Harbour, the Keating Channel, and placed at the spit.

Why Water?

> To begin to glimpse the seas, one must descend rather than transcend, be immersed in highly mediated environments that suggest the entanglements of knowledge, science, economics, and power. Whereas the human alterations of the geophysical landmasses of the planet can be portrayed as a spectacle, the warming and acidifying oceans, like the atmospheric levels of CO_2, cannot be directly portrayed in images but must be scientifically captured and creatively depicted. The depths of the ocean resist flat terrestrial maps that position humans as disengaged spectators. [...] The substance of the water itself insists on submersion, not separation. Even in the sunlit, clear, shallow waters that divers explore, visibility is never taken for granted, nor does distance grant optimal vision.[3]

I've been told in the past that research is an iceberg — an analogy that takes its cue from the proportions of what lies above and below the water; read: above and below human visibility. The transference of meaning from this feature of icebergs has similarly been taken up by motivational vernaculars to talk about success but also popular psychology in addressing feelings of isolation, depression, or anger. Without reading too much into the parallels between these psychic states and the process of research and writing, it is an analogy that has had its uses for me; yet not as an indicator of what percentage of the work ends up seen or unseen in the case of publishing or sharing work. Rather, I identified with the idea of diving deeper and deeper without necessarily knowing what forms would present themselves

---

3   Stacy Alaimo, "Your Shell on Acid: Material Immersion, Anthropocene Dissolves," in *Anthropocene Feminism*, ed. Richard A. Grusin (Minneapolis: University of Minnesota Press, 2017), 107.

because it is only possible to see so far ahead at any given time, and after coming up for air, choosing a different point of entry entirely.

As an educator, and particularly as a cultural producer who works along the lines of ecofeminism, I've also wondered how the rising generation of scholars will receive this analogy now that icebergs are melting, collapsing, and boosting sea-levels even faster than popular science and climate change research espoused. The irony of invoking this image here does not escape me. What if I were to replace the iceberg-as-research with the Great Pacific Garbage Patch or trash vortex — a swath of debris bound by an ocean gyre, which is a system of circular ocean currents formed by wind patterns and planetary rotational force. Non-biodegradable particles that accumulate, never fusing, but breaking down into tinier and tinier pieces until these micro and nano-plastics are too small to be seen by the naked eye but the perfect size to become flesh within global food webs.

* * *

As an exhibition, *Learning from the Lake* grew out of a case study of the Greater Toronto Area ravine system I undertook as a means of understanding how different physical topographies might shape or give way to the lived experiences of its habitants. How might the entanglement of myth, poetics, and story-telling about the ravines influence the social or cultural imaginary? What began as a fixation on landmass and psychogeography developed into the unearthing, so to speak, of the driving force behind my impulse to focus on these spaces — the watersheds so intimately tied to these ravines or the very elemental force that carved them out so many years ago. In Toronto, the ravine system branches off from the six watersheds of the city: Highland Creek, the Rouge Valley (and Rouge River), the Don River, the Humber River, Mimico Creek and Etobicoke Creek. These bodies wind through residential, commercial, and industrial areas; parks, trails, railways, golf courses, cemeteries, hydro corridors, and former landfills — all before feeding Lake Ontario, Lake of Shining Waters.[4] A bedrock depression forty-seven fathoms deep; fathom or faethm — the nautical unit of outstretched arms. Dunes, lagoons, wetlands, pannes. Water from all of the Great Lakes flows through Lake Ontario before passing into the Atlantic Ocean.

What may seem like a natural progression from one site-responsive project to another signifies a greater conceptual shift or turn. A turn away, that is, from the terrestrial and geologic figurations of man and rock that sit heavy at the core of techno-normative or masculinist approaches to the Anthropocene. Anthropocene is a term that will be used sparingly in this context, despite its usefulness as a popularized shorthand for the proposed current geologic epoch. However, the centrality of the *anthropos* or "human" man as a geophysical force on the planet works to reinforce subject-object dualisms that support domination of the more-than-human world through assumed unilateral agency. Donna Haraway offers up an alternative in the form of Cthulucene, while Capitalocene and Platationocene hover on standby but unfortunately miss the mark in this context. This sentiment is ech-

---

4   The origins of Lake Ontario's name come from the Iroquoian language; see "Lake Ontario," *Lake Ontario Waterkeeper,* http://www.waterkeeper.ca/lake-ontario/.

oed in Isabelle Stenger's suggestion that political theory decenter from the abstract concept of "humans," correlative to the problem of inclusion of "nonhumans."[5]

Instead, I consider the speculative imaginings of queer and feminist knowledge production and an ethos of disruption; the liquidity of entanglement and change; supporting the agency of the compromised, circulating substances, materialities, and forces in a human and more-than-human world. Is there a means by which the act of contemporary art might embody an ontological relationality and entanglement with aquatic or marine ecosystems, the plastic-made-flesh of polluted bodies and reverberations of catastrophe in the hydrosphere?

* * *

There is no shortage of artists or curators who have committed their practices to water as a principal concern, sharing an investment in the conditions of the bodies of water on which we as humans so greatly depend. They come quite literally in waves, these exhibitions which gather up artworks responding to the aqueous, and for good reason. Water has always been more than a necessary resource for living: it can serve as an emotional, elemental, or spiritual home, a fact that is reflected across time, across cultures. More recently, for artists living through the global water crisis, a growing interest in water is connected to the development of strategies for visualization or affective representation of the changes occurring in bodies of water, the element which has become one of the most urgent, visceral, and ethically fraught sites of political and theoretical inquiries.[6]

How, then, can water be adopted as the topic of inquiry in a field that is saturated with work that takes up this element as a means of consciousness-raising or promoting environmental literacy and responsibility? What would the implications be of mobilizing water not just as a literal subject but also as an elemental metaphor to inform curatorial methodology, process, and practice? What is at stake in this process? Or, even more critically, how can the efficacy of an epistemological or methodological shift be measured in the context of a public-facing exhibition? If stories, knowledges, and representations help us to make sense of the world, it is because they foreground aspects of a phenomenon while backgrounding others. Elizabeth Grosz suggests that "concepts do not solve problems that events generate for us" but "they enable us to surround ourselves with possibilities for being otherwise."[7] Investigating an elemental metaphor as a cultural producer will not solve the global water crisis. It will not replenish dwindling ground water or repair damaged ecosystems, but it does hold the potential to present possibilities for being otherwise, to prefigure certain kinds of ethical relations with water or watery others.

<hr>

5   Isabelle Stengers, "Including Nonhumans in Political Theory: Opening Pandora's Box," in *Political Matter: Technoscience, Democracy, and Public Life*, eds. Bruce Braun and Sarah J. Whatmore (Minneapolis: University of Minnesota Press, 2010), 3–33.

6   Katie Lawson, "Learning from the Lake," *Art Museum at the University of Toronto*, https://artmuseum.utoronto.ca/exhibition/learning-from-the-lake/.

7   This version of Elizabeth Grosz's quotation is drawn from Astrida Neimanis, *Bodies of Water: Posthuman Feminist Phenomenology* (London: Bloomsbury Academic, 2017), 168.

Liquid Logic(s)

Asking such questions within walking distance of one of the world's largest bodies of fresh water offers the opportunity to oscillate between the general and specific — water as an elemental force or abstract — but also situating the project in the context of the place where the project develops, an urban center built on the shore of one of the Great Lakes. Changes in the contour of Lake Ontario's edge have come to pass on varying scales of time. The shoreline has shifted geologically over the span of millennia; in the case of human intervention, decades. This space is representative of the ecological principal of the edge effect or ecotone — the meeting of two distinct elements and of bordering communities, resulting in diverse and productive habitats. They are hotbeds of energy and material exchange, thriving and teeming with life.

The shore is neither land nor water but somewhere in between, it is both and countless variants. The conditions of one become the necessities of the other and vice versa. Shore or coastlines are merely one example of the meeting and mixing of different organisms and natural features that occurs where edges meet as ecotones operate on every conceivable scale and produces an overwhelming variety of networked relationships and conditions. Yet this type of zone in the more-than-human world seems like a suitable site to push back against the oppositional, binary logic that, as the foundation of Western thought, has led to the divisions of self–other, subject–object, man–woman, mind–body, discursive–material, and nature–culture. While this list is by no means exhaustive, it is representative of key distinctions within the logic of dualism, variants of the same basic form and implicit assumptions connecting them as linking postulates.[8]

In its varying and malleable forms and iterations, feminism has organized around the question of who: who speaks, for whom, and whose subjectivity is presupposed in the very grammar of the question?[9] When it comes to considerations of difference, feminist strategies fall along a sliding scale, at one end operating based on the claim that woman is not subsumable beneath the figure of man, at the other is the insistence that women cannot be set apart or excluded from the world of man. Yet both of these forms work within the very logics of domination and oppression through polarity and hierarchy that found the grounds of Western philosophy. The feminist flight from nature[10] is understandable, given the

8   It should be noted that not every dichotomy is a dualism. Making non-hierarchical distinctions and recognizing differences has its uses, and Plumwood provides an extensive account on the features of dualism (e.g., backgrounding, radical exclusion, incorporation, instrumentalism, homogenization, or stereotyping). Denial of difference and the elimination of distinction (i.e., merger strategy) results in an entirely new host of issues. For more, see Val Plumwood, *Feminism and the Mastery of Nature* (New York: Routledge, 2015), 45.

9   Linda Alcoff, "The Problem of Speaking for Others," *Cultural Critique* 20 (Winter 1991–1992): 5–32.

10   While nature has accumulated a confusing array of meanings, the nature which feminists have avoided is the one which is positioned as "the excluded and devalued contrast of reason, includes the emotions, the body, the passions, animality, the primitive or uncivilized, the non-human world, matter, physicality and sense experience, as well as the sphere of irrationality, or faith and of madness. In other words, nature includes everything that reason excludes." Plumwood,

inferiorizing history of feminine connection with nature that has functioned as a regressive tool or relic of patriarchal domination. Yet the result of this impulse is work done within rather than against predominant dualisms, upholding a rigid opposition between nature and culture and all of its linking postulates. By way of Luce Irigaray, Stacy Alaimo suggests that women should inhabit the feminine space in discourse in order to transform it and that ecofeminism[11] is embraced as a serious contender in matters concerning strategic essentialism, performative identities, postmodern feminism, difference, and reworking the very matrix of power by which all are constituted.[12]

The writing of Luce Irigaray is founded on the very potential of the elemental to destabilize the insularity of human thinking in her critiques of phenomenology and ethics. For her, all intersubjective relations are situated within elemental phenomena (light, water, and air).[13] Out of her elemental trilogy (*Marine Lover of Friedrich Nietzsche, Elemental Passions,* and *Forgetting of Air*) emerges a powerful metaphor to encourage this transition from binary to fluid logic in relation to how we understand the world around us and our relationship to it. Binary logic would insist that it is always either raining or not-raining, A or not-A, one defined by the lack of the other. But, Irigaray asks, alongside all those who read and interpret and think-with her, what about the drizzle? How hard does it have to drizzle for the drizzle to be rain? How light is the drizzle that constitutes not-rain? What would be the implications of replacing the binary with a logic of fluidity?

Writing in the 1980s, Irigaray was theorizing sexual difference and is understandably critiqued for a certain essentialism which is pervasive in her work. Contemporary readings[14] contemplate strategies for extending Irigaray's work beyond the idea of sexual difference and to read alongside her and to open the application of fluid logic to other forms of domination and discrimination rooted in the system of binary logic. If even one dichotomy can be unraveled, unfurled, dismantled, it could signal the fall of other dichotomies. A ripple effect that moves toward a horizon of becoming.

Feminism and the Mastery of Nature, 20.

11   Of all the variants that fall within the broad intellectual tradition of ecofeminist theory, Trish Glazebrook provides a succinct definition of a methodological basis which most closely aligns with my own, based on the belief that more-than-human entities warrant moral consideration with a refusal to reduce nature to its instrumental value and a feminist ethics of care. For more, see Trish Glazebrook, "Ecofeminist 'Cityzenry,'" in *The Natural City: Re-Envisioning the Built Environment,* eds. Ingrid Leman Stefanovic and Stephen Bede Scharper (Toronto: University of Toronto Press, 2012), 174–90. Similarly, Sherilyn MacGregor, "Only Resist: Feminist Ecological Citizenship and the Post-politics of Climate Change," *Hypatia* 29, no. 3 (Summer 2014): 617–33.

12   Stacy Alaimo, *Undomesticated Ground: Recasting Nature as Feminist Space* (Ithaca: Cornell University Press, 2000), 172.

13   In her study of the ethics of historical and contemporary earth art, Amanda Boetzkes extends the elemental work of Irigaray to ask what part elementals may play in developing an ethical stance toward the earth: "If elementals afford a sense of alterity, is it possible that they could also evoke an ethical mode of contact with the earth?" See Amanda Boetzkes, *The Ethics of Earth Art* (Minneapolis: University of Minnesota Press, 2010), 107–61.

14   Hanneke Canters and Grace M. Jantzen, *Forever Fluid: A Reading of Luce Irigaray's Elemental Passions* (Manchester: Manchester University Press, 2005).

Irigaray's proposition is, of course, one model among many that proposes alternatives to hierarchical, binary logic in keeping with the plurality and speculation which foregrounds feminist epistemologies. Take, for instance, Haraway's figurations of the cyborg, onco-mouse, companion-species, the modest witness, and other hybrids as figures of radical interspecies relationality. They blur and destabilize categorical distinctions (human–nonhuman, nature–culture, male–female, oedipal–nonoedipal, European–non-European) in attempting to redefine a program of feminist social justice through what she calls boundary creatures.[15] She provocatively suggests that A and not-A are likely to be simultaneously true, an exaggeration which insists that feminist analysis requires contradictory moments and a wariness of claims of resolution, dialectically or otherwise.

A second provocation along these lines of alternate logics: what might the interaction be between Haraway's figurations and Alaimo's suggestion of the theoretical site of trans-corporeality as the time-space that human corporeality inhabits, opening out into a more-than-human world — a move to shift material fleshiness as inseparable from differentiated "natures" or "environments"? It is a place where corporeal theories and environmental theories meet productively, an entangled territory or contact zone. Alaimo seeks ways of knowing that do not foreclose the actions, relations, significance, and value of the more-than-human world.[16]

One final alternative in this survey of feminist meaning-making: Mielle Chandler and Astrida Neimanis propose the consideration of water as a site of material sociality for the cultivation of a plural future and as an alternative mode of being that problematizes logics of domination and oppression. This mode of being is framed as gestational, defying the either-or structure of activity and passivity as it is neither yet both. Sociality refers to qualities of relating, or modes of existence which are fundamentally responsive as a part of kinship between human and more-than-human natures. Chandler and Neimanis insist on untying the connotations of gestationality from what is human, female, and reprosexual — it is more so a form of logic tied to the hydrological cycle as a means of encouraging kinship and responsive sociality.[17] These varying alternatives work within different pockets of feminist theory to ease hyper-separation of difference in a way that bypasses merger strategies.

To return to and to read Irigaray's proposition in light of these knowledge practices that understand difference as fluid, unfolding, and situated and, in the context of this work on the Lake, I might understand the interstitial drizzle as the

15   Donna J. Haraway, *Simians, Cyborgs and Women: The Reinvention of Nature* (New York: Routledge, 1991).

16   Stacy Alaimo, "Trans-corporeal Feminisms and the Ethical Space of Nature," in *Material Feminisms,* eds. Stacy Alaimo and Susan Hekman (Bloomington: Indiana University Press, 2008), 237–65. See also Karen Barad, "Posthumanist Performativity: Toward an Understanding of How Matter Comes to Matter," in *Material Feminisms,* eds. Stacy Alaimo and Susan Hekman (Bloomington: Indiana University Press, 2008), 120–57.

17   Mielle Chandler and Astrida Neimanis, "Water and Gestationality: What Flows beneath Ethics," in *Thinking with Water,* eds. Cecilia Chen, Janine MacLeod, and Astrida Neimanis (Montreal: McGill-Queen's University Press, 2013), 61–84. For Margrit Shildrick, it is the leaks and flows of the human corpus that disrupt the structure of the Western logos. See Margrit Shildrick, *Leaky Bodies and Boundaries: Feminism, Postmodernism and (Bio)ethics* (New York: Routledge, 1997).

shore, the shore as the drizzle. This overlapping of or transition between land and water provides a model or metaphorical structure through which to reconsider curatorial practices which seek to address sustainability, climate change, and environmental activism through cultural production.

Dissolve the border between
identities, between human and more-than.
The space of the in-between as the locus for transformation;
      subversion for processes of becoming
that which is not a space, a space without boundaries of its
own, which takes on and   receives itself, its form, from the
outside, which is not its outside
      whose form is the outside of identity, not just of an other but of others
      relations of possibility define, by default, the space
that is constituted as in-between
assimilation to space as a state of mind — expansive consciousness,
physical boundaries:
dissolving, eroding, crumbling, slipping, tripping, melting, spilling, pooling, drip —

Partial knowledges: Think-with, Read-with, Write-with

It matters what matters we use to think other matters with; it matters what stories we tell to tell other stories with; it matters what knots knot knots, what thoughts think thoughts, what descriptions describe descriptions, what ties tie ties. It matters what stories make worlds, what worlds make stories.[18]

This sentiment, in varying forms and iterations, echoes through Donna Haraway's most recent book as a means of punctuating propositions with a summoning of those she has thought alongside. This first instance allows Haraway to conjure the social anthropologist Marilyn Strathern, who embodies the art of feminist speculative fabulation in a scholarly mode. It matters what matters we use to think other matters with. It matters who we think-with, read-with, write-with.

It matters, and because of this, I selected artists based not on existing works but on the conceptual underpinnings of their ongoing practices, inviting them to think with me, tell stories with me. The impetus or emphasis in the context of this project is not so much the art objects themselves but the ways of thinking and being that support their coming together in space. In his manifesto for the twenty-first century, Rasheed Araeen sees this as the role that artists should inhabit on a damaged planet: "it is in fact artistic imagination, not art objects, which, once

---

18   Donna J. Haraway, *Staying with the Trouble: Making Kin in the Chthulucene* (Durham: Duke University Press, 2016), 12.

freed from the self-destructive narcissist ego, can enter this life and not only offer it salvation but put it on the path to a better future."[19] It matters.[20]

As an exhibition, the fixed elements of *Learning from the Lake* are rooted in the contributions of two Canadian visual artists — Maggie Groat and Kelly Jazvac. Each has demonstrated an ability to engage with unique sites at both a material and conceptual level while respecting the delicate ecologies they encounter with reverent response-ability. With the gathering of relational ecological knowledge through field studies, Groat and Jazvac both work alongside the specificity of place, visualizing the information that they acquire in a way that may be accessible to varying publics.[21]

Groat and Jazvac possess a certain sensibility or sensitivity when it comes to the complication of disciplinary boundaries, as artists who complicate distinctions between different modes of practice, suggesting that something is gained in bringing them into conversation with one another. While Jazvac works with a team of scientists, artists, and writers on plastic pollution research, Groat's highly interdisciplinary work engages with site-responsiveness with regard to shifting territories, alternative or decolonial ways-of-being, methodologies of collage, and the transformation of salvaged materials into utilitarian objects for speculation, vision and action.

These two artists embrace the privilege of partial perspective and situated knowledges, recognizing the network of connections that flourishes when the Western promise of objectivity is set aside in favor of "contestation, deconstruction, passionate construction, webbed connections, and hope for transformation of systems of knowledge and ways of seeing" — feminist epistemologies of location, positioning and situating are multidimensional and attuned to resonances rather than dichotomies.[22] They are marked knowledges which facilitate the mapping of consciousness, experiences, and separations in fields of meaning and fields of power.

19 While Araeen takes this to the extreme in suggesting that artists abandon their studios altogether, the sentiment of collectivity and shift in ways that we think, initiate, and create is very much at the heart of this work. See Rasheed Araeen, "Ecoaesthetics: A Manifesto for the Twenty-first Century," *Third Text* 23, no. 5 (September 2009): 679–84.

20 Despite my conviction: sometimes it matters less who we think-with and more so how we think-with. There is no greater example of this, in my mind, than Elizabeth Grosz, who proposes a reading of Darwin's work despite the mobilization of Darwinism in support of relations of domination and subordination. Yet in Grosz's reading, he offers a critique of essentialism and teleology based on the formation of a dynamic and open-ended understanding of the intermingling of history and biology. Darwin's work can be understood as a complex account of the movements of bifurcation, and becoming that characterize all forms of life; elements of productivity, chance, repetition and pure difference. Grosz takes the principle of evolutionary unfolding and encourages that feminism look to processes of revision and revitalization as a model for the consideration of a thorough self-transformation of the discipline's basic presumptions, methods, and values. See Elizabeth Grosz, "Darwin and Feminism: Preliminary Investigations for a Possible Alliance," in *Material Feminisms,* eds. Stacy Alaimo and Susan Hekman (Bloomington: Indiana University Press, 2008), 23–52.

21 Lawson, *Learning from the Lake.*

22 Haraway, "Situated Knowledges," 858.

Amplification, Communication, Contamination, Dissolution, Destruction, Gestation

At the core of my curatorial practice is the question of whether it may be possible to move beyond the illustrative or thematic models of exhibition-making to develop ecofeminist methodologies. When water is mobilized as literal subject and as metaphor and as process, what kinds of strategies could be developed in working with, rather than against, fluidity as a guiding principle? What are the creative possibilities and the difficulties of integrating a fluid logic into curatorial methodologies? What are the implications of making room for conceptual seepage, flooding, or moisture in the process of research and the development of an exhibition? How do we understand the agency and significance of elemental forces in relation to trans-corporeality, or movement across bodies and nature? Could a form of curatorial gesture prompt an Irigarayan drizzle? Where does the drizzle fall — between artworks, between visitors, through conversation, in writing, in movement and activation and performance? How could the efficacy of water as metaphor and as process be measured?

The use of metaphor in ecofeminism has been, for some, grounds for repudiation. In *Rethinking Ecofeminist Politics,* Janet Biehl rejects the inclusion of metaphor in radical, political movements as she sees the function of these forms of organizing to be to explain the world rather than obscure it. Yet here I am inclined to align myself with Alaimo and with Haraway, in their insistence that most ways of thinking — within ethics, politics, physics, social sciences — are shaped by metaphors, and theoretical work comes through figuration and imagining.[23] Concepts rest on material metaphors as a means of expression, as a reference to embodied experience. In this particular case, my words and ideas shape and are shaped by waters, a more-than-human collaboration or intra-action.[24]

23 Alaimo, *Undomesticated Ground,* 172.

24 In considering performativity and matter from a posthumanist, naturalist, and materialist position, Karen Barad proposes the "intra-activity" (in contrast to "interaction," which presumes the prior existence of independent entities/relata) of becoming of all substance — human and nonhuman. This iterative intra-activity is closely related to boundary-making practices, or discursive practices — practices of knowing and being are not isolatable, but rather, mutually implicated. "We do not obtain knowledge by standing outside of the world; we know because "we" are of the world. We are part of the world in its differential becoming." Barad, "Posthumanist Performativity," 147.

References

Alaimo, Stacy. "States of Suspension: Trans-corporeality at Sea." *Interdisciplinary Studies in Literature and Environment* 19, no. 3 (Summer 2012): 476–93. DOI: 10.1093/isle/iss068.

———. "Trans-corporeal Feminisms and the Ethical Space of Nature." In *Material Feminisms,* eds. Stacy Alaimo and Susan Hekman, 237–65. Bloomington: Indiana University Press, 2008.

———. *Undomesticated Ground: Recasting Nature as Feminist Space.* Ithaca: Cornell University Press, 2000.

———. "Your Shell on Acid: Material Immersion, Anthropocene Dissolves." In *Anthropocene Feminism,* edited by Richard A. Grusin, 89–121. Minneapolis: University of Minnesota Press, 2017.

Alcoff, Linda. "The Problem of Speaking for Others." *Cultural Critique* 20 (Winter 1991–1992): 5–32. DOI: 10.2307/1354221.

Araeen, Rasheed. "Ecoaesthetics: A Manifesto for the Twenty-first Century." *Third Text* 23, no. 5 (September 2009): 679–84. DOI: 10.1080/09528820903189327.

Barad, Karen. "Posthumanist Performativity: Toward an Understanding of How Matter Comes to Matter." In *Material Feminisms,* edited by Stacy Alaimo and Susan Hekman, 120–57. Bloomington: Indiana University Press, 2008.

Bennett, Jane. *Vibrant Matter: A Political Ecology of Things.* Durham: Duke University Press, 2010.

Boetzkes, Amanda. *The Ethics of Earth Art.* Minneapolis: University of Minnesota Press, 2010.

Canters, Hanneke, and Grace M. Jantzen. *Forever Fluid: A Reading of Luce Irigaray's Elemental Passions.* Manchester: Manchester University Press, 2005.

Chandler, Mielle, and Astrida Neimanis. "Water and Gestationality: What Flows beneath Ethics." In *Thinking with Water,* edited by Cecilia Chen, Janine MacLeod, and Astrida Neimanis, 61–84. Montreal: McGill-Queen's University Press, 2013.

Cheetham, Mark. *Landscape into Eco Art: Articulations of Nature since the '60s.* University Park: Pennsylvania State University Press, 2018.

Gaard, Greta. "Ecofeminism and Climate Change." *Women's Studies International Forum* 49, (March–April 2015): 20–33. DOI: 10.1016/j.wsif.2015.02.004.

Glazebrook, Trish. "Ecofeminist 'Cityzenry.'" In *The Natural City: Re-Envisioning the Built Environment,* edited by Ingrid Leman Stefanovic and Stephen Bede Scharper, 174–90. Toronto: University of Toronto Press, 2012.

Groat, Maggie, and Kelly Jazvac. *Learning from the Lake: Maggie Groat and Kelly Jazvac.* June 14–July 7, 2018. Art Museum at the University of Toronto, Toronto, Canada.

Grosz, Elizabeth. "Darwin and Feminism: Preliminary Investigations for a Possible Alliance." In *Material Feminisms,* edited by Stacy Alaimo and Susan Hekman, 23–52. Bloomington: Indiana University Press, 2008.

Haraway, Donna J. Simians, *Cyborgs and Women: The Reinvention of Nature.* New York: Routledge, 1991.

———. "Situated Knowledges: The Science Question in Feminism and the Privilege of Partial Perspective." *Feminist Studies* 14, no. 3 (Autumn 1988): 575–99. DOI: 10.2307/3178066.

————— . *Staying with the Trouble: Making Kin in the Chthulucene.* Durham: Duke University Press, 2016.

Irigaray, Luce. *Marine Lover of Friedrich Nietzsche.* Translated by Gillian C. Gill. New York: Columbia University Press, 1991.

Jazvac, Kelly. "Noni Knows." In *Plastiglomerates,* 11-17. Toronto: Durable Good, 2017.

"Lake Ontario." *Lake Ontario Waterkeeper.* http://www.waterkeeper.ca/lake-ontario/.

Lawson, Katie. "Learning from the Lake." *Art Museum at the University of Toronto.* https://artmuseum.utoronto.ca/exhibition/learning-from-the-lake/.

MacGregor, Sherilyn. "Only Resist: Feminist Ecological Citizenship and the Post-politics of Climate Change." *Hypatia* 29, no. 3 (Summer 2014): 617–33. DOI: 10.1111/hypa.12065.

Neimanis, Astrida. *Bodies of Water: Posthuman Feminist Phenomenology.* London: Bloomsbury Academic, 2017.

Plumwood, Val. *Feminism and the Mastery of Nature.* New York: Routledge, 2015.

Rios, Lorena. Interview by Christina Battle. Gallery TPW, June 24, 2017.

Shildrick, Margrit. *Leaky Bodies and Boundaries: Feminism, Postmodernism and (Bio)ethics.* New York: Routledge, 1997.

Stengers, Isabelle. "Including Nonhumans in Political Theory: Opening Pandora's Box." In *Political Matter: Technoscience, Democracy, and Public Life,* edited by Bruce Braun and Sarah J. Whatmore, 3–33. Minneapolis: University of Minnesota Press, 2010.

Tuana, Nancy. "Viscous Porosity: Witnessing Katrina." In *Material Feminisms,* edited by Stacy Alaimo and Susan Hekman, 188–214. Bloomington: Indiana University Press, 2008.

CHAPTER 12

Lagomorph Lessons: Feminist Methods for Environmental Sensing and Sensemaking

Maya Livio

The Great Blue Heron is not a symbol. Wandered inadvertently or purposefully inland, maybe drought-driven, to a backyard habitat, it is a bird, Ardea herodias, *whose form, dimensions, and habits have been described by ornithologists, yet whose intangible ways of being and knowing remain beyond my — or anyone's — reach.*[1]

Introduction

Scientific research on indicator species, organisms studied for the purpose of assessing or predicting environmental health, has increased sharply over the last several decades.[2] Reasons for this shift towards monitoring individual species may range from cost efficiency to desires for more straightforward findings that can easily be shared with regulatory organizations and the general public.[3] More charismatic indicator species can also be harnessed by environmental organizations as public-facing "issue animals" with the hopes that they motivate climate action. Serving as proxies for their ecosystems, indicator species have been mobilized as living environmental sensors — beings-cum-technology. And while they no doubt provide meaningful ecological data points and environmental talking points, their use is not without limitations, for example by oversimplifying ecological complexity.[4]

The study of indicator species is just one of many ways in which nonhuman beings have been mobilized for human sensing. There are more overt strategies,

---

1   Adrienne Rich, *What Is Found There: Notebooks on Poetry and Politics* (New York City: W.W. Norton & Company, 2003), 7–8.

2   Stuart R. Borrett, James Moody, and Achim Edelmann, "The Rise of Network Ecology: Maps of the Topic Diversity and Scientific Collaboration," *Ecological Modelling* 293 (December 2014): 111–27.

3   Ahmed A.H. Siddig et al., "How Do Ecologists Select and Use Indicator Species to Monitor Ecological Change? Insights from 14 Years of Publication in 'Ecological Indicators,'" *Ecological Indicators* 60 (January 2016): 223–30.

4   David B. Lindenmayer and Gene E. Likens, "Direct Measurement versus Surrogate Indicator Species for Evaluating Environmental Change and Biodiversity Loss," *Ecosystems* 14, no. 1 (January 2011): 47–59.

such as applying or implanting biosensors onto or into nonhuman beings in order to quantitatively detect their environmental or physiological conditions. There is also biomimicry, the study of beings as prototypes for technological development, often those beings with sensing capacities that exceed or operate differently from those of humans. For example, millimeter wave scanners, the machines deployed at airports for searching passengers' bodies, were inspired by the sensing mechanisms of the Brazilian free-tailed bat (*Tadarida brasiliensis*).[5] And on the more abstract end of the multispecies sensing spectrum, nonhuman organisms have been looked to for enhancing human understandings of our shared world. Such an approach has long been integral to Indigenous knowledge practices, and in scholarly writing has recently been articulated in the "nonhuman turn," the interdisciplinary move which has sought to decenter human animals in theory and practice.[6] In short, nonhuman perspectives are used not only for human sensing but for human *sensemaking*.

But what is at stake when already marginalized nonhuman beings are leveraged as sensemaking apparatus? In this chapter, I argue that sensing and making sense through nonhuman beings in research requires acknowledgment of those beings as knowledge coproducers. My aim is not to argue against nonhuman knowledge coproduction but to highlight and attend to the embedded power relations among species in knowledge exchange. I do so by surveying my own research alongside a biologist on a small mammal called the American pika, which led to an intermedia project called *Thermopower* (2020–2021). Using the project as a case study, I will outline some of the methods for multispecies sensemaking that I began to develop that are informed by feminist methods. Far from a complete or comprehensive set of strategies, I present these as a few preliminary tactics that might serve as methodological breadcrumbs towards more ethical sensemaking with nonhuman beings.

The Backstory on Pikas and Heat

The American pika (*Ochotona princeps*) is a small lagomorph, a relative of rabbits and hares who lives in the mountains of western North America (see Fig. 12.1). Rotund herbivores, their diet consists of wildflowers, forbs, grasses, and moss. They typically live at high elevation, at or above tree-line, and do not burrow but live amid deposits of broken rock called talus.[7] Pika populations are severely threatened by the climate crisis, a recent study suggests that under moderate carbon-emission predictions they will be lost from more than half of currently suitable habitats by the year 2100, and under high-emission predictions, they may be lost entirely.[8] These factors in combination make the American pika particularly well-

---

5   "Bat Inspires Space Tech for Airport Security," *European Space Agency,* October 10, 2005, https://www.esa.int/Space_in_Member_States/Ireland/Bat_inspires_space_tech_for_airport_security.

6   Richard A. Grusin, ed., *The Nonhuman Turn* (Minneapolis: University of Minnesota Press, 2015), vii.

7   Andrew T. Smith, "The Distribution and Dispersal of Pikas: Influences of Behavior and Climate," *Ecology* 55, no. 6 (November 1974): 1368–76.

8   Donelle Schwalm et al., "Habitat Availability and Gene Flow Influence Diverging

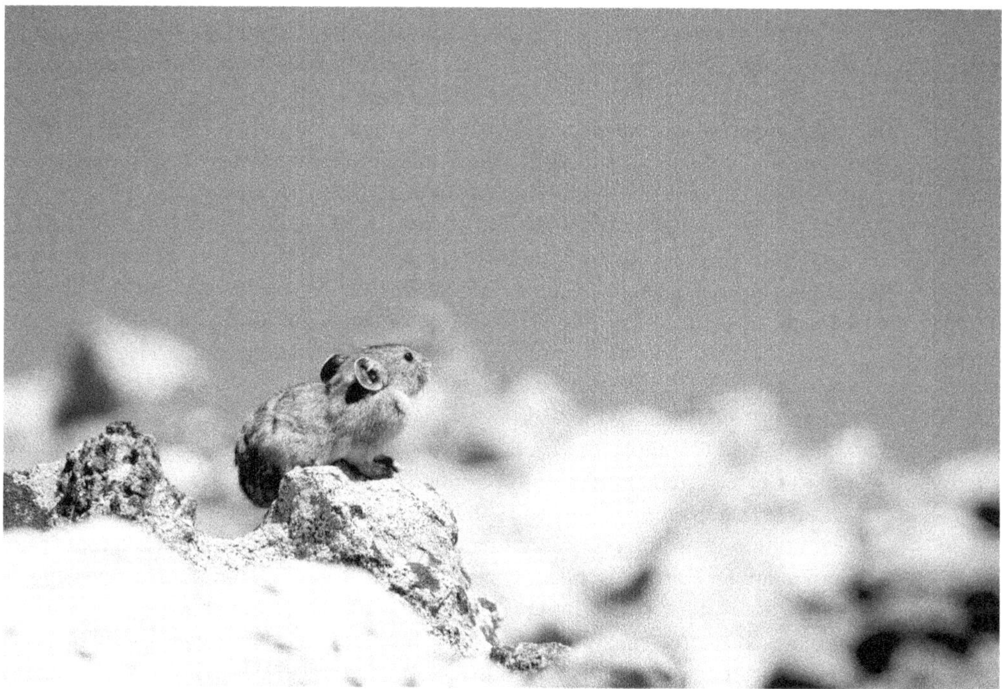

Fig. 12.1. An American pika in the Colorado Rocky Mountains, 2018. Photograph by the author.

suited as a climate change indicator species, studied to sense the environmental health of their mountain ecosystems. Their perceived cuteness also leads them to be activated as charismatic issue animals for climate causes.[9]

My research on American pikas was initiated in the context of field and lab research conducted with evolutionary biologist Ashley Whipple, who studies their thermal stress, and resulted in an intermedia research-creation project called *Thermopower*. The project, which commingles scientific, creative, and technological approaches, animates a conversation on the role of technology in maintaining livable temperatures by weaving the concept of thermoregulation through the practices of mammals and machines. It consists of a short film told through four lenses — a networked research camera, imaging satellites, an on-location camera, and screen-recording. The images are paired with a conceptual score that blends the sounds of a chamber music ensemble, pikas, air conditioners, and algorithmic processes. The work also exists as a multimedia performance in which the ensemble and narration are performed live. Before diving deeper into the project, an outline of thermoregulation and its relationship to the American pika will be useful.

Local Population Trajectories under Scenarios of Climate Change: A Place-based Approach," *Global Change Biology* 22, no. 4 (April 2016): 1572–84.

9   Esther Weltevrede and Sabine Niederer, "Issue Animals Research," *Digital Methods Initiative Wiki,* April 2, 2008, https://www.digitalmethods.net/Dmi/IssueImageAnalysis.

Pikas' vulnerability to warming temperatures, as well as their capacity to live at high elevation, are results of the mechanisms they use to thermoregulate. Thermoregulation is the means by which some organisms maintain livable body temperatures — means that are typically classified as either physiological or behavioral. Some physiological thermoregulation processes include evaporation via sweating or panting, tapping into stores of fat or blubber, shivering, and trapping or releasing heat by moving feathers, fur, or hair (note that fur and hair are chemically indistinguishable and are merely markers to differentiate nonhuman from human animals). Some behavioral thermoregulation mechanisms include seeking sun or shade, moving to lower or higher ground, huddling, or otherwise sharing or stealing warmth from other organisms (amusingly called kleptothermy), or dormancy to avoid hot or cold temperatures for either long periods of time (hibernation) or short ones (torpor).

In order to endure the harsh cold of their alpine tundra habitats, American pikas use a combination of both physiological and behavioral strategies. They do not hibernate, but they do spend some of their days under talus in winter months, with the snowpack serving as an insulating blanket. They have a dense coat of fur and maintain a high resting body temperature of 40.6° Celsius, only a few degrees shy of their upper lethal limit, 43° Celsius.[10] To ensure enough food for the frigid months, pikas *haypile,* or collect plants for food reserves. Remarkably, some of the plants they collect are toxic to them, and these plants both act as preservatives for the haypile and likely prevent other herbivores from eating it. As the toxins decrease over winter, pikas are able to consume the formerly toxic plants at the end of the season.[11]

Pikas' physiological and behavioral strategies make them uniquely suited to tolerate cold winters, but in order to survive warm temperatures, they are mostly reliant on behavioral thermoregulation alone. Their coat does thin a little in a summer, but their primary thermoregulation in heat consists of reducing activity to short bursts, sometimes only four minutes at a time, and spending much of the day staying cool in the shaded microclimates under talus.[12] This reliance on behavioral thermoregulation to endure hot weather, coupled with their high resting body temperature, is what makes American pikas particularly vulnerable to thermal stress under a warming climate, as it leaves them with a narrow range of options for maintaining livable temperatures. Given that pikas already live at high elevation, their upslope mobility, a behavioral thermoregulation strategy available to some other species, is limited. The fragmented availability of the talus they require as habitat, as well as their territorial nature, further limit their capacity to disperse in search of shade.

10   Robert A. Macarthur and Lawrence C.H. Wang, "Physiology of Thermoregulation in the Pika, 'Ochotona Princeps," *Canadian Journal of Zoology* 51, no. 1 (1973): 13.

11   Andrew T. Smith, "The Distribution and Dispersal of Pikas: Influences of Behavior and Climate," *Ecology* 55, no. 6 (November 1974): 1368–76.

12   Lukas Moyer-Horner et al., "Modeling Behavioral Thermoregulation in a Climate Change Sentinel," *Ecology and Evolution* 5, no. 24 (December 2015): 5815.

Embodied Engagement

I was drawn to the American pika not for their thermoregulatory specificities, but because of their use as an indicator species, organisms leveraged for sensing and sensemaking that hover at an interstice between biology and technology. Still, thermoregulation became impossible for me to ignore during the research phase of the *Thermopower* project when my own thermoception was unexpectedly foregrounded.

The project took up Whipple's recent work, which centered on testing a hypothesis that pikas who live on active rock glaciers suffer less climate-related stress than those living in other microclimates because they benefit from the glaciers' more-stable year-round temperatures.[13] Whipple's methods included long-term observation of pika habitats and the collection of fecal samples durationally from a number of talus sites which were identified by satellite to either overlap or not overlap with active rock glaciers. By measuring the glucocorticoid, a stress hormone, in the fecal samples collected and comparing them spatially and temporally, pika stress levels could be approximated across locations and time.[14] Furthermore, Whipple's continuous observations of pikas in situ provided meaningful qualitative data of their potentially shifting habits and well-being. As all of Whipple's methods relied on slow, sustained observation of pikas, I myself spent slow time with pikas in the field.

In the summer months, I was able to visit the pika neighborhoods in person, and the embodied experience of doing so provided vital information and context. Specifically, the combination of high elevation, strong winds, and intense solar radiation makes thermoregulation unnervingly noticeable in the alpine tundra. In the field, I found myself continuously adding and removing layers to maintain thermocomfort, which quickly led me to note the relative ease with which I was able to do so by comparison to pikas.[15] A seemingly banal gesture suddenly took on greater significance. Noticing my alternatingly cold and hot body drew my attention to the role that clothing and other coverings play in thermoregulation. Clothing is a technology that is so obvious that it no longer seems like technology but rather is seamlessly (pun intended) integrated into daily life. As my body made visible this particular thermopractice, I considered what other technological thermoregulation strategies exist.

Not limiting a notion of technology to humans alone, I researched and developed a preliminary list of technologically inflected thermoregulation across animal species. The list includes practices such as building insulated burrows, nests, and houses, constructing or using pools, waterholes, and baths,[16] making and using

13   Jennifer L. Wilkening, Chris Ray, and Johanna Varner, "Relating Sub-Surface Ice Features to Physiological Stress in a Climate Sensitive Mammal, the American Pika ('Ochotona Princeps')," *PLoS ONE* 10, no. 3 (March 24, 2015): 2.

14   Jennifer L. Wilkening, Chris Ray, and Johanna Varner, "When Can We Measure Stress Noninvasively? Postdeposition Effects on a Fecal Stress Metric Confound a Multiregional Assessment," *Ecology and Evolution* 6, no. 2 (January 2016): 504.

15   (*Ochotona princeps*) American pika, 2019.

16   "The Elephants of Africa: Tale of the Trunk," *PBS: Nature*, November 16, 1997, https://www.pbs.org/wnet/nature/elephants-africa-tale-trunk/11391/.

umbrellas,[17] and designing and using heating and cooling systems that use materials such as electricity, fossil fuels, water, steam, or refrigerants (e.g., HVAC units, incubators, radiators, and fans). Here, collapsing the distinction between human and nonhuman reveals a tension. While asserting that humans are not the only animals who design and implement technologies is vitally necessary for recognizing nonhuman intelligences, human-designed technological thermoregulation does diverge from other species' strategies. To unpack the difference, I will turn to a ubiquitous example, the air conditioner.

Air conditioners were invented in 1902 and reached commercial enterprises first, then movie theatres — where the "summer blockbuster" was invented due to the cooling refuge that theatres provided in summer — before finally making it into private homes.[18] By 2018, almost 90 percent of American homes included air conditioners.[19] While that number has remained relatively low outside of the United States by comparison, air conditioners worldwide are predicted to rise from 1.6 billion to 5.6 billion units over the next thirty years.[20] With the bitterest irony, the refrigerants used by air conditioners, called hydrofluorocarbons, are potent greenhouse gasses that amplify a warming climate. As the number of air conditioners worldwide increases over the next three decades, the greenhouse gasses they emit are expected to nearly double, contributing to a rise in global temperatures, and further raising demand for air conditioners.[21] While scientists are actively searching for replacement refrigerant fluids with a lesser environmental impact, recent research at the National Institute of Standards and Technology in Colorado, adjacent American pika habitats, has concluded that few good alternatives currently exist.[22]

An even more insidious example of the specificities of human-designed technological thermoregulation is that of technologies which themselves *require* thermoregulation. Computers, for example, use fans and other cooling mechanisms to prevent overheating and malfunction. Computer components have increased in power consumption, speed, and heat production over recent decades and so can no longer rely on passive cooling alone to maintain adequate temperatures.[23] On a much larger scale, the internet requires tremendous cooling to work efficiently. In 2015, the data centers on which most of the internet operates consumed at least 2 percent of the world's electricity, an amount expected to triple by the year 2030.[24]

17   "Orangutans," *National Geographic*, n.d., https://www.nationalgeographic.com/animals/mammals/group/orangutans/.

18   Marsha Ackermann, *Cool Comfort: America's Romance with Air Conditioning* (Washington, DC: Smithsonian Books, 2010).

19   "The Future of Cooling: Opportunities for Energy-efficient Air Conditioning," *International Energy Agency*, May 15, 2018. https://www.iea.org/reports/the-future-of-cooling.

20   Kendra Pierre-Louis, "The World Wants Air-conditioning: That Could Warm the World," *The New York Times*, May 15, 2018, https://www.nytimes.com/2018/05/15/climate/air-conditioning.html.

21   Pierre-Louis, "The World Wants Air-conditioning."

22   Mark O. McLinden et al, "Limited Options for Low-global-warming-potential Refrigerants," *Nature Communications* 8 (February 2017).

23   Kakaç, Sadik, Hafit Yüncü, and K. Hijikata, eds. *Cooling of Electronic Systems* (Dordrecht: Springer, 1994), 97.

24   Tom Bawden, "Global Warming: Data Centres to Consume Three Times as

This estimate does not take into account the energy consumed by individual devices, cellular networks, or technology manufacturing. Data centers also accounted for 2 percent of global carbon emissions, a similar carbon footprint to the aviation industry.[25] And while some data centers are now built in places such as Sweden and Iceland, where cool climates can reduce cooling needs, many data centers are still cooled by air conditioners and fans. Quickly, the multiplying global effects of human-designed technological thermoregulation become evident.

These examples illustrate that though the practice of technological thermoregulation is shared across many animal species, there is a notable feature of the human variants: Unlike all other forms of thermoregulation, human-designed technological strategies are the only ones with the potential to change not only individual, local, and immediate temperatures, but also global temperatures across greater timescales. This tension, between collapsing human-nonhuman difference in order to acknowledge nonhumans as technology-makers, while at the same time identifying that human-designed technologies cause a great deal more harm, illustrates how framings of "entanglement" can foreclose important exclusions.[26]

In *Thermopower*, I suggest that classifying thermoregulation as merely "behavioral" or "physiological" may be insufficient, and that specifying "technological" thermoregulation, and perhaps more specifically "human-designed technological" thermoregulation, may more fully describe the conditions at hand. Here, centering embodied knowledge as a means of seeking common or disparate grounds with pikas is what enabled me to cultivate more nuanced attention to these concerns.

Pikas and Power

After spending some time with pikas in their environments, I also developed a greater awareness of how power plays out in even the most innocuous instantiations of nonhuman research. Though Whipple and I were exceedingly careful not to disturb pika habitats or haypiles, we were still entering their communities uninvited. In the case of those pikas living within a long-term ecological research (LTER) site, we were also among countless researchers to do so. Such low-impact intrusions may indeed be fully justifiable considering the need for pika conservation but should be reflexively considered and accounted for, even within arts and humanities work. To more fully map pika research and power, I also looked to foundational pika studies, particularly around thermoregulation, in order to attend to those histories and relations.

Much of what is presently known about American pika thermoregulation was learned in a frequently cited set of studies from 1974, in which a captive animal was embedded with a telemeter (a radio-controlled sensor) to detect resting body

Much Energy in Next Decade, Experts Warn," *The Independent,* January 23, 2016, https://www.independent.co.uk/climate-change/news/global-warming-data-centres-to-consume-three-times-as-much-energy-in-next-decade-experts-warn-a6830086.html.

25 James Bridle, *New Dark Age: Technology, Knowledge and the End of the Future* (New York City: Verso, 2018), 63.

26 Eva Haifa Giraud, *What Comes after Entanglement: Activism, Anthropocentrism, and an Ethics of Exclusion* (Durham: Duke University Press, 2019), 2.

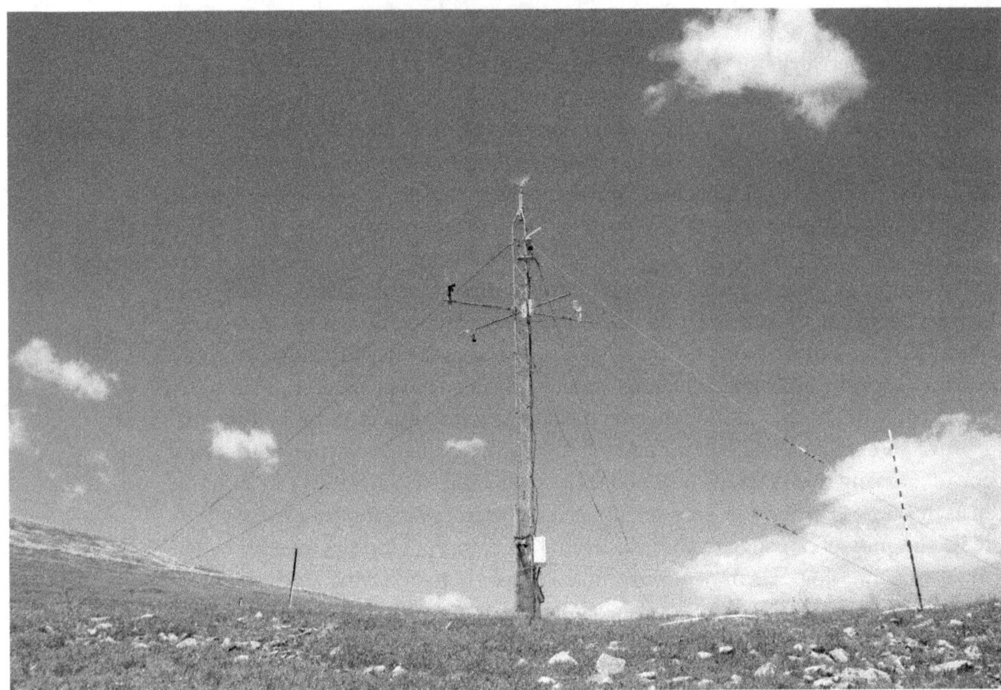

Fig. 12.2. View of the TundraCam, 2018. Photograph by the author.

temperature changes over time. Pika resting body temperatures were also deter-mined in that study by shooting or trapping them in the field, where "their rectal temperatures were taken with a quick-reacting mercury thermometer within ten seconds of their instantaneous death."[27] In order to establish the upper lethal limit of pika body temperatures, another study in that set held pikas captive in wire mesh cages placed in the full sun:

> When the caged pikas were confined in the sun at the lower altitude site they died in six hours. On both days the animals were placed in the sun at 0630-hr when the shade air temperature was 17 Celsius (62 Fahrenheit). They were initially active, then calmed down for most of the experiment. The half hour before death was marked by extreme activity and salivation. Death occurred at almost exactly 1230-hr on each day. The ambient shade temperature at time of death had reached 29.40 Celsius (85 Fahrenheit) in one case, and only 25.50 Celsius (78 Fahrenheit) in the other.[28]

In the *Thermopower* film, I acknowledge these pikas. To be sure, animal research in the United States must meet much higher welfare standards today, and indeed welfare is of utmost importance to Whipple and her colleagues. Her research does not directly manipulate pika bodies in any way but only collects fecal samples. It is worth mentioning, however, that the kits used to analyze the glucocorticoid in the samples contain antigens and antibodies derived from species perceived to

27   Smith, "The Distribution and Dispersal of Pikas," 1374.
28   Ibid.

be less at risk — sheep and donkeys.[29] The kit, known as an Enzyme-linked Immunosorbent Assay (ELISA), is a commonly used protocol in biology, as well as to study multispecies, including human, immunology. While the ELISA kit does not harm pikas specifically, it makes visible how pikas fit into hierarchies of more and less valued bodies, even across conservation efforts. Donna Haraway's framing of "noninnocence," in which "the accountabilities are extensive and permanently unfinished,"[30] becomes well-illustrated here, as does Alexis Shotwell's call for a move "against purity." Shotwell reminds that "we do better to start from an assumption that everyone is implicated in situations we (at least in some way) repudiate" and insists that the impossibility of purity should not paralyze action, in this case conservation research.[31]

Mediated Mammals

In order to minimize intrusion and foreground different kinds of pika relations, I explored other forms of observation for *Thermopower*. Among the project's aims were methodological experimentation, testing interdisciplinary approaches for collaboration among scientific, cultural, and creative modes of knowledge production. As such, part of my work included translating Whipple's scientific methods into a media-based territory more familiar to me. Just as I had mimicked Whipple's slow observation in the physical field and followed her to research sites and the lab, I developed similar methods in a mediated "field," using a steerable online camera called TundraCam (see Fig. 12.2).

TundraCam streams a live feed from the long-term ecological research site in Niwot Ridge, Colorado, where one of the pika talus habitats included in Whipple's study is visible. The camera is attached to a 10-meter weather tower and sits in the high-altitude tundra region, 5.5 kilometers from the Continental Divide.[32] What is particularly remarkable about the camera is that, unlike most networked cameras, its steering and zoom can be controlled by any internet user, though it is typically used by scientists like Whipple for real-time environmental monitoring of changes such as cloud cover, vegetation, and snow. Nearby sensors measure local data and maintain an ongoing climate record. Over the course of nearly a year, I developed a slow, daily, observational practice using TundraCam. This, in tandem with the embodied understandings I gained in the field, was at the heart of the *Thermopower* project.

Pikas are not actually visible through TundraCam because they are so small. In fact, besides weather, most of what can be seen through the camera changes at a scale too slow to observe with the unaided eye, but there are occasional moments of more easily perceptible excitement such as marmot or human sightings (see Fig. 12.3). Following the TundraCam's slow pace over time enabled me not only to con-

---

29   "DetectX: CORTICOSTERONE Enzyme Immunoassay Kit — Species Dependent" (Ann Arbor: Arbor Assays, 2009), 4.

30   Donna J. Haraway, *Staying with the Trouble: Making Kin in the Chthulucene* (Durham: Duke University Press, 2016), 114.

31   Alexis Shotwell, *Against Purity: Living Ethically in Compromised Times* (Minneapolis: University of Minnesota Press, 2016), 5.

32   "TundraCam," *Niwot Ridge LTER*, n.d., https://nwt.lternet.edu/tundracam.

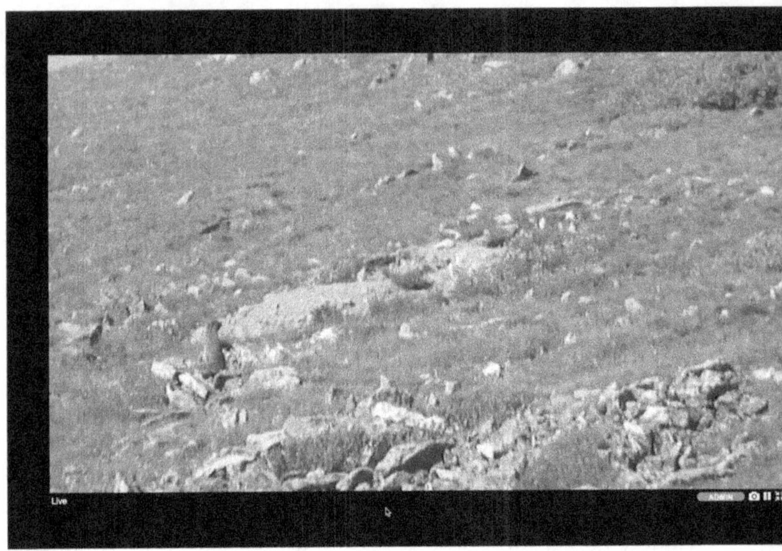

Fig. 12.3. Yellow-bellied marmot (left) and person jogging (right) as seen through the TundraCam. Still from *Thermopower*, 2019.

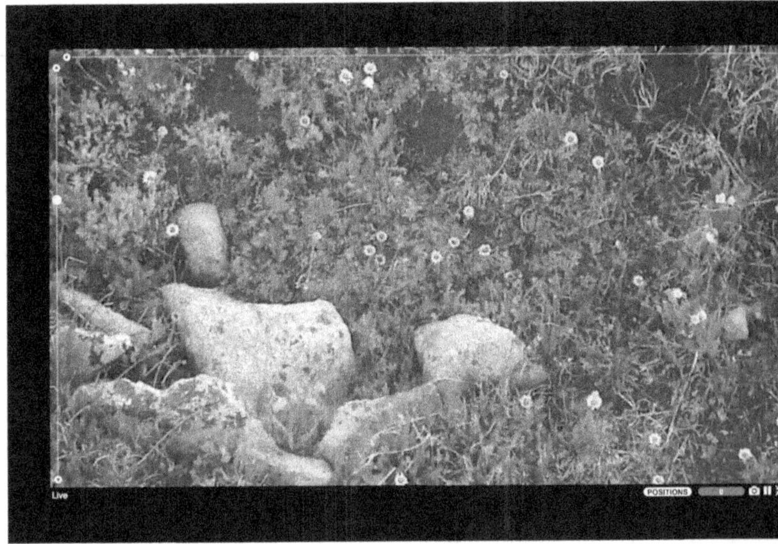

Fig. 12.4. "Green-up" (left) and "green-down" (right) as seen through the TundraCam. Still from *Thermopower*, 2019.

nect with Whipple's approach to the place through methods closer to my own, but also to pay careful attention to subtle events and shifts such as the slow transition between the plant color-changing cycles known as "green-up" and "green-down" (see Fig. 12.4). This sustained attention provided a different perspective on the conditions in which pikas live and ensured that I could continue observing the site over the course of the year, even in the bitter cold when Whipple and most other scientists no longer visit.

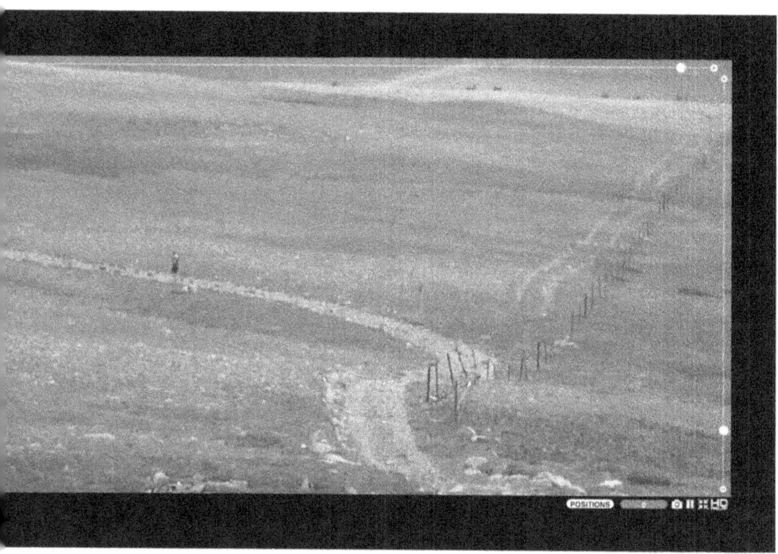

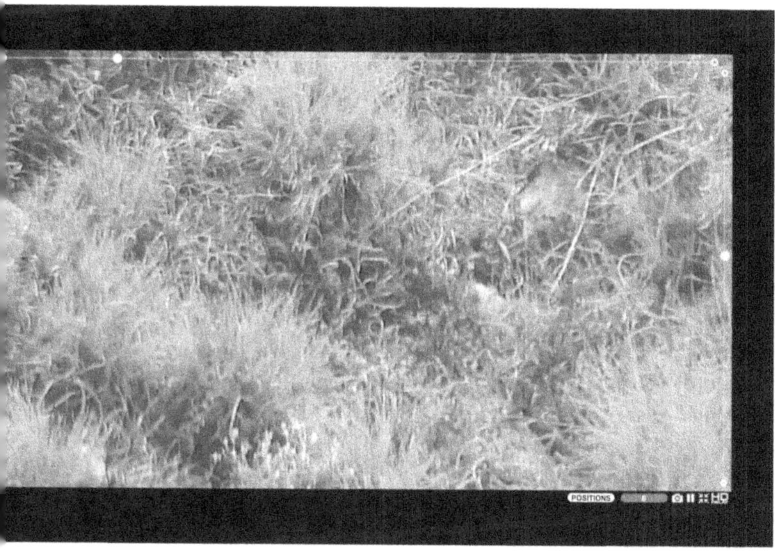

To further complicate questions surrounding thermoregulating technologies, *Thermopower* combines the footage I recorded from TundraCam observations together with a screen-captured recording of Google Earth observations of the exact same site. Scrolling through historical Google Earth data reveals how the site was documented across seasons by satellites, mirroring both the TundraCam's chronological capture and the longitudinal study by Whipple. Like TundraCam, satellites are a sensing tool used by researchers to monitor environmental change, and in the case of Whipple's study of the American pika, satellite imagery was pivotal for identifying which habitats overlap with active rock glaciers. The distanced mediation afforded by both Google Earth and TundraCam facilitated a less intrusive and more holistic engagement with the ecologies and histories of pikas. Moreover, it allowed me to engage with pikas without the expectation that they perform cuteness, as often happens when they are mobilized for climate causes. *Thermopower* features very few close-up shots of pikas for this reason.

As a reflexive note on methods here, both satellites and TundraCam require robust thermoregulation strategies in order to function in the intense environmental conditions in which they operate. The carbon emissions produced by building and operating the networked cameras, satellites, and sensors used for pika conservation, and for the *Thermopower* project, should also be included within a mapping of power.

Notes on Nonhuman Knowers

By now you have likely noticed that I have zoomed out significantly from the American pika, but pikas were crucial beacons in this work. They encouraged me to better understand thermoregulation and shifted my attention to the role that human-designed technologies play within it. They did so not through any specific action, one can only assume through no intention, and not through "collaboration," a term all-too-casually used in multispecies projects. Collaboration requires consent, an ongoing process that is difficult, though perhaps not impossible, to achieve with nonhuman beings. Rather, pikas were a kind of accidental tour guide, in the manner of Haraway's "thinking with" companion species[33] or Tsing's following the matsutake mushroom via the "arts of noticing."[34] Such an approach treats multispecies kin as knowledgeable and recognizes that their ways of being have something to offer towards refocusing on planetary and interdependent matters of concern.[35] Following this reasoning, if multispecies kin are contributive to knowledge work, should they not be considered as knowledge participants? Echoing Vinciane Despret, we should not "take [nonhumans] as hostages in our problems,"[36] nor should we instrumentalize them as teachers or rely on them for solutions. Moreover, if pikas, albeit inadvertently, provided new lenses for me to think through biological, ecological, and technological questions, should they receive some form of attribution and reciprocity as contributors? Without these, does multispecies knowledge-building not simply replicate the extractive logics of colonial science, hinging on questions such as: What can they teach us? What can we gain from them? What can we "discover"?

So far, I have touched on a few methods that I used as counter-tactics to these logics throughout the research and production of *Thermopower*. I will now outline

33   Donna J. Haraway, *When Species Meet* (Minneapolis: University of Minnesota Press, 2008).

34   Anna Lowenhaupt Tsing, *The Mushroom at the End of the World: On the Possibility of Life in Capitalist Ruins* (Princeton: Princeton University Press, 2015).

35   Bruno Latour, "Why Has Critique Run out of Steam? From Matters of Fact to Matters of Concern," *Critical Inquiry* 30, no. 2 (Winter 2004): 225–248.

36   Vinciane Despret, "Politics of Terristories," lecture at Multispecies Storytelling in Intermedial Practices Conference, Linnæus University, Växjö, Sweden, January 23, 2019.

a few additional strategies that I have considered and implemented in the dissemination phase of the project as initial attempts toward attribution and reciprocity.

Attribution and credit are of course among the core interventions of feminist methods, making visible the knowledges and labors of those who have contributed to research, particularly in the case of marginalized populations whose knowledges are rarely or sufficiently acknowledged or valued.[37] To that end, I have made a point of citing the American pika in writings about *Thermopower*, though I recognize the absurdity of such an approach (and it surely makes citation management software tricky to navigate!). Clearly, citing pikas probably yields no benefits to them — I prefer not to make assumptions about what pikas care about, but it seems unlikely that citations are pika priorities or that they function as currency in pika value systems. Nevertheless, citations function as an epistemological gesture, and in this case, I view them as a kind of performance that reiterates nonhuman beings as knowledge producers and contributors.

Challenging the distinctions between human and nonhumans both conceptually and through meticulous language choices is also a part of this practice, something often taken up in multispecies writing but rarely made explicit. Examples include the incorporation of nonhuman-made technologies within technological framings, using words such as "who" rather than "that" or "which," and defining terms to expose where language has previously worked to maintain species hierarchies, as is the case with the distinction between hair and fur. Specificity with language decenters human animals and further champions nonhuman knowledge production. Again, it is unlikely to benefit the particular pikas I observed for this project, or perhaps even pikas in general, and it may therefore seem unnecessarily laborious. However, it may serve as a kind of long-term micro-contribution toward the cultural shifts necessary for valuing nonhuman beings and their knowledges, perhaps to the benefit of some future pikas or other species.

While these language-based strategies operate on more illustrative and longer timescales, immediate and concrete approaches for working with nonhuman knowledge ethically outside of the sciences are also needed, such as the well-established feminist-informed methods of reciprocity[38] and activism.[39] These are of course more difficult to implement or even conceptualize with nonhuman rather than human participants, especially those who share little time and space with us. It may be easier to enact care with those nonhumans we have more intimate relations with, such as the companion animals or plants who share our habitats, but performing actions of care toward American pikas, for example, is far less straightforward. Beyond communication difficulties, our value systems are not always in alignment: can one compensate a pika, for example, in a way that is

---

37 Carrie Mott and Daniel Cockayne, "Citation Matters: Mobilizing the Politics of Citation toward a Practice of 'Conscientious Engagement,'" *Gender, Place & Culture: A Journal of Feminist Geography* 24, no. 7 (2017): 954–73.

38 Alison Wylie, "A Plurality of Pluralisms: Collaborative Practice in Archaeology," in *Objectivity in Science: New Perspectives from Science and Technology Studies*, eds. Flavia Padovani, Alan Richardson, and Jonathan Y. Tsou (Cham: Springer International Publishing, 2015), 189–210.

39 Patricia Maguire, "Feminist Participatory Action Research," in *Just Methods: An Interdisciplinary Feminist Reader*, ed. Alison Jaggar, 2nd edn. (Boulder: Paradigm Publishers, 2014), 417–32.

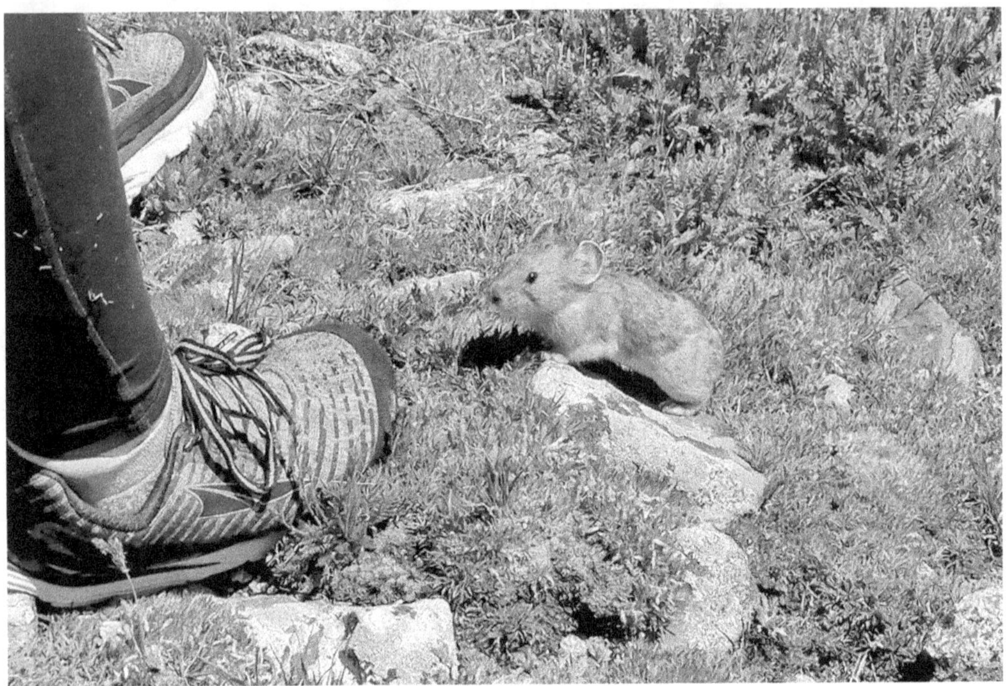

Fig. 12.2. American pika with the author during field research, 2018. Photograph by the author.

meaningful and also does not produce more harm? For *Thermopower*, I decided to implement reciprocity through an intermediary that has closer relations with American pikas and to work with the Front Range Pika Project, a citizen-science research organization focused on conservation of pikas in the Colorado Rocky Mountains.

Activist commitments are not only important for the sake of reciprocal exchange, but also for developing a research agenda that insists on not decoupling research from intervention.[40] Here, I do not mean to center individual responsibility or to suggest that researchers are always able to, or should always be expected to, take on direct action on behalf of their nonhuman research participants. A commitment to any intervention in the systems affecting nonhuman participants could also be an approach for embedding reciprocity and activism into a nonhuman research agenda. In the case of the American pika, for example, voting for political candidates or contributing to campaigns invested in increasing regulations against oil and natural gas drilling in the Rocky Mountains could be one such strategy, activities which put pikas at immediate risk,

Conclusion

The American pika has contributed to sensing and sensemaking for countless human animals. As climate change indicator species, they have been used as a kind of sensor technology, providing information about the health of their environment

40   Giraud, *What Comes after Entanglement*, 22–23.

much in the way that canaries were used in coal mines and other sentinel species are used to monitor pollution of the air or water. As charismatic issue animals, environmental organizations have relied on them to help the public make sense of the climate crisis. Through sensors placed inside their bodies, biologists have learned about thermoregulation. More ambiently, pikas have contributed to my making sense of multispecies thermoregulatory processes and to noticing how technological thermoregulation maps thermopower across species lines. Pikas have also drawn my attention to thermoregulation as an instance where technology can be challenged in terms of human exceptionalism and have inadvertently guided me through concretizing tactics for more ethical nonhuman research (see Fig. 12.5).

To be certain, leveraging pikas and other nonhuman beings in order to sense the environment in scientific research is often motivated by efforts to conserve their populations, habitats, and ecologies. Sensemaking with and through pikas and other nonhumans also typically stems from well-intentioned, if noninnocent, goals: desires to cultivate attunement to ecological interdependence. Yet, American pikas, along with all other nonhuman beings, are not teachers, collaborators, technologies, metaphors, symbols, or solutions, they are living beings with concerns of their own. The complex power relations around nonhuman sensing and making sense should not be grounds for ceasing these practices altogether; rather, making these relations explicit is a crucial first step for taking them into better account.

Throughout the *Thermopower* project, I experimented with tactics that move toward a recognition of pikas as nonhuman knowledge producers and participants, including centering embodiment, mapping power, mediating intimacy, and thinking through attribution and reciprocity. Often drawing from feminist values as a point of departure, these methods must of course each be situated within specific research contexts and are laid out here as initial probes for working towards greater consideration for nonhuman knowers.

References

Ackermann, Marsha. *Cool Comfort: America's Romance with Air Conditioning.* Washington, DC: Smithsonian Books, 2010.

"Bat Inspires Space Tech for Airport Security." *The European Space Agency,* October 10, 2005. https://www.esa.int/Space_in_Member_States/Ireland/Bat_inspires_space_tech_for_airport_security.

Bawden, Tom. "Global Warming: Data Centres to Consume Three Times as Much Energy in Next Decade, Experts Warn." *The Independent,* January 23, 2016. https://www.independent.co.uk/climate-change/news/global-warming-data-centres-to-consume-three-times-as-much-energy-in-next-decade-experts-warn-a6830086.html.

Borrett, Stuart R., James Moody, and Achim Edelmann. "The Rise of Network Ecology: Maps of the Topic Diversity and Scientific Collaboration." *Ecological Modelling* 293 (December 2014): 111–27. DOI: 10.1016/j.ecolmodel.2014.02.019.

Bridle, James. *New Dark Age: Technology, Knowledge and the End of the Future.* New York City: Verso, 2018.

Despret, Vinciane. "Politics of Territories." Paper presented at the Multispecies Storytelling in Intermedial Practices Conference, Linnæus University, Växjö, Sweden, January 23, 2019.

Giraud, Eva Haifa. *What Comes after Entanglement: Activism, Anthropocentrism, and an Ethics of Exclusion.* Durham: Duke University Press, 2019.

Grusin, Richard A., ed. *The Nonhuman Turn.* Minneapolis: University of Minnesota Press, 2015.

Haraway, Donna Jeanne. *Staying with the Trouble: Making Kin in the Chthulucene.* Durham: Duke University Press, 2016.

———. *When Species Meet.* Minneapolis: University of Minnesota Press, 2008.

Kakaç, Sadik, Hafit Yüncü, and K. Hijikata, eds. *Cooling of Electronic Systems.* Dordrecht: Springer, 1994.

Latour, Bruno. "Why Has Critique Run out of Steam? From Matters of Fact to Matters of Concern." *Critical Inquiry* 30, no. 2 (Winter 2004): 225–248. DOI: 10.1086/421123.

Lowenhaupt Tsing, Anna. *The Mushroom at the End of the World: On the Possibility of Life in Capitalist Ruins.* Princeton: Princeton University Press, 2015.

Lindenmayer, David B., and Gene E. Likens. "Direct Measurement versus Surrogate Indicator Species for Evaluating Environmental Change and Biodiversity Loss." *Ecosystems* 14 (January 2011): 47–59. https://www.jstor.org/stable/41505949.

Macarthur, Robert A., and Lawrence C.H. Wang. "Physiology of Thermoregulation in the Pika, 'Ochotona Princeps.'" *Canadian Journal of Zoology* 51, no. 1 (1973): 11–16. DOI: 10.1139/z73–002.

Maguire, Patricia. "Feminist Participatory Action Research." In *Just Methods: An Interdisciplinary Feminist Reader,* edited by Alison Jaggar, 417–32. 2nd edn. Boulder: Paradigm Publishers, 2014.

McLinden, Mark O., J. Steven Brown, Riccardo Brignoli, Andrei F. Kazakov, and Piotr A. Domanski. "Limited Options for Low-global-warming-potential Refrigerants." *Nature Communications* 8 (February 2017). DOI: 10.1038/ncomms14476.

Mott, Carrie, and Daniel Cockayne. "Citation Matters: Mobilizing the Politics of Citation Toward a Practice of 'Conscientious Engagement.'" *Gender, Place & Culture: A Journal of Feminist Geography* 24, no. 7 (2017): 954–73. DOI: 10.1080/0966369X.2017.1339022.

Moyer-Horner, Lukas, Paul D. Mathewson, Davin M. Jones, Michael R. Kearney, and Warren P. Porter. "Modeling Behavioral Thermoregulation in a Climate Change Sentinel," *Ecology and Evolution* 5, no. 24 (December 2015): 5810–22. DOI: 10.1002/ece3.1848.

"Orangutans." *National Geographic,* n.d. https://www.nationalgeographic.com/animals/mammals/group/orangutans/.

Pierre-Louis, Kendra. "The World Wants Air-conditioning: That Could Warm the World." *The New York Times,* May 15, 2018. https://www.nytimes.com/2018/05/15/climate/air-conditioning.html.

Rich, Adrienne. *What Is Found There: Notebooks on Poetry and Politics.* New York City: W.W. Norton & Company, 2003.

Schwalm, Donelle, Clinton W. Epps, Thomas J. Rodhouse, William B. Monahan, Jessica A. Castillo, Chris Ray, and Mackenzie R. Jeffress. "Habitat Availability and Gene Flow Influence Diverging Local Population Trajectories under Scenarios of Climate Change: A Place-based Approach." *Global Change Biology* 22, no. 4 (April 2016): 1572–84. DOI: 10.1111/gcb.13189.

Shotwell, Alexis. *Against Purity: Living Ethically in Compromised Times.* Minneapolis: University of Minnesota Press, 2016.

Siddig, Ahmed A.H., Aaron M. Ellison, Alison Ochs, Claudia Villar-Leeman, and Matthew K. Lau. "How Do Ecologists Select and Use Indicator Species to Monitor Ecological Change? Insights from 14 Years of Publication in 'Ecological Indicators.'" *Ecological Indicators* 60 (January 2016): 223–30. DOI: 10.1016/j.ecolind.2015.06.036.

Smith, Andrew T. "The Distribution and Dispersal of Pikas: Influences of Behavior and Climate." *Ecology* 55, no. 6 (November 1974): 1368–76. DOI: 10.2307/1935464.

"The Elephants of Africa: Tale of the Trunk," *PBS: Nature,* November 16, 1997. https://www.pbs.org/wnet/nature/elephants-africa-tale-trunk/11391/.

"The Future of Cooling." *International Energy Agency,* May 15, 2018.

"TundraCam." *Niwot Ridge LTER,* n.d. https://nwt.lternet.edu/tundracam.

Weltevrede, Esther, and Sabine Niederer. "Issue Animals Research." *Digital Methods Initiative Wiki,* April 2, 2008. https://www.digitalmethods.net/Dmi/IssueImageAnalysis.

Wilkening, Jennifer L., Chris Ray, and Johanna Varner. "Relating Sub-Surface Ice Features to Physiological Stress in a Climate Sensitive Mammal, the American Pika ('Ochotona Princeps')." *PLoS ONE* 10, no. 3 (March 24, 2015). DOI: 10.1371/journal.pone.0119327.

———. "When Can We Measure Stress Noninvasively? Postdeposition Effects on a Fecal Stress Metric Confound a Multiregional Assessment." *Ecology and Evolution* 6, no. 2 (January 2016): 502–13. DOI: 10.1002/ece3.1857.

Wylie, Alison. "A Plurality of Pluralisms: Collaborative Practice in Archaeology." In *Objectivity in Science: New Perspectives from Science and Technology Studies,* edited by Flavia Padovani, Alan Richardson, and Jonathan Y. Tsou, 189–210. Cham: Springer International Publishing, 2015. DOI: 10.1007/978-3-319-14349-1_10.

The Blattarians

Adam Dickinson

We write our environment as our environment writes us. The carbon cycle has been hijacked. Buried sunlight pours back into the atmosphere in the form of carbon dioxide from burned fossil fuels. The nitrogen cycle, the water cycle, and many other planetary metabolic flows have been similarly disrupted. In the Anthropocene, these effects are magnified by the circulation of capital and its attendant concentrations and deprivations that reinforce other kinds of metabolic rifts, including those associated with income inequality or food insecurity. Indeed, the global metabolism of energy and capital is inextricably linked to the local metabolism of human and nonhuman bodies. We see this in the form of petrochemical pollution accumulating in our flesh (DDT, PCBS, and heavy metals) or in shifted gut microbial communities associated with industrialized food production and an increasingly ubiquitous Western diet high in sugar, salt, and fat. Similarly, it is fair to say that the spread of the novel coronavirus via transnational travel and shipping corridors is as much a product of global metabolism as it is a product of human metabolic susceptibility.

What I call "metabolic poetics" is a research-creation practice concerned with the potential of expanded modes of reading and writing to shift the frames and scales of conventional forms of signification in order to bring into focus the often inscrutable biological and cultural writing intrinsic to the Anthropocene and its interconnected global and local metabolic processes. I see metabolic poetics at work in Jen Bervin's *Silk Poems,* which is a nanoscale poetic work on a silk biosensor designed to be implanted as a metabolic monitoring device into a human body.[1] I also see it in a number of works published and produced by Dea Antonsen and Ida Bencke as part of the Laboratory for Aesthetics and Ecology. In particular, Morten Søndergaard's *Sugar Poems,* which is an edible book that looks at the metabolic effects of sugar, Amanda Ackerman's *Air Kissing,* which examines the history of perfume and the biology of scent, and Karin Bolender's *R.A.W. Assmilk Soap,* which explores the poetics of soap making and how human historical myths and memories are part of landscapes "inextricably intertwined with the fleeting, unwritten, embodied blood vessels and mammary glands of many species."[2] Recent examples of my own explorations in metabolic poetics include *The Polymers,*

---

1   Jen Bervin, *Silk Poems* (New York City: Nightboat Books, 2017).

2   Karin Bolender, *R.A.W. Assmilk Soap* (Berlin: Broken Dimanche Press/Laboratory for Aesthetics and Ecology, 2016), 16. See also Morten Søndergaard, *Sugar Poems* (Berlin: Broken Dimanche Press/Laboratory for Aesthetics and Ecology, 2017), and Amanda Ackerman, *Air Kissing* (Berlin: Broken Dimanche Press/ Laboratory for Aesthetics and Ecology, 2016).

which combines the discourses, theories, and experimental methods of the science of plastic materials with the language and culture of plastic behaviour, and *Anatomic,* which incorporates and responds to the results of chemical and microbial testing on my blood, urine, feces, and skin.[3]

More recently, I have been exploring the metabolic poetics of heat. How does heat, for example, or the thermoregulatory process of humans and nonhumans constitute forms of writing? In a warming world, how might heat be invited into renovated poetic forms and compositional methods? I have pursued some of these questions through a series of recent experiments. In one case, with the assistance of the Environmental Ergonomics Laboratory at Brock University, I undertook several heat-stress trials, raising my internal body temperature by around 1.5 Celcius through active heating (cycling in controlled conditions) and passive heating (wearing a specialized hot-water-piped garment). At various intervals, during all these trials, I wrote, took cognitive tests, and measured my core temperature, skin temperature, blood pressure, carbon-dioxide uptake, and brain blood flow, among other data. Using this data, I wrote poems inspired and informed by the signifying framework of temperature extremes. The heat stress trials were taxing, especially the passive heating, which required me to sit still for many hours as my body's ability to cool itself was slowly overwhelmed. I experienced prolonged exposure to the critical wet-bulb temperature of 35 Celcius, the point at which the human body can no longer cool itself by sweating. This is a weather phenomenon that climate change is expected to make more frequent and widespread. In 2015, the Iranian city of Bandar Mahshahr reached 46 Celcius with a humidity of 50 percent, which combined to create a wet-bulb temperature of 34.6 Celcius. Even healthy people sitting in the shade will die within six hours in these conditions. I felt extreme anxiety during the heat stress trials. It was difficult to concentrate on writing. I wanted to strip off the wires and tubing. My heart was racing. I couldn't wait for the trials to end.

In another experiment, I turned to cockroaches. Cockroaches are hearty creatures and their distribution around the planet has occurred in conjunction with colonial conquests and the spread of multinational capitalism.[4] Common cockroach species first came to North America on slave ships.[5] Wherever people have travelled or exchanged large quantities of goods, it is safe to assume cockroaches have accompanied them. Consequently, they are part of the global metabolism of trade. They are also adaptive and likely to survive extreme climate change; they do well in hot and humid environments and are famously more resistant to radiation than humans. What lessons do their thermoregulatory processes offer us for thinking responses to heat? In my experiment, I measured the change in biomass with two different groups of cockroaches (*Blaptica dubia*) living for five weeks on top of the first two pages of Kafka's *The Metamorphosis,* a story about a man who turns into an insect commonly assumed to be a cockroach. I had a control group at 30 Celcius along with another group at 32 Celcius. This was, in part, an experiment

---

3   Adam Dickinson, *Anatomic* (Toronto: Coach House Books, 2018), and *The Polymers* (Toronto: House of Anansi Press, 2013).

4   W.H. Robinson, *Urban Entomology: Insect and Mite Pests in the Human Environment* (London: Chapman and Hall, 1996), 134.

5   Richard Schweid, *The Cockroach Papers: A Compendium of History and Lore* (New York: Four Walls Eight Windows, 1999), 11.

responding to climate change and the 2-degree escalation in global temperature that is expected, at least, in the next few years. The small experiment produced inconclusive results in terms of biomass change — they all produced many offspring regardless of the temperature — but all groups defiled the text: they ate parts of it, and they defecated on large swaths of it. In fact, those at the most elevated temperatures appeared to defile it the most. What literary potential lurks in their capacity to digest and otherwise live with literary texts in a hotter world?

Heat is often associated with transformation and metamorphosis, whether through the engine of metabolic action and stress or through the cascade of chemical changes involved with cooking. Kafka's text is a kind of apocalyptic narrative of metabolic proportions: man turns into bug, man fails to provide for family in the expected way, and, as a result the metabolic mechanisms of exploitive employment begin to be exposed. Moreover, the text invites us to consider the "bad dream," the feverish vision of transformation. The entire novella is bookended by dreams: the "uneasy dreams" from which Gregor awakens at the beginning, to the concluding sentence and its "confirmation" of the "new dreams and excellent intentions" which await the bright future of Grete, now that the nightmare of her brother's life is behind the family. Global warming is a future of bad dreams, a future of addled, feverish thinking as vulnerable populations begin to experience tension and pressure. Conspiracy theories thrive in such pressurized moments. In *Suspicious Minds: Why We Believe Conspiracy Theories*, Rob Brotherton points out that "[a]mbivalence threatens our sense of order, so, to compensate, we can seek order elsewhere."[6] We can only expect conspiracy theories to grow more prevalent as climate change increases.

The cockroach has deep roots in the metabolism of culture: at once a trickster figure in Caribbean folklore, a poet imagined in the Archy poems by Don Marquis, and a "roach" in the clips and butt-ends of marijuana culture, to name but a few of the cockroach's many influences.[7] Moreover, Kafka's story purportedly influenced Gabriel García Márquez in his early innovations with magic realism. Just as the cockroaches living on Kafka's text in the laboratory digested a story of conflicting dreams, how can we cook the fever dreams of conspiracy theories to imagine something else, some other possibility? Cockroach feces have an attractant in them that draws other roaches to the scene.[8] The drawing together of particles — increasing pressure — is expressed as heat. What can be drawn together from the stained feces on Kafka's text? How can the cockroach make our dreams grow wings, flightless as they may be?

The first poem below is made by drawing together legible words and letters unobscured by excrement from the first two pages of Kafka's *The Metamorphosis*, which I used to line the base of each cockroach enclosure. (I chose the widely available version of the story translated into English by Will and Edwin Muir in 1961.)[9] The second poem is made by bringing together barely legible words and

6   Rob Brotherton, *Suspicious Minds: Why We Believe Conspiracy Theories* (London: Bloomsbury, 2015), 13.

7   Schweid, *The Cockroach Papers*, 120, 101.

8   Robinson, *Urban Entomology*, 137.

9   Franz Kafka, *The Metamorphosis*, trans. Willa and Edwin Muir, in *Franz Kafka: The Complete Stories*, ed. Nahum N. Glatzer (New York: Schocken Books, 1971), 89–139.

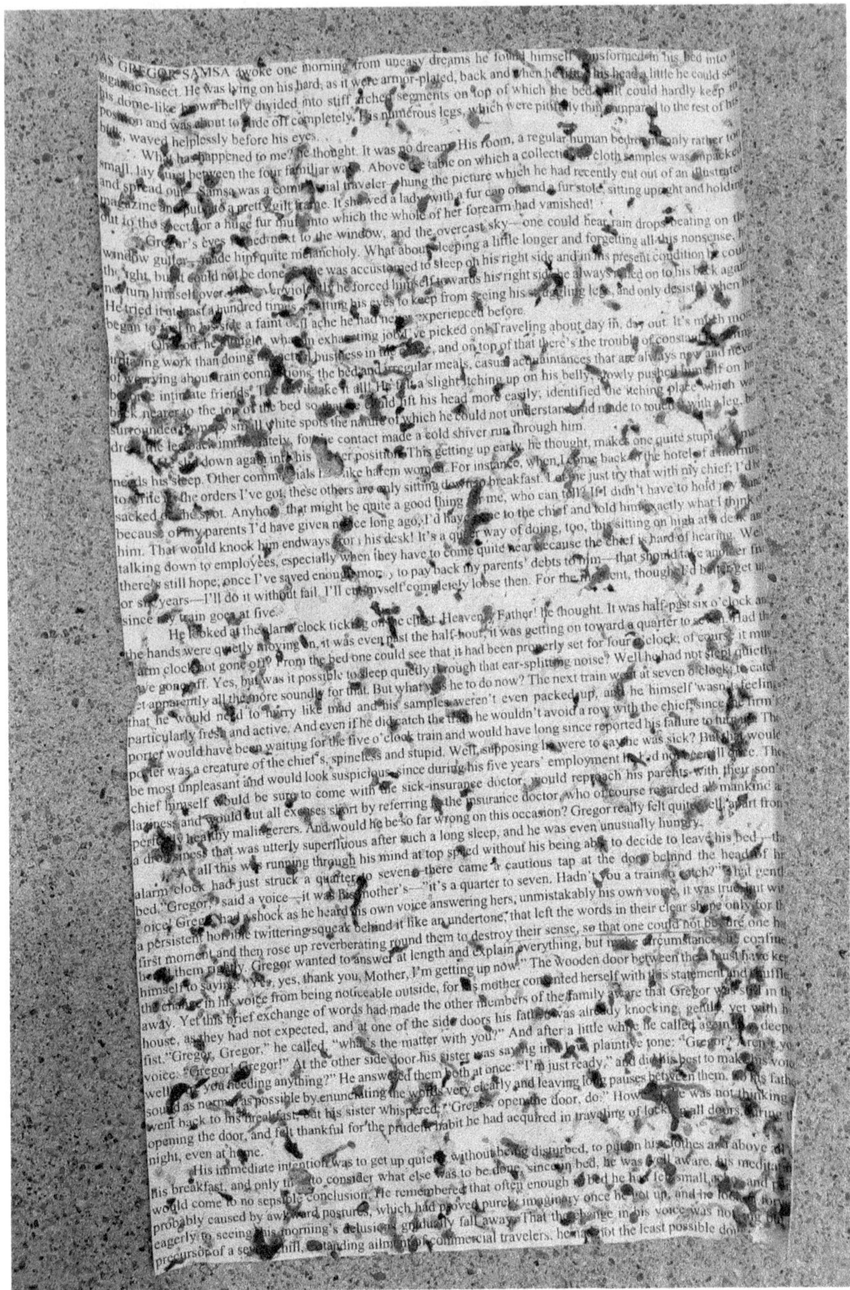

Fig. 13.1. A section of Franz Kafka's *The Metamorphosis* after 5 weeks of exposure to cockroaches. Photograph by the author.

letters that were largely obscured by excrement. The final poem is a fever dream that takes its title, "Instar," from the term used to describe the developmental stage between each molt in which a cockroach sheds its exoskeleton and grows another of altered proportions.

Awakened

            As grass
            as smoke
            one morning
            dome-like
            divided by
            a bed

            numerous legs
            waved a regular
            human
            recently cut
            out of a
            forearm

            raindrops beat
            a little longer
            forgetting
            this accused sleep
            thought
            didn't hold

sacked spot
cut clock
possible ear
packed up
a row
of waiting spines

far wrong
after a long
sleep
a cautious tap
at the head
of a voice train

the matter
called
the other side
thankful
for habit
to get up quietly

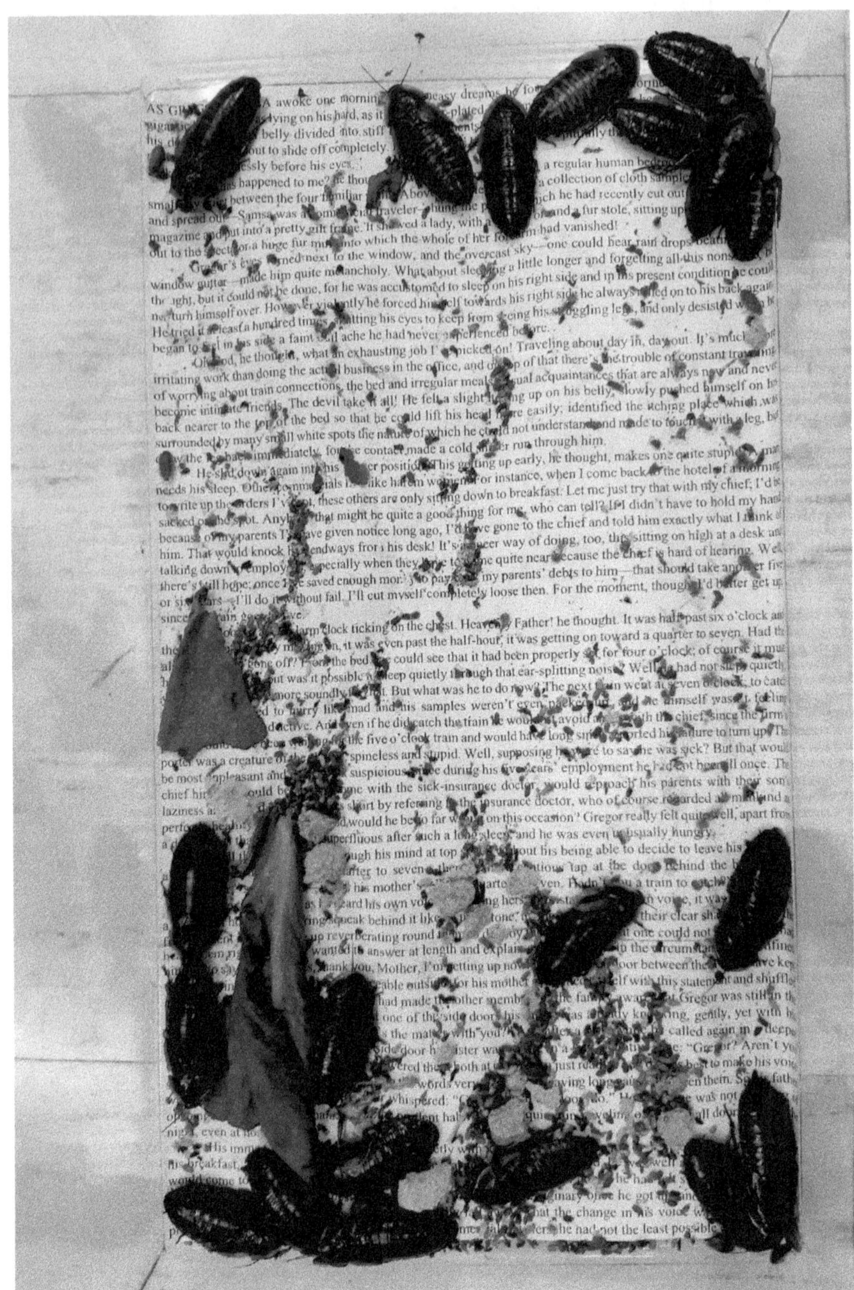

Fig. 13.2. Experiment in progress. Each roach bin lined with Kafka's story, 20 female roaches added to each bin and provided approximately 4 g of rat chow and half a leaf of romaine lettuce (supplemented weekly). Photographed at regular intervals. 2 bins set at 30°C and 2 bins at 32°C. Biomass was approximately 50 g per bin at the outset. Photograph by the author.

Asleep

Bulk dream
bedroom traveler
illustrated
drops
beating
the irregular top

of sleep
cut loose
thought
any train
the alarm ticking
on the bed

        sleep
        splitting
        soundly was
        made fresh
        turned drowsy
        running

        speed door
        contented
        deeper
        in an answer
        whispered
        precursor

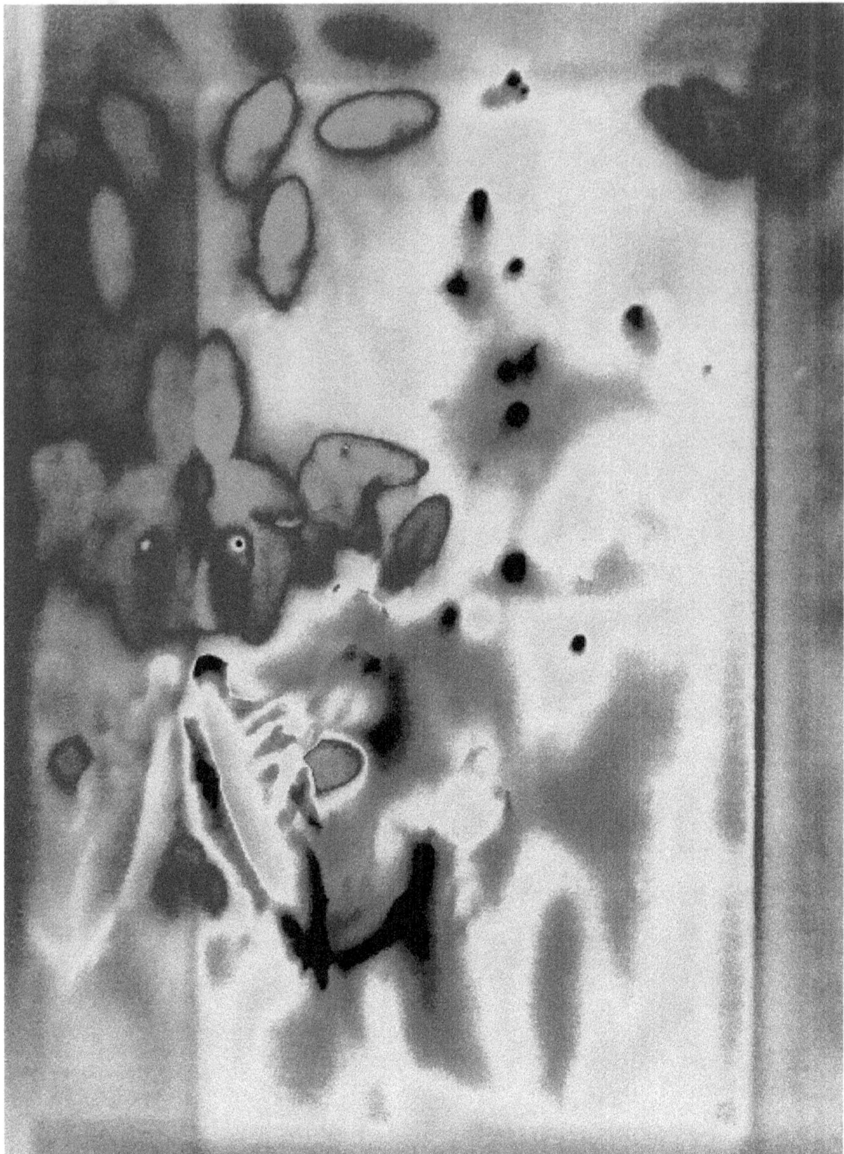

Fig. 13.3. Thermal camera image of the cockroaches during the experiment. Experimental and photographic assistance provided by Dr. Glenn Tattersall. Photograph by Wynne Reichheld at the Tattersall Lab at Brock University.

Instar

How easily
we consider
what is already
in our mouths
to be food
the birds
are in on it
the government
is feeding
them dirt
on the latest
guano albedo
I feel
like a radio
licking static
from the microwave
while a bug
crawls
into my ear
and my attention
span is lit
linoleum
laying waste
to the leapt thought
moving in a single
nerve through
wall voids
black pepper
and horned coffee
how many horses
does it take
to make
enough glue
to keep your mouth
shut
live births
thread the dampness
they dump
the dark rank
of demoted generals
for every winged
adult
the earth is as flat
as a soft drink's
croup cure
they show us
the stool strength

of the interior
shed
we feel its acids
and police
learn
to defecate
in unassigned
cramps
my memory
touches me
in the atlas
of my moult
giving off
its own heat
flameless
we are carriers
for our genres
I take my heartrate
at its word

References

Ackerman, Amanda. *Air Kissing.* Berlin: Broken Dimanche Press/Laboratory for Aesthetics and Ecology, 2016.

Bervin, Jen. *Silk Poems.* New York: Nightboat Books, 2017.

Bolender, Karin. *R.A.W. Assmilk Soap.* Berlin: Broken Dimanche Press/Laboratory for Aesthetics and Ecology, 2016.

Brotherton, Rob. *Suspicious Minds: Why We Believe Conspiracy Theories.* London: Bloomsbury, 2015.

Dickinson, Adam. *Anatomic.* Toronto: Coach House Books, 2018.

Dickinson, Adam. *The Polymers.* Toronto: House of Anansi Press, 2013.

Kafka, Franz. *The Metamorphosis.* Translated by Willa and Edwin Muir. In *Franz Kafka: The Complete Stories,* edited by Nahum N. Glatzer, 89–139. New York: Schocken Books, 1971.

Robinson, W.H. *Urban Entomology: Insect and Mite Pests in the Hunan Environment.* London: Chapman and Hall, 1996.

Schweid, Richard. *The Cockroach Papers: A Compendium of History and Lore.* New York: Four Walls Eight Windows, 1999.

Søndergaard, Morten. *Sugar Poems.* Berlin: Broken Dimanche Press/Laboratory for Aesthetics and Ecology, 2017.

CHAPTER 14

WERT: Interspecies Weaving and Becoming

Carol Padberg

To weave is to breathe. In and out. Up and down. Over and under. Over and over. The loom holds the warp in tension, while the weft slowly accumulates through the back-and-forth movement of the shuttle. A balance emerges between the fixed structure of the warp's length and the fluid energy of the weft's width. The rhythmic clattering sounds of a floor loom make soothing repetitions. Weaving such as this gradually allows two dimensions to become three, then four. The weaving begins as a length and width binary, but place any weaving on human skin and the cloth drapes into a volumetric form of clothing. Add mycelia to the warp and weft, and you have another dimension of exchange and expansion: the topological space of consideration that we make and inhabit. Weaving provides a space in which our multispecies collective—humans, mycelia, and more—can consider sprawling topics while employing concise, repetitive motions. We consider the temporal history of weaving as mythical worldmaking, and a vast open space appears over the loom beam's horizon.

Our crafting is rooted in Nook Farm House, our living studio home and small backyard in inner-city Hartford, Connecticut, a mid-sized city in a small state on the Northeast coast of what is now called the United States. Here, we produce weavings designed and implemented by *Pleurotus ostreatus* mycelia and *Homo sapiens* hands (see Fig. 1). Our wearable sculptures have an ongoing life cycle and are grounded in a system of backyard regeneration and care. Our ecological weaving practice is four years old and it includes sheep; pollinator honeybees; dye plants from our garden; and the chickens, insects, worms, and protozoa that maintain our soil's vitality. Our creative group has representatives from each major family of Eukaryota organisms: animals, fungi, plants and protists. With the exception of our six Leicester Longwool sheep, who live a rural life, we move together through urban life as a communal indoor and outdoor household. This land is dense with community and trauma. It is, and always will be, unceded Algonquin territory and was one of the first places of American settler colonial violence. In the nineteenth century, this place became a part of a community called Nook Farm, an abolitionist literary colony founded by Harriet Beecher Stowe and Samuel Clemens, also known as Mark Twain. Currently, it is part of the Asylum Hill neighborhood of Hartford, Connecticut. Amid corporate parking lots, our gritty lot includes a modest Victorian house and a small de-paved yard right next to the freeway. This is where we live, spin, weave, and die, as part of the circulation of Earth's nutrients.

The process of making our weavings includes the sheep growing the wool, the humans shearing the sheep and then spinning and dyeing wool. It includes plants

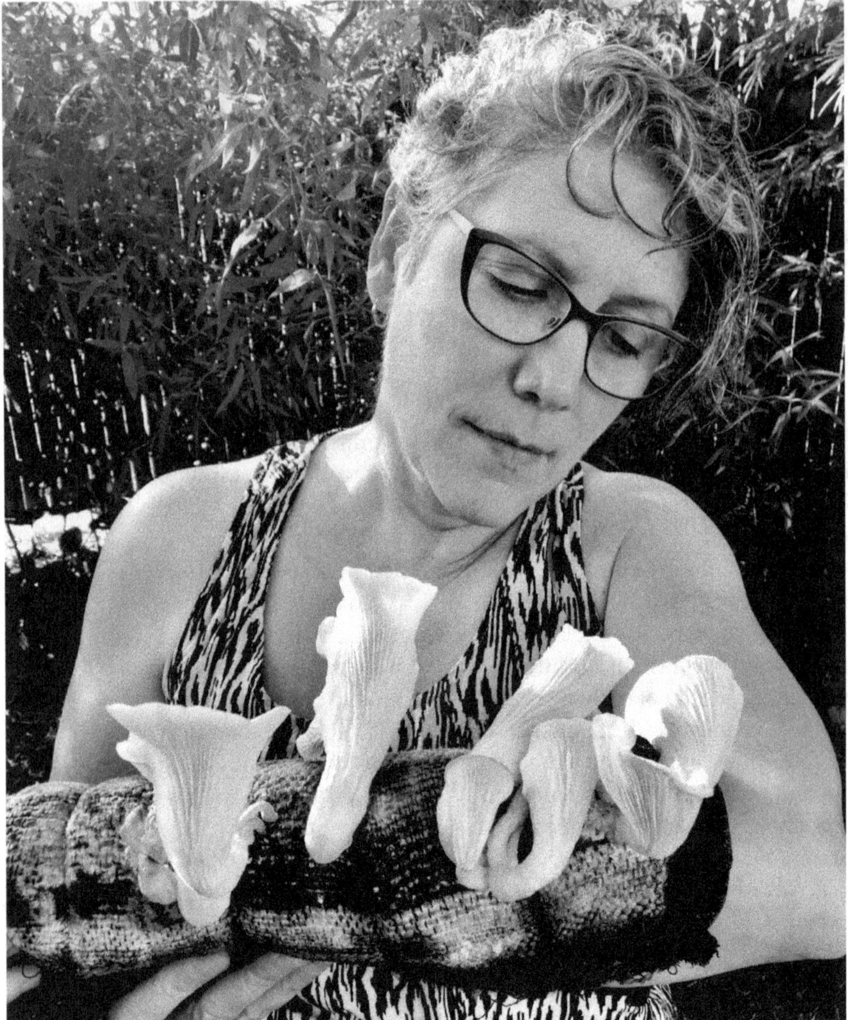

Fig. 14.1. The author wearing a mycelial woven sculpture, in her backyard, July 2019.
Photograph by the author

reaching their roots to find water and human hands harvesting plant dyes from the garden. All of this world weaving then enables the loom weavings of simple cloth, which is sewn into wearable sculptures. When we make the wearable sculptures, the humans integrate the fabric with mycelial substrate and keep the sculptures moist, until the mycelia spin their own woven forms of life amidst the woolen fibers, creating an inner web.

Once fruiting, the sculptures are used for workshops which allow humans to get to know the many roles fungi play, within our bodies and within the Earth's metabolism. At the point that the weavings have become depleted and digested, we leave them atop the soil in our dye and herb gardens, to continue their life cycle underground, contributing back to the plants' own weaving of roots.

Our loom, the space of action between A-threads and B-threads, is located in a garden shed that works as a tiny studio, looking out onto the contained living

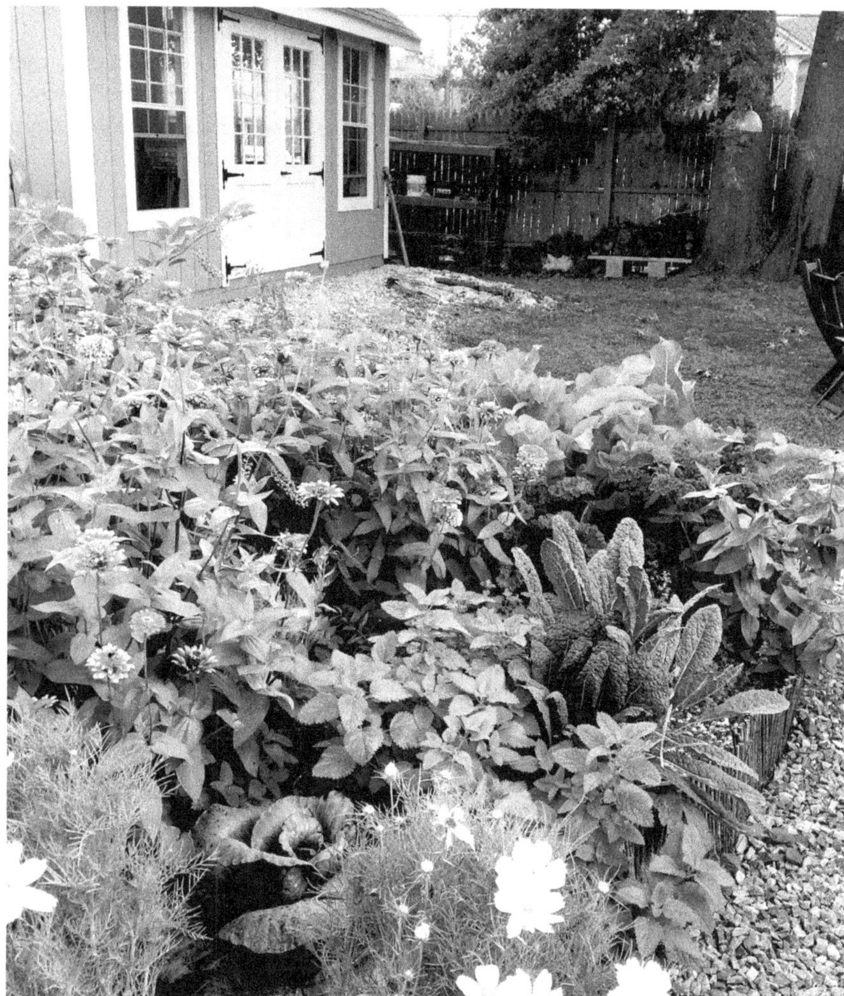

Fig. 14.2. The backyard studio of Nook farm House in Hartford, Connecticut, June 2018. Photograph by the author

tapestry of mycelia, plants, bees, chickens and soil critters that inhabit our patch of Earth. This is a tightly designed space, with edged borders set up to maximize life force in a small place (see Fig. 2).

Weaving is about edges, boundaries, and growth. The edges matter. The side edge of a conventional weaving is called a selvedge. In traditional weaving this should be as straight as possible. In contrast, our working group makes weavings that are full of dissolving, unpredictable edges. The resulting mycelial forms eventually digest the edges and shapeshift altogether. They create thresholds into new awareness when worn. In these forms, boundaries and categories become questions, questions of self-edge, selvedge no more. The fuzzy mycelial webbings of rhizomatic forms confuse the grid of warp and weft, as mycelia pulse in all directions. Undoing uniformity and predictability with mycelial digestions reminds our human artist to release the colonial conditioning of perfectionism and control, as she focuses instead on emergent and collaborative currents.

For mycelial weavers such as oyster mushrooms, to weave is to eat. The mycelial body spreads its hyphal threads in multiple directions. Then, releasing enzymes, the hypha breaks down the host (in this instance, wool saturated with grain substrate), and absorbs its nutrients to grow the webby worlds that produce mushrooms. In our workshops, humans have the opportunity to wear the living mycelial cloth, even feel the hyper fast growth of the fruiting bodies through their mammal skin. If the humans pay attention, they may feel an energy exchange as a subtle current.

This ultrathin, interspecies frequency can be experienced and understood as a shimmering. Deborah Bird Rose brought this term into multispecies writings in 2017, writing "shimmer is an Aboriginal aesthetic that helps call us into these multispecies worlds."[1] Shimmer, or Bir'yun in Yolngu, is an embodied tip to toes experience:

> *Bir'yin*, or shimmer, or brilliance, is — people say — one's actual capacity to see and experience ancestral power. This is to say that when one is captured by shimmer, one experiences not only the joy of the visual capture, but also, and more elegantly as one becomes more knowledgeable, ancestral power as it moves actively across the world.[2]

Weaving is ontological and narrative, as well as biological. For millennia, human ancestors have understood weaving to be an essential part of cosmological storytelling. In North America, weaving is foundational to the creation stories of many Indigenous cultures. In Hopi culture the figure of *Kokyangwuti*, a spider grandmother, gives birth to the world. In the Diné worldview, *Na'ashjé'íí Asdzáá*, spider woman, is a powerful world-maker and world-protector.

And in the Dakota story of the Woman in the Cave the regenerative power of the world is explained through the image of the old woman who is weaving a most beautiful garment. When she goes to tend the fire, the black dog comes to unravel the weaving. She pauses, finds the loose thread, and becomes inspired to weave an even more beautiful garment. This cycle of creation and destruction continues in the dynamic interplay of deep time.

In European Pagan creation stories, images abound of goddesses who spin worlds into being, weave the future and knot fate. As Max Dashú writes, the importance of textile processes in European pagan creation stories is well established. "Women's craft of spinning, weaving, plaiting, wickerwork and knotting reflected a central sacrament of tribal European religion. It was the image of the Fates' transformative power, under whatever names they were known."[3] Dashú shows how the ancestral pagans of Europe considered words for spinning to be verbs for becoming and that those words carried stories of magical transformations. Specifically,

1   Deborah Bird Rose, "Shimmer: When All You Love is Being Trashed," in *Arts of Living on a Damaged Planet: Monsters and Ghosts of the Anthropocene*, eds. Anna Lowenhaupt Tsing, Heather Swanson, Elaine Gan, and Nils Bubandt (Minneapolis: University of Minnesota Press, 2017), G53.

2   Ibid., G53–G54.

3   Max Dashú, *Witches and Pagans: Women in European Folk Religion, 700–1100* (Richmond: Veleda Press, 2016), 47.

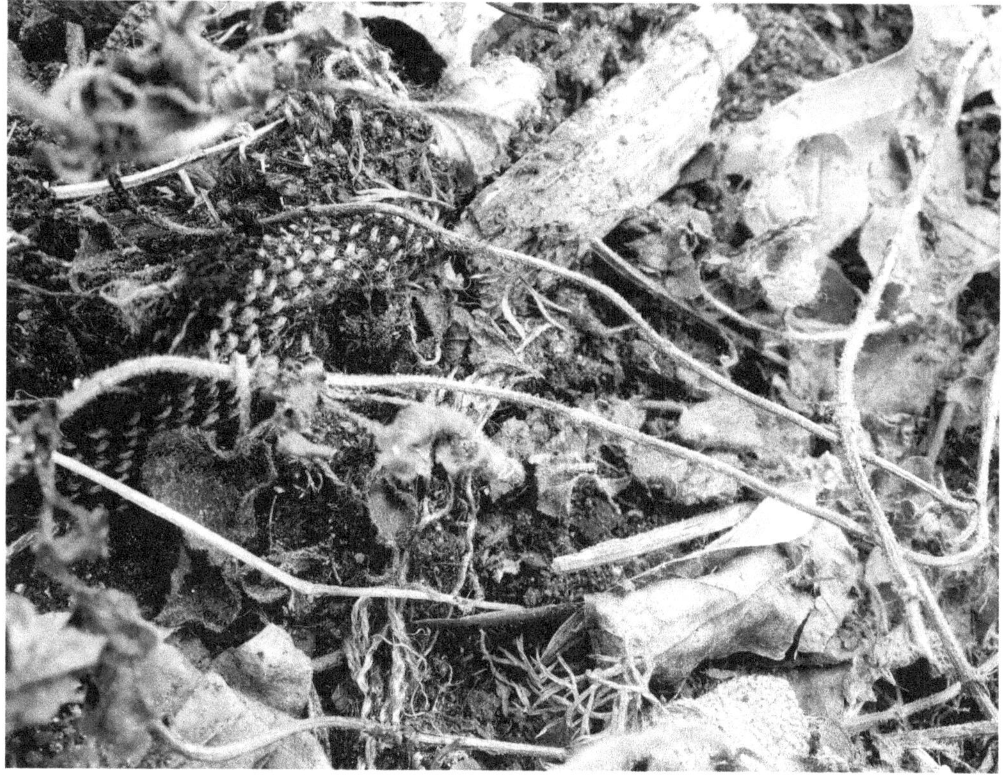

Fig. 14.3. Decomposing mycelial sculpture in dye garden at Nook Farm House, March 2020. Photograph by the author

Dashú explains, "from the Proto-Indo-European root Wert arose verbs of turning, being, and becoming."[4]

Aidan Wachtner writes about the mythic figure of Verthandi, whose name shares the Wert/Vert root. In tribal Northern Europe, before Roman colonization, Verthandi was widely recognized as the weaver of the emerging present moment. She would weave alongside two other mythical weavers: Urda, the weaver of the past and Skuld, the weaver of the future. Wachner writes, "My preferred story is that the Weavers weave in all directions at once and that time and our lives within the weaving are multi-dimensional ripples in a vast sea of possibilities."[5]

Our twenty-first-century, myco-ecological weavings are in conversation with these old ways. While Oyster Mushrooms weave through digesting and dissolving, humans weave through accumulation and addition and this creates a luscious tension. The two types of weaving exist in our creative works as an interspecies reciprocity. Our textiles' fuzzy lateral structures function as relational webs of symbiosis. Here the line between life and death grows blurry. Whether understood through the body of a mycelium or human, we are constantly living-dying. The mycelial woven forms we create are composed to compost (see Fig. 3). These weavings on the garden floor bring bits of human and mycelia DNA with them from the

---

4   Ibid., 27.
5   Aidan Wachter, *Weaving Fate: Changing the Past & Telling True Lies* (n.p., Red Temple Press, 2020), 32.

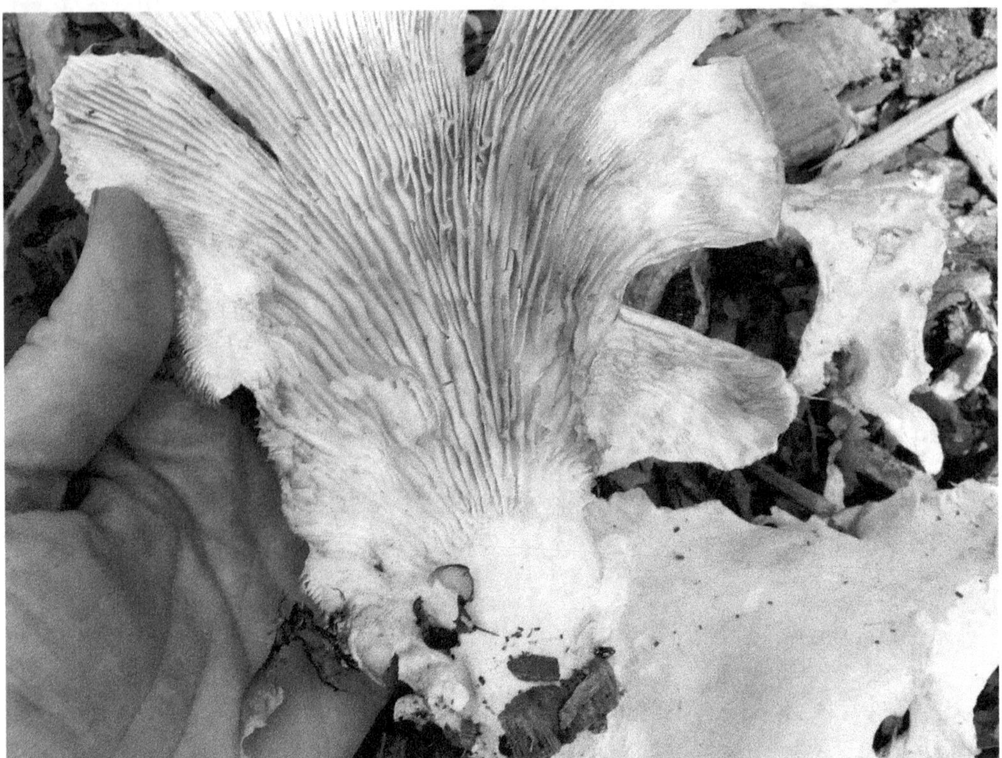

Fig. 14.4. An Oyster mushroom cluster that appeared in a separate area of the yard, across from the dye garden. Nook Farm House, summer 2021. Photograph by the author

workshop participants into the soil community to biodegrade. There in the soil, over the seasons, the weavings rot, keeping the roots of the dye plants moist and nourished. Once these mycelially digested nutrients are released into the garden soil, the cycle begins again as the dye plants use those nutrients to make color for future woven mycelial textiles.

This art is as deeply rhizomatic as it is regenerative. Using nonlinear functions such as whole-lifecycle design, emergent theory for social change, and preindustrial agricultural practices, we have established a sprawling creative process with ever multiplying nodes that include herbalism, beekeeping, and social activities such as selling goods at our local farmer's market, and a community-activated free food pantry in our front yard. Mycelial organisms are webby root structures, thus the conceptual frame of the rhizome suits us. In their 1987 text, *A Thousand Plateaus,* Gilles Deleuze and Félix Guattari lay out the philosophical concept of the rhizome.

Deleuze and Guattari proposed the rhizome as a generative metaphor for an encompassing nonlinear way of knowing and doing.[6] They described the rhizome's inherent multiplicity, an attribute we appreciate as a diverse working group dedicated to recursive interspecies understanding. The rhizome's focus is on non-

6   Gilles Deleuze and Félix Guattari, *A Thousand Plateaus: Capitalism and Schizophrenia,* trans. Brian Massumi (Minneapolis: University of Minnesota Press, 1987), 7–8.

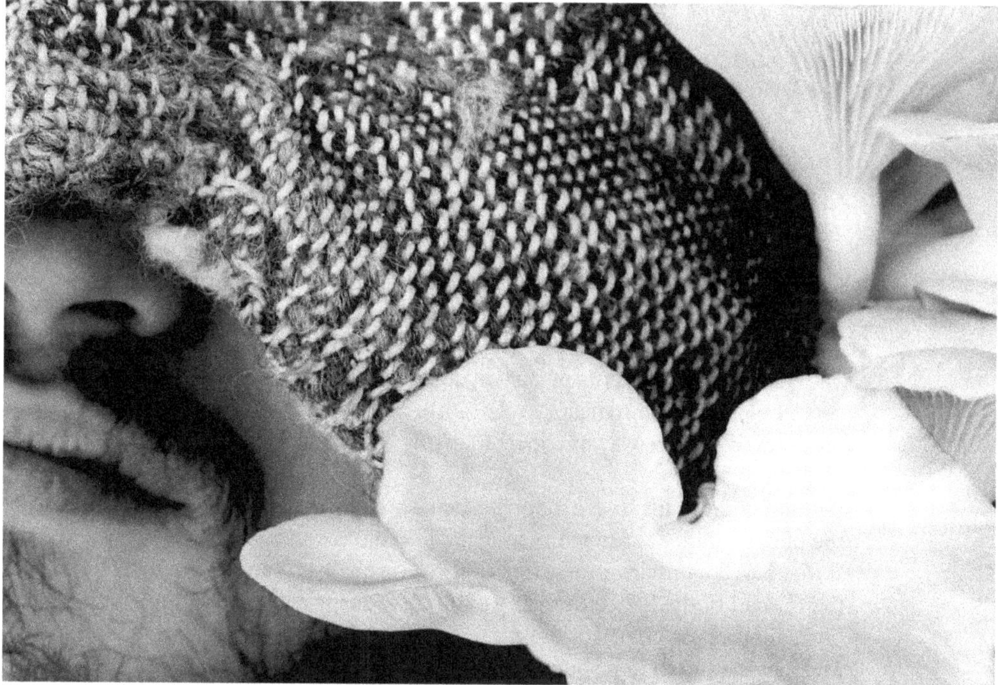

Fig. 14.5. Participant wearing a myceliated headset, spring 2021. Photograph by the author

hierarchical connectivity. This connectivity includes endless links between boundless assemblages, which provides a fertile metaphor for our woven nonlinearities and dispersed yet potent creativity (see Fig. 4).

Although we can function easily within a theoretical paradigm, we are first and foremost a pragmatic enterprise. We are quietly participating in a slow, ecological revolution in our city. Our efforts are becoming visible, not unlike the underground mycelial run of *Pleurotus ostreatus* that are now fruiting mushrooms in unexpected parts of our backyard. Our practice can be entered and understood by interacting with any node in the rhizome. This latticework of endeavors include the wearable mycelial sculptures, the workshops using these sculptures, and all the backyard activity that supports and decomposes our symbiotic sculptures.

This web of beekeeping, herbal medicine making, dye color brewing, food growing, and sheep and chicken raising is sensually rich and yet somewhat unusual to those around us, and we find that the public is keen to relate with us. We are bringing back the old ways of growing materials for a household and a community. Our methodology has no beginning or end, and the edge between our art and lives is indeterminate.

Our workshops invite humans to close their eyes and consider the multispecies nature of the human body, by *thinking with* the skin's mycobiome as it establishes direct physical contact with our growing *Pleurotus ostreatus* fungi (see Fig. 5).

Our experimental headsets, masks, and sleeves are worn on faces and arms during these somatic workshops. With these wearable textiles we reach our human audience through their senses of touch and smell. We posit that if "one" can begin to understand the body as a multiplicity rather than an individual, "one" is better able to understand the symbiotic nature of life on our planet.

We ask humans to consider themselves more accurately — as holobionts rather than individuals. The fallacy of biological individuality is described by Scott F. Gilbert as follows:

> When you think of a cow, you probably envision an animal grazing, eating grass, and perhaps producing methane at her other end. However, cows cannot do this. Their bovine genome does not encode proteins with the enzymatic activity needed to digest cellulose. What the cow does is chew the grass and maintain a symbiotic community of microorganisms in her gut. It is this population of gut symbionts that digests the grass and makes the cow possible. The cow is an obvious example of what is called a holobiont, an organism plus its persistent communities of symbionts. The notion of the holobiont is important both within and beyond biology because it shows a radically new way of conceptualizing "individuals."[7]

By helping humans to sense fungal beings through their skin, we are cultivating the human ability to know the fungal communities that already live right on their skin, as well as micro-organisms that live in their gut and other mycobiomes in the human body. Rehabilitating these senses helps to increase human awareness of the interconnectivity of the myriad forms of life on planet Earth.[8] As Michael Meade has written in response to the climate catastrophes of our current era, "We don't see the world as it is, we see the world as we are. How we see the Earth must change before we can learn how to heal the Earth."[9] In other words, if we see the world through the eyes of a biological individual, this holds us back from being able to create the relational transformations that are needed.

It is important to point out that this expansion of sensing is at least a two-way street. Nook Farm's weavings establish multispecies reciprocal touch. Oyster mushrooms thrive through touch, reaching out in order to literally take in the world. So who is touching whom? Karen Barad, Donna Haraway, and Anna Tsing have used the spatial metaphor of entanglement to theorize interspecies relationality. In *Matters of Care, Speculative Ethics in More Than Human Worlds,* Maria Puig de la Bellacasa works with Barad's theory of intra-activity: "The reversibility of touch (to touch is to be touched) also inspires the troubling of such assumptions: Who/what is *object*? Who/what is *subject*? It is not only the experimenter/observer/human agent who sees, touches, knows, intervenes, and manipulates the universe: there is intra-touching."[10] Ours is a constant practice of such intimate

7   Scott F. Gilbert, "Holobiont by Birth: Multilineage Individuals as the Concretion of Cooperative Processes," in *Arts of Living on a Damaged Planet: Monsters and Ghosts of the Anthropocene,* eds. Anna Lowenhaupt Tsing, Heather Swanson, Elaine Gan, and Nils Bubandt (Minneapolis: University of Minnesota Press, 2017), M73.

8   I am indebted to the work of Maria Andreotti and the Gesturing Towards Decolonial Futures Group, for their framing of the concept of rehabilitating lost capacities. See https://decolonialfutures.net/

9   Michael Meade, "Climate Change and the Mythic Imagination," *Mosaic Voices,* August 26, 2021, https://www.mosaicvoices.org/climate-change-and-mythic-imagination.

10   Maria Puig de la Bellacasa, *Matters of Care: Speculative Ethics in More Than Human Worlds* (Minneapolis: University of Minnesota Press, 2017), 114.

intra-actions. As the human works the garden and feels the dirt, the dirt microbes work the skin and nibble a cellular snack. As the fungus colonizes woven wool structures with its hyphae, the antimicrobial agents within the wool keeps green mold at bay to allow healthy myceliation of the wool. As the slug eats the decomposing mushrooms of mycelial weavings left on the garden floor, the mushroom is spreading its spores via the slug's droppings. These actions ground an intellectual discussion of entanglement in the bodies of relating, living beings.

Our public interspecies engagements establish reciprocal mycelia-skin contact. In this way, our workshops help restore diminished human capacities for ecological connection, and help develop *Pleurotus ostreatus*'s direct knowledge of human bodies.

Our human workshop participants include mycophiliacs, mycophobes, and folks who approach mushrooms with neutral curiosity. Surveys from workshop attendees indicate that our cooperatively woven forms entice interactions that surprise and soothe:

> As someone who has an interest in nature and art, but no formal training in either, I welcomed the opportunity to have an interdisciplinary learning experience outside of a classroom where my lack of credentials did not feel like a barrier. This fungi workshop challenged me to think differently and deeper about how I view my relationship with the natural world. By inviting people to participate to the extent they are comfortable, they made the workshop more accessible than if everyone had been required to wear a mask covered in mushrooms, for instance. Being able to dip my toe in the water made it possible for me to have this thought-provoking and memorable experience.[11]

Humans who already love mushrooms seem prone to positively charged experiences, such as these comments indicate: "Personally, I had a profound experience with the eye mask wearable. I literally felt the organism pulsing on my eyelids. This developed into a realization to listen closely to what is around me that I cannot hear." And:

> For years I've foraged mushrooms. I've spent hours in the forest seeking choice edibles. Though I will taste mushrooms in the field, inhale the rich earthy odors of the fungi gathered in my basket, the truth is that I navigate the forest with a sort of laser focus and purpose. I've never really taken the time to commune with these remarkable fungi. I've never considered the possibility of becoming a part of their miraculous mycelial network. This work changed my relationship to mushrooms. The myco-encounter began with awe. I was presented with a series of delicate objects, stunning pink oyster mushrooms growing out of hand- woven garments. I carefully placed the mask on my face and slid one of the sleeves onto my arm for a slow sensory encounter. As I relaxed, the tactile and olfactory qualities of this intimate, physical contact, calmed me. In a state similar to yogic sleep, the mushrooms literally entered my body through my nose and nerve endings.

11   Carol Padberg, unpublished survey of workshop participants, September 2019.

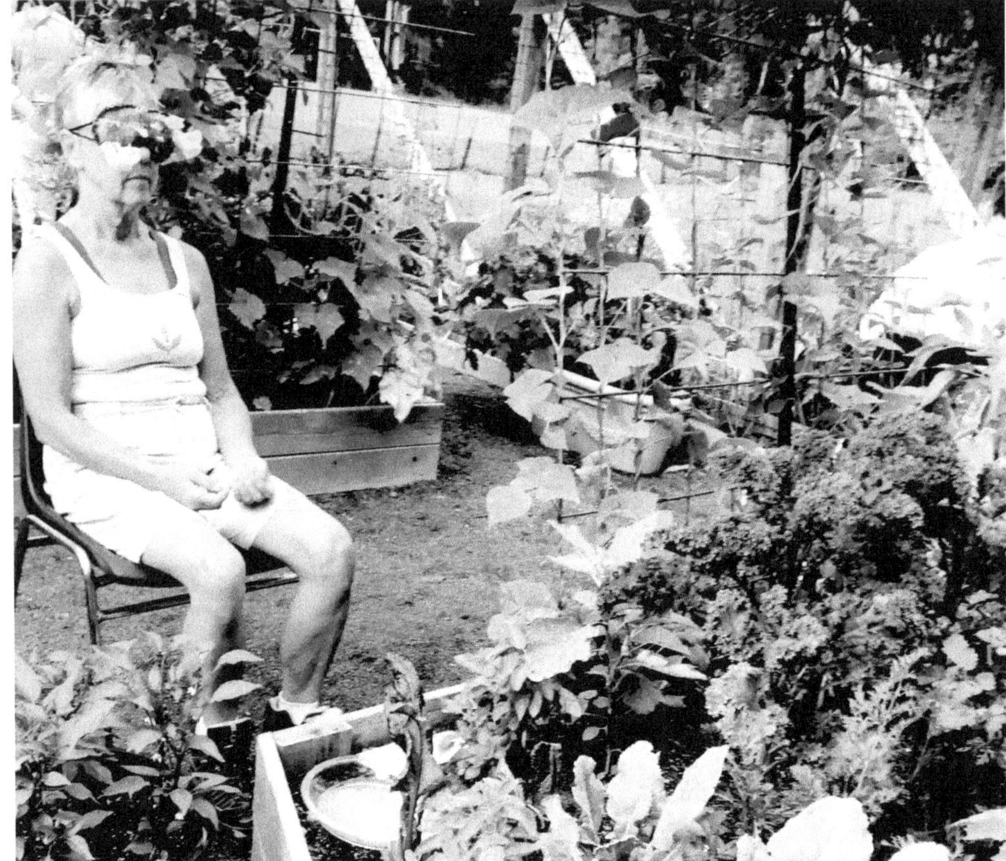

Fig. 14.6. Community garden workshop participant, summer 2019, New Paltz, New York.
Photograph by the author

> For a time the mycelial network was the same as my nervous system. The experience of sloughing off my sense of self was beautiful and humbling.[12]

Our human-fungal workshops are slow, silent, and self-guided. Brief text prompts ask human participants to quietly engage with our curious, fruiting headsets, mycelially pinning forearm sleeves, as well as whole-face masks (see Fig. 6). The prompts provide information about mushrooms, as well as the human microbiome and mycological skin landscapes. This somatic experience has unleashed curiosity and stimulated novel experiences for each fungal workshop participant. The workshops encourage Oyster Mushrooms use their tentacular senses to explore human skin, a rare experience. Rita Hayward has described using "fingeryeyes" as she uses her human senses to make sense of cup corals.[13] Borrowing Hayward's entangled synesthesia, our workshops ask fungal and human beings to use a kind of "see-ingtouch" to explore the vivid yet nuanced sensation of intimately encountering

---

12   Ibid.
13   Rita Hayward, "FINGERYEYES: Impressions of Cup Corals," *Cultural Anthropology* 25, no. 4 (2010): 580

bodies across species. As such, our workshops include a modality of interspecies care that exists outside of solutionist, theoretical, or scientific approaches. This is art with human eyes closed. This is art infused with intimate, reciprocal touch.

Our art raises neglected questions, refuses the status quo, and brings forth new knowledge regarding non-linear protocols. These nonlinear thinking modalities are well suited for interspecies research and raise useful questions about common research methodologies. Our non-linearity returns us to the realization that independent lines do not make a strong weave. We need to usher the thread through the warp to the left, and then back to the right many times to achieve the accumulation of a weaving. Only through an accumulation of multidirectional lines do we make a plane, a volume, and a meditative space of consideration.

We like to describe this as Lateral Research. Not governed by a central research question, it moves mycelially in multiple directions at once, like Medusa's hair of snakes. This methodology allows us to make several refusals as we define our interspecies practice. We have eschewed the dry and sterile space of the white cube art gallery, and have chosen soil instead. We deny the orthodoxy of mono-species authorship, just as we refuse the idea of biological individuality. In this way, we exercise symbiosis as an essential plurality of knowledges. Inspired by Lynn Margulis's work on cell symbiotics, and Suzanne Simard's writings about forest communications, we continue to weave, dissolve, digest, and interconnect our worlds. By working holistically, we hope to afford deeper multispecies capacities through empathy and touch. In fact, our human team member believes that through these weavings she is developing new neural pathways.

Perhaps this experiential capacity is actually an increase in interspecies neural plasticity. Maintaining a rhizomatic process of improvisational weaving keeps us probing, sensing, and wondering. Just as Pauline Oliveros's Deep Listening techniques expand perception until it is much larger than hearing, our more-than-rational research methodologies expand how we think beyond our brains. What powers of knowing might be unleashed as we continue to craft a wider set of interspecies research methodologies? How might weaving with *Pleurotus ostreatus* help humans disrupt and digest toxic individualism? And how might other interspecies co-craftings help humans extend additional abilities towards mutuality and symbiosis?

We believe that this moment on Earth requires us to think and make differently, to move beyond the disastrous human confines of separation and extreme individualism. Through forming our long-term interspecies weaving team, we have begun such an exploration. Our human-mycelial weaving is a place where we find the turning, being, and becoming of *Wert*. Through craft, these interspecies weavings create a site, a process, and a metaphor for developing nonlinear knowledges and rhizomatic systems of care.

References

Dashé, Max. *Witches and Pagans: Women in European Folk Religion, 700–1100.* Richmond: Velona Press, 2016.

Deleuze, Gilles, and Félix Guattari. *A Thousand Plateaus: Capitalism and Schizophrenia.* Translated by Brian Massumi. Minneapolis: University of Minnesota Press, 1987.

Gilbert, Scott. "Holobiont by Birth: Multilineage Individuals as the Concretion of Cooperative Processes." In *Arts of Living on a Damaged Planet: Monsters and Ghosts of the Anthropocene,* edited by Anna Lowernhaupt Tsing, Heather Swanson, Elaine Gan, and Nils Bubandt, M73–M89. Minneapolis: University of Minnesota Press, 2017.

Hayward, Eva. "FINGERYEYES: Impressions of Cup Corals." *Cultural Anthropology* 25, no. 4 (2010): 577–99. DOI: 10.1111/j.1548–1360.2010.01070.x/.

Meade, Michael. "Climate Change and the Mythic Imagination," *Mosaic Voices,* August 26, 2021. https://www.mosaicvoices.org/climate-change-and-mythic-imagination.

Puig de la Bellacasa, María. *Matters of Care: Speculative Ethics in More Than Human Worlds.* Minneapolis: University of Minnesota Press, 2017.

Rose, Deborah Bird. "Shimmer: When All You Love is Being Trashed." In *Arts of Living on a Damaged Planet: Monsters and Ghosts of the Anthropocene,* edited by Anna Lowenhaupt Tsing, Heather Swanson, Elaine Gan, and Nils Bubandt, G51–G63. Minneapolis: University of Minnesota Press, 2017.

Tsing, Anna Lowenhaupt. "Arts of Inclusion, or, How to Love a Mushroom." *Australian Humanities Review* 11 (2011). http://australianhumanitiesreview. org/2011/05/01/arts-of-inclusion-or-how-to-love-a-mushroom/.

Wachter, Aidan. *Weaving Fate: Changing the Past & Telling True Lies.* n.p., Red Temple Press, 2020.

CHAPTER 15

Creating Distance or Proximity? How Wild Lives Are Told through Remote Camera Viewing

Elizabeth Vander Meer

Introduction

Camera traps are being used with increasing frequency in conservation in order to capture the lives of species living in remote regions and to limit human disturbances from field observations. Remote camera viewing has also been used as means to engage wildlife tourists in the lives of wild animals, to encourage attitudes of care for conservation without the potential significant impact of tourists being immersed in habitats. This technology allows individual animals' stories to be told in some way, but the benefits of this method are debated. Some research concludes that remote camera viewing creates distance between humans and other animals, continuing a tradition of dominance and commodification.[1] It has also been argued that such viewing can create intimacy, connection, and positionings of care toward other animals.[2] This chapter explores remote camera contact zones and issues of framing power and dualisms as well as the potential for their breakdown in the context of Seabird Education Centre, a center in the UK located near extensive seabird breeding colonies. Research blends media and discourse analysis with autoethnography; observations were made during multiple visits to the center from 2017 to 2019, and the center's name and location have been anonymized.

How can we interpret the visual address of the Seabird Education Centre to understand whether the media they use cultivate distance or proximity between humans and other animals? I consider use of remote camera viewing as central to the visitor experience at the center. At the same time, film, photography and the sounds and the feel of wind become part of the context of this viewing. It is useful here to refer to Jamie Lorimer's identification of four affective logics and micropolitics in moving image, to understand the visual address of the center through the various media that it employs.[3] The four logics are sentimentality, curiosity and

---

1   Charlotte Chambers, "'Well It's Remote, I Suppose, Innit?' The Relational Politics of Bird-watching through the CCTV Lens," *Scottish Geographical Journal* 123, no. 2 (2007): 122–34.

2   Ike Kamphof, "Linking Animal and Human Places: The Potential of Webcams for Species Companionship," *Animal Studies Journal* 2, no. 1 (2013): 82–102.

3   Jamie Lorimer, "Moving Image Methodologies for More-than-human Geogra-

awe, sympathy and shock, and disconcertion. The affective logic of sentimentality is described as evoking emotions such as love, pity, anger, and comedy through fantasy and drama that anthropomorphizes animals, and Lorimer presents Disney characters such as Dumbo to demonstrate how these categories of feeling produce this effect.[4] Curiosity and awe are epitomized in David Attenborough's BBC documentaries, where audiences are intrigued by and in awe of the presented behavior and ecology of other species;[5] this approach can also include crittercams. Animal welfare, protection, and rights organizations often present a visual address that evokes sympathy and shock from viewers, in their exposés based on hidden investigative filming. Here Lorimer asserts that while moving toward sentimentality, this positioning is focused on bringing the lived experiences of individual animals into closer relation with humans.[6] The final affective logic of disconcertion can be seen in "surrealist wildlife documentary and postmodern animal art and experimental video," which present alterity as well as commonalities shared across species to disturb anthropomorphism or boundaries and dualities.[7]

In this study, Lorimer's analysis is deepened by an approach that draws from ideas in biopower and phenomenological performance theory to assess the visual address presented by the Seabird Education Centre. I examine the center as an apparatus that functions in a particular cultural context of the Anthropocene, conservation agendas, and neoliberalism and consider what this means in terms of power relations between humans and other animals. Biopower operates under a system of "normalization." It is the power of the norm, according to Foucault,[8] where power is understood as producing reality, or "domains of objects and rituals of truth."[9] Stephen Thierman describes an apparatus as defining "a field of interactions that enables a particular kind of experience (or perception) [...] bring[ing] a particular environment into focus."[10] It includes "the constellation of spaces and discourses in which various bodies (both human and nonhuman) find themselves enmeshed."[11] These ideas in biopower map onto performance theory and together help to conceptualize the visual address presented at the Seabird Education Centre and the way this address works in a particular cultural context. The Center presents a particular point of view to visitors, a particular visual address, as defined by Maaike Bleeker.[12] Absorption in what is presented can occur and the success of a visual address must be "understood in relation to a culturally and historically specific seer responding to the address presented."[13] The meaningfulness of what is

phies," *Cultural Geographies* 17, no. 2 (2010): 237–58.

4   Ibid., 245.
5   Ibid., 247.
6   Ibid., 248.
7   Ibid., 250.
8   Michel Foucault, qtd. in Paul Rabinow, ed., *The Foucault Reader* (London: Penguin, 1984), 196.
9   Ibid., 205.
10 Stephen Thierman, "Apparatuses of Animality: Foucault Goes to a Slaughterhouse," *Foucault Studies* 9 (September 2010): 90.
11 Ibid., 89.
12 Maaike Bleeker, *Visuality in the Theatre: The Locus of Looking* (Basingstoke: Palgrave MacMillan, 2011).
13 Ibid., 35.

presented is generally related to how much it resonates with a wider public cultural and emotional context within which individuals are immersed.[14]

Drawing on understandings of kinaesthetic empathy influenced by phenomenology and performance theory,[15] I consider how individual animals may be able to captivate in the UK Seabird Education Centre context, "showing themselves" beyond cultural overlays and providing visitors with opportunity for kinaesthetic empathy, potentially a deeper engagement than Lorimer's sympathy. This witnessing is a visceral engagement that involves human viewers in unfolding life stories and may or may not lead to a sense of moral obligation when individual animals are seen to be threatened. Kenneth J. Shapiro has defined kinaesthetic empathy in relation to attunement to others. It requires sensitivity and observation over time "through one's own body to the postures, expressive movements, incipient intentions and actions of the object of study."[16] Maren Wehrle describes "the experiencing body [as] simultaneously habitual and proactive, natural and cultural, passive and active, subjective and intersubjective," all of which makes action beyond the norm possible.[17] Una Chaudhuri describes the "ethical value and urgent need for an approach to animals that is imbued with the traits of performance — embodiment, presence, expressive encounters in shared time-space" — to cultivate intersubjectivity and being attuned to others, countering humanism, that rests on human exceptionalism.[18] These concepts guide the consideration of witnessing that follows.

Discussion starts with investigation of the visual address and power relations presented by remote camera viewing at the Seabird Education Centre, then moves to the wider context of how film and photography showcase indigenous wildlife. I present the cultural norms and power relations that may be expressed within different modes of viewing in the Seabird Centre context and also determine, in what storytelling instances, witnessing is more likely to occur in which animal vulnerability and agency can be seen and has potential to inspire a human positioning of care, which may or may not lead to specific actions on behalf of these animals. I argue that Lorimer's affective logics of sympathy and disconcertion are most evident or cultivated in the visual address or storytelling of the Seabird Education Centre, evoked through remote camera viewing and in the whole center experience. However, the visual address can also evoke curiosity and awe, especially if visits are fleeting. Regular visitors to the center and to online resources can develop a naturalist's view and a related kinaesthetic empathy, in contrast to the collector's gaze associated with zoo contexts.

14   William O. Beeman, "The Anthropology of Theatre and Spectacle," *Annual Review of Anthropology* 22, no. 1 (1993): 380.

15   Maren Wehrle, "Normative Embodiment: The Role of the Body in Foucault's Genealogy," *Journal of the British Society for Phenomenology* 47, no. 1 (2016): 56–71; Kamphof, "Linking Animal and Human Places"; Una Chaudhuri, "(De)facing the Animals: Zooesis and Performance," *The Drama Review* 51, no. 1 (2007): 8–20; Kenneth J. Shapiro, "The Human Science Study of Nonhuman Animals," *Phenomenology and Pedagogy* 8 (1990): 27–42.

16   Shapiro, "The Human Science Study of Nonhuman Animals," 28.

17   Wehrle, "Normative Embodiment," 60.

18   Chaudhuri, "(De)facing the Animals," 9.

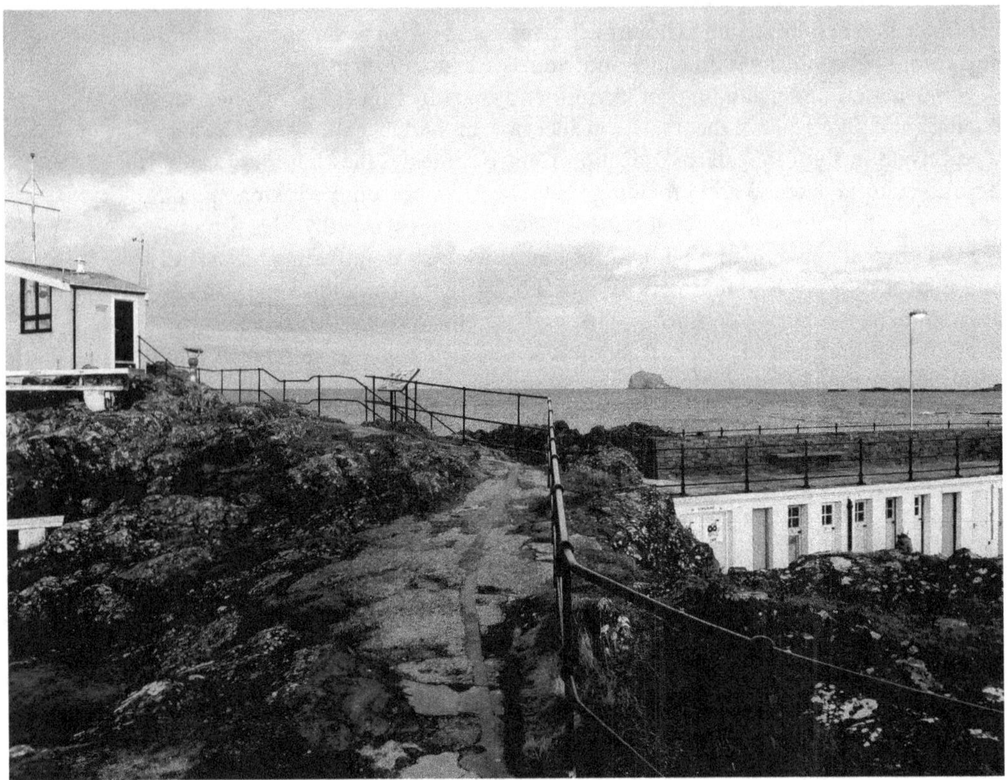

Fig. 15.1. View to a breeding colony island. Photograph by the author.

The Seabird Centre's Audio-visual Address: Remote Camera Viewing

I feel a sense of calmness by the sea, inhabiting the lapping waves against a shoreline, a soothing regular rhythm of touching and pulling away. The wind carries saltiness and that great expanse stretching out to the horizon is awe-inspiring in its reach, so out of reach, and comforting in its liquid solidity. But I grew up in an island nation in the Pacific and on a southern American peninsula, so they became a part of me, coastlines and the whirling and calling of seabirds along them.

As I approach the Seabird Education Centre, these images of childhood rush back to me and fill me with a sense of connection and belonging. The seagulls caw and screech here, and I listen in a way I do not or cannot when I walk through the city, distracted by other sounds and the need to reach destinations. The harbor boasts rows and rows of colorful boats, and the gulls wheel above them in vast numbers. I reach the farthest vantage point into the sea, an outcrop of rocks with a well-worn path to the very edge of water and see in the distance the white-coated volcanic island where the gannets are raising their young. I have watched their mad dives into water, straight down like bullets, wings all tucked in and streamlined. To the west, I can just make out the island that I know the puffins inhabit, but it is too far away for me to see them. This mystery, this knowing without seeing entices, draws me into the center to get closer by way of the cameras.

At first, I find myself hanging back, just barely of a generation to feel equipped to manage any technology that confronts me. I watch children expertly using re-

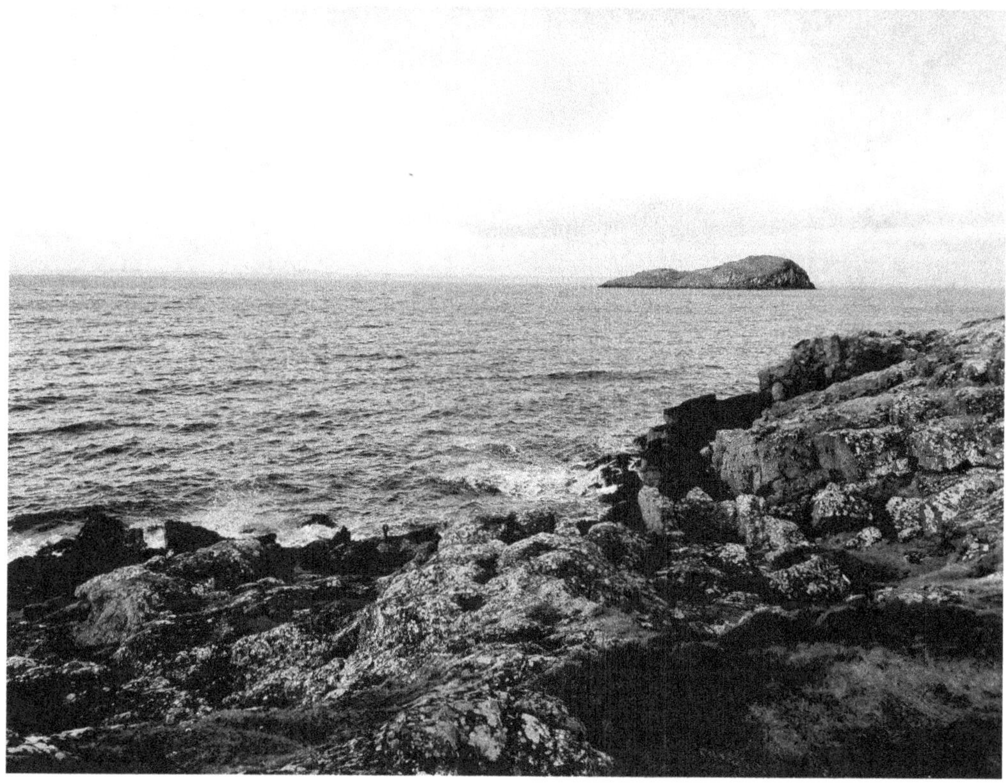

Fig. 15.2. Coastal view from the center. Photograph by the author.

mote camera controls to steer their views toward a gannet chick with open mouth,
or toward a puffin parent with a beak full of tiny glinting sand eels. This mediation
through joystick initially affects my ability to engage with what I am trying to see,
and it feels awkward and involves my concentration on controls. I veer off to a deso-
late rock face accidentally and attempt to redirect the camera's gaze back to the bustle
of gannets. I am lost, though, unsure of where they are and where I am. A member
of staff assists me, to get me back to the action. And then I move controls ever so
slowly, staying still or scanning the area in minute movements. I begin to absorb life
on this island of chattering seabirds, pulsing and bursting with their own particular
interconnected energy and agency.

The Seabird Education Centre aims to bring the seabirds and other wildlife of the
coastal islands closer to visitors through an array of exhibits. But it relies heavily
on presenting real-time remote camera footage of the islands, broadcast on large
screens called a "giant virtual blind." The center provides advice on use of remote
camera viewing technology internationally. The solar powered remote cameras'
main purpose is to capture and display the nesting sites of large colonies of Atlantic gannets (*Morus bassanus*) and Atlantic puffins (*Fratercula arctica*) on the nearby islands, from March or April to September. Cameras have zooming capabilities
to see individual bird's identification rings, as well as sound through a wireless
microwave system similar to mobile phone technology (so instead of wiring, there
are carefully placed microwave dishes). Gannets literally transform one volcanic

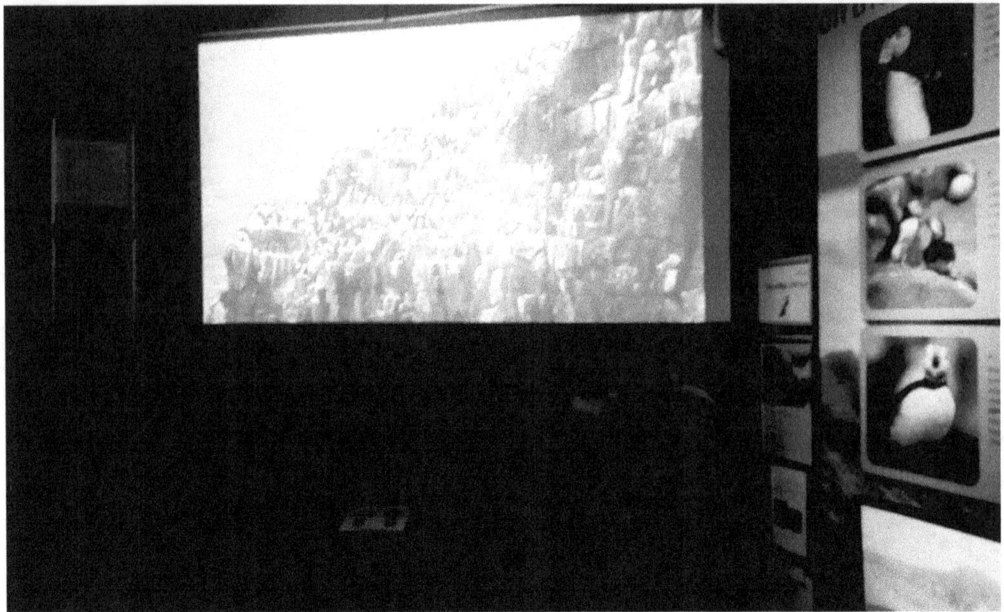

Fig. 15.3. Live remote camera footage of seabird breeding colonies, with sound. Photograph by the author.

island from gray-brown to white with their arrival *en masse* each February. The center describes the excitement around their return every year and the witnessing of bill fencing as established mated pairs reunite and reestablish bonds. The center is able to share individual lives during the breeding season over a long period of time as the gannets have a thirty-year lifespan. Puffins inhabit one of the largest islands off the coast from April to July each year. When they first arrive, these "clowns of the sea" land in flocks and leave in flocks, in flighty fashion, until they settle to breed.`

Gray seals (*Halichoerus grypus*) begin to heavily populate one of the islands during their breeding season from October to December, and the birth and growth of seal pups are events also captured by cameras. These animals are highlights of the center, but other seabirds are brought into focus by the cameras, such as breeding cormorants (*Phalacrocorax carbo*), kittiwakes (*Rissa tridactyla*), guillemots (*Uria aalge*), razorbills (*Alca torda*), shags (*Phalocrocorax aristotelis*), and fulmars (*Fulmaris glacialis*) who nest on the islands. Peregrines (Falco peregrinus) also have become regular visitors, caught on camera year-round. Most of these animals are in the category "of least concern" in the IUCN Red List of Threatened Species,[19] but UK populations of puffins and kittiwakes are now on the red list of UK Birds of Conservation Concern, while gannets, fulmars, and razorbills are on the amber list.[20]

19   "IUCN Red List of Threatened Species: History," *International Union for the Conservation of Nature,* 2021, https://www.iucnredlist.org/about/background-history.
20   "Birds of Conservation Concern 4: The Red List for Birds," *British Trust for Ornithology,* 2015, https://www.bto.org/our-science/publications/psob.

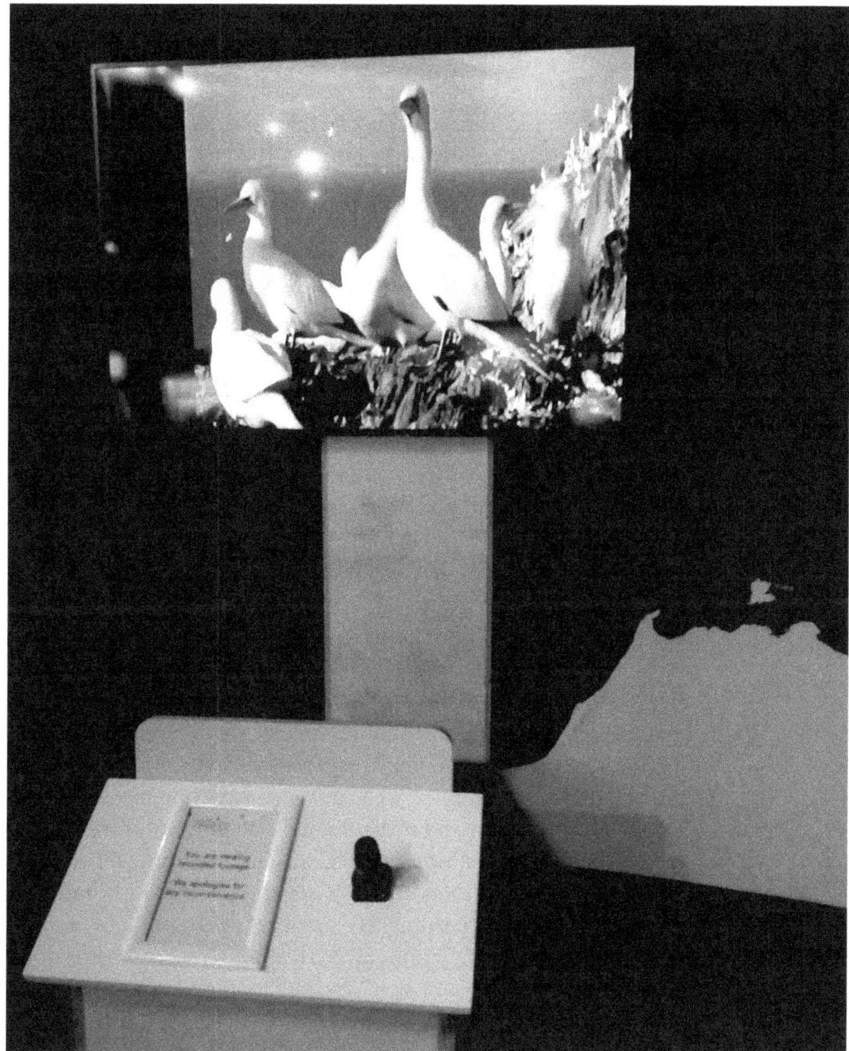

Fig. 15.4. Looped audio-visual recording of gannets from remote camera footage. Photograph by the author.

Remote Camera Viewing and Power Relations: Conservation and Commodity

The Seabird Education Centre's key attraction of remote camera footage streaming in real-time on large screens, and available on the center's website, forms the basis for spectatorship. Is spectatorship likely to be passive and voyeuristic in this context with animals having a fleeting encounter value, and what do the cameras mean for the animals being watched? First it is important to consider cultural context. The increase in wildlife surveillance using a range of technologies — not just remote camera viewing and camera traps — has been associated with a rise in camera-based surveillance within human populations in the Euro-American context, and particularly in the UK.[21] Specifically focusing on migratory species, William Adams has concluded that "effective conservation of [...] species is seen to demand better understanding of conditions on migration routes to target conservation action" and, thus, tracking of these animals.[22] Camera trap and CCTV technologies were first employed by hunters, the military and in police surveillance in the UK context. Conservation has been historically and is currently about control of life, about biopower and biopolitics, valuing particular lives for conservation efforts (e.g., charismatic endangered species in their indigenous contexts or in zoo captivity) while devaluing others (e.g., introduced species). It has been argued that conservation biology aims for an increasingly panoptic view.[23] As Charlotte Chambers points out, Gregg Mitman described this growing impetus over twenty years ago as "the power of an omnipresent and omniscient Being [...] ever watchful and ready at any moment to intervene and impose divine justice."[24] At the same time, a culturally pervasive neoliberalist ideology, again within Euro-American contexts, takes hold and creates spectacular nature for consumption. We can first explore biopower critiques of remote camera viewing and then consider control and consumption in relation to the Seabird Centre.

Ike Kamphof notes that "webcam viewing contains nonhuman animals as objects for spectacle in a viewing space defined by the human eye."[25] Both Chambers and Adams critique the purely visual medium of remote camera viewing as they have encountered it, where smells and sounds have no place in the experience.[26] Disconnection, disorientation, and dissociation can occur through use of this technology, and lack of moral engagement can be seen as inevitable due to the distance from real, tangible experience of another being.[27] Renee Van de Vall points out the potential for webcams and analogue modes of viewing animals to lead to objectification and instrumental conceptions of wildlife.[28] Such distancing and objectification is supported by Chambers. Framing through CCTV-like camera viewing ultimately creates a "hyper-separation" between human seer and animal "other" being seen, according to Chambers's research into viewers' perceptions of birdwatching via "CCTV" cameras.[29] The human seer remains dominant and views

---

21   William M. Adams, "Geographies of Conservation II: Technology, Surveillance and Conservation by Algorithm," *Progress in Human Geography* 43, no. 2 (2019): 337–50.

22   Ibid., 338.

23   Ibid., 340.

24   Chambers, "Well It's Remote, I Suppose, Innit?"; Gregg Mitman, "When Nature is the Zoo: Vision and Power in the Art and Science of Natural History," *Osiris* 11 (1996): 143; see Audrey Verma, René van der Wal, and Anke Fischer, "Imagining Wildlife: New Technologies and Animal Censuses, Maps, and Museums," *Geoforum* 75 (October 2016): 75–86 about increase in use of monitoring technologies.

25   Kamphof, "Linking Animal and Human Places," 82.

26   Chambers, "'Well It's Remote, I Suppose, Innit?'" and Adams, "Geographies of Conservation II."

27   Paul Virilio, *Ground Zero*, trans. Chris Turner (London: Verso Books, 2002); Vivian Sobchack, *Carnal Thoughts: Embodiment and Moving Image Culture* (Berkeley: University of California Press, 2016).

28   Renée van de Vall, "Promises of Presence," *Foundations of Science* 18, no. 1 (2013): 169.

29   Chambers, "'Well It's Remote, I Suppose, Innit?'"

the images in a relationship of consumer to commodity, a point that Adams has recently reiterated.[30] Within this commoditization, viewers may relate to remote camera live images in the way that they relate to television documentaries, and indeed visitors exhibit culturally-defined viewing expectations, which, in the UK, are based on easy consumption of wildlife via wildlife documentaries.[31] These expectations are cultivated by channels such as Animal Planet, where animals *are* in frame, *are* active and spectacular in form and movement. And they carry over into engagements with remote camera viewing footage. Ultimately, nature is "over there" — objectified and packaged in these interpretations.

The camera viewing at the Seabird Education Centre can be considered in contrast to the visual address created at a zoo. This exercise is useful in revealing the center's positioning in relation to wildlife. In both locations other animals have limited or no choice in terms of the surveillance trained upon them. But remote camera viewing could be interpreted as a less symmetrical relationality than that of visitor to a zoo and zoo animal in one sense if we set aside the obvious difference of captivity. Remote cameras allow humans to see the local wildlife, but the animals are unaware that they are being watched, unlike the zoo, which is an embodied experience on both sides; both human and nonhuman animal are present physically and have some, if minimal, potential to interact. Is there also a need for embodied experience, in order for visitors to be "touched" and perhaps changed so that they begin to care about the fate of other animals? Research around the educational and affective value of zoos reveals mixed conclusions on impact.[32] According to comments made at public talks during my visits, a few visitors to the center expressed disappointment at the camera method of seeing seabirds as they somehow expected to get "up close and personal" with puffins and gannets, perhaps thinking that they would be held in enclosures at the center similar to zoo spectatorship. This is an encounter value experienced through close physical proximity and could be considered more about the exhilaration felt by the visitor, rather than care for the animals being seen. I explored this positioning in the context of alligator farm experiences in Florida.[33] Euro-American consumer culture, and technologies that have developed within this culture, prime individuals for instant gratification, and for self-definition through the sharing of spectacular packaged experiences on social media. The growth of social media has led to this focus on the self and image creation: a performance of self through shared content which, in effect, creates or defines the individual as their own carefully crafted product. Getting up-close and personal with wildlife for selfies, for example, has led to the death of other animals in the search for unique and stimulating images,

30   Adams, "Geographies of Conservation II."
31   Chambers, "Well It's Remote, I Suppose, Innit?" 126.
32   See Andrew Balmford et al., "Message Received? Quantifying the Impact of Informal Conservation Education on Adults Visiting UK Zoos," *Zoological Society of London* (2007): 120–36; Eric Jensen, "Evaluating Children's Conservation Biology Learning at the Zoo," *Conservation Biology* 28, no. 4 (August 2014): 1004–11; and Patricia G. Patrick et al., "Conservation and Education: Prominent Themes in Zoo Mission Statements," *Journal of Environmental Education* 38, no. 3 (2010): 53–60.
33   Elizabeth Vander Meer, "Alligator Song: A Challenge to Spectacle, Product, and Menace," *Society & Animals* 28, no. 1 (2017): 1–20.

while also endangering the human selfie-taker.[34] This can be described as a "collector's gaze." The collector's gaze was epitomized by Victorian scientific expeditions, which resulted in specimen gathering and the displaying of animals in zoos and menageries, all of which involved objectification, domination, and distancing.[35] It is a gaze that is still alive today, not only perpetuated by some zoos and zoo-goers but also apparent in the commodification of "biodiversity," for instance.[36] We can see this commodification and packaging of experiences with wildlife as part of social media representations of self.

Chambers argues for tangible experiences but appears not to fully consider what this kind of experience for all might mean for other animals.[37] Humans can be perceived by many non-predator animals as predators and human presence may elicit fight or flight or stress-related coping responses.[38] Human populations have expanded to a point, where no part of the world is left untouched by climate change, plastics, and other forms of pollution. The deleterious desire to experience "in the flesh" could be dampened, however, by an understanding of the negative impact of this significant human presence. The Seabird Education Centre aims to cultivate this positioning in relation to free-roaming indigenous animals. Rhonda J. Green has researched wildlife tourism and its effects on individual animals, also exploring ethical implications.[39] She catalogues breeding failures, death of young at nesting sites, and transmission of zoonotic diseases due to wildlife tourism.[40] A denial of the nature-culture dualism and nature "over there" does not necessarily mean that remote camera viewing is unsuitable in the Anthropocene, which is typified by human-induced, rapid, environmental change. While Chambers de-

34   See for instance Jessica Maddox, "'Guns Don't Kill People … Selfies Do': Rethinking Narcissism as Exhibitionism in Selfie-related Deaths," *Critical Studies in Media Communications* 34, no. 3 (2017): 193–205, and John Pearce and Gianna Moscardo, "Social Representations of Tourist Selfies: New Challenges for Sustainable Tourism," in *Conference Proceedings: BESTEN Think Tank XV* (Townsville: BEST Educational Network, 2015), 59–73.

35   Harriet Ritvo, *The Animal Estate: The English and Other Creatures in the Victorian Age* (Cambridge: Harvard University Press, 1987), 206–26.

36   David Takacs, *The Idea of Biodiversity: Philosophies of Paradise* (Baltimore: Johns Hopkins University Press, 1996).

37   Chambers, "'Well It's Remote, I Suppose, Innit?'"

38   Ursula Ellenberg, "Impacts of Penguin Tourism," in *Ecotourism's Promise and Peril: A Biological Evaluation*, eds. Daniel Blumstein, Benjamin Geffroy, Diogo Samia, and Eduardo Bessa (Cham: Springer, 2017), 117–32; Laetitia Maréchal et al., "Impacts of Tourism on Anxiety and Physiological Stress Levels in Wild Male Barbary Macaques," *Biological Conservation* 144, no. 9 (2011): 2188–93; and Karen Higginbottom and Noel Scott, "Wildlife Tourism: A Strategic Destination Analysis," in *Wildlife Tourism: Impacts, Management and Planning*, ed. Karen Higginbottom (Champaign: Common Ground Publishing, 2004), 253–75; and see also Phillip W. Bateman and Patricia A. Fleming, "Are Negative Effects of Tourist Activities on Wildlife Over-reported? A Review of Assessment Methods and Empirical Results," *Biological Conservation* 211 (July 2017): 10–19.

39   Ronda J. Green, "Disturbing Skippy on Tour: Does It Really Matter? Ecological and Ethical Implications of Disturbing Wildlife," in *Wildlife Tourism, Environmental Learning and Ethical Encounters,* eds. Ismar Borges de Lima and Ronda J. Green (Cham: Springer, 2017), 221–33.

40   Green, "Disturbing Skippy on Tour," 223.

scribes what could be considered a low-impact, "twitcher" experience of being "in it" near home, and thus immersed in a natural context to view and hear birds in close proximity in the flesh, we cannot deny the potential impact of sheer human numbers on other animals.

In contrast to the zoo experience, remote cameras are physically nonintrusive and appear to barely disrupt the daily lives of the seabirds and seals on the islands. Having said that, Bret Mills asks whether animals have a right to privacy and while his discussion is centered on television wildlife documentaries, it does have relevance here.[41] Mills believes that we could apply to other animals the same conceptions of public and private space that are used in relation to humans.[42] This would mean that animals should be filmed in what could be considered public space (walking across a desert or savannah, for instance) but not in what could be considered private space (in burrows or nests, when procreating, and so on). The center's cameras do capture the seabirds and seals at their most vulnerable, during breeding season, and this would be a private space, according to Mills. However, Mills's right to privacy could be seen as anthropomorphism and a particular Christian definition of these spaces, since all other animals do not distinguish between public and private space in the same way that humans do. This is not to say that an animal would not be more relaxed in the safety of a burrow, as would a human in the safety of their own home, for example. The seabirds on the islands cannot comprehend what the cameras mean — that many pairs of human eyes are watching them at a distance — and so their behaviors remain as they would be without cameras present. But their intimate behaviors are being "packaged" in a way and sold to visitors for an educational experience that could lead to public interest and caring for the birds' importance in the UK's ecological communities. Mills's point is well-taken, as it highlights the issue of speciesism[43] and whether it is right to use one culturally specific standard for ourselves and another for other animals; the scientific endeavor and the desire to entertain often involves the complete exposure or manipulation of nonhuman organisms to push the limits of knowledge or the limits of excitement.

What is the affective logic apparent if we consider remote camera viewing at the Seabird Education Centre in a context of biopower that includes commodification of wildlife? We can identify Lorimer's curiosity and awe being cultivated by the visual address of the center, so that visitors are drawn to the chaos of the breeding season on the islands and so to spectacular live images of births, of flights and dives, of struggles for space in the crowds of gannets or of courtship flourishes between mated pairs of puffins. Visitors may have a fleeting relationship with place, as wildlife tourists from distance places, and they may be drawn to the center's easily consumed display of charismatic seabirds, which constitutes their taste of nature in the UK, the collector's view. While on the islands, the birds and seals cannot escape the camera's eye and they become spectacles for consumption onshore. However, the animals' agency, unfettered by this kind of viewing, is equally on display as they move to their own individual and species rhythms on and off screen.

41   Brett Mills, "Television Wildlife Documentaries and Animals' Right to Privacy," *Continuum* 24, no. 2 (2010): 193–202.

42   Ibid., 198.

43   Richard Ryder, *Speciesism, Painism and Happiness: A Morality for the Twenty-first Century* (Exeter: Imprint Academic, 2011).

Remote Camera Viewing and Kinaesthetic Empathy? Conservation and Care

Is it possible for a different relationality to develop through remote camera viewing at the Seabird Education Centre? An alternative paradigm becomes visible upon consideration of shifting cultural norms, the interaction and agency of staff, visitors, and other animals in the lens. In a human-dominated world, growing concern for the plight of other species or biodiversity loss has become increasingly apparent both within and outside of conservation circles in the last decade. References to a human-induced sixth mass extinction event can be found in popular science articles and news media, although there is scientific debate as to whether this is occurring. Are we at the cusp of such an event or is this discourse alarmist or inaccurate?[44] Climate change and biodiversity loss have become regular subjects of news stories in the mainstream media, although conservation in the UK has been a public concern since the nineteenth century. This is evidenced, for example, by the Wild Birds Protection Act, enacted in 1872,[45] and by the establishment of the National Trust for Places of Historic Interest and Natural Beauty in 1895.[46] The Royal Society for the Protection of Birds (RSPB) was created initially by urban, middle-class women to sharpen the often ineffective Bird Protection Action (1872).[47] The National Trust and the RSPB are now ranked in the top ten of the largest UK membership bodies, alongside unions.[48] Urbanization and industrialization in the UK have been linked to a nostalgic view of nature and the desire to preserve or conserve it, as expressed by British Romantic writers.[49] We can locate the development of remote camera viewing of wildlife, specifically seabirds, and the use of camera trap technology within this care for nature. It reflects one aspect of biopower and a relationality that we can now consider, in terms of possibilities for care, in the context of the Seabird Education Centre.

Visitors at the center can control the cameras, to shift view and zoom in or out, so in this sense they are interactive, and views are not fixed. Visitors have

44   Georgina M. Mace et al., "Aiming Higher to Bend the Curve of Biodiversity Loss," *Nature Sustainability* 1, no. 9 (2018): 448–51; Gerardo Ceballos et al., "Accelerated Modern Human-induced Species Losses: Entering the Sixth Mass Extinction," *Science Advances* 1, no. 5 (2015): 1–5; John C. Briggs, "Emergence of a Sixth Mass Extinction?" *Biological Journal of the Linnean Society* 122, no. 2 (October 2017): 243–48; and Pincelli Hull, Simon A.F. Darroch, and Douglas H. Erwin, "Rarity in Mass Extinctions and the Future of Ecosystems," *Nature* 528, no. 7582 (2015): 345–51.

45   Paul A. Rees, "A Chronology of Major Legislation Affecting Animals and Nature Conservation in the United Kingdom," in *The Laws Protecting Animals and Ecosystems* (Chichester: John Wiley & Sons, 2018), 445–48.

46   "Our History: 1884–1945," *National Trust*, 2020, https://www.nationaltrust.org.uk/lists/our-history-1884-45.

47   "RSPB History: From Humble Beginnings to Thriving Today," *Royal Society for the Protection of Birds*, 2020, https://www.rspb.org.uk/about-the-rspb/about-us/our-history/.

48   "Largest 100 UK Membership Bodies (The Influence 100 List)," *Memberwise*, 2020, https://memberwise.org.uk/influence100/.

49   Jonathan Bate, *Romantic Ecology: Wordsworth and the Environmental Tradition* (London: Routledge, 2013).

witnessed the first seal pup birth on one of the islands, reported it, and identified peregrine falcons on camera to the delight of other visitors and staff, for instance. Education Centre staff are on-hand to fill in a narrative for each island covered on camera, describing them in terms of main population of breeding bird species. Staff also seem to know individual animals. For instance, during a visit, I zoomed in on a seal and pup and was promptly told a bit about their brief history on the island and their behavior (the mother was shielding the pup from the onslaught of the incoming tide with her body). During a pan over one of the islands, I also spotted what appeared to be two lifeless, seal pup bodies, and I was told that they were dead, crushed against the rocks during a stormy night when their mothers could not protect them.

I did wonder at this point whether staff would ever intervene if an animal appeared to be in distress. Does the sight of the animal on camera bring with it any responsibility (does actual interaction ever result)? A staff member explained that they or researchers on the islands will intervene in certain circumstances, for instance when a seal pup is seen to be unwell or poorly located when the mother has left or when pufflings become disoriented by lights on shore and fly into the village rather than out to sea. Pufflings have been ushered out of the town's hotels and high street and encouraged in the right direction by center volunteers. The cameras provide a monitoring function, which allows for intervention at critical times for the benefit of the animals. A volunteer project to clear nonnative tree mallow (*Lavatera arborea*) from one of the islands resulted from remote monitoring, which revealed tree mallow blocking puffins' burrows, leading to a population crash. The story of tree mallow's introduction is a familiar one. It arrived on the island through human will, planted by members of a garrison for medicinal use. In recent years, the plant spread from island to island in a process linked to climate change, and this spread led to the crash in the puffin population. The response to this crisis, brought close by remote camera viewing, shows evidence of Lorimer's affective logic of sympathy and shock, witnessing which he considered in relation to investigative, exposé hidden-camera footage in places of captivity such as slaughterhouses, zoos, circuses: "the camera takes us where we would or could not go, revealing spaces, bodies, and events, generally obscured from contemporary visual horizons."[50]

Kamphof has explored the potential for webcams to create affective and ethical space and her research can be considered in relation to the center's project of providing similar real-time images of local wildlife.[51] Unlike the wildlife documentary, which in traditional form chooses viewpoints for audiences through camera shots (i.e., what is or is not shown) and through an overlaid narrative, the webcam images are free to be directly interpreted by the viewer. The lives of the birds or other animals on display at the center slowly unfold on camera in real-time unedited. Kamphof notes that such observation can lead to connection:

50 Lorimer, "Moving Image Methodologies for More-than-human Geographies," 249.
51 Ike Kamphof, "Webcams to Save Nature: Online Space as Affective and Ethical Space," *Foundations of Science* 16, nos. 2–3 (2011): 259–74; Kamphof, "Linking Animal and Human Places," 82–102.

Affective investments are particularly stimulated by the slowness and mundaneness of the scenes that are usually visible on a cam. While some viewers find this boring, regular users are captivated. The close-up view of a bird sitting on a nest, day after day, the minute portrayal of simple physical activities like taking a mud bath or a drink of water, evoke recognition of these activities in the bodies of the viewers. No narrative tensions lead away from this visceral layer of seeing.[52]

The bustle of puffin and gannet breeding and nesting may not appear as mundane as this, but many observed moments will include birds undertaking repetitive activities day to day. In contrast to the captive animal zoo environment that may facilitate the collector's gaze, I would argue that webcam or remote camera viewing in this case can encourage the "naturalist's gaze." The naturalist's gaze relies on immersion based on painstaking observation of and closeness with subjects of study over time and an ecological temporality. The naturalist's view certainly does seem to apply to the staff, volunteers, and some local members of the center who see the day to day of local wildlife and may begin to know individual animals on camera, which leads to kinaesthetic empathy; the spectacle is not the "exotic" ex-situ, and none of the key animal "attractions" are endangered, although they are charismatic. This way of seeing or relating may not be exhibited by all visitors to the center, since some only stay for a few hours and may not return. But there will be that subset who do return and who also engage regularly with real-time images online.

Surrounding Remote Cameras: Exhibition Spaces and the Story of Breeding and Migration

The smallness of puffins immediately strikes me as I walk through the puffin exhibition, just before I reach the flyway tunnel. I expected larger birds, but the image shows a puffin and its eight inches when standing, with an average weight of around one pound. While size should not emphasize or call to mind vulnerability, in this moment it does, but I am soon disabused of this idea as I watch the little birds' sturdy acrobatics in air and learn about their tenacious attachment to place and to specific mates and burrows. When not on land for breeding, puffins spend their lives out at sea, this is their element and a time when they become solitary and out of reach. Not much scientific research has been undertaken on their lives in the open ocean. I move on to the flyway tunnel, past the cinema that is already playing Clowns of the Sea, a film highlighting puffin behavior during the breeding season when they can be closely watched.

I notice a wind as I step into the tunnel, and the darkness is in equal parts soothing and mysterious, which creates an atmosphere of nonhuman otherness. The screeching and cawing of seabirds reach my ears, and it is a cacophony of communication swirling around me, as if carried on that artificial wind. To my left, I see a display titled, "Arrivals and Departures," and I am transported into an airport, which jolts me out of this othered place for a moment and into the nowhereness of Heathrow or Miami International. I understand the use of this storyline to call to mind mass transits and landings, the international and the far flung.

52   Kamphof, "Webcams to Save Nature," 264.

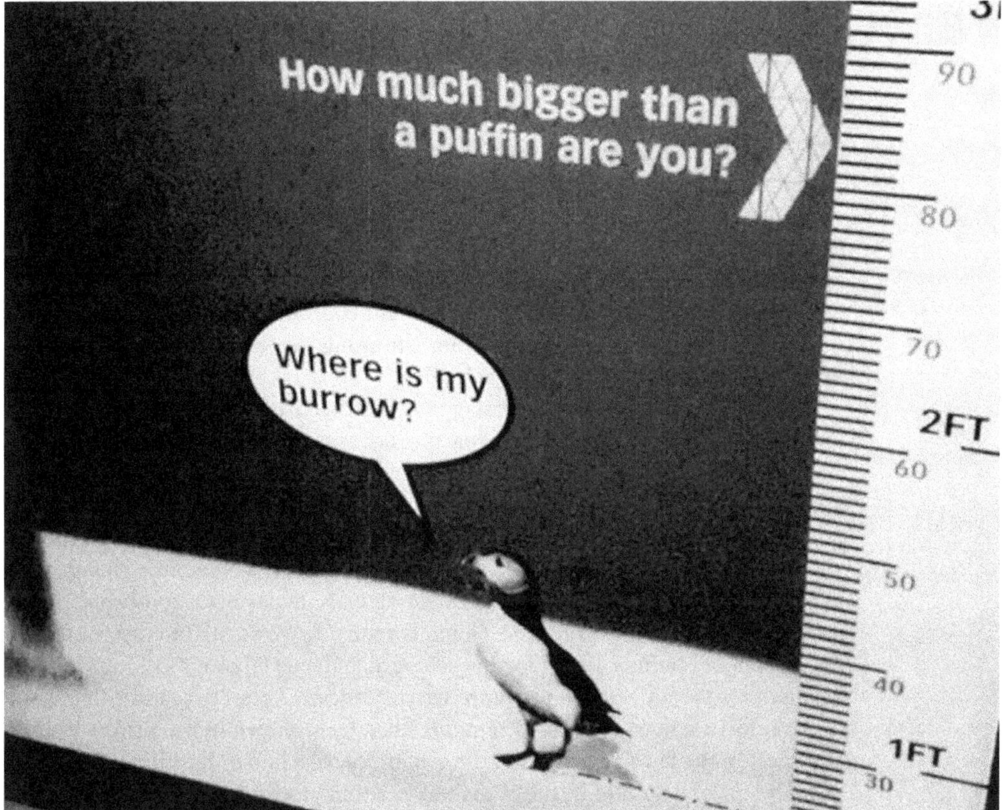

Fig. 15.5. Puffin exhibition displaying the birds' average size. Photograph by the author.

The Seabird Education Centre includes permanent exhibits around remote camera viewing, describing seabirds' life cycles, particularly breeding on the islands, and projects underway such as tree mallow eradication, to protect and support them which link to local human communities. Center exhibits and visitor guides provide explanations and further details, for instance describing the story of the gugas, the name for young gannets, as fraught with danger and risk. When they leave the nest, they must plunge from the rock into the sea before they are able to properly fly due to their weight. These same young birds, if they survive, will return to their birthplace once they reach the age of two in order to nest and eventually breed. Gannet bodies are celebrated as precisely designed through evolution to survive dives into water from air at up to sixty miles per hour. Puffin mating rituals are described in detail to make sense of what is seen in remote camera footage. As with gannets, puffins return to the same mates each year and to the same burrows. Puffin bodies come to life through descriptions of these little birds flying underwater, propelled by their short wings to depths of almost fifty feet to fish.

Accessible via the center website, researcher blogs reveal unique characteristics of birds as well as interaction so that these are not just birds "over there" and at a distance from human contact. Blog posts not only focus on charismatic puffins and gannets but also try to draw readers into the life cycles of fulmars and kittiwakes who arrive later and perform the serious task of raising chicks when the puffins have left. The stories told are of breeding successes for the most part, and islands teeming with activity at certain times of the year. Writers convey the flux of the seasons and cycles with the excitement of the abundance of seabird life on the island giving way to a winding down as seabirds leave to migrate to distant destinations. On Facebook and Twitter pages for the center, a story unfolds of interventions and interactions with members of the public. An image of a young puffin hiding in a rock crevice is received on social media with comments of love, awe, and sympathy. This is an individual with a story of vulnerability captured on camera. The bird is the last little puffling to leave the island. Among these accounts are dramatic photos of individuals, such as a gannet surfacing from a dive, fish in mouth, and water droplets creating silver glints around the bird in a thrashing, white capped sea. Reactions range from "stunning" to "beautiful" and "amazing." These photographs are close and visceral.

The flyway tunnel takes center stage as a multi-sensory exhibition space, bringing to life the yearly arrivals and departures of seabirds using sights, bird sounds, and simulated wind. Emphasis is placed on the feat of migration throughout this and other exhibits. The panel similar to the arrivals and departures board in an airport presents times that different species will alight on the islands and when they will leave. The center presents the analogy with airports as the birds' perspective, the town akin to a global hub of frequent arrivals, departures, and brief transits for rest before journeys continue. Gannets return to West Africa after the breeding season and puffins depart for the sea. A map depicts flyways for other seabird destinations too, in North and South Africa, Canada, Antarctica, and Norway.

The documentary, *Winged Migration*,[53] had been shown in its entirety for several years in the flyway tunnel, but the center now displays only a clip, though they play *Ocean Wonderland* in full.[54] Visitors continue following the winding tunnel and discover dolphins, whales, seals, turtles, and rays in dramatic photographs and descriptions on the walls and in documentaries that are displayed on in-set screens. Quotes from well-known naturalists are scattered throughout the flyway exhibition space. The exhibit leads to stairs heading to the ground level and a scoping deck, providing telescopes and binoculars to view seabirds on the nearby islands.

The Whole Center Story: Film and Other Media in the Flyway Tunnel and Disconcertion?

Chambers and Adams do not locate their examples within particular and whole experiences of viewing in their critiques of remote camera viewing or CCTV-style cameras used to view wildlife. This is the visual address and the apparatus that we are considering in the example of the Seabird Education Centre. Not including this full visual and other sensory field or contact zone is problematic. It is to this context that we turn to now. *Winged Migration* had been a central item in the flyway tunnel. The ninety-eight-minute *Winged Migration* is meant to present the bird's-eye view, particularly through the innovative filming of geese and other migrations using cameras on remote-control gliders and ultra-lights. It also provides

---

53 Jacques Perrin, Jacques Cluzaud, and Michel Debats, dirs., *Winged Migration* (BAC Films, 2003).
54 Jean-Jacques Mantello, dir., *Ocean Wonderland* (Universal Pictures UK, 2003).

minimal narrative overlay with equally minimal human presence in the frame in order to become more of a visceral experience of birds' experiences of migration. Many segments include music to heighten awe, mystery, drama. As Mathew Lerberg notes, "human and nonhuman animals migrate together co-creating footage through their intra-actions not only with each other but also with the multiple environments they traverse."[55] However, this co-creation is only apparent in the "Making of" documentary of the documentary. *Winged Migration* instead presents a spectacular nature and a romanticizing of children's and rural communities' relationships with that nature. Using Lorimer's affective logics theory, it can be seen to evoke curiosity and awe, at both the ingenuity of filming techniques and the migratory journeys of the birds, as well as a controlled sympathy for a human-degraded nature "over there."

Ocean Wonderland 3D takes a slightly different position, while it also overlaps with the spectacular vision of *Winged Migration*. It embraces an anthropomorphic characterization of a sea turtle, who becomes guide to the viewer-as-diver in the Great Barrier and Bahamas coral reefs. The sea turtle invites the viewer to explore the beauty of his ocean home, with minimal narration and an overpowering, dramatic soundtrack. Narration that is provided by the sea turtle focuses on describing characteristics of coral reefs and their inhabitants in brief, relying on music and three-dimensional imagery to tell a story of beauty. The film runs for a short forty minutes and can be easily dipped into by visitors to the flyway tunnel, its three-dimensional format attracting viewers and attempting an immersive perspective in ocean life. Here again we can identify an affective logic of curiosity and awe, as well as a logic of sentimentality as the narrating, anthropomorphized sea turtle describes threats to and degradation of his ocean home. The film appears to be geared more toward children than adults with this anthropomorphizing and three-dimensional effect. Both films rely on the aesthetic appeal of imagery presented and are contradictory in their attempts to stay with the animals while also overpowering them with emotive music and particular image framings.

We can compare these documentary formats with *Bear 71*, a documentary that I argue delivers Lorimer's affective logics of sympathy and disconcertion and presents a visual address similar to the whole center experience.[56] The twenty-minute-long *Bear 71* does not rely on a fully linear storyline and uses digital technologies such as camera traps and an interactive platform to draw viewers into the wanderings and challenges faced by a young female grizzly bear in Banff National Park as she navigates an increasingly human- and tech-dominated landscape. A narrative runs through the interactive display, voiced by the bear from an omniscient, anthropomorphic perspective. The documentary begins with footage of Bear 71 being radio-collared with voice over explaining the drugs and technology being used to subdue and track her. The view then shifts to an interactive digital map, visualized by dots and lines representing the regional geography, with radio collar transmission beeps sounding and a locator tag representing Bear 71 moving through the digital landscape. *Bear 71* describes the technologies that are shaping wild lives. Other animals such as hares, cougars, ravens, and wolves appear in similar

---

55   Mathew Lerberg, "Animals, Actors, and Agency: Navigating 'Winged Migration,'" *Green Letters* 12, no. 1 (2010): 44.

56   Jeremy Mendes and Leanne Allison, *Bear 71* (Montreal: National Film Board of Canada, 2012).

fashion, tracked and moving within the map's boundaries. A click on the moving animal will open camera trap footage and individual and species-level details such as Latin name, weight, age, population trend, and conservation status. Individual human viewers will also be tracked and numbered if they agree, their webcams capturing their image and shared with other viewers watching at the same time. A framing point is made in the narration that animals learn in many instances not to do what comes naturally in order to survive in a human-dominated landscape. The interactive film concludes with the bear's account of her own death, when she roars and charges a train to protect her cubs as they feed on grain that has spilled from a transport carriage on train tracks. This last natural act was caught on train camera footage but was not shown in its entirety. When she talks about her surviving cub and the cubs she will have, Bear 71 explains in narration that, "the wild is not where she lives. [… T]hey'll have to learn not to do what comes naturally."

Bear 71 has potential to shift human perspective to the positioning of the bear, to understand the ways in which she moves through Banff National Park and the many ways in which she is bounded by roads, train lines, and human settlements. She must adapt to those things which are not part of her natural repertoire of threat responses, those things she has not been evolved to confront, for instance, a face off with a train. This vulnerability in the face of human technology can have a profound effect on the viewer who is familiar with these technologies and perhaps has only considered them in terms of their value to human users.

This leads to disconcertion but also to sympathy. An affective logic of disconcertion is associated with experimental image-making, in which other animals are not anthropomorphized according to Lorimer.[57] *Bear 71* is experimental while it also anthropomorphizes, giving the bear a human voice and human understandings of the technologies around her. However, this positioning, as noted by Gwendolyn Blue, works to disrupt the typical narrative voice in wildlife documentaries, "typically an older human man, who makes assertions that are supported by visual evidence," and makes apparent Bear 71's subjective, first-person aliveness. She "is decidedly situated in her story and its implications."[58] The narrative in fact evokes disconcertion through its perspective-taking alongside the trail-camera, trap footage and digital mapping. Here digital technologies, including remote camera footage, bring the shared vulnerability and alterity of bear and other animal individuals closer to the human viewer.

The Seabird Education Centre uses a wide range of media and experiences to tell the stories of seabird lives on nearby islands. This approach borders on delivering an affective logic of disconcertion, close to achieving the positioning in *Bear 71*. Migration is a key and defining aspect of the seabirds' stories as they are told by the center. With their flyways and breeding patterns, these migratory birds link land, sea, air, and countries vastly different both culturally and ecologically, thousands of miles away from each other. The center uses the multi-sensory, multi-media flyway tunnel, including photographic images, to chart journeys, human-related challenges, and links. Similar to Finis Dunaway's description of

---

57   Lorimer, "Moving Image Methodologies for More-than-human Geographies," 250.

58   Gwendolyn Blue, "Public Attunement with More-than-human Others: Witnessing the Life and Death of Bear 71," *GeoHumanities* 2, no. 1 (2016): 49.

photographer Subhankar Banerjee's visual politics,[59] the center attempts to provide a global ecological context for and understandings of interconnectedness that will upset the notion of nature separate and "over there." Migration could pervade the center's visual address more strongly and move the viewer alongside or with the seabirds without reference to airports that anthropomorphize the animals. This story can be framed to show commonalities while also showing alterity. Migration is a story of attachments and relationships, of place as meaningful. These seabirds exhibit site fidelity, the need for the presence of conspecifics at those sites, and pair bonding. Thom Van Dooren's storytelling around Little Penguins brings this approach to life:

> Only one colony is "home" and, within it, likely only one burrow. More than the sum of their ecological parts, these places carry penguin histories and stories. In focusing exclusively on "habitat" in accounts of penguin breeding places, we provide a framework of thought in which it is far easier to deny, or conveniently forget, both the real significance of penguins' relationships with these *particular* places and the fact that penguins inhabit their own richly meaningful and storied worlds.[60]

Conclusion

Animals captured by camera traps or CCTV-style camera viewing have visible agency, interacting with the cameras in some cases and moving in and out of frame. The human spectator is not privy to all. This can be said of the animals captured by remote cameras at the Seabird Education Centre even though visitors can zoom in and move the field of vision. The seabirds are migratory and do leave the islands, flying out of sight for long periods of time. The seals also come and go, and when they go, they live their lives, for the most part, beyond the human gaze. Staff and volunteers at the center have been moved by what they see through remote cameras to act with care toward seabirds and seals in their community; rather than evoking merely curiosity and awe at spectacle, this visual address can evoke sympathy and a deeper kinaesthetic empathy leading to action. Regular visitors to the center have opportunity to develop a naturalist's view rather than collector's view as they witness the cyclical unfolding of individual seabird and other lives on nearby islands.

Remote camera viewing at the Seabird Education Centre cannot be divorced from the full context within which it is located. Other media forms aim to supplement and add to the story. This is the audiovisual or sensorial address of the center. It functions within a particular UK cultural context that is dominated by consumer culture, aligning with it, while also capitalizing on a growing concern for other animals in the Anthropocene based on sense of loss of and disconnection from nature and disconnection from slower temporal scales and life cycles. The center

---

59   Finis Dunaway, "Reframing the Last Frontier: Subhankar Banerjee and the Visual Politics of the Arctic National Wildlife Refuge," *American Quarterly* 58 (March 2006): 159–80.

60   Thom Van Dooren, *Flight Ways: Life and Loss at the Edge of Extinction* (New York: Columbia University Press, 2014), 80.

could be seen to verge on the interactive approach of the documentary *Bear 71* and its shift to bring to life an individual amid human-dominated and -constraining contexts. Lorimer's affective logic of disconcertion almost becomes apparent in the overarching theme of migrations, also supported by the shift from Winged Migration to *Ocean Wonderland*, which while anthropomorphic attempts to reorient the viewer to the positioning of sea life it portrays.

The story of migration could be told in a way that brings human viewers closer to the experiences of seabirds and to develop positionings of care, while also maintaining other animal alterity. Migration away from the UK provides a valuable ecological story that connects individual animals to remote regions and shows our interconnectedness and shared vulnerabilities in the face of human-induced, rapid environmental change. Unique places and relationships are meaningful to seabirds, are central to migration, and the vast, interconnecting journeys undertaken by seabirds speak to alterity. Further research is needed to explore center intentions and how they have changed the telling of these multi-species stories over time in response to cultural and ecological pressures. Van Dooren's approach to Little Penguins describes a valuable positioning to refine within the context of the Seabird Education Centre, not only in terms of the local lives of seabirds but also in terms of their migratory journeys, which can bring closer other, particular places storied by these seabirds once they leave their breeding grounds:

> Thinking through the lens of storied-places enables us to appreciate some of the ways in which penguins, places and the stories that connect them are all at stake in one another, all reshaped through ongoing patterns of attachment and relationship.[61]

61   Ibid., 73.

References

Adams, W.M. "Geographies of Conservation II: Technology, Surveillance and Conservation by Algorithm." *Progress in Human Geography* 43, no. 2 (2019): 337–50. DOI: 10.1177/0309132517740220.

Balmford, Andrew, Nigel Leader-Williams, Georgina M. Mace, Andrea Manica, Olivia Walter, Chris West, and Alexandra Zimmermann. "Message Received? Quantifying the Impact of Informal Conservation Education on Adults Visiting UK Zoos." *Zoological Society of London* (2007): 120–36.

Bate, Jonathan. *Romantic Ecology: Wordsworth and the Environmental Tradition.* London: Routledge, 2013.

Bateman, Philip W., and Patricia A. Fleming. "Are Negative Effects of Tourist Activities on Wildlife Over-reported? A Review of Assessment Methods and Empirical Results." *Biological Conservation* 211 (July 2017): 10–19. DOI: 10.1016/j.biocon.2017.05.003.

Beeman, William O. "The Anthropology of Theater and Spectacle." *Annual Review of Anthropology* 22, no. 1 (1993): 369–93. DOI: 10.1146/annurev. an.22.100193.002101.

"Birds of Conservation Concern 4: the Red List for Birds." BTO — *British Trust for Ornithology,* 2015. https://www.bto.org/our-science/publications/psob.

Bleeker, M. *Visuality in the Theatre: The Locus of Looking.* Basingstoke: Palgrave MacMillan, 2011.

Blue, Gwendolyn. "Public Attunement with More-than-human Others: Witnessing the Life and Death of Bear 71." *GeoHumanities* 2, no. 1 (2016): 42–57. DOI: 10.1080/2373566x.2016.1166976.

Briggs, John C. "Emergence of a Sixth Mass Extinction?" *Biological Journal of the Linnean Society* 122, no. 2 (October 2017): 243–48. DOI: 10.1093/biolinnean/ blx063.

Ceballos, Gerardo, Paul R. Ehrlich, Anthony D. Barnosky, Andrés Garcia, Robert M. Pringle, and Todd M. Palmer. "Accelerated Modern Human-induced Species Losses: Entering the Sixth Mass Extinction." *Science Advances* 1, no. 5 (2015): 1–5. DOI: 10.1126/sciadv.1400253.

Chambers, Charlotte N.L. "'Well It's Remote, I Suppose, Innit?' The Relational Politics of Bird-watching through the CCTV Lens." *Scottish Geographical Journal* 123, no. 2, (2007): 122–34. DOI: 10.1080/14702540701624568.

Chaudhuri, Una. "(De)facing the Animals: Zooësis and Performance." *The Drama Review* 51, no. 1 (2007): 8–20. DOI 10.1162/dram.2007.51.1.8.

Dunaway, Finis. "Reframing the Last Frontier: Subhankar Banerjee and the Visual Politics of the Arctic National Wildlife Refuge." *American Quarterly* 58, no. 1 (March 2006): 159–80. https://www.jstor.org/stable/40068352.

Ellenberg Ursula. "Impacts of Penguin Tourism." In *Ecotourism's Promise and Peril: A Biological Evaluation,* edited by Daniel T. Blumstein, Benjamin Geffroy, Diogo S.M. Samia, and Eduardo Bessa, 117–32. Cham: Springer Publishing, 2017.

Green, Rhonda J. "Disturbing Skippy on Tour: Does It Really Matter? Ecological and Ethical Implications of Disturbing Wildlife." In *Wildlife Tourism, Environmental Learning and Ethical Encounters: Ecological and Conservation Aspects,* edited by Ismar Borges de Lima and Rhonda Green, 221–33. Cham: Springer, 2017.

Higginbottom, Karen, and Noel Scott. "Wildlife Tourism: A Strategic Destination Analysis." In *Wildlife Tourism: Impacts, Management and Planning*, edited by Karen Higgenbottom, 253–75. Champaign: Common Ground Publishing, 2003.

Hull, Pincelli M., Simon A.F. Darroch, and Douglas H. Erwin. "Rarity in Mass Extinctions and the Future of Ecosystems." *Nature* 528, no. 7582 (2015): 345–51. DOI: 10.1038/nature16160.

"IUCN Red List of Threatened Species." *IUCN Red List*, 2021. https://www.iucnredlist.org/about/background-history/.

Jensen, Eric. "Evaluating Children's Conservation Biology Learning at the Zoo." *Conservation Biology* 28, no. 4 (August 2014): 1004–11. DOI: 10.1111/cobi.12263.

Kamphof, Ike. "Animal Studies Journal Linking Animal and Human Places: The Potential of Webcams for Species Companionship." *Animal Studies Journal* 2, no. 1 (2013): 82–102. https://ro.uow.edu.au/asj/vol2/iss1/8.

Kamphof, Ike. "Webcams to Save Nature: Online Space as Affective and Ethical Space." *Foundations of Science* 16, nos. 2–3 (2010): 259–74. DOI: 10.1007/s10699-010-9194-7.

"Largest 100 UK Membership Bodies (The Influence 100 List)." *Memberwise*, 2020. https://memberwise.org.uk/influence100/.

Lerberg, Matthew. "Animals, Actors, and Agency: Navigating 'Winged Migration.'" *Green Letters* 12, no. 1 (2010): 36–49. DOI: 10.1080/14688417.2010.10589062.

Lorimer, Jamie. "Moving Image Methodologies for More-than-human Geographies." *Cultural Geographies* 17, no. 2 (2010): 237–58. DOI: 10.1177/1474474010363853.

Mace, Georgina M., Mike Barrett, Neil D. Burgess, Sarah E. Cornell, Robin R. Freeman, Monique Grooten, and Andy Purvis. "Aiming Higher to Bend the Curve of Biodiversity Loss." *Nature Sustainability* 1, no. 9 (2018): 448–51. DOI: 10.1038/s41893-018-0130-0.

Maddox, Jessica. "'Guns Don't Kill People … Selfies Do': Rethinking Narcissism as Exhibitionism in Selfie-related Deaths." *Critical Studies in Media Communication* 34, no. 3 (2016): 193–205. DOI: 10.1080/15295036.2016.1268698.

Mantello, Jean-Jacques, dir. *Ocean Wonderland.* Universal Pictures UK, 2003.

Maréchal, Laeticia, Stewart Semple, Bonaventura Majolo, Mohamed Qarro, Michael Heistermann, and Ann MacLarnon. "Impacts of Tourism on Anxiety and Physiological Stress Levels in Wild Male Barbary Macaques." *Biological Conservation* 144, no. 9 (2011): 2188–93. DOI: 10.1016/j.biocon.2011.05.010.

Mendes, Jeremy, and Leanne Allison. *Bear 71.* National Film Board of Canada, 2012.

Mills, Brett. "Television Wildlife Documentaries and Animals' Right to Privacy." *Continuum* 24, no. 2 (2010): 193–202. DOI: 10.1080/10304310903362726.

Mitman, Gregg. "When Nature Is the Zoo: Vision and Power in the Art and Science of Natural History." *Osiris* 11, no. 1 (1996): 117–143. DOI: 10.1086/368757.

"Our History: 1884–1945." *National Trust*, 2020. https://www.nationaltrust.org.uk/lists/our-history-1884-1945.

Patrick, Patricia. G., Catherin E. Matthews, David Franklin Ayers, and Sue Dale Tunnicliffe. "Conservation and Education: Prominent Themes in Zoo Mission Statements." *Journal of Environmental Education* 38, no. 3 (2010): 53–60. DOI: 10.3200/JOEE.38.3.53-60.

Pearce, John, and Gianna Moscardo. "Social Representations of Tourist Selfies: New Challenges for Sustainable Tourism." In *Conference Proceedings: BESTEN Think Tank XV,* edited by Rachel Hay, 59–73. Townsville: BEST Education Network, 2015.

Perrin, Jacques, Jacques Cluzaud, and Michel Debats, dirs. *Winged Migration.* BAC Films, 2003.

Rabinow, Paul, ed. *The Foucault Reader.* London: Penguin Classics, 2020.

Rees, Paul A. "A Chronology of Major Legislation Affecting Animals and Nature Conservation in the United Kingdom." In *The Laws Protecting Animals and Ecosystems,* 445–48. Chichester: John Wiley & Sons, 2017.

Ritvo, Harriet. *The Animal Estate: The English and Other Creatures in the Victorian Age.* Cambridge: Harvard University Press, 1987.

"RSPB History: From Humble Beginnings to Thriving Today." *The RSPB,* 2020. https://www.rspb.org.uk/about-the-rspb/about-us/our-history/.

Ryder, Richard D. *Speciesism, Painism and Happiness: A Morality for the Twenty-first Century.* Exeter: Imprint Academic, 2015.

Shapiro, Kenneth J. "The Human Science Study of Nonhuman Animals." *Phenomenology and Pedagogy* 8 (1990): 27–42.

Sobchack, Vivian. *Carnal Thoughts: Embodiment and Moving Image Culture.* Berkeley: University of California Press, 2016.

Takacs, David. *The Idea of Biodiversity: Philosophies of Paradise.* Baltimore: Johns Hopkins University Press, 2016.

Thierman, Stephen. "Apparatuses of Animality: Foucault Goes to a Slaughterhouse." *Foucault Studies* 9 (September 2010): 89–110. DOI: 10.22439/fs.v0i9.3061.

van de Vall, Renée. "Promises of Presence." *Foundations of Science* 18, no. 1 (2013): 169–72. DOI: 10.1007/s10699-011-9265-4.

Vander Meer, Elizabeth. "Alligator Song: A Challenge to Spectacle, Product, and Message." *Society & Animals* 28, no. 1 (2017): 1–20. DOI: 10.1163/15685306-12341480.

Van Dooren. Thom. *Flight Ways: Life and Loss at the Edge of Extinction.* New York: Columbia University Press, 2014.

Virilio, Paul. *Ground Zero.* Translated by Chris Turner. London: Verso Books, 2002.

Verma, Audrey, René van der Wal, and Anke Fischer. "Imagining Wildlife: New Technologies and Animal Censuses, Maps and Museums." *Geoforum* 75 (October 2016): 75–86. DOI: 10.1016/j.geoforum.2016.07.002.

Wehrle, Meran. "Normative Embodiment: The Role of the Body in Foucault's Genealogy: A Phenomenological Re-reading." *Journal of the British Society for Phenomenology* 47, no. 1 (2016): 56–71. DOI: 10.1080/00071773.2015.1105645.

Dancing Is an Ecosystem Service, and So Is Being Trans

Loup Rivière

This lecture was first presented at the Multispecies Storytelling conference at Linnaeus University in January 2019. A French version of the text was presented in May 2019 at La Gaîté Lyrique (Paris) for an event that gathered Anna Lowenhaupt Tsing, Vinciane Despret, and Loup Rivière. This is an assemblage of excerpts from this second version translated back to English by Deborah Birch in conversation with the author.

In 2001 the United Nations defined the notion of Ecosystem Services (ES) as "the benefits people obtain from ecosystems." They give as examples the production of oxygen in the air, the natural purification of water, the biomass that feeds domesticated animals, the pollination of crops, and so on. Also included are the "cultural services such as spiritual, recreational, and cultural benefits."[1]

I don't know what it's like for you, but I noticed that the idea of ES often has a disturbing effect on people. I think, for example, of Donna Haraway speaking about the moment she first heard about the concept of ES and saying, "I remember how depressed I was."[2] What struck me when I heard her — beyond the emotional aspect of the reaction, which I think is not completely innocent — was that personally, I felt exactly the opposite. The day I first heard the expression "ES," I had a revelation: "ha, so there exists a concept to speak about what I do in life." It sounded like a magic formula. Later, I looked for the actual definition and obviously found it really creepy, but it didn't depress me. In fact, it rather excited me. I said to myself, "so they found the words, but they still don't really understand what they mean." It's kind of like that strange moment when my queer ancestors said to themselves, "Wow, that insult, that word queer that people spit in my face, I like it. It is as if it is describing exactly what I am and maybe even what I need to be in this world, the way in which I want to be seen and understood, the relationship I want to nurture in and around what is said to be normal. Yes, I am, queer as fuck." And so I decided to reclaim the term. Just as the process of reclaiming queerness was a super-empowering movement to celebrate our bodies and our "unnatural" practices, this questionable branding of ES has become the very spell I needed in

---

1   "Ecosystems and Human Well-being: A Framework for Assessment," *Millennium Ecosystem Assessment,* https://www.millenniumassessment.org/en/Framework. html#download/.

2   Donna Haraway et al., "Anthropologists Are Talking — About the Anthropocene," *Ethnos* 81, no. 3 (2016): 535–64.

order to acknowledge, to make visible, and to share my daily work. Dancing is an ES. And so is being trans.

The thing that attracts me in this idea is precisely its catastrophic aspect, its drama, its somatic propensity to provoke emotions and sensations. If I find energy in this misery, it's in realizing that the situations that capture most insidiously are often the most empowering when it comes to break the spell. They are able to shift, with the same rigor and efficiency, from one spiral to another.

It is in its intimacy with our sneaky system that the notion of ES seems to me to hold the promise of a counter-spell just as dramatic, allowing for the emergence of precisely the kind of conceptual lever that could become a decolonial apparatus.

An ecosystem is a given intermingling of a plethora of more-or-less biotic beings. Thinking with an ecosystem means to be immersed in the complexity of its more-or-less durable benefits, dubious love stories, partial digestions, and half-innocent services. Whether human, nonhuman, or not-quite-human-but-not-quite-nonhuman, whether enormous, invisible, tiny, quick, and silent or slow and very loud, every body in a given space is intra-acting constantly with everything else. We can even say that those bodies' relations precede their existence as distinct entities. I guess that it is only from this muddy entanglement that a decolonized, thus potentially decolonial, ES can start to emerge. One that would allow us to think not only with human or nonhuman knowledges and practices but weaving and woven through more-than-human collectives; or rather, in our case, more-than-nonhuman ones, which we can call ecosystems.

This brings us to ask a fundamental feminist question: *Cui bono,* who benefits? In our case, it is not only who benefits from a given ES but, also and above all, who benefits from such a tool, and who pays the price?

One thing I do in life is dancing for plants. Since the creation of the collective *dance for plants* in 2016, one of our favorite activities is to let relationships generated by this very statement unfold, to allow the emergence of slightly secret stories, those at the threshold of the sayable or hearable. In general, just before admitting that they talk to their plants when they are home alone, people start by posing questions; often, notably, the question of who really benefits? Who pays for the service and why? Can you heal my plants? Do you dance for the plants for yourself?

My dances are addressed to plants. I dance for them, but I don't really see myself dancing in their name or in their place (as the second meaning of the word "for" sometimes implies) because I don't quite feel they need me in order to move. Incidentally, I am not one of those people convinced that plants dance when they move, and it is for that reason that I dance *for* and not *with*. In fact, I wouldn't advise dancing with someone who doesn't clearly want to because I care about consent. However, I do suggest trying to dance *for* someone who doesn't know it, doesn't want it, or doesn't really expect it — maybe who doesn't even see you or notice your dance; for example, a person with their eyes closed, someone who is really far from you, miles away, someone who is dead or who forgot you; it could be a lover or a stranger, a cat, a cloud, a computer, a city, or, possibly, a plant. Rather than a molecular call for "becoming-plant," the proposition would be to become capable of dancing in their presence, not seeking to transform into them or to imitate them but rather to present yourself to them, to dance for them and *because* of them, to let them become, for a while, a reason for you to be in the world.

Something that the plants, or at least dancing for them, have taught me is that the movement of giving is also simultaneously a movement of receiving. Giving is often first receiving, to let oneself become interested, as if being opened to receive the receiver. When I dance for plants, I make the plants capable of making me do things that I wouldn't do otherwise. In the words of Vinciane Despret, plants enable me to "gain a body that does more things, that feels other events."[3] I don't dance *their* dance but a dance they make me capable of dancing or that they allow me to dance for them. I am danced not only by them but by what I allow them to make me become. There is no imitation or even inspiration in my experience. I just listen, and it moves me.

I understand dance as a more-than-human technology of facilitation. When I am asked to dance, I am invited to facilitate some kind of transition. Whether it's a meeting, a talking circle, a gathering, a rehearsal or a coincidence, to facilitate something is to be given a certain role or a certain power by a group or situation. When given this responsibility, I am rendered capable of enabling a given assemblage of things or people to listen, to listen to invitations issued by everything in this assemblage that is momentarily "other," including oneself or, more precisely, what the "self" is becoming in this process. The person that facilitates, or that dances, is a relay. The work of relaying can be performed by any person, object, or entity that is offered the role. In short, I could describe dancing as a process of being rendered capable by any given group or ecosystem in order to render it capable of listening to itself. Sometimes I call this a "diplomacy of the invisible" or a "facilitation from the interstices." Other such examples of facilitations could include storytelling, making magic, putting on a good show, being a whore in the sense of being a sex worker, cooking for guests, dramatizing, dying (being buried or burned, for example), gardening, or healing.

Strangely, I could describe certain aspects of my socialization as a trans person in almost the same way as what I live when I dance. My experience of being "gender non-conforming," of not being recognized either by models of femininity or models of masculinity in the local performative libraries, of being visibly femme and visibly hairy, of not making the necessary efforts to become a woman, of not making the necessary efforts to become a man or, in short, being both way too much and not enough, seems to correspond quite well to this kind of *facilitation from the interstices* I have just described.

In my experience, dancing with people and being trans with people (we can speak about what it means to dance and "be trans" far from others another time) are two things that can be particularly exhausting and extraordinarily empowering, each in their own way. Each triggers intense emotions and unexpected secretions in the bodies of other humans. They both thicken the milieu, provoking at once a hyper-agitation and a radical slowing down of things and signs. Both are extremely demanding forms of work and, I dare say, fundamentally necessary ones.

(Just to be clear, "being trans" corresponds to an extraordinary number of situated and distinct experiences, the variety of which is infinitely precious and delicate. What I am sharing here today is not solely bound to me but based on my

3   Vinciane Despret, "The Body We Care For: Figures of Anthropo-zoo-genesis," *Body & Society* 10, nos. 2–3 (2004): 111–34.

own experience and ability to articulate it, both of which depend on a unique assemblage of privileges, oppressions, and specific utterances.)

At this stage, it is important to clarify that being trans, contrary to dancing, is not a choice, nor a practice in and of itself, no more than being a girl, being bisexual, white, in love, or sick. These are not things that you choose, like you would pick a dress to wear today, even though one could argue that some of these things are the complex results of a certain number of complex choices. And yet, each of these things does and undoes a tremendous number of other things and therefore is in a way inevitably associated with a range of situated practices. Each form and inform its milieu while being formed and informed by it.

"Trans," for me, is the name of a hole, a rift, a gap. It is the name of the distance that separates me from what I am not (and what I am not sorry not to be). "Trans" is the name of the difference between the strange moving and unfinished thing that I am and the quite ambitious project of bringing together the teeming multiplicity of animal lifeforms into two dubious categories. It's the name of a structural defect of the imagination.

This distance, this hole, this gap, between the norm and me, only exists in relation to this norm. If the norm disappears, there is no more in between, nothing to exist outside of, there is no more gap, nothing more to name. It is important for me that this is clear. It's not *me* who is trans. I am trans, as long as *you* continue to make the correlation between genitals, a pronoun, a geography of hairs, and a social role. "Trans" is the name for what you see in me, as long as you don't learn to see me for myself. It's not *me* who is trans, it is all of those who are not trans yet. You are precisely *transitioning* toward your own ability to think and organize collectives without the help of the embarrassing, binary myths that we have been pedaling the last few centuries while colonizing the planet. "Trans" is the name of a transition that is not just mine. A systemic transition from a single binary world to a multitude of multiple worlds. What I propose to call an ecological transition or an ecology of transitions. Being trans is not about transitioning; it is about making things transition, about facilitating an ecological transition. (And that's good, we already have a ministry for that!)[4]

For a long time now, I have had the feeling that I dance for plants because I am trans. The question of understanding if I am trans because I dance for plants would require more time and more ghosts. I spend the Transgender Day of Visibility in the forest, and I am sure that the trees know why. Coincidentally, all members of *dance for plants* are queer, and I wonder if I should even wonder why. I do not believe that coincidences need to be commented or explained. Rather, I am convinced that they need to be fomented, generated, and narrated without a specific chronological order. Coming across a person you know while crossing the street *is a practice*, neither accident nor fate.

The family of practices that I am invoking here, demand, I believe, the joyous, insidious becoming, and the particular thickness of conspiracy. And it is from this place of conspiracy (etymologically *con-spirare*, breathing-together) that I would like to characterize the type of enmeshing necessary for the activation of a decolonial ES.

Before finishing, I need to backtrack to honor a delicate, terrifying, and crucial question that I didn't dare pose earlier. It has less to do with "who might receive" a

---

4   In France the Ministry of Ecology is called *Ministère de la Transition Écologique.*

given ES than with "who can really give, and give what?" This is perhaps the golden spike of our epistemic stratigraphy, the ultimate hesitation of the Uroboros about to bite its own tail, as one ends up wondering, *and me, what do I give to the world?* Indeed, the question is not a light one and can easily lead to a form of despair or panic. And, still, I propose to ask it and to actively caress the risk of letting it lure its own answers. The urgency to take the time to become responsible entails a concomitant urgency to eventually feel capable — that is to say, to no longer allow ourselves not to team up with those susceptible of rendering us capable. It is an urgency to ground, to listen.

Perhaps the most beautiful thing that your body can give to the world is in becoming capable of listening. Serving, entering an ecosystemic commerce is becoming capable of sabotaging the infernal alternative, the one that would have us replace our current destiny of profiting, pumping, extracting, emptying, mining, tearing down, exterminating, *ad libitum,* with a providential role of protection, regulation, preservation, management, and salvation as if being content to stop destroying was our best bet at this point.

If I have spoken a lot about listening while supposedly talking about dancing, it's an attempt to articulate something that for me is physically evident but that I continue to find cosmologically precarious. Listening is an active gesture. It is a form of receiving so dense that it cannot not simultaneously be the gesture of a radical gift. To listen is to become the intimate of things, it is a metonymic adventure of the milieu. It is necessarily an ES. To listen is to hear oneself breathing-with, it is literally to be conspiring. It is to let oneself be invaded by the world. To let oneself be mutated, to choose to be transformed by what you could have just ignored. It is becoming an ecosystemic Trojan Horse: if I'm part of the world and I let myself be disrupted by it, I technically disrupt the world, or at least part of it.

The verb "to heal" has two meanings, and it is ecologically impossible to silence one when you beckon the other. To heal oneself is to heal the world, to take care of things is already taking care of oneself. To listen deeply to oneself, to let one's needs bloom and ask for the space of their actualization is to grow ears in the depths of the world. Any performative listening, the one that moves bodies when it happens or that triggers hurricanes in the collective mitochondria, is a modern anomaly, a bug in the heteropatriarchal matrix, an epistemic mutation. I argue that any mutation, any facilitation of transition from a single binary world to a multitude of multiple worlds is an ES. Reseeding our ontologies-in-ruins is to make worlds flourish in basins of glyphosate, a kind of mundane transubstantiation that loses the Absolute of the miracle in order to become the muck of magic once again.

When you are asked to use a neutral pronoun in place of he or she: do it.
Do not start wondering why, just do it.
Get used to asking people that you meet what pronoun they use, even if it may
seem obvious to you — especially if it seems obvious to you.
Denaturalize your perceptions.
If that requires a lot of effort, acknowledge it.
And if you're able to, do it anyway.
Or rather, do it precisely because it is not yet easy.
Slow down.
Make mistakes, then make fewer.

The gender binary as we know it is a colonial apparatus created by Europeans to control, abuse, and kill in the name of progress and civilization.
And this massacre continues.
Every day.
The people that in our current moment we call trans, intersex, or "gender non-conforming" have existed everywhere at all times and, in any case, way before the epiphany of the Enlightenment.
If we are "non-conforming" to something, it is to a colonial ontology that is relatively recent and it's time to let it finish collapsing.

Let yourself be contaminated by the epistemic doubt that you slowly become capable of manifesting.
And you, what part of yourself are you mourning because of "gender" as you know it?
Listen to your gut.
Give way to resurgences.
Give up your quest for heterosexuality, allow your body to be attracted to what you have not been invited to desire.
Bruno Latour almost wrote it, "We Have Never Been Heterosexual."
Nothing obliges you to be a sexual creature.
If you choose to be, foment a desire that is etymologically hetero, a desire of others in all their otherness.
Take the time to allow more and more bodies capable of arousing desire in you.
Turn this process into a party.
Celebrate and contaminate.
Reclaim the splendors of what you've been taught to find repulsive.
Rejoice in the bizarre.
Create beauty in all the interstices, facilitate transitions everywhere and all the time.
Cultivate the practices of disidentification,
Fluidify your gender expression, learn how to dare to be vulnerable.
Listen to everything without your ears, especially that which makes no noise.
If you don't do it for yourself, do it for the climate.
Do it for the trees and butterflies.
Choose for whom or what you are doing it at this precise moment, even if it's always for everyone at once.
Become capable of addressing things.
Do it as an ecosystem service.
The climate crisis is a heteropatriarchal, colonial project, a manifestation of white supremacy.
Every concrete action against your own racism, your own transphobia, misogyny, ableism, classism, your own self-hatred, is a concrete action of climatic resurgence, a direct and immediate gift to the koalas.
While you were grieving the extinction of the white rhinoceros last week, three Black trans women were killed in different regions of the most brilliantly developed of all colonies (the United States of America).
Three Black trans women killed within eight days.

(This was written two years ago. In 2020 at least thirty-three trans feminine people [of course mostly Black and Latinx] have been murdered so far [October 2020] in the US. In France, trans youth commit suicide at a terrifying rate. Every November it takes a whole evening to pronounce the names of all of us who died this year on the Transgender Day of Remembrance.)

If you feel powerless in light of the sixth mass extinction, understand that providing financial or organizational assistance for trans femmes to thrive and working actively to dismantle everyday transphobia within yourself and your social circles is not just another umpteenth cause to support, a.k.a. "we can't do everything," a.k.a. "there are already so many."
It is urgent to acknowledge the entanglement of massacres.
Monoculture crops and the non-consensual operations on intersex people are part of the very same epistemic machine systematically eradicating resurgences, a.k.a. life.
Fighting for social justice is a service that is literally ecosystemic.
If you experience white/cis or whatever kind of structural fragility, relax your sphincter.
Breathe.
Feel the air surrounding you.
Listen to objects and things.
Don't create guilt.
Nobody wants that here.
The plants don't need your guilt.
The ice caps don't either.
Learn to love yourself, it is an ecological responsibility.
Get indebted.
Make yourself immensely and joyfully indebted: indebted to the plants that make you breathe, to your microbiota, to the people that you don't quite understand yet.
Even in a closed room in the middle of the city, remember that there is not a single dioxide molecule that you breathe that wasn't produced by a plant or by phytoplankton that hasn't passed through their bodies at some point in time on earth before going through yours.
Make space for this cellular intimacy in your daily life.
Acknowledge your interdependences in order to celebrate them.
Give thanks, create new ways to give, over and over again.
Foment strategies to become capable of feeling it in your body.
Dance for plants.
Dance for yourself, dance for the world, dance for this tiny part of the world that you are. Move your body like a giant articulated ear, an ultra-sophisticated receptive technology; move as a precise gift to everything, as a manifestation of structural gratitude, move to invent new places of pleasure in the muscles of things.
Dance with other people, foment factions to share more-than-sexual pleasures.
Organize.
Connect people that want to dance together, create moments to dance in the shadows. No need for classes or institutions to gather.
Dance in a room, in the shower, in the metro, in the park.

Dance as an ecosystem service.

As a conspiratorial technology accumulating revolutionary methodologies in your bones.

Think like an ES. Make art, science, and stories as ES. Give the land back. Dismantle the police and the prisons systems as an ES. Fight in order to facilitate any form of repair or structural healing.

Make of love the ES that love has never stopped being.

Require consent at every stage of all of your choices. Imagine new ways to feel seen, to acknowledge your work and have it acknowledged.

Our practices bring us together, they make swarms of us, they mix our bodies and the forms of our thoughts. We have never been individuals, and we have what it takes to reinvent that every day.

Names are vicious and magnificent movements, monsters doomed to decay and devour each other. Let your names go extinct. Foment a joyful vigil, allowing other strange names to flower from the flesh and bones of your dead ones.

Don't forget to check out the performance of things.

It is moving, and you are part of it.

References

Despret, Vinciane. "The Body We Care For: Figures of Anthropo-zoo-genesis." *Body & Society* 10, nos. 2–3 (2004): 111–34. DOI: 10.1177/1357034X04042938/.

"Ecosystems and Human Well-being: A Framework for Assessment." *Millennium Ecosystem Assessment.* https://www.millenniumassessment.org/en/Framework.html#download/.

Haraway, Donna, Noboru Ishikawa, Scott F. Gilbert, Kenneth Olwig, Anna L. Tsing, and Nils Bubandt. "Anthropologists Are Talking — About the Anthropocene." *Ethnos* 81, no. 3 (2016): 535–64. DOI: 10.1080/00141844.2015.1105838/.

Contributor Biographies

Ida Bencke holds an MA in Comparative Literature. She is co-founder of the curatorial platform Laboratory for Aesthetics and Ecology. Her curatorial work spans experimental exhibition formats, care activism, and speculative feminist aesthetics. Her recent exhibition projects investigate domestic technologies of resistance and insurgent practices of m/otherhood. Research interests include radical practices of mourning, play and pleasure, shared vulnerabilities, and soft resistance tactics. Currently, she holds a position as in-house curator with the Center for Arts and Mental Health in Copenhagen investigating the exhibition as a site of repair.

Melanie Boehi is a historian, Postdoc.Mobility fellow of the Swiss National Science Foundation (SNSF), and visiting postdoctoral fellow at the Wits Institute for Social and Economic Research (WISER) at the University of the Witwatersrand in Johannesburg. She has an MA from the University of the Western Cape and a PhD from the University of Basel. Her research is concerned with environmental and multispecies history, archives and journalism. She published several articles about plant histories of Southern Africa, and co-edited the book *The Politics of Nature and Science in Southern Africa* (Basler Afrika Bibliographien, 2016).

Karin Bolender (aka K-Haw Hart) is an artist–researcher who seeks untold stories within meshes of mammals, plants, pollinators, microbes, and many others. Since 2008, K-Haw's projects have come under the auspices of the Rural Alchemy Workshop (R.A.W.), a homegrown, collaborative living-art practice that explores dirty words and tangled wisdoms of earthly ecologies through performance, writing, video/sound installation, and experimental book arts. Durational and site-specific projects and performances include *R.A.W. Assmilk Soap, Gut Sounds Lullaby,* and *Welcome to the Secretome.* K-Haw has an MFA in Interdisciplinary Art from Goddard College and a PhD in Environmental Humanities from UNSW in Sydney. 3Ecologies/punctum books published *The Unnaming of Aliass* in 2020. The R.A.W. herd resides in patchwork forested hills between the ocean and mountains in western Oregon.

Jørgen Bruhn is professor of Comparative Literature at Linnæus University, Sweden. His two latest monographs are *The Intermediality of Narrative Literature. Medialities Matter* (Palgrave Macmillan, 2016) and, with Anne Gjelsvik, *Cinema Between Media: An Intermedial Approach* (Edinburgh University Press, 2018). With Beate Schirrmacher he edited Intermedial Studies. An Introduction to Meaning across Media (Routledge, 2022). His main research areas are literary theory, intermediality and media studies, ecocriticism and environmental humanities. He is currently writing a book under the working title *Intermedial Ecocriticism: Anthropocene Representations across Media* (with Niklas Salmose) to be published at Lexington Books in 2023.

After philosophical and psychological studies, **Vinciane Despret** specialized in ethology, the study of animal behavior, and became fascinated by the humans who work with animals. Borrowing a path from philosophy of sciences, her work combines ethological and psychological research with the goal of understanding and explaining how scientists build their theories, how they interact with historical and social contexts, and what relation is established between them and animals. She is currently Maître de Conférences at the University of Liège and at the Free University of Brussels. Despret is the author of numerous articles and books, some of them having been translated in English: *Our Emotional Makeup*, trans. Marjolijn de Jager (Other Press, 2004); *What Would Animals Say If We Asked the Right Questions?*, trans. Brett Buchanan (University of Minnesota Press, 2016); *Living as a Bird*, trans. Helen Morrison (Polity, 2021), *Our Grateful Dead: Stories of Those Left Behind,* trans. Stephen Muecke (University of Minnesota Press, 2021) and, with Isabelle Stengers, *Women Who Make a Fuss: The Unfaithful Daughters of Virginia Woolf,* trans. April Knutson (University of Minnesota Press, 2014).

Adam Dickinson is the author of four books of poetry, including *Anatomic* (Coach House Books, 2018), a finalist for the Raymond Souster Award and winner of the Alanna Bondar Memorial Book Prize from the Association for Literature, Environment, and Culture in Canada. His work has been nominated for the Governor General's Award for Poetry, and twice for the Trillium Book Award for Poetry. He was also a finalist for the Canadian Broadcasting Corporation (CBC) Poetry Prize and the K.M. Hunter Artist Award in Literature. His work has been translated into Chinese, Dutch, French, German, Norwegian, and Polish. He has been featured at international literary festivals in Canada, Germany, the Netherlands, Norway, and the United States. He teaches English and Creative Writing at Brock University in St. Catharines, Ontario, Canada.

Ute Hörner and **Mathias Antlfinger** are artists and professors of Transmedial Spaces/Media Art at the Academy of Media Arts Cologne. Their installations, videos, and sculptures deal with the relationship between humans, animals, and machines and provide both critical perspectives on changeable social constructs as well as utopian visions of fair terms of interaction between these parties. Together with the African grey parrots Clara and Karl they have founded the Interspecies Collective CMUK in 2014, a collaborative project of parrots and humans that promotes the decentralization of human animals as superior creators and opens up the perspective towards an overwhelming productivity by a non-human agency. Their work has been presented in many international exhibitions and festivals including, CCA Tbilisi, Porto Design Biennale, ZKM Karlsruhe, Shedhalle Zürich, NMFA Taiwan, Werkleitz Biennale Halle, Museum Ludwig Cologne, KAC Istanbul, Ars Electronica Linz, Video Dumbo New York, Shift Electronic Arts Festival Basel, International Short Film Festival Oberhausen, and Transmediale Berlin. Hörner/ Antlfinger are members of the Minding Animals International Network. They live and work in Cologne, together with their flock.

Fröydi Laszlo is a Norwegian visual artist living in Sweden. Her main interest is art and sustainability, she leads a transdisciplinary group called Club Anthropocene, and she runs the publishing company 284 publishers.

Katie Lawson is curator of the Toronto Biennial of Art, collaborating with Candice Hopkins and Tairone Bastien on the inaugural 2019 and 2021 editions. She is a graduate of the Master of Visual Studies Curatorial program at the University of Toronto, where she previously completed her Master of Arts in Art History. A researcher, curator, and art educator, Lawson works within the tradition of eco- and material feminisms. She has held curatorial and programming positions at the Art Gallery of Ontario, Doris McCarthy Gallery, the Power Plant Contemporary Art Gallery, bodega (NYC), and the University of Toronto. She has lectured and participated in programming with Images Festival, The Gladstone Hotel, The Power Plant Contemporary Art Gallery, the Laboratory for Aesthetics + Ecology and Universities both nationally and internationally. She has curated exhibitions at the MacLaren Art Centre, Barrie; Y+ Contemporary, Scarborough; RYMD, Reykjavik; the Art Museum, Toronto; and the Art Gallery of Ontario, Toronto. She was the Art Editor for the *Hart House Review* from 2016–2019.

Péter Kristóf Makai recently joined the Kulturwissenschaftliches Institut as a KWi International fellow to study how theme parks are transmediated into digital and board games. He finished his Crafoord Postdoctoral Fellowship in Intermedial and Multimodal Studies at Linnæus University in Växjö, Sweden in 2020, where he studied how evolutionary theory is being communicated across media borders. He earned a PhD in English Literature from the University of Szeged, Hungary, where he wrote a dissertation on how cognitive literary theory, clinical psychology, disability studies, and contemporary English and American middlebrow novels represent autism spectrum conditions and fictional mental functioning. As a science fiction and fantasy scholar, he wrote on Tolkien's legendarium and its legacy in worldbuilding and gaming for *Tolkien Studies* and Wiley-Blackwell's *A Companion to J.R.R. Tolkien*; he has also published studies on Isaac Asimov and Philip K. Dick's work.

Emily McGriffin has held teaching and research positions at the Universities of British Columbia, Ghana, and Edinburgh and is currently a Research Fellow at University College London. Her monograph, *Of Land, Bones, and Money: Toward a South African Ecopoetics* (University of Virginia Press, 2019), examines the environmental politics of South African poetry. She is also the author of two poetry collections.

Carol Padberg is an artist, writer, educator and founding director of the Nomad MFA. Padberg has an art and ecology studio where she weaves with living oyster mushrooms, using yarn that is colored by plants from her back yard dye garden. She uses regenerative agricultural strategies to maintain a city micro-farm called Nook Farm House. She is an herbalist and witch, and sells homemade herbal remedies that she crafts from cultivated and foraged herbs. Her art practice includes making textiles with living organisms, creating drawings with homemade inks, and raising sheep for the homespun yarn that she makes to use in her multispecies weavings. Her art has been the subject of exhibitions at the Minneapolis Institute of the Arts, and the New Britain Museum of American Art. Her initiatives have been featured at the Walker Art Center, MoMA, and the Creative Time Summit at the Venice Biennale. Recent papers and presentations have been featured in the Social Theory in Art Education Journal; the Center for Sustainable Practice in the Arts Quarterly; STREAMS: Transformative Environmental Humanities, KTH Environmental Humanities Laboratory, Stockholm; the InSEA European Congress, Aalto University; the Multispecies Storytelling Conference, Linnæus University; and Imaginative Futures: Arts Based Research as Boundary Event Symposium, Arizona State University.

Helen V. Pritchard is an artist-designer and geographer whose work considers the impacts of computation and digital media on social and environmental justice. Their research addresses how practices configure the possibilities for life—or who gets to have a life—in intimate and significant ways. As a practitioner they work together with companions to make propositions and designs for environmental media and computing otherwise, developing methods to uphold a politics of queer survival and practice. They are currently working on the book project "Animal Hackers and Critter Compilers"; and together with Cassandra Troyan a research project across their institutions entitled, "Multispecies Methods for Solidarity Stories" which seeks to use transdisciplinary methods as part of a virtual lab, to allow writers, scholars, artists, designers, and theorists to build collective practices. Helen is an Associate Professor of Queer Feminist Technoscience & Digital Design at i-DAT, University of Plymouth and a research fellow at Goldsmiths University of London. They are the co-editor of *Data Browser 06: Executing Practices,* published by Open Humanities Press (2018) and *Science, Technology and Human Values: Sensors and Sensing Practices* (2019).

Loup Rivière is a dancer and a poet. She lives in rural Massif Central (France). She founded the collective dance for plants in 2016, which offers workshops and performances in gardens, universities, forests, apartments, and museums. She is currently touring her solo armes molles and training to become a death doula. She recently published the texts "I'm Not Trans in the Forest" and "Geological Lesbians: Girldicks and Other Stories."

Cassandra Troyan is a writer, artist, organizer, and educator whose work explores the intersections of gendered violence, radical histories of resistance, sex work, and speculative futures beyond capital. They are the author of several books of multigenre work, including *Freedom & Prostitution* (2020), *A Theory in Tears* (2016) and *KILL MANUAL* (2014), and have presented, performed, and screened their multimedia work internationally. Forthcoming in 2021 from Veer2 is *Against Capture,* a collection about trauma, love, isolation, and abolitionist dreaming for the end of incarceration, captivity, domestication, and borders towards trans-species solidarity. In collaboration with Helen Pritchard, they work on the on-going research project across their institutions entitled, "Multispecies Methods for Solidarity Stories" which seeks to use transdisciplinary methods as part of a virtual lab, to allow writers, scholars, artists, designers, and theorists to build collective practices. They live in Kalmar, Sweden and teach theory, practice, and creative-critical writing as a Senior Lecturer in the Department of Design at Linnæus University.

Elizabeth Vander Meer has a PhD in Environmental Policy and Ethics from Lancaster University, an Anthrozoology MA from the University of Exeter, and is now in the second year of a PhD in Anthrozoology at Exeter. Her research is multidisciplinary, drawing on anthropology, compassionate conservation, performance studies, philosophy, and social theory. She combines interests in biodiversity conservation with human-animal studies, conducting multispecies ethnographic studies that focus on human–wildlife conflict and co-existence and captive wild animals in circuses, rescue centres and zoos.

Kristina Van Dexter is a poet–researcher whose writing focuses on the ecocidal destruction of forests and their own relational poetics of resistance, including narratives and political and ethical projects that emerge through human and non-human collaborations in forests' relational worlds. Her experimental and poetic ethnographic research and projects involve relational practices of collaboration that are guided by and grow from forests themselves. Van Dexter is the founder of Paz con la Selva, a collective for an insurgent poetics in the defense of forests. She lives and works in Colombia (and Indonesia) where she is completing a Ph.D. in Environmental Studies. She is currently working on a collection of insurgent poetics that entangles ecological narratives of witness to forest destruction and the forests' own poetics expressed through its diverse registers, temporal relations, and ceremonial encounters with forest spirits.

Gillian Wylde is an artist and researcher, central to her practice is an engagement with technologies, performativity and otherwise thinking. Her portfolio as an artist includes international exhibitions, commissions, and residencies. Dissent, queerness, and feels are constants through most of the work like maybe a wild smell or hairy logic.

www.ingramcontent.com/pod-product-compliance
Lightning Source LLC
Chambersburg PA
CBHW081432250726
48662CB00009B/2764